DARK DESIGNS AND VISUAL CULTURE

MICHELE WALLACE

DUKE

UNIVERSITY

PRESS

DARK DESIGNS AND VISUAL CULTURE

DURHAM

AND LONDON

2004

© 2004 Duke University Press. All rights reserved.
Printed in the United States of America on acid-free paper. ∞
Designed by Rebecca M. Giménez. Typeset in Minion by Tseng
Information Systems. Library of Congress Cataloging-in-
Publication Data appear on the last printed page of this book.

TO BURDETTE RINGGOLD, the father I knew best, and who dropped the wisdom on me with beneficent regularity. Without him, all our lives would have been an unimaginable tragedy. Forgive me for not having understood this before.

CONTENTS

ACKNOWLEDGMENTS

I would like to begin by acknowledging and honoring the patience and the fortitude of my family, the most important single force in my life. In particular, I owe a great debt to my niece, Faith Wallace Gadsden, who helped me to prepare this manuscript and in almost all regards has been like a daughter to me. Her strength and perseverance through her years of boarding school and college have been an inspiration to me. I love and admire her. Also, my mother (Faith Ringgold, who supplied many of the images and ideas in this book) and my sister Barbara Wallace have stood by me, as always. While not as involved in the actual preparation of the book, I, nevertheless, could not have done all these years of writing without their support.

I would like to thank my many wonderful students, in particular, my special favorites LeRonn Brooks, Anne Rice, Stacey Williams, Ira Dworkin, Lowell Coleman, Rezwan Ahmed, Ronaldo Wilson, and Catherine Bowles, who very kindly did some of the last-minute typing and copyediting for me.

This book includes previously published materials from *Women's Review of Books, October, Transition, Renaissance Noire, Village Voice, New York Times, Social Text, Entertainment Weekly, Aperture, AfterImage, Art-in-America, Ms. Magazine, Emerge*. During my sojourn as a Ph.D. candidate in Cinema Studies at New York University's Tisch School of the Arts, I learned more than I can say from my advisors and teachers there, in particular Christine Straayer, the director of my dissertation committee, and my always benevolent, always indispensable mentor Manthia Diawara. The great theoretical minds that gather on the 6th floor of Tisch—among them Annette Michelson, Antonia Lant, Bob Stam, Robert Sklar and Jim Hoberman, Richard Schechter, Peggy Phalen, Ngugi Wa Thiongo, Jose Munoz, Barbara Kirschenblatt-Gimblett and Brooks MacNamara just down the hall in Performance Studies—helped give my thinking on many aspects of cultural ritual, performativity, and visual representation a kind of depth and exhaustiveness I had only dreamed of achieving before.

The chance to study ethnographic and documentary film with the important anthropologist Faye Ginsberg and David and Judith MacDougall, the famous ethnographic film team, was something I will cherish all my life. These programs offer marvelous opportunities to study the politics and construction of global trends in visual media. My only regret was that advanced degree work there was often so harried and pressured for time because of the necessity most students have of earning a living. Unavoidably, it takes time to learn, time to assimilate new ideas, regardless of whether you have the time or not. Meanwhile, these programs continue to offer some of the most important cultural events to the public in the city.

I would like to thank my dear friends Coco Fusco, Jim Hoberman, Margo Jefferson, Eve Sedgwick, E. Ann Kaplan, Robert Reid-Pharr, and Diane Harriford for their advice and input in regard to a range of ideas included in this book. Needless to say, they hold no responsibility for my many mistakes.

I would like to thank my editor at Duke University Press, Ken Wissoker, for his patience and support. Also I would like to thank Karen Durbin, Angela Ards, Tim Haslett, Moira Roth, Brian Wallis, Anne Snitow, Maurice Berger, Donna de Salvo, Lisa Yee, David Theo Goldberg, Henry Giroux, Peter McLaren, Phil Mariani, Russell Ferguson, Trinh Minh-ha, Carolyn Korsmeyer, Linda Nochlin, and Lisa Jones for editorial assistance and guidance at various times.

INTRODUCTION

I

In June of 2003, I visited Black River, Jamaica, the birthplace of my father's parents. My niece, Faith, who was a twenty-one-year-old college student, and I traveled there with a distant cousin, Carol, the daughter of my grandfather's sister, a seventy-year-old retired college librarian. Although my parents divorced when I was only two years old, and I had almost no relationship with my father, a heroin addict, after that, I knew and kept in touch with my paternal grandparents over the years. My father's mother is still alive. Over one hundred, she is now senile, disabled, and incapable of communication. My father's father died when I was twenty-seven and I had just published *Black Macho and the Myth of the Superwoman* (1979), the book that jump-started my career as a writer. It was the cousin who traveled with us to Jamaica who, over twenty years ago, had asked me to deliver the eulogy at my grandfather's funeral.

My grandfather, Robert Earl Wallace, was a literate, scholarly man who enjoyed studying languages. He was a musician, a gardener, and a tinkerer who suffered, I believe, from periodic bouts of depression that rendered him incapable of doing more than minimal jobs. Whatever else they may or may not have accomplished in their lives, both my father (who was both a classical and a jazz pianist) and my grandfather were hopelessly scarred and traumatized by racism, colonialism, and Jim Crow oppression both in Jamaica and in the United States. Even though others from similar backgrounds — such as Harry Belafonte and Colin Powell—may have fared better, they are the exceptions from the islands, not the rule. Grandpa Bob lived until he was seventy-eight, just long enough to tell me how pleased he was by my book and that I was a writer. I think perhaps he now told me this in the hopes that one day I would tell his story and the stories of others like him.

Carol told me that, for the last three years, a literary festival called Calabash had been held near Black River, in the remote fishing village of Treasure Beach. Treasure Beach is on the south-central coast of the island where tourists rarely venture. Carol suggested we plan a trip to the festival that included exploring Black River, visiting existing family still in Jamaica (her family on her father's side) in Kingston, and examining genealogical records in Spanish Town. In late May 2003, we set out via Air Jamaica to Montego Bay, spent two days in this tourist town, and then were driven to Treasure Beach.

From the first moment I arrived in Montego Bay at midday, I knew I would have difficulty with the environment from a health standpoint. It was very hot, extremely humid, and there was no air conditioning. I arrived with an intellectual understanding that Jamaica was a third world country but I did not realize what that meant on the ground. I had never been in such a place before. Because of the precariousness of my health, there are many places I have not been. I tend not to take chances.

From the airport, we took a cab to the Glouschester, a hotel where our accommodations were much more comfortable than where we would subsequently be. The three of us shared a large room with a wall air conditioner. Our hotel was located along a commercial strip with lots of tourist shops and bars, everything gaudy and overpriced and designed to appeal to American college students or other tourists who pursued the havoc and abandon they mistakenly like to refer to as a vacation. There was little activity along the tourist strip, however, while we were there. It was off-season, summertime, and very hot. We were across the street from Doctor's Beach, a famous watering hole where you have to pay to enter. For an additional fee, you can rent a chair and an umbrella and a man will set it up for you.

After three days of this, a driver came from Treasure Beach to take us to the Southeast Coast. His car was a struggle buggy with no air conditioning, and the sun grew hotter and hotter as we drove across the island through the mountains. Obviously impoverished people lived in corrugated tin huts along the road, selling fruit and other foods from roadside stands.

The temperature was in the 90s in the shade, very humid, precisely the environment that someone with lupus should avoid. When we got to Treasure Beach, there was barbed wire around all the lots of dried-out grass. On some of them were partially built concrete structures or buildings and establishments that had been abandoned, presumably because of lack of business or because it was off-season. Whatever the reason, it gave the place a forlorn quality. Here and there stray dogs bayed and howled. This area of the country was known for its population of descendants of stranded Scottish sailors who had interbred with the locals to produce Jamaican-African peasants with blonde or red hair and blue eyes. The driver drove slowly and carefully down a rough, rocky dirt road to a large cement blockhouse, which was brightly painted in light pastels but had no air conditioning and no screens. There were lights and ceiling fans in the ceiling but no bulbs in the lights. I found the bulbs where they had been placed under the sink.

The beach was down a steep slope and just beyond the visible horizon, an uncomfortable distance for anyone not youthful and limber. Moreover, the information sheet that came with the house warned us that it wasn't safe to swim there because there was a very bad undertow. All around the house were goats and chickens; the rooster was crowing. Wasps and other flying insects flew in and out of the wood slat windows. Inside and outside was intensely hot and humid. I found myself appalled by the desperate conditions that were visible everywhere, that this place which seemed so incomplete in so many ways in terms of infrastructure and civility had been presented to me as a country, a sovereign nation, a place that my ancestors had voluntarily come from, and to which they would often return on holiday. No one had ever mentioned this omnipresent environment of desperation and poverty. All I ever heard about were the beautiful flowers, the beautiful houses, trees, and fruit. The picture postcards were accurate in their details, but in the postcards you couldn't see the harshness and despair of the locals who had produced the tourists' bounty—the wonderful foods that they laboriously prepared.

Suddenly, I understood how and why my own family, and all the other West Indians who lived in Brooklyn and Queens and Harlem, had fled this island. As a writer, it grieved me to see no bookstores, no libraries, no universities, so few books in general—even at the literary festival, which was given over more to spoken word and music (the oral tradition) than it was to the pursuit of the life of the literate mind. The Nobel Prize winner Derek Walcott, who was to be featured at the conference, did not show up. His slot was occupied instead by bell hooks, who did an excellent job of presenting her recent work on love and self-esteem among black people. Our trek to and from the conference was about a mile over rough, unsteady terrain, and on the second day of the festival it began to rain heavily, which brought out an entirely different assortment of flying insects; the festival grounds turned to thick, slippery mud. Jakes, the hotel where the festival was actually being held, was obviously the most comfortable habitation in the area with cute little colorful cottages arranged on a beautiful beachfront, but they were totally booked, as were most of the nearby hotels. That they were already full when Carol made our reservations meant that we were placed in more direct proximity to the local population and had no hot water (superfluous because of the heat), no air conditioning or much electricity, and no transportation.

The plan had been for us to spend about a week in Kingston after the festival. Because I was tolerating the heat and humidity so poorly in Treasure Beach, growing weaker and weaker in a place where it would be impossible to survive if one were not strong, I decided to return to Montego Bay almost immediately. The disappointments of this trip filled me with despair such as I have rarely felt. The mystery of my birth father and my father's ancestors was finally settled. This was the end of the line or at least as far as I dared explore given my age and health. We passed through Black River, which looked entirely uninhabitable to me. What shocked me the most was to have been so rudely awakened from my fantasy of the idyllic fatherland. When I complained to my cousin that it wasn't going to be possible to read (my major occupation and entertainment under all circumstances) or do anything at night because there were no screens and the bugs were intense, she said to me, "of course not, you're in the country, you're home," as though that would settle everything. But it isn't my home. For better or for worse, I'm dependent on the class-based comforts that I take for granted (however hard-won they are) back in New York. Meanwhile, I could not forget how the place reeked of the hard lives and precipitous deaths of the slaves and their descendants.

II

Like travel to another country, an autobiographical text is a potential minefield for those who may wander naively among its pleasures. It does not combine well with either psychological innocence or the kind of publicity-making machinery associated with celebrity. Nonetheless, when appropriately handled, it can be an essential work of intellectual history, with a kind of information that can be found nowhere else. As someone who is fascinated by cultural history, as well as the personal histories of cultural producers, I look to autobiography in search of the kind of knowledge that other established disciplines and more clearly delineated subject areas ordinarily overlook. Many very smart people find autobiographical or biographical criticism problematic because of the temptations of having an excess of information superfluous to the interpretation of the work of the artist or the intellectual. Yet the fact remains that an individual life, the day-to-day grind of being a person, is the basic unit of experience for each of us. In thinking about black culture and history in particular, it is important to remind ourselves that black people, regardless of their struggles and obstacles, always live individual lives in their individual skins; they process and assimilate the difficulties of their time in ways as unique as every other facet of human existence.

We, who think of ourselves as black scholars, academics, and thinkers, have not had enough serious or rigorous intellectual narratives of our lives. We have been forced to make do too often with polemical approximations (such as the current usually platitudinous wisdom concerning the lives of such black leaders as Paul Robeson, Malcolm X, and Martin Luther King Jr.) and incomplete translations from the world of once dominant discourses (i.e., black appropriations of poststructuralism and deconstruction in the late '80s). What makes it so easy for people to lie, dissemble, and fabricate mythical structures concerning Afro-Americans has directly to do, I believe, with this tendency we have as a people to leave so many blanks in the record through an excess of discretion, even humility. We Afro-Americans (and others of the African diaspora in the Caribbean, Latin America, and Canada as well) find ourselves with one foot in and one foot out of the modern world. On the one hand, we hark back to the rhythms and the caveats of African-derived oral traditions in which tone, repetition, and permutations of style and enunciation, body language and demeanor differentiated your story from that of anybody else's. It was a performance that survived your own existence through retelling by friends and children, in a manner designed to be unnoticeable to the master class (white folk or their surrogates). On the other hand, we continue to exist uncomfortably, especially now that we are nominally integrated, in a world in which the only kind of record that really matters is the one that is written.

In this society, to which we are inextricably bound as modern westerners of African descent, what is written (or videotaped) is privileged as fact, as reality, as evidence in a manner in which the impermanence of the ethereal performance can never hope to touch. At the same time, the universe of inscription has always been much smaller and more exclusive than the world most of us have always inhabited. In this age of globalization, digitalization, and computerization, the challenge is to find adequate translations for every sensation, mood, and aspect of experience and reality so that we can all be adequately represented, equally able to express our wishes and desires and the fullness of our being. But this is far from the situation at the moment.

After years of speculation and wondering, the shelves of the bookstores are finally bursting with new information about the once nearly forgotten Afro-American writer Zora Neale Hurston — her letters, a new biography, a collection of folklore that had been hidden away in a fellow anthropologist's papers since it was first written in 1927, previously unpublished materials from her work for the Florida WPA in the 1930s. It has been fascinating to absorb all this new material. Has it made a difference to have access to so much information about her? Yes, it has, but I cannot help think about how such an apparently secretive woman might have orchestrated these revelations differently if she had been given the opportunity to do so. Also, it feels as though the essential key that might make sense of these disparate pieces of the puzzle is still missing. Why had she wanted to conceal certain crucial facts about herself, such as her marriages or that she was really born in Alabama instead of Eatonville, Florida, or when she was actually born? And from whom did she wish to conceal this knowledge? It seems apparent to me that she probably wanted to hide certain information because it could lead us to jump to the wrong conclusions. Most disturbing about all this information on Hurston is that the readings of her motives have not become any more psychologically complex.[1] She was never the primitive that she and Godmother so much wanted her to be but rather, adapting yet another version of the Du Boisian mask of double consciousness, she was sometimes "going native" or sometimes just plain lying. Hurston cunningly manipulated discourses of anthropology and ethnography in order to knit together a life for herself as an artist who was also dedicated to documenting and reinventing an acutely and riotously improvisational Afro-American oral tradition. Her informants throughout the South and the Caribbean were scarcely primitives either by any stretch of the imagination, despite her endeavor to cast them as such. Rather they were fully ensconced in the twentieth century as the descendants of slaves, forced into the convoluted and complex underdevelopment and servility of Jim Crow laws and conventions.

Notions of primitivism or the primitive are peculiar relics of an earlier social science organization of knowledge and the cultures of the world. They no longer satisfactorily describe or denote cultural differences today, and yet it remains clear that many descendants of the African diaspora are not meaningful participants in modernity. Where does the difference lie, and what does it signify to the life of the black intellectual?

We black people, owing to our history of oppression and persecution, are particularly sensitive to any kind of perception of dishonor, notoriety, or indiscretion. We feel vulnerable to public disclosures of a personal or private nature. At the same time, smear campaigns remain a uniquely effective form of stigmatization in black communities.

In the pieces gathered in the first section of this book, I've tried to tell the truth. Not the whole truth but the portion of it that I could bear to tell and that you could bear to hear. By way of introduction to this work, I will fill in a few personal details that I have been reluctant to disclose in an effort to help you understand the meaning and ramifications of such disclosure. Some time in the future when more time has elapsed I hope to write my autobiography and elaborate further on these moments. In the meantime, I hope these notes will clarify the present picture sufficiently.

I turned fifty-one years old in January 2003. I am hoping I will live a good deal longer, although the world I inhabit (by which I mean the geopolitical United States) has become a deeply unsettling place. Both the spiritual and physical environments suddenly seem more precarious than I ever could have anticipated. I live on the 14th floor of an apartment building in the center of Harlem on what used to be called Sugar Hill. From my window, I can see Manhattan, New Jersey, and the Bronx for miles around. I don't particularly enjoy heights or appreciate urban views yet I find myself here in the apartment in which I spent most of my childhood under the care of my parents, Burdette and Faith Ringgold (the well-known artist). I returned here after breaking up with my husband Eugene Nesmith in 1999. We had an amicable and peaceful separation followed by a divorce that was three years in the making. We had irreconcilable differences when it came to living together—differences of taste and material values too far apart to bridge. We remain friends.

From 1981, when my maternal grandmother (Momma Jones) died and I left Yale in the middle of my first semester as a Ph.D. candidate in American Studies because I had a nervous breakdown, through the present, my life has been shaped by the realities of being chronically ill. My foremost priority has become maintaining my physical and mental health, regardless of what may be going on in the world around me. If I am not well, I cannot do anything for anyone, including myself.

In 1993, just as I entered the Ph.D. Program in Cinema Studies at New York University, I was diagnosed with lupus during a very severe attack of it. I think I have had lupus at least since 1981 (when I was twenty-nine), and perhaps even earlier. Although this aspect of it is controversial, it seems as though my lupus affects my central nervous system and has psychiatric ramifications. The internist I began to see the year after I graduated from college, and whom I still see periodically, had apparently suspected I had lupus since 1981 because, during my hospitalization then, I had been switched from the psychiatric ward to the medical ward owing to a severe and inexplicable fever (one of the symptoms of lupus) that would not go away. This fever had rendered me delirious and unable to communicate for about a month. My family thought I was dying and no one could fathom why. Despite the fact that it seemed as though every manner of specialist available then at Harlem Hospital was consulted at one point or another, the word "lupus" was never mentioned.

I left Harlem Hospital on my thirtieth birthday in 1982 weighing 113 pounds (the lowest weight I have ever been as an adult), without any kind of medication or any comprehension of what had happened to me or of what I was about to face in the next two decades in terms of my health. From 1982 through 1984, I dropped out of the Ph.D. program at Yale and lived with my family in Harlem (first with my sister, who had her first child in 1982, then my Mom and Dad). Whatever money I had made from *Black Macho* was long gone (the surviving edition with Warner Books would soon be out of print), and I continued to owe an unwieldy sum to the IRS. It was a depressing time during which my family was very supportive of me. The great light of my life was my newborn niece, whom we called Baby Faith. Because of my own indigence, I was honored to be included among her primary caretakers at this stage of her life. She was bright, quick, delightfully funny, and alive, and I fell hopelessly and completely in love with her (as did everyone), and remain so to this day.

At the same time, Moira Roth, who was chair of the Art History Department at the University of California at San Diego (UCSD) in La Jolla, came into our lives. She was a great admirer of Faith's painting, sculpture, and performances, and she wanted to recruit her as a professor of art. Mom had never been to California and could not drive; she found it difficult to imagine what it would be like to make such a transition, although there were no jobs for her closer to home. Indeed, at that time, she had quit the Board of Education, was doing freelance lecturing at colleges, and had even begun to do some substitute teaching at a local high school. It would also mean temporarily leaving her husband, my stepfather Burdette. Mom was still grieving the death of her mother and the death of her sister in the following year (1982). Having been to California a number of times myself (either on reporting assignments or to do lectures or book-signings associated with the publication of *Black Macho*), I was very much in support of her pursuing this opportunity. New horizons always seemed like a splendid idea to me. Moira Roth hooked me up with Sherley Williams, who was then a Professor of Literature at UCSD and needed someone to replace her while she was on a Fulbright. As a consequence, I ended up going to UCSD as a Visiting Lecturer in Literature with Faith, who went as a Visiting Professor in Art. This was my great chance to get back into college teaching (I had taught journalism at NYU from 1976 through 1978 before publishing *Black Macho* but had abandoned the job to promote the book and move to New Haven).

During that spring in La Jolla, I met the poet Jerome Rothenberg who put me in touch with George Economou, then chair of the English Department at the University of Oklahoma, who asked me to come there to be a Visiting Professor in English and Writing. That became a permanent tenure-track job in the spring of 1985, the same year in which I met Gene. Soon after we met I got sick again and had to be hospitalized for two weeks during a spring vacation visit to San Diego. This time Mom insisted on a private hospital, which was as different from Harlem Hospital as night is from day. These periodic illnesses have come and gone with great regularity ever since, particularly when I am under a lot of stress and burning the candle at both ends, which was something I used to do all of the time. Yet in the process, I have also learned a great deal about how to control and regulate my health by simplifying my life and downsizing my expectations in general.

From that time on, I would get fevers occasionally, take an aspirin, and sleep them off until one day in 1993 when the fever would not go away, no matter what I did, no matter what I took. I developed swollen glands in my throat (as though I had the mumps), itchy, unsightly patches of eczema all over my body, a huge butterfly rash on my face, and my hair came out in handfuls.

After a month or so of trying to get the doctors at Health Insurance Plan (HIP) to do their job (which was the caliber of medical coverage one could obtain as an employee of the State of New York), I finally returned to my faithful internist (at full cost) who tested me for lupus and confirmed that I had it. By that time, both my liver and my kidney were endangered from the amount of Tylenol and ibuprofen I had been gulping in order to control the fever. I guess I was the last person in the world to discover that both drugs are poisons when taken excessively.

When I returned to New York in 1989, the year Gene and I got married, to teach at the City College of New York, I began to see a therapist whom I still see and who has added a great deal of order and discipline to my life. While he was my husband, Gene was always supportive and understanding and an excellent nurse when I needed him to be. Since my illness in 1993, I have continued to see a rheumatologist, a dermatologist, a psychiatrist, a psychologist, a gynecologist, and an internist, none of whom is covered by my current health insurance. By means of this invariable routine of tests, medication, and doctors' visits at great personal expense; by sleeping more than most people and eating regularly; by avoiding stress and staying out of the sun, I am able to remain reasonably well. Most black women are not able to control their day-to-day lives as rigorously as I can. I think of lupus as an occupational disease. If you have any occupation that is overly demanding of your time, and at all outside the shade of a well-maintained home, then you will find it difficult to control the illness.

When Gene and I married, my family was present, including Barbara, my sister, and her three kids: Baby Faith (who was seven), Teddy, and Martha (who was two). Most important, after almost three years of being out West, moving back to New York gave me the chance to get to know Mom and Dad (my stepfather) in a way I could never have known them as a child. I began then and still do find them endlessly fascinating, never dull, always surprising and intriguing.

Early in the '90s, Barbara helped Faith and Birdie (Burdette) to find and buy a little house that sat on almost an acre of wooded land in Englewood, New Jersey, about fifteen minutes by car from our old neighborhood in Harlem. It was Faith's intention to remodel and expand the house to include a studio and larger living quarters. She also added an extraordinary and extensive garden, which I had no concept of until it was finished about four years ago. Each summer it grows fuller and more resplendent; it seems to me to epitomize why physical and material beauty are so essential, whether via nature or what Walter Benjamin called "mechanical reproduction."

I love this house and love to visit it; to luxuriate and meditate in the wonderful Japanese-inspired garden with its waterfall, pond, and gazebo amid the many plants and flowers; and to observe the animals scurrying from bush to bush. It takes me back to fond childhood memories of an all-black sleep-away camp called Camp Craigmeade in the heart of the Catskills, with neither electricity nor hot water nor indoor bathrooms. The place was run by three Aunties — Aunt Helen, who wore shorts, a polo shirt, and her hair slicked back regardless of the chill in the air; and two older women, perhaps her sisters, who did all the cooking in the nineteenth-century kitchen. The best part of being there was feeling dwarfed yet coddled by the environment of lots of young adults (teenage counselors) with warm laps and warm arms; miles of trees, rivers, steaming earth, cows chewing their cud; the songs we sang together around the campfire, the bugler playing reveille under the stars.

You didn't have your mom and dad, but then you had all these other delicious, fabulous-smelling new people who knew your name and held your hand and reassured you that you would never die of homesickness, and thus you first learned that it could be fun and safe to wander away from home.

There is not a lot of grass in Mom's garden because Mom and all of us are allergic to it. There are lots of rocks and chairs to sit on, and a great deal of shade and trees, as well as a closed-in back porch, something I particularly appreciate because, due to the lupus, I can't be in direct sunlight. The entire house has central air and heat and lots of natural light, something perhaps the rest of the United States takes for granted but seems a divine luxury in the New York tristate area where so many of us have air conditioners hanging in our windows. When I stay there with my parents, my whole body changes. My occasional bouts of eczema go away, my allergies go away. Mom has created a perfect and beautiful and complete environment, which has changed the way I see the world and the way I regard aesthetics. Remove the noise and the mayhem and everything is infinitely better, even if it is all a mere fifteen minutes away.

It is possible to escape the rat race and to live in a way that swaddles and comforts the psyche by virtue of an artistic and architectural concept. It was this nurturance that enabled me to come through the events of September 11 relatively unscathed.

It was also this sense of strategic location that allowed me to weather the profound disappointment in learning that the world that had produced my father's people had not been one of glory and nobility but one of suffering and exploitation. Whether my father's people were part of the minuscule class of mixed-blood Jamaicans who exploited all the others (although my father was very dark skinned he apparently had Indian and European ancestry) or part of the huge class of Jamaican peasants who were exploited (over 90 percent of the population according to a Lonely Planet guide), the prospect was equally depressing. Either way, it was a nightmarish past to contemplate, something I am not sure to which I will ever grow accustomed.

III

The morning of September 11, 2001, I was fast asleep and completely impervious to the momentous events that took place right outside my window. At the time, it was not unusual for me to sleep late. Since Gene and I had broken up immediately after I defended my Ph.D. in December 1999, and I had gone to live in the family apartment in a Harlem high-rise, I had been in the habit of sleeping ten, sometimes even twelve, hours per night. Since I never went to sleep before midnight, reading in bed from about nine until I fell asleep, I frequently woke up at noon or sometime after. Morning was a time

I completely missed. On the practical level, I regretted this practice, but on the emotional level, I had always hated morning. Also, I really needed the sleep.

September 11 was a Tuesday, the day I always see my therapist at 1:15 P.M. But on this particular day, I woke up so late that I had time only to dial her number in order to take my appointment over the telephone. I began to speak to her in the normal way. She quickly interrupted me to ask me if I knew what had happened. I said no. Then she told me. I believe in miracles, or at least I do now. I will always think it a miracle of divine intervention that she, the person I probably rely on and confide in more than anyone else on this earth, was the one to break this awful, terrifying news to me. I was drawing on the full weight of the entire twelve years of our relationship in order to believe the words she then said. She ended with the suggestion that I turn on the television. I did so and the whole nightmarish scenario came flooding into my bedroom. She said she needed to leave the telephone line open for patients who might be particularly upset. In that moment, I felt an overwhelming sense of relief regarding my relative safety, glad that it wasn't me who needed emotional, spiritual, or physical triage. It began to dawn on me then how well I was becoming, how strong and even resilient. Still, as I watched the unfolding situation on a variety of channels, it took me hours to understand that the buildings had already fallen before I awoke. It seemed as I watched the footage on television that they fell again and again. Also, it took me several more hours to finally look in the direction of the World Trade Center from my bedroom window in order to see the black smoke that was still rising.

Harlem was extremely quiet that day. Harlem can be so quiet sometimes, especially if there is a catastrophe elsewhere in New York. There were no buses and few cars, no subways running, and no way to get off Manhattan because all the bridges were closed. I wanted to flee to my parents in New Jersey, but I had to wait.

Now I am saying all this because perhaps, like many New Yorkers, I have been in shock over this event and its many economic, political, and military ramifications. The first thing I did, once I realized that I was becoming mesmerized, was to turn off the television and turn off the radio and not watch or listen to any news for over a year. This may seem like a politically irresponsible act (I, myself, would have regarded it as such before then), but I knew I needed to pull myself all the way together if I was going to get through it as a functioning intellectual; having a play-by-play breakdown on events was not going to help me do that. I am, and have been for some time, a student of political history and current events and have been fascinated by their relationship to cultural production. Living fifty years on this planet and my experiences of the Gulf War; the Vietnam War; Contragate; Irangate; Watergate; the Anita Hill–Clarence Thomas hearings; Attica; the Cuban Missile Crisis; Lumumba; Idi Amin; the March on Washington; the Freedom Riders; and the murders of Emmett Till, Medgar Evers, John and Robert Kennedy, Malcolm X, Martin Luther King, and so forth, was enough to keep me more aware than I needed to be of the broad outlines of what was likely happening.

I have never been a political optimist, so knowing every detail could easily have sent me into an immobilizing depression. For me, if the cost of knowing the full story would be catatonic depression, I think at this point restricting the flow of information made sense. Now that I have just come out of my news embargo, I suspect I am looking at an entire adult population largely suffering from the very thing I was trying to avoid. A lot of folks seem to be sleepwalking. I am not quite sure what can be done about this. I don't think it is a good idea to awaken sleepwalkers abruptly, especially as I spent several years of my life (in my twenties and thirties when I wrote and suffered through *Black Macho*) sleepwalking. Sleepwalking is a tender but potentially creative state poised between unconsciousness and death. You should walk around a sleepwalker if you can. It is as if she is in a chrysalis. She is leaving one state and becoming something else. She is in limbo or transition and is not to be interrupted during the transition.

When I stopped reading the news, watching television, and listening to the radio — the absolute staples of my existence in the ten years prior to September 11 — I turned to my love for music. I gathered up all the music that sustained me through difficult times in the past. In particular, I started with opera in an attempt to probe the emotional depths I was beginning to suspect I possessed. I followed up on a lifelong desire to know more about Maria Callas who held out the promise of the drama I was looking for. I bought a CD of her most famous arias and a CD of *Carmen*, my first and favorite opera. Mom had taken my sister and me to see it when we were very small because a daughter of a friend of hers sang in the children's chorus. I never forgot this, especially because from then on the recording of the opera was played and replayed in our house. When I studied French in school, I frequently sang along with the recording, trying to figure out what would make Carmen and Don Jose so obsessed with ruining one another's lives.

The Callas version did not disappoint me. The dark richness of her voice matched the bitterness of my own tears. I cried a lot in those first months. I cried alone. Every time I cried (which was something I was told as a child one should never do for fear that you would never be able to stop), I felt better afterward and I got stronger. Of course, this was only after years of therapy dealing with the issues that had held me back all my life and taking the time to understand how important it was to finally mourn for the loss of the life I had never had a chance to live, that other life of my dreams as a dancer or a singer or a pianist.

From Callas, I returned to my greatest love, the late Nina Simone, whose lyrics and peculiar voice had always nurtured me in times of personal difficulty. One could hardly choose a better friend in sad and lonely times. I returned as well to Donny Hathaway, Lou Rawls, Mahalia Jackson, Sarah Vaughn, Billie Holiday, and Miriam Makeba. Because my father was a jazz pianist I have always loved the piano and great pianists such as McCoy Tyner, Bud Powell, Thelonious Monk, Art Tatum, Count Basie, and Duke Ellington. I love, as well, the music of John Coltrane, Eric Dolphy, Dizzy Gillespie, Miles Davis, Sonny Rollins, Art Blakey, and the incomparable early works of Louis Armstrong. Armstrong's singing voice and his presence on stage are particularly appealing. I think he must have been very attractive to women in his prime.

These days, as I am increasingly likely to ponder the ultimate meaning and purpose of existence, I have found myself more and more interested in a phenomenon called the "gospel blues," that great era of black religious music led by gospel composers such as Charles A. Tindley, Lucie E. Campbell, Thomas Dorsey, and Roberta Martin, which took off with the rise of the recording era and ended more or less in the mid '70s with Aretha Franklin's *Amazing Grace* album. Out of this same music, and at the same time, came an extraordinary archive of recorded blues and the development of rhythm and blues with such crossover artists as Sam Cooke, Aretha Franklin, and Dinah Washington leading the way.

My latest musical interest is prompted by my recent trek to Jamaica— reggae by the culture hero Bob Marley and the more recently popular Lauryn Hill. Rastafarianism is a strangely mystical religion pursued by only a small minority of Jamaicans, perhaps 100,000 out of a population of over 2 million. There is a mystique about it that begins to make sense once you are in Jamaica for a while. Rastafarians have no church and no official doctrine except for the belief that Africa is the spiritual home of the black race to which all are destined to return. This notion of a spiritual return to Africa is characteristic of a variety of apocalyptic cultural forms in the African diaspora: Back in the past somewhere, someone made a wrong turn toward slavery or toward emigration, and if he had not, if we could retreat to some time in Africa before the wrong turn took place, then an effortless nirvana would be the result.

It makes sense that the harsher the realities of everyday life are in the present, the more unrealistic and imaginative the vision of transcendence is through an exploration of the past. Infused with the Garveyism of the '30s, Rastafarians regard Marcus Garvey as a prophet and Haile Selassie as God incarnate. They are known by their dreadlocks, their distrust of white interpretations of the Bible, and their belief that smoking ganja provides an opportunity to commune with God. I understand Bob Marley's music better now that I have seen the conditions of poverty and desperation in his native land. The music is fundamentally sacred and religious. Also clarified for me has been the recent turn of Lauryn Hill's career as seen in her fascinating performance on MTV's *Unplugged* in 2002.

Rising to fame via the enormous success of the release of *The Miseducation of Lauryn Hill*, the stunningly beautiful dark-skinned Lauryn Hill was suddenly featured on an array of magazine covers wearing skimpy designer fashions. After working with the Haitian artist Wyclef Jean as a member of the Fugees, Hill left Jean to pair up romantically with one of Bob Marley's sons, who sometimes accompanies her on drums. By 2002, after she gave birth to her third child, Hill cut her dreadlocks, scaled back her elaborate stage act, and sang simple, politically inflected songs to the accompaniment of her not particularly accomplished acoustic guitar playing. The presentation emphasized spiritual purity, emotional authenticity, and not aesthetic expertise. When one considers the signal effort of her success—the non-profit Refugee Project designed to help save and educate poor children in Haiti and elsewhere throughout the third world—the attempt to cleanse and purify her practice was stunning, albeit via a religion in which such female assertion was unprecedented. One of the songs on *Unplugged* is a cover of Bob Marley's "So Much Things to Say," in which she sings, "I'll never forget no way the way they crucified Jesus Christ," implying some comparison to the awful paradox of being rich and celebrated in a world in which being black continues to be a living hell for most. I won't try to defend the preaching and sermonizing that destroys the quality of much of the *Unplugged* CD, but I can say that I look forward to her survival as an artist, and I anticipate that her future development will be stunning to watch.

MY FOREMOST PRIORITY is taking care of myself and keeping my soul intact now that I am fifty-one years old and have had the unpleasant experience of watching so many of my contemporaries and immediate elders die. In recent years, the legions now include Addison Gayle, Larry Neale, Marlon Riggs, Essex Hemphill, Audre Lorde, June Jordan, Barbara Christian, Sherley Anne Williams, Claudia Tate, Toni Cade Bambara, David Jackson, and Joe Wood.

Black people die relatively young. Our life expectancy is not what it should be, even under the best of circumstances. Nobody really definitively knows why, except that I suspect that the world puts too much on us, and we are always all too willing to take it on. I do not want to join this crowd of short-lived lives. I am sad that the United States has gotten mixed up in so much global unpleasantness but, after all, it was to be expected when Congress decided to override the popular vote and put Bush into office. Now we citizens are paying the price and will continue to do so.

In the process, however, of this disaffection with the political climate, I have come to see and understand Afro-American music and Afro-American culture in a way I thought I never would, to empathize with its resilience and its ability to accommodate all manner of temporal circumstances. I think that with a better understanding of this musical legacy—and through the encouragement of those among the hip-hop generation such as Lauryn Hill, Meshell N'degeocello, Angie Stone, the Roots, Prince, Erykah Badu, Common, and other innovators who take their lead from the great Afro-American music of the past—that we will survive on the planet.

IV

In the first section of *Dark Designs*, you will encounter a brief essay I wrote for the photography magazine *Aperture* in which I use my last conversation with my paternal grandfather, who was from Jamaica, to talk about the alienation I felt from discussions around anti-Semitism that went on in New York in the wake of the Crown Heights riot, Skip Gates's critique of Afrocentrism in the *New York Times*, and Leonard Jeffries's unfortunate speech at the Black Arts Festival in Albany in 1991, which found its way onto the cover of the *New York Post*. Chapter 2—"Places I've Lived"—is an excerpt from an experimental memoir I've worked on for years, which pairs family photographs with text. In this section, I wrote about the first place I can remember living, in Momma Jones's apartment on Edgecombe Avenue. The picture is of myself and my sister Barbara, three and two years old respectively, my only first cousin Cheryl (Uncle Andrew's only child), who is five years older, Cheryl's mother Aunt Berneice, and my mother Faith, both of whom are twenty-four in the picture, and Momma Jones, the matriarch who is fifty-one, the same age I am now. The picture's fascination for me is that all the women in it are so different, gazing differently at entirely different things it seems, but what are those things? The situation mirrors the complicated ties of affiliation among the members of my family. The men are absent but, nevertheless, implied.

Chapter 3—"Engaging and Escaping"—is a set of responses to a series of questions *The Women's Review of Books* proposed to feminists about their reading and media watching habits in 1994. It was just at the point at which O. J. mania seemed endless. Forever the contrarian, I was into reading every news item except those about O. J. I had finally been diagnosed with lupus the year before, which I still believe was largely brought on by workaholism, exhaustion, an abusive diet, and stress, so I was not running around in the streets to the theatre and so forth as much as I had once done with Gene. But in place of that, I was doing all this promiscuous reading of the news, which was often so emotionally disquieting. I now think you have to seek a balance in life (given our endless access to information) between knowing all you can know and establishing and attempting to also maintain a central tranquility in your everyday existence. It sounds idealistic and utopian but unfortunately such loftiness is essential to meaningful and continuous intellectual production.

Chapter 4 is another excerpt from my ongoing experimental memoir project. I self-published this segment and sold it to the audiences at Yari-Yari, a conference of African diasporic women writers, which was held in 1998 at New York University by a special committee invited to do so by the department of Africana Studies under the mentorship of Manthia Diawara. The next essay, chapter 5, "Censorship and Self-Censorship," is the address I delivered at the conference, in which I talk about "a totalitarianism of the mind" in order to characterize the forces within the self that continue to inhibit black women around the world from engaging in free expression. Chapter 6 is an interview, which has never been published, with me for *The Harvard Advocate*, in which I talk about connections between my life and my work.

My move back to Brooklyn in 1989 facilitated a reunion with my old friend Susan McHenry. Susan had lived in Park Slope since 1979 back when she had first started as an editor at *Ms. Magazine* after completing her M.A. in English at Harvard. She was just then engaged in the startup of a new black magazine called *Emerge*. For the inaugural issue, she asked me to write about the then-hot phenomenon Arsenio Hall (chapter 7), who had achieved the miraculous distinction of being the first black person to ever host a nighttime talk show that was competitive in the ratings with both Johnny Carson and David Letterman. What is more, the show was hip, politically adventurous, and timely. You could say it had a hip-hop format slightly more sophisticated than *In Living Color* but similar in genre. Gene and I argued about whether it was defensible politically as it was commercial television par excellence.

One of the inherent difficulties with television history and criticism is that the real moments of distinction in the medium tend to be comparatively brief. As a consequence, when you see a serious catalogue of the best of television, it is composed largely of shows you've never heard of because in the blink of an eye you would have missed them. Therefore, I knew it didn't matter if Hall's moment lasted. Indeed, if it did turn out to be as fleeting as I suspected, that would be one of the signs of its significance. On the other hand, few people (only those who were paying attention at the time) would be able to remember it. And the reruns would be slow in coming. Thirteen years later, cable TV is splattered with Arsenio Hall spin-offs and look-alikes, but the only sign of Hall himself is in a series of tiresome "1–800-collect" commercials. I like to think, however, that somewhere behind the scenes, given his close ties with Eddie Murphy and the rest of the new funny boys, Arsenio is hooked up and wealthy on the down low.[2]

Meanwhile, I continued to write off and on for the *Village Voice*. I had written for it since 1975 after I met Ross Wetzsteon at a dinner party at Mark Mirsky's house. I had just graduated from City College in 1974 and fancied myself an accomplished writer of both fiction and new journalism. I told Ross I wanted to write for the *Village Voice* and he made it happen for me, as he did for so many others. His death a few years ago was an incalculable loss for constructive voices on culture at the *Voice*.

In 1989, I got to write two little pieces about film as my interest in the medium was growing post–*The Color Purple* and because of the innovations of Spike Lee and other young black filmmakers. The first piece (chapter 8) was on "Black Stereotypes in Hollywood Film," in which I basically repeated the conventional wisdom about stereotypical images. The particular occasion for rehashing the matter was the enormous success of Morgan Freeman and Jessica Tandy in *Driving Miss Daisy*. Indeed, I don't remember the film editor at the *Voice* then, but I can remember standing in his cramped office listening to him talk proudly about how, as a Southerner, he had really loved *Driving Miss Daisy*. Meanwhile, every black actor I knew was retching over it. Many blacks, I think, will never forgive Morgan Freeman, who is a perfectly superb actor, for taking that part. It was just one of the many times that I have had an occasion to marvel at the fact that often the "back of the book" cultural sections at any publication are in the hands of dinosaurs.

The other piece that year was on *The Group*, the movie (1966) and the book by Mary McCarthy. The movie, directed by Sidney Lumet, showcased the luminous Candace Bergen as the perfect blonde dyke goddess who dominated a circle of girls that graduated from Vassar together in 1933. The book was a page-turner and a veritable compendium of proto-feminist thought for the monied classes. I saw the movie in the theatre when I was fourteen and loved it. I would even go so far as to say that it was one of the signature pieces of my adolescence. At the time I wrote about it in 1990, I had finally mastered VCR technology so that I could obsessively review all my favorite films and show them to Gene.

"Storytellers" (chapter 10) was written after the conclusion of the Clarence Thomas–Anita Hill hearings. Like a lot of feminists I suppose, I fell hook, line, and sinker for Hill. I found her beauty and visual coolness arresting and her highly public victimization irresistible. Yet the trouble with publicly declaiming your victimization is that it often is hard to avoid reenacting that victimization. Of course, the political consequences of that moment of tragic TV drama have been almost too terrifying to contemplate. Clarence Thomas was installed on the Supreme Court permanently as the opening salvo in a rightward swing at the top that has not stopped yet.

"Conversations on the Gulf" (chapter 11) was another piece written in the heat of the moment when we had first gone to war with Saddam Hussein. At the time, I guess I was preoccupied with being among those who could get a chance to say something publicly about unfolding national and international situations, although now I am perfectly content not to take that call. There is very little that I have ever written under the deadline pressures of popular journalism that I haven't lived to deeply regret, but I am still proud of this piece on the Gulf War. I am proud of the fact that I understood even then how devastating a war in the Gulf would continue to be. War doesn't work well. The stated reasons for the war are imaginary and visionary while the real reasons are always mundane and material, such as oil or some such indispensable commodity. Nonetheless, war remains a holdover from a more primitive time. It continues to be outrageously wasteful, ridiculous, and totally ineffectual in terms of improving life on the planet.

So why do "we" do it? I don't know (and I don't include myself in that "we" either), but I think it parallels the interest in large sports events and the rise and fall of the stock market, both of which I also have little appreciation for. I think cryptic symbols and ornery ghosts motivate our collective lives. These entities move us around like chess pieces on a large fairytale chessboard, back and forth with no real advances. We live life with our backs against the wall. On one side, the harsh material realities; on the other, the symbols we don't understand and can't control.

Perhaps the piece that best epitomizes my feelings of regret concerning pop journalism is "For Whom the Bell Tolls," a literary profile of bell hooks (Gloria Watkins) that I wrote in a fit of pique for the *Voice Literary Supplement* (chapter 14). To their credit, both of the people I consulted about it —

Susan McHenry and Mom—told me *not* to go ahead with it, and I didn't tell my therapist about it until after it had closed.

If there were one thing I had ever written that I could un-publish and un-write, it would be this piece on bell hooks. Despite the fact that many black women of note privately thanked me for writing it, I think its real impact was to strike terror in the hearts of the many, even perhaps especially the ones who thanked me. I now think it is simply wrong to attack anyone in a piece of published writing for anything other than the most severe and extreme political disagreements. In other words, such ire should be reserved for dangerous reactionaries exclusively, the idea being to reserve one's bullets for real and present danger. No matter whatever bell might have done or not done—whatever direction she wanted to take her work in—it wasn't my place to chastise her publicly. All I did was humiliate myself publicly. Yet now that it is done, it cannot be undone.

I guess what made the way I acted feel inevitable was the publication of her book *Killing Rage*, which I read vociferously from cover to cover. Two things I thought I knew: (1) nothing good could ever come of a woman's rage, and (2) it is impossible to eradicate rage with more rage. I needed so badly to publicly dissociate myself from bell's feminist positions at that point—and the feeling that I was being engulfed by bell's reputation—that I just could not resist the urge to go on the offensive. Indeed, the whole thing is a perfect illustration of how rage can stem from a narcissistic wound to self-esteem, which often may have nothing to do with the particular situation at hand but with deep-seated feelings of inadequacy and inferiority. I am afraid that all too much race talk is tied up with the externalization of such internal psychological dynamics. What I did, and what I wrote, seems rather ridiculous to me now, but much intellectual history, once you separate it from its accoutrement of footnotes and self-perpetuating rhetoric of objectivity and critical distance, is often composed of a great deal that is patently absurd.

So I got bell and in the process, as much as I had wanted to get out of the attack business, I inadvertently reenlisted for yet another decade of service. Mea culpa. What else can I say? Perhaps I should not have included this essay but I felt as though it would be akin to Judy Garland trying to do a concert without singing "Somewhere Over the Rainbow" or "Melancholy Baby."

Which brings me to the greatest joy of this section, chapter 15—"Miracle in East New York," the first in a series of "Invisibility Blues" columns I wrote while substituting for Lisa Jones during her leave-of-absence from the *Voice*. This was absolutely the best and most spiritually empowering experience I have ever had of deadline journalism writing. One of the things that made it so great was having this incredible young editor—Angela Ards. Sometimes God just sends you an angel. Angela was that angel for me for pretty much the entire year during which I wrote this series of columns, beginning with this one about a production of Langston Hughes's *Black Nativity* in Reverend Johnny Ray Youngblood's maverick church in East New York during Christmastime in 1995. It combined many of my favorite elements of performance: Christmas, modern and African dance, gospel music, black Brooklyn, black church traditions, and a whole lot of other things. I owe this collaboration to one of my oldest cohorts in crime, Karen Durbin, who was my first editor at the *Village Voice* in 1975 and who briefly became editor-in-chief of the *Voice* at this time. Karen Durbin, Ellen Willis, and M Mark were the feminist editors at the *Voice*—all of them had stood by me at various crucial times in my career as a writer, and I watched them leave the *Voice* in utter frustration. We could name names but why bother? We know who and what they are. The real villain I believe is the very concept of commercial journalism, which has become a kind of monster in the arms of computer technology and global capitalism.

A former student, from the early days when I taught journalism at New York University (1975–1978), David Hadju, reemerged in my life as an editor at *Entertainment Weekly* and as the author of the brilliant Billy Strayhorn biography, which taught us all just how important the young Strayhorn had been to Duke Ellington's prodigious music writing talents. Soon after our reunion in 1993 (I believe I just called him up), he asked me to write a short feminist response to John Singleton's *Poetic Justice* for *Entertainment Weekly* (chapter 13). My take on it was that it was a failed women's film, (à la, for example, *A Star Is Born* or *Terms of Endearment*) as first defined for me by Molly Haskell in *From Reverence to Rape: The Treatment of Women in the Movies* (1973), and that issues of race were really secondary to the shortcomings of the film. In retrospect, I think it was such a star vehicle package for Tupac Shakur and Janet Jackson that generic considerations were ultimately drowned out. One of the biggest problems that black films continue to have in breaking away from the Hollywood mold, or setting some alternative agenda, is this obsession with recycling proven box office stars.

In the process of writing this short piece, I inadvertently sideswiped the poetry of Maya Angelou, who is the source of the poet's writings in the film. Despite her infinitely famous performance of the inaugural poem at the beginning of Clinton's presidency, I still think of the stellar Angelou as predominantly a wonderful essayist and autobiographical writer, as well as a riveting speaker and performer. Since 1990, however, I have come to have a much greater appreciation of the roots of the poetic sensibility she celebrates, which stems from the unjustly neglected writings of Paul Lawrence Dunbar—in particular his poetry in dialect. In turn, his work has its roots in a largely unexplored tradition of African American orality and folklore.

I guess the biggest break in this section, and the most widely read piece was "When Black Feminism Faces the Music, and the Music Is Rap" (chapter 9), which was published in the "Arts and Leisure" section of the *New York Times* in 1990. It was around the time that 2 Live Crew made everybody crazy with its misogynistic and sexually explicit rhetoric. To drive the stakes even higher, Henry Louis Gates Jr., who was fast becoming the most famous black academic anyone had ever seen from his perch as the chair of the newly refurbished Afro-American Studies at Harvard, decided to testify on their behalf in a suit brought against them on charges of pornography. It wasn't in the least surprising that the black feminist battle-ax (me) would be dragged out once again to do the heavy swinging, but the resulting damage turned out to be irreparable in many respects.

Honestly, I knew virtually nothing about rap at the time but couldn't say no to a chance to call its misogynism on the carpet, so I had to stumble through a series of idiosyncratic spellings of group names. It was inevitable that I would make mistakes, and I did, weakening my reputation with the young white editor whom I was assigned to work with. I can't recall her name but, with my luck, she's probably head of Condé Nast or is somebody equally powerful by now. Yet I couldn't turn and walk away from this sense of feeling personally persecuted by the "bitches and whores" rhetoric of some rappers. Even though I understood on some level that these weren't the major voices in this newish medium, they always seemed to get the biggest airtime in my neighborhood in the middle of the night when a black feminist was trying to sleep. Moreover, I have always despised loud music of any kind, and this nasty rap in particular is just plain loud for the sake of being loud. So here I go shooting off my mouth again. Yet I think I have learned a thing or two since then about the still newish music of hip-hop from an interview with Chuck D I once had the pleasure of reading. He said something like this: that hip-hop is either good or bad, on the side of doing right or doing wrong, and that there really isn't a lot of middle ground, which makes sense to me in terms of what I know about the streets. On the streets, there is not much moral ambivalence or a lot of nuance. So if you keep that in mind, you will be all right in terms of choosing what to listen to.

The seven essays in the third section of this book came out of a convergence of a series of related events. First, I presented a paper on Michael Jackson and the Grammys in 1988 at a Conference on Postmodernism and Television at SUNY, Buffalo, where I was then teaching American Studies.[3] At this conference, I met Maud Lavin, who was then working with Brian Wallis on *Global Television* (Wedge/MIT 1988), an anthology on TV in which the Michael Jackson piece was eventually included. Through Maud and Brian, I also met Philomena Mariani who organized many events at the Dia Center for the Arts, including assisting me monumentally in the planning of the Black Popular Culture Conference, which took place at the Studio Museum in Harlem and at Dia in Soho in 1991.[4] It was for Mariani's conference "Critical Fictions," which brought together political writers from around the world (including Angela Carter whom I got one chance to run with before she died), that I wrote "Black Feminist Criticism: A Politics of Location and Beloved" (chapter 17), a meditation on the political ramifications of Toni Morrison's *Beloved.*

Chapter 20, the short essay on "Political Correctness," was written for a forum on this subject at the instigation of Robert Stam (who was the first to suggest that I might seek a Ph.D. fellowship in Cinema Studies at NYU) in *Social Text* in 1993. But perhaps the key essay in this section is chapter 16, "The Politics of Location: Cinema/Theory/Literature/Ethnicity/Sexuality/Me," a heartfelt piece presented at a Cultural Studies conference in Birmingham, England, in 1989. On this occasion, I met Stuart Hall for the first time and got to spend more time with British filmmakers Isaac Julien and John Akomfrah. These young men, as well as their whole fascinating circle of British Blacks (anyone who wasn't white in Britain), helped me to imagine the life of the minority in a capitalist stronghold as one of subtlety, grace, and wit. Much like Afro-Americans, they were stylish folk in terms of hair, dress, and carriage but with just a twist of a difference. The effect was to clarify for me the potential for a worldwide Afro-diasporic, or even a worldwide people-of-color, aesthetic consciousness as a viable alternative to Anglo- or Eurocentrism.

I was also fascinated by the black appropriations of the British cultural studies of Raymond Williams and Terry Eagleton, in particular by theorists Paul Gilroy, Hazel Carby, and Kobena Mercer with Hall as their role model. The theoretical investigations are only fully understood through consideration of the substantial role played by the anecdotal and the autobiographical. Most useful in this light for me was, in particular, an autobiographical essay Stuart Hall wrote for *October* several years back in which he described the circumstances under which he left his homeland in Jamaica and embarked on his university education in Britain.

Hall continues to remind me, in terms of both intellectual style and substance, of precisely the kind of men the Wallaces were—my father and my grandfather before him, both of whom hailed from Black River in Jamaica.

Hall and I both had Portuguese Jewish great-grandfathers. At the time, Black British interrogations of theoretical discourses such as postmodernism and cultural studies around issues of race seemed to me the height of intellectual sophistication, and I suppose it still is. On the other hand, I have since come to suspect that there are more direct ways of making the same kinds of points. Nonetheless, it was an intervention in terms of academic language that was absolutely necessary to the future of the Left in doing intellectual work in the United States.

In any case, by the time my husband and I arrived in London for the conference, I was prepared to say two things. The first was to point out what I then considered the unmerited influence of Adrienne Rich in black feminist circles. Quite simply, I thought it unjustified because her camp gave *Black Macho* short shrift. At the time I didn't understand Rich's status as well as I do now, having since met her and served as her faculty host when she was awarded an honorary doctorate at CCNY. She taught at CCNY in the early open enrollment days; was one of the sweetest, most generous people anybody has ever met; was enlightened on issues of race, gender, and sexuality long before most whites; and had certain well-maintained loyalties to some of the early stars of black feminism such as Audre Lorde and June Jordan. The second point I sought to make in Birmingham, which has proven longer lasting in value, is that popular cultural images of black women circulate in insidious ways that are designed to exacerbate our political and intellectual silence. In the final analysis, it isn't such a great piece but it does capture something of the moment.

The most recent work I did under Brian Wallis as my editor is chapter 21, "The Culture War within the Culture Wars," for *Art Matters: How the Culture Wars Changed America* (NYU 1999). This essay is as accomplished and to the point as "The Politics of Location" is rough and improvisatory. I was disappointed by its non-reception, nevertheless. How does one get people who have only the vaguest sense of what race is to believe that not only does it exist in some real way but also that it is of great importance to be familiar with its historical and emotional repertoire? I don't know. I don't feel as though I have ever come close to accomplishing this.

The first conference I participated in at Dia was in 1988 on postcolonialism and film, and it was organized with consummate brilliance by Yvonne Rainer, the filmmaker and former dancer, and Berenice Reynaud, film critic for *Cahier du Cinema*. During these proceedings, I first met the fabulous Cuban-American diva, curator, and performance artist Coco Fusco who had organized a black British film series in the United States and introduced me to Isaac Julien, John Akomfrah, Martina Atille, and Ada Gay Griffith (who then worked for Third World Newsreel, the sponsor of the series). We had a chance to hang together at Coco's spot in Williamsburg and our place in Cobble Hill, making the trip to London and Birmingham (largely facilitated by Coco's efforts) a reunion of sorts. I also got to see bell and Kobena in action in response to a stodgy panel on feminist film criticism and psycho-analysis. Yvonne and Berenice maintained an admirable and exemplary cool throughout. It was their conference that I emulated in putting together *Black Popular Culture*. The afterword from the anthology, "Why Are There No Great Black Artists?" (chapter 18, which was delivered on the final day of the conference), and "*Boyz N the Hood* and *Jungle Fever*" (chapter 22), which was delivered on the first day on the first panel, are included in this section.

Multiculturalism was one of the themes in cultural work of the '90s along with, and interwoven with, postmodernism, poststructuralism, and post-colonialism. Institutional strategies and discourses of multiculturalism were most forthright about issues of diversity and the problem of how the United States would need to change in order to accommodate increasing popula-tions of color. In 1989, Jim Drobenick interviewed me on multiculturalism and postcolonialism for an obscure dance magazine. "Multiculturalism and Oppositionality" (chapter 25) was written in response to a series of multicul-tural events: Reynaud's and Rainier's film festival and conference on post-colonialism at Dia in 1989; "The Decade Show," a joint exhibition at the New Museum of Contemporary Art, the Museum of Contemporary Hispanic Art, and the Studio Museum in Harlem; and Rainier's film *Privilege*. It is inter-esting to look back at this time and to realize how much everything about the art scene has changed; how the spaces that were then available for intel-lectual inquiry into issues of multiculturalism and diversity, particularly at the Dia Center for the Arts and the Whitney Museum of Art, have dried up along with the availability of creative and adventurous funding from the National Endowment on the Arts.

"Race, Gender, and Psychoanalysis in Forties Film" (chapter 23) was writ-ten for Manthia Diawara's *Black American Cinema* (Routledge 1993). It deals with my longing to know more about the racial repertoire of '40s films, in particular film noir. I wanted to figure out whether noirish technique might have a racial correlate. Although I did not realize this at the time I wrote this, I now believe that it does through the mechanism of the McCarthy Era Black Lists. Many black performers', writers', and intellectuals' lives were changed, and their careers circumscribed, by the witch-hunts of the McCarthy Era, in-cluding Lena Horne, Paul Robeson, and W. E. B. Du Bois. Others simply ran for the hills—to Canada, Europe, or the relative safety of early retirement and married life in the suburbs. The double message of political pessimism as expressed through a darkly layered aesthetics is part of what film noir was all about. The other part was that Hollywood films were at the peak of their success and thus strong enough to launch plainly subversive offshoots or, that is, noir films that, more or less, plainly engage in political assaults on the status quo (*Criss Cross* et al.).

In 1995, when I was a Visiting Scholar at Douglass College, I delivered "Black Women in Popular Culture" (chapter 26) as my public address, in which I analyzed some of the consistent features, from the heroic to the absurd, of the image of the black woman in mass culture. "The Search for the Good Enough Mammy" (chapter 27) was an attempt to use some ideas borrowed from object-relations psychoanalysis to investigate racist assumptions about black mothers and black women in black film and U.S. culture.

In 1990, I was assigned by *Emerge* to interview Henry Louis Gates Jr., which I was very eager to do. I had last seen Skip when he was a new assistant professor, with his dissertation from Oxford barely finished. I was living in New Haven and going to graduate school at Yale. Since then he had taught at Yale, moved on to Cornell and then Duke, won a MacArthur, and was beginning to make a major splash in the *New York Times* as well as academia for his considerable entrepreneurial capacities. I studied Gates's important anthology *Black Literature and Literary Theory* (1984) while at the University of Oklahoma until the pages were dog-eared. Almost every essay is still a gem in my estimation. Gates's introduction appropriates stellar Deconstructionist Gregory Hartman's project in rereading Matthew Arnold in order to point to the "irony implicit in the attempt to posit a 'black self' in the very Western languages in which blackness itself is a figure of absence, negation" ("Criticism in the Jungle," 7). All the extremely then-fashionable structuralist and poststructuralist rhetoric and machinations still leave some people reeling, but it was intoxicating to discover such texts from a black writer who sought a way to establish a critical voice. Gates's books *Figures in Black: Words, Signs and the 'Racial' Self* (1987) and *The Signifying Monkey: A Theory of Afro-American Literary Criticism* (1988) were impressive as well, far and away the most important black publications in the humanities in the '80s. Since then, I had returned to the Northeast and was beginning to access some of the rumblings in the art world about whether poststructuralism could be appropriated for what we used to call "liberatory discourse." In other words, was poststructuralism just more bars on the cage or was it a tool that could finally bring down the master's house? I tried to argue something of the latter in the pages of my master's thesis (1989), which was republished as the last two chapters in *Invisibility Blues: From Pop to Theory* (Verso 1990).

Aunt (paternal) Doris, Doris Rhino (about twenty years old), b. 1906 in Jamaica. Cameo Photo Studio in Harlem.

Momma T (paternal grandmother), b. 1903, Theodora Grant, about twenty years old on a Harlem rooftop (1920s).

Grandpa Bob (paternal), b. 1895, Robert Osmond Wallace, about twenty-five, the '20s in Momma T's apartment at 365 Edgecombe Avenue in military uniform.

Grandpa Bob (paternal) in bohemian calypso outfit with guitar, about thirty, the 1930s in Harlem.

Earl as an infant with Christmas toy in Kingston, Jamaica, living with grandparents then. Morais Photo Studio, photographer: W. G. Morais, circa 1930.

Earl, my father at about ten with his mother, Theodora,
standing in front of a Christmas tree at 365 Edgecombe
Avenue during the Depression.

Earl, at about ten with his cousin Carol and Momma T on unspecified waterfront.

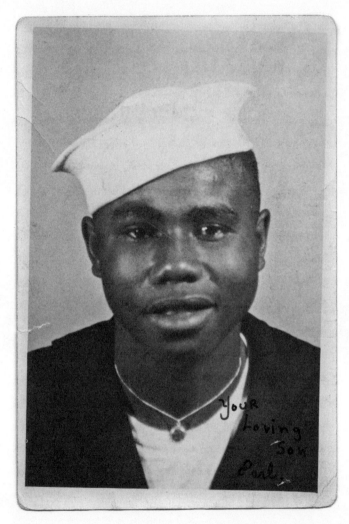

Earl in the navy at sixteen in 1943. He lied about his age to get in and then went AWOL constantly because he was homesick.

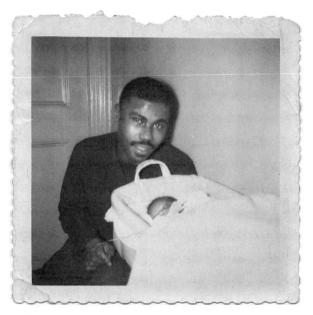

Earl with his newborn daughter, Michele, January 1952, at 365 Edgecombe Avenue.

Above: Michele, almost one year old at Momma Jones's apartment, 363 Edgecombe Avenue, awaiting the arrival of her new little sister, Barbara, born December 15, 1952. *Opposite, top:* Momma Jones feeding Michele with Mr. Morrison looking on, 1952. *Opposite, bottom:* Momma Jones as Mme. Willi Posey, all dolled up in her own fashions, about 1950 at 363 Edgecombe Avenue. Photo by Thomas Morrison.

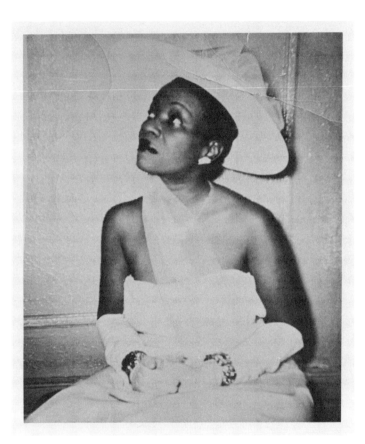

Above: Momma Jones, Mme. Willi Posey, in a fashion pose photographed by Thomas Morrison, about 1950. *Opposite, top:* Uncle Cardoza, Momma Jones's oldest brother, with Faith at her college graduation, B.S. City College, 1955. *Opposite, bottom:* Aunt Barbara at her graduation from Hunter College with the M.S. in Education about 1955.

Ann Porter, Momma Jones's favorite model, at 363 Edgecombe Avenue in 1954.

January 1955 at 363 Edgecombe Avenue. Clockwise: Aunt Berneice, Michele (third birthday), Barbara (with head turned looking at Aunt Berneice), Cousin Cheryl, Mom Faith, and Momma Jones.

Barbara and Michele with Mme. Willi Posey (Momma Jones) at a fashion show in 1959. Mom Faith in sunglasses in the background.

Mme. Willi Posey in sunglasses with Mr. Morrison and a favorite model, Margaret. Circa 1960. Photo by George Hopkins.

Faith when she was still a Wallace, modeling in one of Momma Jones's fashion shows, circa 1960.

APRIL 1972

Michele at twenty modeling a Mme. Willi Posey design at a fashion show, 1972.

Barbara on a bike in London, 1977, while in graduate school.

Michele with Momma Jones in blonde wig at graduation from City College, outside of Madison Square Garden, June 1974. Photo by Faith Ringgold.

Margo Jefferson, Michele, Carol Lee, and unidentified woman posing at 345 West 145th Street. When you're young, everything is potentially funny. It is 1975 and I was twenty-three. Photo by Faith Ringgold.

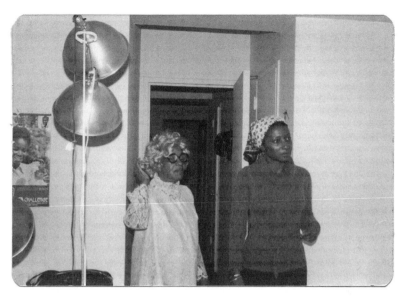

Momma Jones and Michele awaiting photographic session with Faith. For Momma Jones it was her wedding (to Mr. Morrison) pictures and for Michele, an author's photo for the back of *Black Macho*. At 345 West 145th Street in Harlem. Photo by Faith Ringgold.

Michele on the terrace at Washington Square Village, while teaching journalism at NYU. Spring of 1978. Photo by Barbara F. Wallace.

Momma Jones, Momma T, and Faith with Michele, 1978. Photo by Anthony Barboza, used in *Ms. Magazine* layout for *Black Macho*.

Overhead. Michele reading from *Black Macho* at the Feminist Salon in Westbeth, fall 1978. Photo by Barbara F. Wallace.

Gloria Steinem introducing the *Black Macho* cover issue of *Ms. Magazine* at the Women's Bank with Dorothy Height, December 1978. Photo by Barbara F. Wallace.

Michele signing cousin Cheryl's book at the Women's Bank. Photo by Barbara F. Wallace.

Michele with Momma Jones and Mr. Morrison at the Women's Bank. Photo by Barbara F. Wallace.

My bulletin board at Washington Square Village, December 1978. Photo by Barbara F. Wallace.

Michele in Washington Square Park. 1979. Photographer unknown.

Michele on the *Donahue Show*. Photo by Barbara F. Wallace. 1979.

Michele and David Baldwin. Photo by Barbara F. Wallace.

Faith Ringgold soft sculpture group in house in New Haven, 1982. Photo by Barbara F. Wallace.

Barbara pregnant in her apartment after Momma Jones's death in 1981. Cousin Mildred in the background, Cheryl and Aunt Berneice.

Momma T, Baby Faith, and Michele, 1982. Photo by Barbara F. Wallace.

Baby Faith at the Bronx Zoo, 1983. Photo by Barbara F. Wallace.

Faith (Professor Ringgold) among the eucalyptus at UC San Diego with mask, 1984. Photo by C. Love.

My future husband Gene, almost thirty, on the beach in La Jolla, California, 1985.

Faith with her new baby sister Teddy, in Harlem, 1985. Photo by Barbara F. Wallace.

Faith on the terrace in Harlem, 1985. Photo by Barbara F. Wallace.

Gene with his Mom and his niece, Neisha, in 1987 in a La Jolla hotel room.

Michele with Baby Faith in office at UC San Diego, 1987. Photo by Barbara F. Wallace.

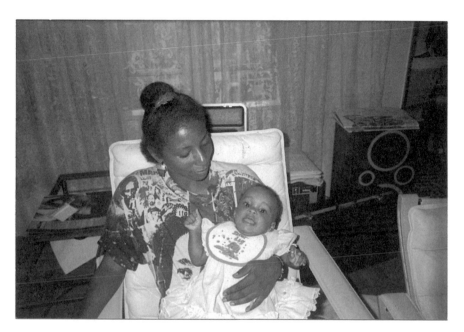

Michele with Baby Martha. Photo by Barbara F. Wallace.

Michele in the Florida Everglades, 1988. Photo by Gene Nesmith.

Gene with his brothers Terry, Nathan, and Art, and his mother at his father's funeral in Naples, Florida, 1989. Gene is the most handsome one.

Barbara and Sandy (Martha's Dad) with Faith, Teddy, and Martha, 1989.

Virginia, Gene, Birdie, and Faith with me at Gene's and my wedding, December 1989. Photo by Corinne Jennings.

Grandma with Faith and Theodora in downtown New York.

Black Writers Conference at Medgar Evers, 1990. Michele on the panel with Quincy Troupe, Steve Cannon, David Bradley, Arthur Flowers. Photo by Eugene B. Redmond.

Michele at Grand Army Plaza, 1991.

Faith at fourteen.

Slave Rape #1, Faith Ringgold self-portrait, in Brooklyn apartment, 1992. Photo by Michele Wallace.

Yari-Yari International Black Women
Writers Conference. Panel with Paula Giddings,
Sapphire, Ama Ata Aidoo, and Michele, 1997.
Photo by Geeta Citygirl.

Ph.D. Defense Party at Professor Jane Marcus's house, 1998.

Bamboozled Panel, NYU: Eric Lott, Margo Jefferson, Stanley Crouch, and Clyde Taylor, 2000.

Jamaica—the hillside shanties, 2003. Photo by Faith Wallace-Gadsden.

Jamaica—the road stands, 2003. Photo by Faith Wallace-Gadsden.

Treasure Beach—barbed wire fences, 2003. Photo by Faith Wallace-Gadsden.

To make a long story much too short, Gates was always someone to be excited about among black scholars in the humanities. Where he seems to get in the most trouble is when he wanders away from our cozy circles by making grand statements concerning the territories of black scholars in other more policy-driven fields, such as politics and the social sciences. Both were at issue in his *Encyclopedia Africana* project, which is the subject of chapter 35 and published here for the first time. Included in this section as well are two short pieces on the Million Man March, which raised some protests among black feminists because of the numbers of otherwise laudatory black activists, such as Derrick Bell and Cornel West, who seemed to accept the idea that black men needed to publicly atone for their sins and that black women should be excluded from the process. Chapter 33, "The Problem with Black Masculinity and Celebrity," and chapter 34, "The Fame Game," consider the devastating negative impact of modern celebrity on depth and seriousness in black discourses.

The final section of this book on "Queer Theory and Visual Culture" gathers together nineteen essays in which I take on various issues of visual culture, sometimes also in relation to my interest in queer theory via feminist theorists Eve Sedgwick and Judith Butler. Although I received my Ph.D. in Cinema Studies under the mentorship of Manthia Diawara and Christine Straayer, I discovered conclusively that I am no major theory head but that there are some qualities in the way queer studies uses theory that I find rather useful to my way of looking at black feminist studies. The problematization of essentialism and identity feels necessary to me as a product of a mixed marriage (Caribbean and Afro-American) and as a descendant of a Portuguese Jew, an Ashanti, and myriad African and Native American tribes.

Chapter 36, "Defacing History," was written under the editorship of Brian Wallis for *Art-in-America* in 1990. It commenced my foray into the world of the image of the black in nineteenth-century American art and facilitated my discovery of the important work of Afro-American art historians Albert Boime, Judith Wilson, Rick Powell, and Lowery Sims. Chapter 37, "When Dream Girls Grow Old," was written on the death of the actress Butterfly McQueen (who played Prissy in *Gone with the Wind*) by fire in 1995. Chapter 38 was written in 1991 about *The French Collection*, a series of paintings by Mom, in which she imagines a black female character in Paris in the '20s who combines the vocational characteristics of herself, my grandmother Momma Jones, and Josephine Baker.

Chapter 39, "Modernism, Postmodernism, and the Problem of the Visual in Afro-American Culture," was written at the request of Cornel West, for inclusion in the collection *Out There: Marginalization and Contemporary Culture* (1991). It was my first meaningful attempt to make a statement concerning the position of Afro-American painters within the realm of visual modernism and in relation to European primitivism's appropriation of African art.

Chapter 40 was written as an obituary for the extraordinary filmmaker Marlon Riggs, whom I first met at a film event at the Whitney Museum and whom I subsequently knew as a result of his participation in the Black Popular Culture conference. Chapter 41 is a review of the republication of *Harlem on My Mind* on the anniversary of the famous exhibition at the Metropolitan Museum of Art in 1978, which launched the protest movement against major museums in the black art world.

Chapters 42 through 47 and chapters 51 through 53 have all been published before. "Questions of Feminism" (chapter 42) first appeared in *October* as part of a discussion about essentialism. "Feminism, Race, and the Division of Labor" (chapter 43) was a catalogue essay for an exhibition at the Bronx Museum on feminist art in the '70s. In it, I wrote for the first time about my unwitting participation in my mother's arrest by the district attorney's office for desecration of the flag at the Judson Memorial Church in 1971. Chapter 44, "*Doin' the Right Thing*," is a profile of Spike Lee that I wrote for the *Village Voice* at the time that *Girl 6* came out. "The Gap Alternative" (chapter 45) was written as a catalogue essay for a portraiture show at the Southampton Museum on Long Island. "Art on My Mind" (chapter 46) is a review of the bell hooks book of the same title for the *Women's Review of Books*. Chapter 51 is a review of director Cheryl Dunye's first feature film, *The Watermelon Woman* (1997). Chapter 52, "The Prisonhouse of Culture: Why African Art? Why the Guggenheim? Why Now?" is an essay that first appeared in *Renaissance Noire*. "Black Female Spectatorship and the Dilemma of Tokenism" (chapter 53) considers the problem of tokenism in the world of academic feminist film criticism.

Of the essays not published previously, chapter 48, "*The Hottentot Venus*," is an essay on the practice of human display with a particular focus on the first historical example of Saartje Baartman, who was brought from South Africa to France and England where her large buttocks were put on display in the eighteenth century. Chapter 49, "*Angels in America, Paris Is Burning*, and Queer Theory," considers the politics of the AIDS crisis in relationship to representations of AIDS and homosexuality in Tony Kushner's plays *Angels in America* and Jane Livingstone's documentary *Paris Is Burning*. Chapter 50, "Toshi Reagon's Birthday," is about Reagon's annual birthday concerts. Chapter 54 is a review of "*Bamboozled*," in part previously published in *Renaissance Noire*. The themes in visual culture explored in this section will be further elucidated in future publications.

Notes

1. Valerie Boyd, *Wrapped in Rainbows: The Life of Zora Neale Hurston* (New York: Scribner, 2003).
2. Raymond Williams, *Television, Technology, and Cultural Forms* (London: Fontana/Collins, 1974).
3. Reprinted in *Invisibility Blues* (New York: Verso, 1990; reissued edition forthcoming).
4. Gina Dent, ed., *Black Popular Culture: A Project by Michele Wallace* (Seattle: Bay Press, 1991; reprint, New York: New Press, 2000).

I.

1.

Whose Town? Questioning Community and Identity

When I was twenty-seven years old, a few days before Grandpa Bob (my father's father) died, he called to tell me about a Portuguese Jew, a slave owner who settled in Jamaica in the early nineteenth century and who had children with an Ashanti woman. After the Ashanti rebellion and the emancipation of the slaves in the British West Indies in the 1830s, this Portuguese Jew married the Ashanti woman. They became my grandfather's grandparents — my great-great grandparents. That day on the telephone, Grandpa Bob gave me the keys to learning something I've never forgotten about identity and community: both are realized through processes, the former of accumulated information and self-revelation, the latter of competing group conceptualizations and interests. Neither is immediately understood but rather unfolds over time, each in tension with the other, according to how curious and open one is to becoming aware of the inner logic and evolution of both.

My artist mother had divorced my musician father when I was two. I had grown up in Harlem knowing my mother's family best. They were originally from Florida and transplanted to Harlem in the 1910s. When Momma Jones, my mother's mother, would entertain us on Thanksgiving with stories about how Betsy Bingham, her grandmother (who seemed so very black in her photographs), was half Cherokee, everybody would collapse with laughter. But perhaps because of these same stories, when I was in a position to pay attention to Native Americans, I did. Living in Oklahoma, the state that almost entered the union as Sequoyah, a Native American State, and in Buffalo, where there is a large Native American community, I studied the history of the Cherokee, their sojourns in Georgia, Tennessee, and Oklahoma, the forced removal of their Trail of Tears, and I learned that Momma Jones was probably telling the truth.

A socialist, an atheist, an astrologer, a musician, a painter, and a horticulturist who was well read in several languages, Grandpa Bob strived to teach me, as I was growing up, a comparative sense of black community. With his facility for accents and his knowledge of the guitar, he recreated Jamaica for my childhood entertainment as an anarchic patchwork of ethnicities, dialects, and songs. Moreover, his stories about Harlem and the United States in the 1920s and 1930s made clear that such diversity was effectively transplanted and further variegated in its new setting. On the telephone on that particular day, the last time we ever spoke, he told me many things about his own and his family's history that he hadn't told me before. He had just finished reading my first book, *Black Macho and the Myth of the Superwoman*, and it must have occurred to him that as the family writer, I could make some immediate use of the information he was giving me.

Grandpa Bob's and Momma Jones's revelations led to my wanting to know how many great-great grandparents I'd had (everybody has sixteen) and how many I could account for. From then on, I began to wonder what a great-great grandparent was, indeed what a parent was. How many great-great grandparents determine one's identity? How many family locations in history determine one's community? How many races determine one's ethnicity?

Of course, the overwhelming majority of my ancestors were black and I grew up in a black neighborhood, which makes me black. But I like to think of myself as mixed and as a citizen of the world. I never forget, have never forgotten since my grandfather told me, that I had a great-great grandfather who was a Portuguese Jew, anymore than I would forget that I had a great-great grandmother who was Ashanti or another great-great grandmother who was half Cherokee and half African.

When events began to occur in Crown Heights and when Leonard Jeffries began to appear regularly on the evening news, and the assumption became law in the press — "high" and "low" — that blacks have become haters of Jews, for the hundredth time in the last decade I felt at a loss for "community." This feeling was only amplified when I saw that the hoards in the streets of Crown Heights — both the West Indian youth and the Hasidic youth — were predominantly male. No self-respecting woman could have any identification with such vigilante tactics on either side. Again I began to wonder about the nature of community and identity. Are these established through class, race, turf, gender? Or is each mutually exclusive of the rest? Cries of racism were sparking debate at the City College of New York (CCNY) long before Leonard Jeffries's infamous speech on July 20, 1991, at the Black Arts Festival in Albany. Dr. Michael Levin, a white professor of philosophy, had been publishing articles contending that "it has been amply confirmed over the last several decades that on average, blacks are significantly less intelligent than whites." Meanwhile, the black Dr. Jeffries was espousing his views with regard to the materialistic, greedy "ice people" — those of European descent — versus the humanistic, communal "sun people" — those of African descent. American Jews as a "community" since World War II have managed to transform their experience of oppression into a state of privilege, in part through their unconscious identification with a national system of white elitism. Yet some black Americans may have been reacting to world systems of white dominance by an unconscious identification with anti-Semitism.

Twenty years ago, Jeffries was installed as permanent head of Afro-American studies at City College in Harlem (where I also teach). He was given tenure and a full professorship without publications. The Afro-American studies paradigm which Henry Louis Gates Jr. at Harvard University, Houston Baker Jr. at the University of Pennsylvania, and even Molefi Asante at Temple University have advanced is a program in which faculty are initially appointed in traditional disciplines in the humanities or the social sciences. Their courses are then cross-listed with Afro-American Studies and/or Women's studies and/or Latino studies. As a consequence of Jeffries's leadership style, most black professors in the conventional disciplines at CCNY choose to disassociate themselves from Afro-American studies. Nevertheless, the continued presumptions in the press that Jeffries's speeches stand for "black community" in Harlem and at CCNY may destroy us and, in the process, many good people who wish to preserve the delicate equilibrium of intelligent discussions about "identity" and "community." Whereas Crown Heights and Jeffries were local New York fiascoes — albeit with national implications — whose focuses were primarily racial "communities" and where a few voices were said to represent many, the Anita Hill–Clarence Thomas hearings threatened (happily) to fully demystify the myth of a national black identity or black community.

Besides the experience of sexual harassment, I share with Hill and with all other black women the negative "community" and negative "identity" of being a silenced black female subject in a world in which we continue to be represented only as objects. This is why, incidentally, our voices are so rarely heard in the press in times of national or local crisis. This is why nobody knows what informed female intellectuals of color think about Crown Heights, or Leonard Jeffries, or Hill-Thomas. Most black women — as their response to the hearings and their distrust of Hill proved — are unaware of their membership in a "silenced" community, their stake in a negatively constructed "identity." But some black women — as it happens the educated ones, the professional ones, the married and unmarried, heterosexual and lesbian ones who have touched the glass ceilings, floors, walls, and locked doors with their fingertips, and, indeed, rammed against them with their skulls — know that Hill is one of us. Despite Hill's Bible Belt conservative Republican politics, and despite all the floating, socially and culturally constructed and negotiated identities of race, gender, class, sexuality, she has begun to learn the one thing that unites us as a conceptual "community," which we might call the black feminist community. The difference between black women who are pro-Thomas and anti-Thomas cannot be fully explained by our membership in communities of race, gender, class, or sexuality — or identities forged in the mantle of same — but by how deeply we, as individual subjects, have had to become aware of the following painful fact: it is our job to fight for justice for black girls because no one else will. What often has joined people together — forming perhaps the most powerful sense of community — has been the need to be heard. This fight for a voice is what black feminists, myself included, have in front of them. Hill, and white feminists, may call it the fight against sexual harassment. They may call it the fight to displace the members of the Senate Judiciary Committee. They may call it anything they like.

Originally published in *Aperture*, spring 1992, 31–39.

2.

Places I've Lived

As a child, I felt as though I knew everybody on Edgecombe Avenue. From 145th street to 155th street, Harlem was divided into Sugar Hill and the Valley by a body of land that descended as sharply as a canyon. This land, which included several stone stairways connecting Sugar Hill and the Valley, was called Colonial Park. Colonial Park was a dense, lush wonderland sprinkled with one or two playgrounds for children and a large swimming pool heavily used in the summertime.

On one side of the park at the bottom of a hill was the crowded, chaotic, and poor Bradhurst Avenue, where Aunt Berneice and my only first cousin Cheryl lived. Cheryl was five years older than I was and Momma Jones's only other grandchild besides my sister Barbara and myself.

The story I remember best about Cheryl's father, my uncle Andrew, my mother's brother, is about how a naked woman once chased him down the street. It was my impression that the story was always told in order to illustrate how attractive he was and how no good he was. I have often imagined the woman running naked and barefoot down the gloomy un-sunlit streets of the Valley, a crowd of people watching her, talking about her, and pointing at her.

On the other side of the park at the top of the hill was Edgecombe Avenue, which was always sunlit and clean. West of Edgecombe, including Edgecombe, was Sugar Hill.

Edgecombe Avenue was a street that ran about twenty blocks with apartment buildings on one side, park benches and the trees of Colonial Park on the other. There was only one store on Edgecombe Avenue: a small candy store run by a dark-skinned old man with a face like a prune who never smiled, who smoked a cigar, and who sold Coca-Colas from an ice-filled chest.

From the time I was two until I was seven years old, from 1954 to 1959, my mother Faith, my sister Barbara, and I lived with my grandmother Momma Jones in a five-room apartment on the fourth floor of a walk-up at 363 Edgecombe Avenue in Harlem. 363 was one in a series of three five-story buildings—the other two were 365 and 367—which were exactly alike. Before I was two, and before Faith and my father broke up, we had lived principally in Momma T's apartment on the third floor in 365 with my father, a jazz musician. These buildings, all of which had stoops, four apartments on each floor with fire escapes in the front, were much like any number of tenement buildings you've seen in photographs of apartment buildings in Harlem, or anywhere in New York during the '30s, the '40s, or the '50s. They weren't sad little railroad flats with the toilets in the hallway, but they were small, cramped, and roach-ridden.

Many of the buildings on Edgecombe Avenue were better looking, broader or taller, or with elaborate courtyards or lobbies, or doormen or elevators. Edgecombe had once been much more distinctly upper middle class around the turn of the century before blacks moved in. Even after blacks had moved onto Edgecombe, it continued to be a prestigious and elegant neighborhood. But by the '50s, Edgecombe was more working class than bourgeois although in black neighborhoods, the two are by no means mutually exclusive.

I think I can remember more about Momma Jones's apartment and her neighbors on Edgecombe Avenue than any place I've ever lived. Upstairs, there was a young couple named Porter—the husband was tall, thin, and light complexioned and the wife was dark with beautiful skin and innocent mournful eyes, fat with several small babies. Regularly, I could hear them fighting through the walls and him beating her. Next door to us was a buxom woman named Rovena. She was glamorous with dyed red hair, and she sometimes got drunk on the weekends. Underneath us was a very light-skinned woman with straight hair (she looked practically white) who came to the door in an apron and was always cooking. She also drank. She had an interesting daughter, a teenager with long, thick dark hair and circles around her eyes. Everybody said she was off. Later, when she became an adult, she lost her mind and roamed the streets begging. But first she got married and Momma Jones, who was a fashion designer, did the wedding gown.

Also on the third floor was a woman whose face I can't remember who used to make powdered milk for me because I was allergic to regular milk. She would bring it in a large glass bottle, cold and frothing at the top. I remember liking the rather sweet taste of it, but little did I know that I was allergic to powdered milk as well, and it was partly the cause of the very bad eczema I had. Another reason for my eczema might have been the chronic dust in the building, on the stairways, and behind the radiators especially, which also contributed to my mother's asthma.

On the second floor there was an entire family about which I was eternally curious. The mother looked rather like the mother on "Lassie," except that she was brown. The children, who were all teenagers when I first remember knowing them, were all very large and very dark. The two boys were like giants. The oldest one soon turned out to be a criminal and a thief who went in and out of jail. The youngest one was retarded and never spoke but hung around in front of the building. Sometimes children teased him, but I never saw him get angry. The girl, who was between the two boys in age, was constantly in the company of boys from the age of thirteen. A few years later she became a drug addict and a prostitute.

My best friend Dede lived on the first floor with her mother, her father, and several other people. Almost the only thing I can remember about Dede is that she had fantastic energy and later on it turned out that she was much poorer than I was. My sister and I never went to school with anybody who came from Edgecombe Avenue because from the time we were first sent to nursery school when we were two and three, we were always sent to private schools.

Originally published in *Assemblage: A Critical Journal of Architecture and Design Culture* 20 (1993): 86–87.

3.

Engaging and Escaping in 1994

My morning paper of choice is, of course, the *New York Times*. Ages ago I used to get up and watch *The Today Show*—I was so much younger I can no longer remember why. I guess, like a lot of other feminists, I had a thing for Jane Pauley. Now I rarely ever rise before 9:00 A.M., and if I do, the last thing in the world I want to hear is the sound of a television. In fact, I never read the morning paper in the morning. I read it, quite deliberately, in the afternoon or even at night. Around 10:00 or 11:00 A.M. or so, I turn on WINS on the radio (a truly provocative station in regard to political matters in the city) for the sake of learning the weather forecast, without which I can no longer conceptualize the rest of my day.

As soon as I've discovered the weather and, hopefully, in the process, the traffic report telling me which subway is not running because it has had a fire or a flood or a bomb (I live in Brooklyn, so I have to take the subway to get to Manhattan), if I still feel as though I want more chat and information, and I don't have to rush from the house just then to teach or go to the dentist or to my therapist, I turn to National Public Radio. In particular, my favorite is Lenny Lopate, whom I regard as a close personal friend (I have been interviewed by him twice), spiritual guide, and fellow traveler.

Occasionally, especially if I've missed my NPR fix, I will also take a peek at *McNeil/Lehrer* in order to feel as though I am catching up on the progress of international events. Not that watching the show generally helps much, but I always feel more virtuous afterward, especially if Charlayne Hunter-Gault does a segment with a black dignitary from somewhere.

The next possible option is *Nightline* with Ted Koppel at 11:30 P.M. on ABC. I never watch any TV during the day, and won't watch most things at night. I have come to abhor all talk and game shows and most new situation comedies. The best shows, if I have time, which I usually don't, are the reruns: *Barney Miller, Jackie Gleason Show, Taxi, Roc, The Cosby Show, The Odd Couple,* and so forth. The only new show I absolutely love is *Star Trek: Voyager* (a real feminist breakthrough with a middle-aged female captain and a sweet black Mr. Spock-type as her second in command), and, of course, I am a fan of all the other *Star Trek* formats.

MY NEWS ORGAN of choice is the *New York Times* unless sudden, large-scale genocide, death, or disaster occurs in Waco, Oklahoma City, South Central LA, Tokyo, Bosnia, Rwanda, India, or China, in which case I tune into CNN like everybody else. In the face of what sometimes seems to be perennial world disorder and widespread mayhem, personally, I find the formulaic calculated ministrations of the CNN news team, with its canned commercial breaks and its repetitive news briefs, oddly reassuring. My thinking goes something like this: If CNN is still breaking for a Jack LaLanne ad, or whatever, then the airport is still open, the Congress must still be screwing around with the new Surgeon General's confirmation hearings, and Clinton is still in the White House.

But while I'll admit it can be both entertaining and calming (although not necessarily informative) to watch the TV newspeople fumbling over the facts and getting hysterical over rumors in the first throes of a breaking story (e.g., the widespread but totally unconfirmed rumor that Arab terrorists were responsible for the Oklahoma bombing), frequently I just don't have the hours it generally takes to see them through it and must settle for the synopsis in the morning paper (always read in the afternoon, in any case). Given this scenario, I much prefer my news predigested, suitably picked over, salvaged and dressed up, which is why I generally stick with the *Times.*

After all, it is still the paper of record, isn't it? I like the sense of order that having the *Times* delivered to my house, and reading it every day, gives me. Although my teachers were always yapping about reading it, I did not grow up in a household in which the *Times* was religiously read, although I did grow up in New York, in Harlem, in fact. My family preferred the *Herald Tribune* before it went out of business, and then the *Daily News.* (They also preferred *The Steve Allen Show* to *The Ed Sullivan Show*, whatever that means.)

But, for me, the *Daily News* has always seemed too local, too provincial, too much like papers all over the country. I want the sense that I know what is going on in the world when I read a paper, even if I really don't. I always tell my students that they must read the *New York Times* if they are to have any hope of being informed. I feel about the *New York Times* kind of like Lacanian feminist film critics used to feel about the "symbolic" and "the Law of the Father." You damn well better know it.

Since I have been reading the *Times* for so long now, I can say that I find it weirdly titillating to keep track of its agonizingly slow (sometimes non-existent) progress over the years on feminist issues, gay issues, AIDS issues, race issues, welfare, the homeless, and so forth. Increasingly, I believe that the only life worth living is one lived in the expectation of progress and improvement on certain fundamental social problems. In the absence of any concrete evidence of progress, supposition, speculation and even fantasy will do. Whatever it takes to remain reasonably positive is justified because from the moment you nut out on the end-game scenario, you're useless. So my particular thing has become reading the *Times* with a light heart, telling myself that they are shifting inexorably to the left but they don't want anybody to know just yet.

On the other hand, while I have almost totally resisted O. J. Simpson TV mania (COURT TV, E!, CNN, etc.), I can fully appreciate the general fascination. I couldn't resist even a moment of the Clarence Thomas–Anita Hill serial, and the Oklahoma bombing was absolutely gripping at first. Jackie Kennedy's brief illness, death, and extended memorial were also personal favorites. (Did she ever take a bad picture?)

Obviously, real life, even in its distilled video version, is much more intriguing and surprising than any soap opera, any game show, any talk show, or situation comedy. Real life may be messy and disturbing: black ex-football heroes being charged with the murder of their beautiful blonde wives, only for the trial—inundated by adoring fans of the accused—to provide an endless source of perverse humor and speculative TV commentary. Then some white supremacist redneck types decide to shift the focus of the country and the media by blowing up a federal building in Oklahoma City (where?), killing hundreds of people including a large number of children (who were unlucky enough, on this particular day, to be the recipients of the now mixed blessings of the daycare centers federal employees had fought so hard to obtain), reputedly in revenge for the FBI's handling of the Waco, Texas, situation, which ended in a blaze of fire, two years before to the day! No soap opera, no nighttime drama, ever had writing like that.

I CAN'T SAY much about the funniest/best time of the last six months — there have actually been so many, including Christmas Eve, Christmas Day, New Year's Eve and New Year's Day with my husband, my mother (Faith Ringgold), and my stepfather in their home in scenic Englewood, New Jersey (or, in other words, without my sister and her kids). Because Faith is still renovating the house and settling in, we had no tree, no lights, no decorations, no hollow holiday cheer, no Christmas carols, or other excess holiday folderol. Just the birds singing, the trees, and the quiet. We took all our meals in one of a number of local restaurants and diners, where it appeared that the rest of the entire bourgeois population of Bergen County was also consuming its holiday fare.

I found it surprisingly enjoyable not having to endure all of the hyperintensity of a children's Christmas, to have my first adult Christmas ever. Shouldn't we go get Barbara and the kids, I asked. No, they have their presents from everybody, their tree, their fathers to visit them, and their toys to play with, Faith and Birdie said. Let's do our own thing. Our own thing, I thought. What would that be on a Christmas?

As a child I had always pitied adults that they were not, themselves, children, wondering what they would find Christmas morning under the tree. In particular, I felt sorry for the adult who didn't even have a single child. Who would wreck the house, make all the noise, knock the tree over, and eat too much candy?

But now I see that whole thing of being a child at Christmastime as pretty stressful. I was never able to sleep, always got up too early, and always ended up being disappointed, no matter how many gifts I had or how much I ate. What I didn't understand as a child, which enables me now to be happy at Christmastime or any other time, is that life is inherently sad, really. I was bourgeois enough as a child to believe in the possibility of unadulterated happiness. Now if the bills are paid and I don't burn dinner, I am thrilled. My expectations are entirely of a different kind. I am forty-three years old, I am never going to have any children, and I won't die of loneliness either. My first adult Christmas turned out to be a relief.

WHAT I MOST need to escape from these days is right-wing talk radio. Luckily, I still have access to unlimited NPR and Pacific Radio during my waking hours, since I live in New York. But if I needed to escape, where I would most like to escape to is across the street to Prospect Park, where I used to take long walks for which I never seem to have time any more.

I'D RATHER NOT mention the books I am not reading (*The Bell Curve*, et al.), since part of the reason I am not reading them is because they are mentioned far too much by everybody else. Of course, right-wing intellectuals have all the support they could ever use.

Rather, I would prefer to provide my own top ten list at the moment. Not only what I am reading but what I find myself reading again and again because the information and sensibilities these books provide are so important to me. They are instructive, informative, well written and, as always, about the really important things that may or may not be visible to the human eye.

1. Paula Giddings. *When and Where I Enter: The Impact of Black Women on Race and Sex in America*. Morrow, 1984. Still the reigning intellectual and cultural history of black women and black feminism from the close of the Civil War until the early seventies, by a wonderful writer who is currently completing a much-anticipated biography of the great antilynching journalist Ida B. Wells. Giddings is one of the great secret weapons of black feminist thought.

2. Jacqueline Jones. *Labor of Love, Labor of Sorrow: Black Women, Work, and the Family From Slavery to the Present*. Basic Books, 1985. Another essential historical text. Lots of rigorous detail, lots of speculation, fascinating.

3. Elizabeth Fox-Genovese. *Within the Plantation Household: Black and White Women of the Old South*. University of North Carolina Press, 1988. Despite this woman's academic politics (conservative), this book is still a lush, adventurous social history of slave women and slave mistresses that asks the right questions about their bonds and antagonisms. The final chapter is devoted to a truly stunning combination historical/literary interpretation of Harriet Jacobs's *Incidents in the Life of a Slave Girl*.

4. Patricia Morton. *Disfigured Images: The Historical Assault on Afro-American Women*. Greenwood Press, 1991. This slim volume from Greenwood Press literally stopped my heart on first reading. Here was the trail, well-documented and clearly articulated, of how black sociologists and historians came to share many of the paternalistic and racist assumptions of the white elite in regard to the black woman and her role in the family. From the historian U. B. Phillips to sociologist E. Franklin Frazier to politician and policy adviser Patrick Moyni-

han, Morton explores how the stereotype of the careless, oversexed, single, black mother originated in a series of virtually undocumented generalizations about the promiscuity and inappropriate mothering of slave women, which no one ever bothered to check.

"By blending the image of 'matriarchy' into the Negro pathology thesis," Morton writes, "black departures from patriarchal gender relations and white defined sexual norms became equated with the Negro's cultural inferiority and, therefore, inequality."

But perhaps even more useful for me, ultimately, has been her tentative suggestion that "Mammy" is something infinitely more complex, important, and real than a flat, stock character who can be dismantled and dismissed. "Both stereotypes and myths," Morton writes, "are fundamentally pictures in the mind created out of imagination, although while the myth tends to mystify reality, the stereotype tends to simplify reality. However, both have pervaded the story of black women's history in a way that leads today's scholars to use these terms interchangeably." This book is quite literally worth its weight in gold. It is written by a representative of what I hope will turn out to be a new, bold generation of black feminist historians.

5. Ann Douglas. *Terrible Honesty: Mongrel Manhattan in the 1920s.* Farrar Straus Giroux, 1995. A truly stunning and handsome book by the author of *The Feminization of American Culture*, who argues that New York became a "mongrel" city in the twenties in the sense that it was the heyday of the Black Renaissance and a time in which the white elite made nightly trips to Harlem nightclubs. While conservative race ideologies predicted the imminent era of miscegenation, more carefree whites idealized and revered black culture. Most important and interesting to me is this work's emphasis on social history, performance, and music as part of the background to the Harlem Renaissance, usually portrayed by academics as an entirely high cultural affair. Of course, this is where you find the women.

6. Darlene Clark Hine. *Black Women in America: An Historical Encyclopedia* (two volumes). Carlson Publishing, 1993. Two volumes that all committed feminists should own. Beautifully illustrated and extensively researched, most of what you might have ever wondered about black women is somewhere in there.

7. Sander Gilman. *Difference and Pathology: Stereotypes of Sexuality, Race, and Madness.* Cornell University Press, 1985. This is the book to read that explains the inexorable psychological link between stereotypes of race, gender, sexuality, and pathology. Interestingly enough,

because Gilman's specialty is German literature, as well as the history of psychiatry, he makes a persuasive argument for how present derogatory notions of race/sexuality are descendants of ideas that proliferated in Weimar Germany.

8. Eve Kosofsky Sedgwick, *Epistemology of the Closet*. University of California Press, 1990. If you have a yen at all (I do) for theory and feminist philosophy with a decidedly progressive bent as practiced by a gifted poet, then *Epistemology of the Closet* is the book for you. Into the bargain, you will get a work that is considered one of the founding texts of queer theory. And while she's at it, Sedgwick gives the rest of those landmark theorists (deconstructive/psychoanalytic/postmodern) hell. One of the smartest, most useful, most comforting books I've read.

9. Edward Said, *Orientalism*. Random House, 1978; R. Martin and H. Koda, *Orientalism: Visions of the East in Western Dress*. Metropolitan Museum of Art, 1995; and Ella Shohat and Bob Stam, *Decentering Eurocentrism*. Routledge, 1994. None of these books by itself is quite what each becomes in juxtaposition with one another. Together they achieve critical mass: a mind-boggling critique of how the West has formulated and articulated the East in literature, fashion, film, and popular culture as a place of simultaneous loathing, envy, and desire. Said is no feminist. Nevertheless, he has cleared a persuasive trail through the thickets of this subject matter. The book describing the Fashion Institute exhibition documents just as clearly how the West stole from (borrowed from? reinterpreted?) the East and, in the process, reinvented itself. The Shohat and Stam book gives us some idea of the scope of Orientalism, as one of a number of Eurocentric tools employed in world cinema.

10. Elizabeth Debold, Marie Wilson, and Idelisse Malave. *Mother/Daughter Revolution: Good Girls to Great Women*. Doubleday, 1994. This is a wonderful book for mothers and daughters of all ages, which gives practical advice about how to use some of the findings of Carol Gilligan's groundbreaking research regarding the development of self-esteem in adolescent girls. I gave a copy to each of the women in my immediate family for Christmas, not that anybody read it.

Originally published as "Engaging and Escaping: Forum," *Women's Review of Books* 12, nos. 10–11 (July 1995): 14–15.

4.

To Hell and Back: On the Road with
Black Feminism in the '60s and '70s

It gets harder and harder to say why and how I became a black feminist twenty-six years ago when I was only eighteen. Over the years, I feel as though I have passed through at least three or four different lives; I've been old, over the hill, in despair, and even nearly dead more than once. I have also been reduced to infancy and total helplessness more times than I care to remember. The girl I was at the chronological age of eighteen is only a vague memory to me, someone I once knew and understood a long time ago.

More to the point perhaps, I had no inkling at eighteen that I would still be explaining twenty-six years later why or how I, as a black woman, became a feminist. The necessity of doing so is all the more aggravating as I have come to realize in the past decade that my feminist ethics and my racial pride are no more than the tip of the iceberg as far as my identity goes.

Some unimaginative types, most persistently in the provinces, continue to believe that a black woman must be brainwashed by white culture in order to voluntarily call herself a feminist. In fact, it has never been easier for me to be a black feminist than it is right now. Perhaps because I haven't been anything else for so many years, I find it difficult to imagine how women who are not feminists stand themselves. Essentially, I've given up on most other kinds of speculative political thought or activism anyway so why not go completely futuristic and visionary? You might say that my preferred political perspective has taken on an almost science fiction–type improbability.

Granted I have to admit that part of the security and satisfaction of my present life is inextricably linked to my ten-year-old relationship with the so-called enemy—hubby bear Gene, the love of my life and my soulmate. I am also cognizant of the fact that many Americans, maybe particularly black Americans, are laboring under the misapprehension that feminism precludes marriage or a satisfactory relationship with a male.

But the problem of loneliness and isolation, which is perhaps global, or at least postmodern, hasn't much to do with feminism, or even with its opposition. The odds are very much against any of us finding or remaining with the "right" person (if you still believe in such a thing) for all sorts of substantial socioeconomic and cultural reasons. Start with the fact that looking probably doesn't help, and that nothing in our upbringing, in our culture, or our history (aside from the popular notion of romantic love, always unrequited) teaches us to value our own time enough to want to find the "one" that we're longing to mate with, the other half of our solitude. Is it luck or acculturation that renders some of us blissfully settled with what feels like just the right complement and others of us consigned to roam, or to settle for a restless autonomy? (I don't believe that shit about a Zen-like isolation, such as Zora Neale gave Janey at the end of *Their Eyes Were Watching God*.)

My observation is that those who really need somebody, find somebody. Those who don't, wander, enriching the world all the more as they go, as a result. Apart from everything else that has to do with our complex individual psychological development, as social critic Barbara Ehrenreich has said, the social structure of patriarchy in whatever form you choose—from the U.S. Senate to the church—has become increasingly unstable. This means that the economic and political function of the nuclear family is deteriorating beneath our feet. So what are we, who are so suddenly orphaned, turning into? Nobody quite knows. Basically, you're on your own when it comes to the conceptualization of a mate, or whether or not you even bother.

As it happens, I am a feminist. I have mated, although I haven't had any children. All of this has to do with shifts in the patriarchy, which is to say if the patriarchy (and along with it old-fashioned capitalism) weren't on shifting ground, a woman like me probably would have had children. But, as it happens, I find myself frankly relieved that I haven't dared. Between the needs of my sister's three, the demands of my vocation as cultural critic, and my pleasure at being a perpetual child to my husband's parent and vice versa, there has never been any space. Sometimes I think of the four children I might have had, or of the four abortions, and the fact that they were for three of the brightest, most interesting men I've known. The children would have been fascinating if they had survived their unwilling parents. Which was a risk I still stand unwilling to take. Given that there are so many other unwanted children—visibly grown and otherwise—in need of recognition, courting, and nurturance, I prefer the living to the dead.

FOR THE UMPTEENTH time, I find myself reflecting on the myriad factors that led me down the curious path of my feminist persuasion and, never satisfied with the answer, wanting to tell a story about it that will finally satisfy everybody, including me. I would have to say I have been inclined to revolutionary politics and radical gestures of one kind or another at least since the seventh grade, perhaps in rebellion against elementary school at the exceedingly dull and pedantic Our Savior Lutheran School in the rural Bronx.

To give you some idea of the extent of the brainwashing in this parochial institution, my typically colored family regarded my sister and me with horror as we plastered our bedroom walls with pro-Nixon stickers during the presidential campaign of 1960, which (no thanks to us) Kennedy finally won. When we started bringing home jokes about Jews and Catholics, my mother thought it high time that we move on. Indeed the pivotal occasion was a run-in with the racism of my sixth grade teacher about which I subsequently wrote a short story (my first, a prize-winner and published three times) in my sophomore year at college.

After Our Savior, our next stop was the ultra-progressive, ultra-rad and boho New Lincoln School, no longer in existence but then located in a lovely old building on 110th Street on the mutual borders of black Harlem, Spanish Harlem, and the Upper Eastside. My fellow students ranged from the son of Susan Sontag (David Rieff) and the daughter of Harry Belafonte (Shari Belafonte) to the sons and daughters of the likes of Robert Rauschenberg, Maureen O'Sullivan, and Zero Mostel.

Other luminaries-to-be were Tisa Farrell (sister of Mia), Robin Bartlett and Deborah Offner (actresses), Stanley Nelson (the filmmaker), Jill Nelson (the writer), Adrian Piper (the artist), Billy Boulware (the TV director), Suzanne DePasse (film and TV producer), Thelma Golden (a mere baby), and so on and so forth.

This isn't just a list of the rich and famous but rather is meant to give some idea of how abruptly New Lincoln managed to change my vision of things to come. It was like going from a warm bath to an ice cold shower. Suddenly I was no longer in Dick-and-Jane land but in something like real time. While it may have been the fashion among a certain tier of the well-off and famous to toy with a radical milieu in education, this game didn't cohere with my mother's ambitions for me. She was more serious. Thanks to the rise of unionization among both teachers (my mother and my aunt) and General Motors assembly line workers (my stepfather), financially I regarded us as comfortable, but no matter how much I fantasized, we still weren't rich.

As it so happened, just as we were making the momentous change to New Lincoln, everything else in the world was changing as well, which continued to lend my experience at New Lincoln a certain gravity.

The first year I was at New Lincoln, in the seventh grade, John F. Kennedy was killed in the streets of Dallas. I can remember trying to explain to my best friend of the moment, the daughter of a soap opera star, why I was unable to cry about it—after all, what was he to me? In the same school year, under my most beloved teacher Helen Myers, we studied Eastern cultures, from the food (which we prepared in cooking classes) and religions to the history and literature; for my project, I led my class in a day of Buddhist observance.

During the year I was in the eighth grade, just as I was getting to know him, Malcolm X was shot down like a dog in the Audobon Ballroom. This event positively rocked Harlem, the community I lived in, and my youngish parents with it. No one uptown was ever quite the same. Meanwhile, I was directing my fellow students in a production of "The Diary of Anne Frank," a book I adored, along with the memoirs of Helen Keller, and every other book I could find about the growing up of sad little girls. Once I had lost my religious faith among all those irreligious leftist Jews at New Lincoln, I never regained it.

Going to New Lincoln was the first of many radicalizing transformations, interior and exterior. Among my classmates were Red Diaper babies and the children of those who had been blacklisted by McCarthy, sometimes overlapping with the rich and famous. What may have been happening was that the taint of McCarthy was finally washing away in the blood of the sixties. Our assemblies featured Peace Activist folk singers, speakers from SNCC and the Civil Rights Movement. We listened to the music of Leadbelly and John Cage, and we sang the songs of Pete Seeger in our classes. The first anti-Vietnam War demonstration I attended was a class outing in the eighth grade.

But the major proof I now have that New Lincoln was exceptional is that it no longer exists in these evil times. It simply vanished, like cheap housing.

Meanwhile, as a full-time resident of Harlem, I was going to the Apollo with my neighborhood friends every Saturday afternoon. We watched show after show, as long as they let us, of the Drifters, the Supremes, Jerry Butler, Jackie Wilson, the Temptations, the Marvelettes, Curtis Mayfield and the Impressions, Smokey Robinson and the Miracles, Marvin Gaye, Gladys Knight and the Pips.

Schoolmate Jill Nelson and I started a singing group with two other girls at New Lincoln modeled after the Marvelettes, and we actually dared to perform our version of "Please Mr. Postman" at the eighth grade dance—a humbling experience.

So it should come as no surprise that at the fragile age of thirteen, and in the midst of a local and international world that seemed convulsed with revolution and upheaval, I decided that life would no longer be possible without first meeting Smokey Robinson. I was very much a doer and at least this was something I could do. So it was just the most natural thing in the world for me to call the Apollo Theater while he was featured there and ask to speak to his manager. I told him that I was a reporter for the school newspaper (my school had none), and that I wanted an interview with Smokey.

Having actually gotten an appointment for the next day—somehow arranging to miss school and with my most grown up makeup on—my sister, my best friend, and I trotted over to the stage door of the Apollo, our hearts in our mouths, and were ushered in to meet not only Smokey Robinson and all the Miracles but also all of the various Temptations, and Wilson Pickett. At the time I didn't even know who Wilson Pickett was. That day I had a preview of something I wasn't quite ready to know yet about the second-class world of black celebrity: the fact that they were so accessible, in comparison to what my white classmates went through to get a peek at the Beatles or other white stars, and that backstage at the Apollo was so unbelievably shabby, killed whatever romantic notion I had previously had of their tier of showbiz.

So at fourteen, as we were entering the "Soul" period in popular music, I was already disillusioned about the magical powers of rhythm n' blues. The fan in me was dead. With somewhat more serious political intentions, I took myself alone down to the SNCC office to volunteer to go South on the bus rides. The lessons of the six o'clock news, bringing bulletins from the front in Mississippi and Vietnam, had not been wasted on me. I was genuinely surprised when the workers at the office suggested that I was too young. I have no idea what made me think they needed me, but I was hopelessly in love with Stockley Carmichael.

Then at fifteen, I was sent off to Paris for the summer with my beloved grandmother, Momma Jones, a Harlem fashion designer who called herself Madame Posey, who was most intent on gaining admittance to the showings of the couture collections. My mother Faith Ringgold, the artist, was approaching her mature development as an artist and needed time to paint. It was the summer of 1967, and the revels to come in 1968 were already very much in the air on the Left Bank. At French lessons at the Alliance Françaises on the Boulevard de Raspail, my sister and I rubbed shoulders with an international student clientele, enabling us to escape periodically the protective gaze of Momma Jones.

On those escapades, I was intent on pretending to be older. I have no idea how successful I was, but I remember much of this period as a time when I had no clear boundaries: I had convinced myself that I looked at least nineteen or twenty to the young Africans, Caribbeans, Italians, and Greeks gathered there. Smoking French cigarettes and drinking espresso helped bolster my courage. I have no idea if I fooled anyone. It seemed as though wherever we traveled, the news stands were always screaming the latest scandal of the Civil Rights Movement in the South. Between that and Vietnam, it didn't feel like such a great time to be American.

After the summer of 1968, when I was an assistant dance teacher at the School of Music and Art, I flopped all over the place during my senior year in high school. I was an extremely indifferent student; my one claim to fame was that I managed an incredibly high score on the SATS after two prior attempts. Boyfriends were already comandeering a good portion of my attention.

Having decided somewhat haphazardly to audition for Juilliard, I sabotaged myself by quitting my preparatory work at Arthur Mitchell's new dance school in Harlem in the middle of a class with the ballet master Karl Shook because, I told myself, ballet was simply too apolitical. I ended up at Barbara Ann Teer's New Age National Black Theatre for a spell, where I met the Last Poets and dancers Kimako (Amiri's sister), Michele Murray (Albert Murray's daughter who was with Alvin Ailey then), and Duane Hanson (star of that Bill Gunn movie *Ganja and Hess*).

The National Black Theatre was a cathartic experience for me because of its philosophy that middle-class Negroes were brainwashed and in need of debriefing. It held out the promise of a transformative blackness. Working there was a ritual healing; it was a place where you could discard all your inhibitions, of which I had a ton. I was so incredibly self-conscious, it is hard to imagine now. Meanwhile I was getting a lot of attention, mainly because of the way I looked. I had had eczema in my early adolescence and been as homely as a flea, but I had been cured by a fancy Fifth Avenue dermatologist and now I was beautiful, or so everybody said.

At New Lincoln, since I was seriously getting into my militant and fed-up-with-whitey phase, I started a black student organization that never could find much to protest in a private school that was already 25 percent black. I finally hit on boosting Puerto Rican enrollment as a demand. I'll never forget that it was Nat Hentoff's stepdaughter, Mara Wolinski (perhaps in a foreshadowing of her father's subsequent proclivity for antiblack nationalist rants), who seemed to be the only person in the school who considered the students of color organizing themselves as a personal affront.

By graduation, I can only suppose (since I was in a semiconscious state) the curriculum was in such disarray from keeping pace with the reverberations of JFK's assassination, the Columbia Riots, SNCC, the Peace Movement, the sexual revolution, and the marijuana craze, all of which seemed to come to a head that year, that we hardly managed to produce a yearbook. Classmates Chris Rauchenberg and Tim Lutz took a lot of crazy, lopsided photographs. By June 1969, our principal was black (Harold Haizlip), our assistant principal was black (Mabel Smythe), the head of the high school was black (Verne Oliver, the mother of one of the future leaders of the Combahee Collective), and our keynote speaker at graduation was the newly minted Broadway star (*Great White Hope*), James Earl Jones.

During graduation, I was actually in another zone. I remember that I had begun to wear my hair in an uncombed style, something like the early stages of what we now know as dreadlocks. At the ceremony, Momma Jones complained that the parents looked as bad as the kids. In particular, she pointed out to Faith the tangled hair and blue jeans of Robert Rauschenberg, who was sitting with John Cage just in front of them. "No wonder we can't get Michele to comb her hair." Some of the kids had on jeans. Some were barefoot. Some showed clear signs of the fact that they were smoking marijuana with their parents on a nightly basis. The music had been written by students and was sublimely dissonant and jarring, after Cage.

For me, it was not a sobering moment but the reverse. I had no desire to go to college as far as I knew but wanted to graduate immediately to autonomy and revolution. My guidance counselor, Verne Oliver, had taken the precaution of applying to Howard University (my choice) and the City College of New York on my behalf. I guess Faith was busting out all over in her development as an artist and hadn't the time, energy, or fortitude to devote to my situation after having spent so much money on private schools and camps.

BECOMING A BLACK feminist in the '70s had not only to do with the times but it also had everything to do with being the daughter of the ambitious, fiercely militant, and driven black artist, Faith Ringgold. My family was made up of women who were either superwomen of one kind or another, or women who just couldn't cope on almost any level. From an early age you were expected to declare which one you would be, although I didn't learn this until much later.

In retrospect, I imagine that I was driving my mother, who had never wanted children to begin with, crazy. She seemed to have little idea how bad things could get. Remember this was the '60s, which had followed the '50s, '40s, and '30s, the latter humbling decade, the one in which my mother was born. After so much money spent on private school, etcetera, how much could go wrong?

When Faith sent my sister and me to Mexico for the summer, I can fully understand why she was relieved to finally have us out of her hair for a short time, although in her place, I would not have allowed my girls out of my sight, but then that may also be why I have never had children. I could never stomach the odds.

As for me then, I was seventeen and simply mad for revolution; my sixteen-year-old sister, Barbara, who was nearly fluent in Spanish and French and quick as grease, wasn't much better. Mexico City, which had been the scene of student revolution the summer before, turned out to be precisely the right place to continue my research. Given my sister's facility in Spanish, it didn't take us long to join a commune in the countryside outside of the city. When I told Faith that I had no desire to return to the U.S. but wished to spend the rest of my life in Mexico, I was ordered home not only by her but also by the U.S. government. To make a long story short, I ended up in a facility for juvenile delinquents on 16th Street.

Up until this time, I was no feminist. Rather my thesis had been that me and my generation were reinventing youth, danger, sex, love, blackness, and fun. But there had always been just beneath the surface a persistent countermelody, which was becoming a full-scale antithesis, what I might also call my mother's line, a deep suspicion that I was reinventing nothing but rather making a fool of myself in precisely the manner that untold generations of young women before me had done. The synthesis of the two lines — my mother's cautionary tales and my own joie de vivre — merged into our joint vision of black feminism, the ground on which my mother and I could mutually agree long enough for me to grow up.

Of course, I am saying this in retrospect. We didn't just wake up one morning as a black feminist mother–daughter team. The radical feminist protest at the Miss America Pageant had happened in 1969 and had gotten a lot of attention in the press in New York. Although the press coverage was designed to turn people off, it did just the opposite for me. I remember that being my initial moment of interest because I had always deeply resented the institution of the Miss America Pageant and had already figured out that life was possible for a woman without a bra.

In the fall of 1969, after my adventure in Mexico, and my debriefing in the Sisters of the Good Shepherd Home for Girls on 16th Street, I went off to Howard University, a place designed to acquaint you with the shortcomings of black female status if ever there was one. Between the fraternities and the Black Power antics, misogyny ran amok on a daily basis down there.

In the spring of 1970, I returned to New York and night school at CCNY. In my absence, New York had become a seething hotbed of all kinds of feminist activity. Faith and I were very shortly radicalized within the frenetic and inclusive goings-on of the downtown art scene. A further motivation was the troubles Barbara was having as a runaway and a recalcitrant juvenile. Both she and Faith saw only red when they saw each other. She could no longer live at home but had begun to stay with Momma T, our real father's mother, in Queens.

A major organizing principle during these times, despite the reluctance of present historians to admit it, was the overarching unity of everybody on the Left — feminists, blacks, hippies, druggies, socialists, and Marxists — in opposition to the Vietnam War. If you are too young to remember it, then try to imagine what it might have been like if the pro-Nicaraguan movement or the antiapartheid movement in regard to South Africa had been one thousand times bigger, then maybe you'll be close. Remember also that an astonishing array of major leaders, from MLK, Medgar Evers, and Malcolm X to both JFK and Robert Kennedy had been taken out, more or less, right in front of our eyes. What with a paranoid and closeted J. Edgar Hoover lurking about and watching us all, no one who had any claims to a position of progressive leadership had any idea when their number might also be up. Baldwin's melancholy refrain during this period was, "Martin, Malcolm, Medgar and me."

My recollection has always been that Faith and I came to feminism at the same time, although I now suspect that I was following her lead in the way that an offspring can sometimes follow a parental lead without necessarily being aware of it, especially since I was an inveterate Momma's girl right through my early twenties. Through those early years of the '70s, I frequently accompanied and assisted my mother in her various radical forays into the antiwar, anti-imperialist art movement of the times. With Faith's assistance and support, I founded an organization called Women Students and Artists for Black Art Liberation (WSABAL) as an activist and polemical unit to advocate the kinds of positions in the art world that are now identified with the Guerrilla Girls.

Particular high points were when we participated in raucous art actions at the Museum of Modern Art and the Whitney; when we occupied the offices of Thomas Hoving at the Metropolitan; and when I wrote the words for the poster for the Judson Memorial Flag Show, (participants ranged from Carl Andre to Kate Millett), which was ultimately closed by the attorney general's office, whereupon Faith as well as Jean Toche and John Hendricks (now Yoko Ono's personal curator) of the Guerrilla Art Action Group were arrested and became the Judson Three. Somewhat reluctantly, and with only half my attention, I sometimes collaborated with Faith when she used texts as she did in her "Political Landscapes" series.

In the meantime, I also managed to move slowly but steadily toward completion of a bachelor's degree in English at CCNY, studying creative writing under such notorious enemies of feminist indoctrination as the late Donald Barthelme, Earl Rovit, John Hawkes, Mark Mirsky, and Hugh Seidman. At various events around town, I met Audre Lorde, Toni Morrison, Alice Walker, June Jordan, Nikki Giovanni, Sonia Sanchez, Clayton Riley, who all seemed to me stunningly attractive, articulate, and bigger than life. They used to say what I now realize were perfectly outrageous, revolutionary things and they were photogenic. Clayton had been my sister's teacher; I encountered Walker, who seemed shy and retiring, at meetings of black feminists. Even then, to fledgling black women writers, Morrison was a queen. I, myself, wrote and published relatively often and got the chance once or twice to read my black feminist poetry in the company of such feminist luminaries as Lorde.

Among the many thoughtful editors of my writing during this period were Kathie Sarachild at *Women's World* for whom I wrote my first black feminist essay, "Black Women and White Women," in 1971; Robin Morgan who was associated with *Rat*; and Theresa Schwartz, editor of *The New York Element* for whom I covered the Panther Convention in D.C. in 1974 at which Huey Newton and Jane Fonda made a notorious pair.

My best feminist buddy and mentor then was Pat Mainardi, now professor of art history at CUNY and Brooklyn College, with whom I spent the summers in a country house in a one-horse town called Craftsbury, Vermont. Together she and I, artists Irene Peslikis and Marjorie Kramer, started an ill-fated left wing publication called *Women and Art*. I can remember distinctly Shulamith Firestone; the minimal artist Robert Morris; the then director of the Museum of Modern Art; Robin Morgan; and various New York Panthers visiting our apartment in Harlem. Sometimes I had the sense that we were making history. I certainly thought we were on the verge of a revolution.

In the summer of 1973, Faith and I went to Europe — she to Germany, to Documenta, and I to meet a friend in Madrid where I spent a sybaritic week of dancing all night and sleeping all day. The only touristy thing I did was visit the Prado, and I did that every day like clockwork, in order to inhale the dusky magic of their Zurburan paintings. I felt invigorated by the Prado and by Franco's totalitarian Spain. It was so quiet, so safe and so cheap, unlike the world I'd come from. I made up for the lack of political stimulation by having a passionate affair with a military stranger whom I met in a discotheque. Perhaps a foreshadowing of my future husband, he too was from South Carolina.

Nevertheless, as I grew older, I became more and more aware that I was often operating under the shadow of a heavy funk. I was depressed a lot.

SOMETIMES I LOOK back on the mid '70s and feel as though I spent more time taking cold showers to break through my numbness than anything else. When I finally graduated from CCNY in 1974, it seemed something like a liberation of sorts. I considered myself a veteran feminist by this time. For reasons that now escape me, I was wearing pseudo-African apparel: *geles* (headwraps), long dresses, sandals, no makeup, and so forth. The assumption that was usually made about me was that I was a Muslim, which won me some respect on the street, more than you might get in a miniskirt. Yet here I was, this very opinionated black feminist, who had real problems with the Black Muslim agenda.

The general idea of the long dresses was to cover as much of my body as possible and thereby impede the course of the various sexual propositions from strangers, which followed me everywhere I went. Apparently, it seemed worth being mistaken for a Muslim woman. Meanwhile, I was also occasionally agoraphobic, bulimic, and often had a nightmare of inadvertently strolling the streets in the nude.

By the fall of 1974, new friend Margo Jefferson (then a writer at *Newsweek*) had helped me get a job as a book review researcher at *Newsweek*, which furnished me with entry to all sorts of magic New York worlds from the Newport Jazz Festival to the Public Theatre to a variety of literary shenanigans and shindigs. I worked on both the Erica Jong and the Toni Morrison cover stories. I first met Ishmael Reed on the telephone. From my spartan office in the Newsweek building on Madison Avenue, in the illuminating company of fellow researcher Robert Miner, and under the mentorship of Senior Editor Jack Kroll, I was able to call anywhere in the world, provided I knew the number.

Michael Wolff, a white friend (we were introduced by a mutual black male friend who was gay), worked in a job of similar prestige at the *New York Times*, and we made a habit of chain-smoking, drinking scotch, and crashing high profile New York literary parties together. I kept hoping that I would one day meet Norman Mailer whose antifeminist rants I secretly found hugely entertaining.

It was around this time, I believe, that I became one of the founders of the National Black Feminist Organization along with Faith and a whole bunch of the usual suspects. I was still urgently passionate about a variety of feminist causes in the abstract. Occasionally, I was asked to write sexy, short pieces for *Ms.* I received all sorts of moral support from Margo Jefferson and Marie Brown (then editor at Doubleday) who never stinted on expense-account lunches. As usual, chum since high school Jill Nelson and I continued our protracted commiserations over the fate of black feminism. In particular, I remember Jill, whom I had known since seventh grade in New Lincoln, as somebody who I thought really understood me. Neither of us had yet turned out the way our parents had expected. Jill already had the cutest baby I'd ever seen, whom I adored, named Misambu.

Together with the poet Pat Jones, Faith, Margo, and I organized the Sojourner Truth Festival of the Arts in 1976 at the Women's Interarts Center, at which Ntozake Shange performed something from *For Colored Girls*. This also turned out to be the scene of a major public confrontation between my mother and me, one that resulted in a lot of tears on my part and in my getting my own apartment. About a year later a new group called the Sisterhood began meeting at Alice Walker's house in Brooklyn to talk about what, if anything, black women writers should do or say about feminism. Also, a little later, around 1978, a black feminist study group, which included Susan McHenry and Barbara Omolade, began to meet to discuss black feminist texts and to ponder what our role should be in the movement.

In 1974, I met Ross Wetzsteon at a party at Mark Mirsky's house. If I wanted to write for the *Village Voice*, Ross told me, he would be glad to introduce me there. He took me to a vivacious and saucy Karen Durbin. As feminists, we immediately bonded. I ended up working with her on my first two *Voice* essays—one about being a black feminist called "Anger in Isolation: a Search for Sisterhood" in which I talk about the difficulty of the black feminist movement in that we black women had neither the will nor the means to risk standing together against black men on any issue. The other article explored my experience of growing up a black American princess in the Harlem of the '50s and '60s. Both essays were struggling to articulate the peculiarly paralyzing specialness of being one of the few members of an educated, black, middle-class elite. We were the talented tenth that Du Bois imagined but never really got to see.

It was with the articles in the *Voice* that I first became a public black feminist in New York. Perhaps my greatest hit had been my back cover profile of Frankie Crocker, then the program director and head DJ at WBLS-FM. It was my luck that James Brown just happened by the studio the day I was visiting. Of course, in my article I gave them both black feminist hell, as was my style in those days. So much so that when Ntozake first met me when I interviewed her, she said that she was glad that the *Voice* had chosen me because I was just the person to put an end to all the ridiculous voyeuristic speculation in the mainstream media regarding her various suicide attempts.

Of course, it didn't turn out that way, but that's another story. But I can remember being hungry for the kind of fame she had then. Everybody knew, I thought, that the possibility of radical politics was over. But at least you could be famous and then tell them all to fuck themselves.

The writing for the *Voice* in the mid-seventies got me my editor, Joyce Johnson, who took me with her to Dial Press, which also published most of Baldwin's books. (She had previously worked with Eldridge Cleaver on *Soul on Ice*, Harold Cruse on *The Crisis of the Negro Intellectual*, and Amiri Baraka on *Home*.) Margo introduced me to Maxine Groffsky, who would become my literary agent. In 1975, Maxine helped me draft a proposal for a book on black women, and Joyce got me a modest advance ($12,500), whereupon I immediately quit my job at *Newsweek* and once again moved away from home uptown with Mom to a mouse-ridden apartment on Greene Street.

In a matter of a few months I had whipped up the essential core of what I thought would be a single chapter on black men. But then Joyce argued that it should be the centerpiece of the book and that I needed only another large section on black women. We then began together the laborious process over a period of two years of editing what was called "Black Macho" and constructing the much more difficult to write section of the book that would be called "The Myth of the Superwoman."

Meanwhile since my money was low, my guardian angel Margo recommended me to her friend Helen Epstein for a job teaching journalism at NYU. At twenty-four, I was suddenly a university professor (actually my rank was lecturer) in a school which had almost no black faculty. It was a common occurrence once I moved into the NYU housing in Washington Square Village to be frantically queried by middle-aged white women in mink coats about whether I had any free days for housework. I was always so stunned, I can't recall what I said. I wasn't used to living around white folks.

It was not unusual for my editorial sessions with Joyce to result in tears: mine. Frankly, most of her qualms were over my head as a writer. I had the distinct impression that she might have been perfectly comfortable drawing out our revision process for another year or even two, but I put my foot down. I needed a book as soon as possible. Talk about waiting to exhale.

What helped me conceptualize both my book and my life, as much as anything else during this time, was a book that Helen Epstein, a colleague at NYU, was working on about children of concentration camp survivors. Helen focused her first book on the riddle of her relationship to her own parents who had survived the Holocaust. She set out to discover what made such people so inscrutable and difficult, and how it affected their children. In the process, she was also learning a great deal about who she really was; in particular (or so I imagine now) how to wake up from the pain that survivors and their descendants sometimes find so crippling. For the first time I began to realize, through my discussions with Helen and through therapy, that I too might be considered the adult child of the walking wounded, and that this fact, as well as my feminism and my blackness, had much to do with who I was.

As *Black Macho and the Myth of the Superwoman* approached the galley stage, old friend Robin Morgan submitted my text for review to Gloria Steinem and Alice Walker. Needless to say, they liked it a lot (which isn't to say they wouldn't later change their minds) and, through a process of elimination and the ministrations of a new black female editor who would become another best friend (Susan McHenry), I ended up with a double excerpt and a picture of me on the cover of *Ms.*

Then the whirlwind began over the way I looked and dressed for TV appearances, the way I spoke, what I did and didn't say. *Ms.* asked me to take my braids out so they wouldn't interfere with the cover lines. The *Today Show* insisted that I be interviewed with someone who could debate my inflammatory positions, a certain Bonnie Boswell, the daughter of the president of the Urban League, who turned out to be as upper crust as her name.

Afterward, all I can remember hearing from the publicity people at *Ms.* and Dial was that I was wearing the wrong colors, the wrong accessories, and I didn't smile enough. I am sure I was probably as animated as a piece of wood on camera, so these complaints were merely their best attempts to get through to me. I don't think anybody ever realized how paralyzed with fear I usually was in any kind of public appearance. While Dial Press wondered whether I should be described as a black feminist in their press materials, *Ms.* wondered whether I was up to snuff as a black feminist spokesperson (I was not).

Meanwhile, although I had dedicated the book to her, my relationship with Faith had reached an all-time low. Not nearly as famous then as she is now, she didn't feel as though I had given her sufficient credit for my miraculous feminist rebirth.

I had started therapy with an Adlerian the year I graduated from college. We had put all our eggs in one basket. The theory was that professional success was supposed to cure whatever was ailing me psychologically. Au contraire, I was more a mess than ever. I was drinking and smoking heavily, even doing the occasional illicit drug, and hating myself on a daily basis for not being pretty or smart enough. My boyfriends then are now too excruciating to remember.

Then the sniper attacks started rolling in. But what could I expect after not having given any thought at all to allowing Dial to feature the most inflammatory paragraph in the book on the jacket cover. "I am saying . . . there is a profound distrust, if not hatred," my inner child proclaimed in black type against a white background, "between black men and black women that has been nursed along largely by white racism but also by an almost deliberate ignorance on the part of blacks about the sexual politics of their experience in this country."

In *Black Macho and the Myth of the Superwoman* I had indiscreetly blurted out that sexism and misogyny were near epidemic in the black community and that black feminism had the cure. I went from obscurity to celebrity to notoriety overnight. Quite suddenly, I was a frequent guest on the *Today Show*, *Phil Donahue*, and "the six o'clock news" from Newark to Pomona; I was reviewed, attacked, and debated in *Essence*, the *Nation*, the *New York Times*, the *Washington Post*, and the *Black Scholar*, by my own people more than anyone else; and my photograph was everywhere. At twenty-six I had written the book from hell, and my life would change forever.

When I did readings and talks, black folks came at me with book in hand quoting chapter and verse. Meanwhile I was completely at a loss to explain how the book had actually come about. In a way, I still am. I think now that *Black Macho and the Myth of the Superwoman* was one of those manuscripts that was never supposed to see print, which, indeed, wouldn't see print in today's more competitive and specialized marketplace.

The result of an unhappy alliance between a perfectionist unfeminist aesthete and a young, nihilistic, black, feminist, militant, half-crazed, and sexually frustrated maniac, the text could only hope to crash and burn, which it promptly did after first driving a lot of people crazy, including me.

Nevertheless, it documents a crucial stage in my development, and perhaps in yours, in learning the lesson that human perfectibility is not a possibility, that men are people too, and that there aren't any answers in life yet. While I don't think of *Black Macho* as the Holy Grail, I am not dismissive of the book. Indeed, I believe it to be one of those immortal texts destined to be misread and misunderstood in its own time but to survive whatever onslaughts are hurled at it. Somewhere in the future it will find its home. Or perhaps it will just help make the future. Just because I gave it birth doesn't mean I understand it.

Moreover, *Black Macho* belongs with other celebrated documents of the heady times of the '60s and '70s, most of them not exactly gospel: from Eldridge Cleaver's *Soul on Ice*, George Jackson's *Notes from Solidad*, Amiri Baraka's *Home* and *Dutchman*, and Angela Davis's *Autobiography* to Toni Cade Bambara's *The Black Woman*, Robin Morgan's *Sisterhood Is Powerful*, Ti-Grace Atkinson's *Amazon Odyssey*, and Jane Alpert's "Mother Right."

In the process, I learned a lot of things, many of them impossible for me to verbalize. But one thing I can say is that no matter how you slice it, humanity still has a lot of fixing to do. Although I am hardly dead yet, I am no longer young; nor do I any longer feel as though the burden of change is on my shoulders, or my generation's shoulders, alone. I am prepared to stand aside, to watch others try and, blissfully, to watch the crowd go by. Nevertheless, I continue to believe that feminism, in all its myriad and contentious incarnations, will always be part of, although not the only, prescription, until somebody comes up with a cure.

Originally published in Rachel Duplessis and Ann Snitow, eds., *The Feminist Memoir Project: Voices from Women's Liberation* (New York: Crown, 1998).

5.

Censorship and Self-Censorship

I have been called many things for many reasons, but to be called a "critic/ scholar" sounds so wonderful and noble, despite the fact that it describes something rather uncomfortable, awkward, and sometimes wholly un- wanted. That is, I am in the business of scrutinizing things people would rather not scrutinize, saying things people don't want to hear, and asking them to think about things they would rather leave for another day. In my case, it has been no popularity contest. But I am not here to complain, at least not in the way that by now it has become customary for us to com- plain—I've done enough of that in my writings, many of which are quite difficult to obtain, especially in other countries.

I say this because what I have noticed about the extraordinary increase— at least in this country—of black women's writing, much of it autobio- graphical either in tone or intent, is that so much of it complains of the very things I built my career complaining about: invisibility, erasure, being negated, ignored, and marginalized because of one's status as a woman of color in this society that does not appreciate women of color. But at this point, at least for me who began to sing this song with all my heart in the early '70s, now that the bookstores are filled with glossy books singing this song, it has become a little overly familiar and even rote. Yes, it is true that black women around the world and in the country are held down, abused, erased, murdered, invisible-ized, marginalized, and that their successes are not what they might be. But at the same time, we are enjoying successes just now beyond our wildest dreams. This very conference Yari-Yari at NYU in New York City is an example of that. Who would have imagined such a thing, in this city, perhaps the most hostile and unwelcoming of cities in the world, twenty years ago?

Rather, I would like to make a point that I didn't know how to make when I published *Black Macho and the Myth of the Superwoman* in 1979, and still didn't understand even when I published *Invisibility Blues* in 1990 with Verso Press, and it is this: invisibility, marginality, and silence are not always disadvantages. Visibility, centrality, and voice, or what I would rather call noise, are not always advantages. I take this point from *Unmarked*, a book by the celebrated performance studies scholar Peggy Phelan.

What fascinates me about this panel is the coupling of censorship and self-censorship, because for me at least, they have always gone together. There are so many ways in which, for a black woman writer in this country at this moment, censorship is inextricably coupled with practices of self-censorship–so much so that the two seem almost indistinguishable at times. Count the ways: (1) the censorship and self-censorship of too much to read in too little time; (2) the censorship and self-censorship of the bombard-ment by other media and other genres of messages that very frequently deny the legitimacy of your existence and the possibility of your intellectual and spiritual autonomy; (3) the censorship and self-censorship of trying to figure out what is really important and urgent enough to risk saying as forcibly as possible, given the fact that you know that everyone is distracted and de-ceived by all sorts of problems, such as (for instance) AIDS and our ongoing health crisis as a people and the problems and dilemmas of our youth: teen-age pregnancy, dropping out of high school, gangs, drugs, etc.; and (4) the censorship and self-censorship of the artist versus "scholar/critic" divide.

Quite recently, I decided that the essential difference between the artist and the scholar/critic is that the artist does not wait to be invited to do or say things. The artist takes her own initiative to say things, write things, propel them into the world. Her spirit and her love of herself and the planet tell her what she needs to give to the world, and she makes sure they get it by any means necessary. She does it even if she is pointedly asked not to. Whereas scholar critics wait for the invitation, the venue, the job offers, the anthology request, the publication, to ask them to comment or analyze or scrutinize this, that, or the other thing. Consequently, as I now see it, the major dif-ference is one of ego. The artist has to feel as though her work has a right to exist regardless of whether or not anyone perceives it to be needed. The scholar/critic waits to respond to invitations and perceived demand. This is actually a very sad situation in the case of the scholar/critic who happens to be a feminist such as myself, because women of color generally see little need for such a function as the scholar/critic. I have been told as much in a million ways.

In my case, the censorship of not being asked to write for the *Village Voice*, the *Nation*, *The New Yorker*, *Vanity Fair*, the *New York Times*, the *Daily News*, *Vibe*, or wherever, is accompanied by an almost inevitable lack of confidence, a lack of self-esteem, that is the ultimate and most fatal censorship in the absence of a totalitarian state. Indeed, it is kind of like carrying your own little totalitarian state around inside your head. In any case, I am inaugurating my own press, Olympia Press, and have printed my first book, *To Hell and Back: On the Road with Black Feminism in the 70s and 80s*, which begins a new inner-directed phase of my writing.

Originally published in *Renaissance Noire* 2, no. 3 (1999–2000): 30–32.

6.

An Interview

THE HARVARD ADVOCATE: We're interested in how you were drawn to the field of visual studies as a development and extension of your initial work in black feminist cultural criticism?

MICHELE WALLACE: My interest in visual culture, as we call it now, goes back to my childhood. My mother, Faith Ringgold, is an artist and I was her daughter and her child at a point when she was developing herself as an artist and was trying to find a niche for herself as an artist. I spent a great deal of time in museums and traveling with her to Europe and other places, visiting the great works of art around the world. As she figured out what type of artist she wanted to be, I figured out that I had an abiding interest in visual culture.

Also my grandmother was a fashion designer [a seamstress] and very interested in photography and had a movie camera. You could say that I grew up with a family that was preoccupied with the visual — especially with images having to do with women.

THA: When did this begin to dominate your intellectual production and become a more prominent research topic for you?

MW: I became a feminist in 1969–1970, as I talked about in my first book *Black Macho*, as a result of my experience of being placed in a juvenile home. I became a feminist as a way of articulating and acting upon an interest that

I always had in women. I was raised in a very woman-centered household and family and my earliest involvement in the women's movement in the '70s was connected to activism on the part of visual artists.

Again, I was following my mother's lead. In that context of the women's movement, although initially it was not a field of research for me, it was always there, it was always talked about. For instance, when I was a teenager and a young woman, one of the people who I knew as a colleague of my mother was Linda Nochlin, who wrote the essay "Why Are There No Great Women Artists?" I found that question a very stimulating one and a disturbing one, particularly because in the essay she always qualifies the question "Why are there no great women artists?" with "Why are there no great black artists?" So it was always there.

But I think it took about two decades for me to realize that what didn't fully satisfy me about feminism had to do with visual questions. And the point at which it became the clearest that I wanted to research visual questions was when I did the Black Popular Culture conference. When I gave the conference, I tried to do specific things that would lend themselves to an emphasis on the visual. For me, from the beginning popular culture was a matter of visual culture. However, I found that I was not on the same wavelength as most of the participants in the conference. They saw no need to emphasize visual issues and black visual artists.

So, having given that conference and been involved with the compilation coming out of the conference, I realized that I wanted to pursue further for myself issues in visual culture. During the creation of the anthology *Black Popular Culture*, two things happened that made me realize that issues around visual culture had a special status. One was that Judith Wilson, who had presented on pornography in Romare Bearden's work and had shown slides of work in the conference, found that when it was time to publish the essay, the Bearden estate would not allow her to use images of Bearden's work in connection with the essay. My impression was that it was primarily because she used the term pornography and they didn't want to be identified with that. So her essay ran, and it was a very good essay, but it was published without illustrations.

The second thing was that another presenter at the conference, Margo Jefferson, showed a fascinating clip of John Bubbles, of the vaudeville dance team Buck and Bubbles, tapping down the stairs and singing a song called "Shine," a famous vaudeville number from *Cabin in the Sky*, at the conference and it caused a great deal of consternation. I think a lot of people were confused about why anybody would show this and what

Margo was talking about. As it turned out Margo ended up not submitting to the final volume of *Black Popular Culture*, and so that voice was not represented.

Again, I had the sense that what Judith, Margo, and I had tried to do in terms of the conference was too ephemeral to be captured in this volume on black popular culture, which I'd hoped would be more subversive in its handling of visual issues. Gina Dent and I tried to make up for it with the illustrations we used in the anthology, but visual issues were not integrated into the work in the way I might have hoped. I think that perhaps what is needed is a conference that focuses on black visual culture. And a number of people have tried to consider doing such a thing, but it's very difficult to do. It hasn't happened yet.[1]

THA: What reasons would you identify for that sort of resistance around the visual?

MW: In the case of *Black Popular Culture*, the way I was able to do this was through the Dia Art Foundation, which has tons of money and was willing to support us. It was a period when wealthy visual institutions were willing to underwrite certain kinds of subversive discourse in order to justify their own existence in relation to communities of difference.

I think that time has passed, number one, and *Black Popular Culture* would not have been possible without their support. They gave each speaker $1,000, they paid all travel and hotel expenses for people coming from wherever they were coming from. If you were coming from Timbuktu they paid for it. It's kind of hard to get that sort of arrangement today.

The other thing about visual culture, and the orientation of visual culture, is that you have to deal with the producers and the owners. They have to be included. For instance, if you gave a conference with a focus on African art, then the major people you would have to consult would be the collectors. If you were dealing with traditional African art, you'd be dealing with collectors and art historians who were involved with collectors. You might talk to some critics, but for the most part those critics would be subsidiaries of the collectors and the museums. So there isn't a lot of leeway or freedom for speculation.

If you did a conference on film you would encounter the same issues. In other words what I'm saying is that if you did a conference on visual culture, the people you have to deal with are, for the most part, commercially or financially connected to the work in a way that doesn't promote free exchange or speculative visionary analysis.

THA: It seems that you've also touched on a tendency amongst critics, an inability to deal with the visual along with and in dialogue with other aspects of culture: What do you see as the source of this? A lack of training, of interest, a need to see the visual as merely illustrative?

MW: It's both of those things, training and the problem of seeing visual culture as merely illustrative. The thing that interferes with free exchange or interpretation of the visual in African American culture has to do with the commercial, economic, and even corporate value of visual culture. And I feel somewhat ambivalent about that.

I mean I'm not one of these people who think that the economic value of visual culture is automatically to be despised and disposed of. That this aspect of it exists attests to the fact of its great value. In other words, it's valuable in terms of interpretation; it's valuable in terms of spirit and profound meaning and philosophical perceptions. It makes sense that it would also be valuable economically or materially.

I think that conceivably these issues have to do with training or early training. One of the things I've noticed in the various forays I've made into visual arts training is that there are a number of fields—for instance, preservation in museum studies, or museum studies in general—where they've realized that if you want to get young people interested in doing preservation work or working in museums in art history, you have to get to them before they get to college, certainly while they are undergraduates. Ideally it would be best if you could reach children in elementary school and high school. What happens to a lot of our children is that we have cut off a lot of ways for them to become sensitized to the visual and there is no opportunity to express that sensitivity.

If you expose children to certain types of things they are going to be interested. Children love dinosaurs, and that love of dinosaurs is nurtured by taking them to the natural history museum where they get to see the constructions of large dinosaurs and go to the bookstores or to the museum shop, and it nurtures their initial entry in science. The ones who need to become scientists are helped in identifying their interest through this process. The same type of process happens in visual art. Unfortunately, visual arts museums are generally more elite than a natural history museum. Nevertheless, there is something egalitarian about the museum as opposed to being limited to encountering art in church or in palatial private homes.

I think the main thing is exposure on the part of children. Mostly, black kids don't get that kind of exposure, even middle-class black kids, because it hasn't been something that is important to us as we climb the ladder of success. However that is changing somewhat, particularly with black celebrities with a great deal of money. Some of them are starting to buy art. But that doesn't necessarily make them any more critical. Michael Jordan is an art collector and buys art as part of his financial portfolio. What I hope is that these black millionaires may also learn to donate and get involved in building institutional support for blacks in the arts and for the public good.

THA: So the economic always underscores the different ways that people relate to art and visuality . . .

MW: Being a collector is a particular kind of involvement with art. It's the only kind of relationship that is really privileged. If you own the work, then you control the work. Either you own the work or you made the work. Those are the only two relationships to visual culture that are absolutely respected. But what I'm saying is that neither one of those relationships seen as closest to the work is definitive. To me that's not what's most interesting—whether you made the work or you own the work. Because if you made the work then obviously you're not particularly interested in a certain kind of conversation about it. There are going to be limits to the amount of discourse you want the work to generate. And if you own it, it's the same thing, because debate might potentially change the work's monetary value.

THA: What about the distinction between the visual as we engage it through art versus other aspects of the visual field, the relationship to the visual that exists on streets and through the various images which permeate our everyday culture?

MW: There are ways of making distinctions between different levels, and I'll admit I haven't been satisfied by any of them: popular culture as opposed to mass culture, high culture, elite culture; visual art versus folk culture; material culture as a way of talking about the materiality of visual culture.

There is a kind of approach to mass culture/popular culture that says all of it is advertising and therefore all of it is tied up in corporate endeavors to sell you things and is always trying to pull the wool over your eyes. But I think it's going beyond that and that there's a kind of making the invisible visible that is in excess of advertising, or the sort of mundane role of advertising, and you see it permeating the way some films are presented in movie theaters, or the way passion drives some of the new technologies coming across the computer screen perhaps in relation to hip-hop or other new discourses. The use of the computer screen, the use of the screen in general in the culture points to an ongoing struggle, which largely defines modernity, between visibility, or rather that which is predominantly visible, such as material things, the human body, buildings, furniture, machines, and so on, and the invisible, or that which is predominantly invisible—which is to my mind all the really important stuff like love, passion, wisdom, honor, courage, character, spiritual depth, emotional density, the aspects of beauty that are largely invisible or quixotic, such as performativity, harmony, rhythm, lyricism, resonance, and so on. The battle is between superficiality and depth. What is so confusing especially to young people is that superficiality is always plain to see, whereas depth is not.

I was in a cab going down Broadway and on 42nd Street. Not only do they have a big TV screen where they are always showing the news, but the news is printed out and it goes around in a circle around the building so as you're driving by, you'll see the breaking news that is constantly being spelled out around the building. But there's a kind of accelerating of the level of visuality that is being produced by the dominant culture that is desensitizing us to the codings.

I mean in other words, the more images are thrown at you, the less you're able to distinguish between them and filter them, make informed decisions about what you like and don't like. I guess the more you're bombarded with these images, the more passive you become. Images have histories and narratives of their own. The way not to be totally seduced by them is to keep that in mind.

THA: Could you talk a bit about your most recent work? How did you decide to focus on early twentieth-century black imagery and what role do you feel that early representations of blacks have to play in contemporary artists' work?

MW: The reason I went back to that period was that I had always heard that black stereotypes in film originated at the beginning of film. I wanted to go back and see what they were and if I could find any differences other than the dominant narratives that I knew from Donald Bogle and Thomas Cripps regarding the stereotypes.

Were there other, competing images? What had been the original intention of these stereotypes? This was particularly important since I found that some things that were presented to me as stereotypical were also pleasing to me in various ways. So as someone whose background is in literature and English, I wanted to go back and uncover the narratives that these stereotypes were linked to and also find if there were any images that had been abandoned and had not survived, maybe because they were less stereotypical or were subversive. Also what was the intentionality, what were blacks themselves trying to do or say about themselves through images during this time period?

I found out that it's a very interesting time period, a transition into certain technologies and images. There were fewer images being mobilized and people were much less bombarded by images. However, the bombardment was beginning at the turn of the century through a number of technologies. One was the creation of film, two was the greater circulation of the photograph around the turn of the century. The invention of the half-tone illustration made it possible to reproduce images and words on the same page and gave rise to the illustrated press as a means of circulation. The third thing was a technological advance in lithography which made it possible to reproduce large numbers of illustrations and posters which people displayed in their homes. There was widespread reproduction of certain works of art through lithography. Paintings by certain artists, genre artists, were taken up and circulated in larger editions and people would decorate their homes with them. Naturally all of this fed newspaper and advertising production, which poor people often used to decorate the walls of their humble homes.

It seems in particular that some of the most popular images included racial subjects, such as Eastman Johnson's genre painting *Negro Life at the South* (1859), an extraordinary work which prefigures the stereotypical image of the urban ghetto as later presented in DuBose Heywood's novel *Porgy* (1925), then reprised in the Gershwin musical *Porgy and Bess* (1935) and again in the Otto Preminger/Samuel Goldwyn film *Porgy and Bess* (1959) with an all-star black cast (including Dorothy Dandridge and Sidney Poitier). Again and again, the original is reprised in photo after photo by WPA photographers and a host of others, almost as if the fiction had created the sociological fact.

The original painting, which portrays the slave quarters of the Washington, D.C., home of Johnson's father in 1859, is gorgeous to see, yet so dark it is impossible to view properly in reproduction. Nevertheless, the entire tableaux, or details from it, were widely reproduced for commercial distribution.

And then of course the turn of the century is the period when advertising began to really use combinations of text and visual images and the time during which some of the uses of black stereotypes in advertising came about [such as the Gold Dust Twins, Uncle Ben, and Aunt Jemima]. At the same time jazz was coming into view, blues was coming into view. As recording develops and more blacks are recording, this gives a certain kind of weight to some of the images of blacks, particularly since so much of the "stereotypes" among blacks have to do with their performance, dancing or singing. As you get sound in conjunction with images of the moving black body, it's almost as if the goal of representation of blacks is to communicate the movement of the black body and the sound that the voice is able to create. So the images try to communicate visually what that sound and impression of movement is like. You also have a lot of images of blacks connected with sheet music. And you've got black performers writing and performing coon songs and images coming out of that. It was a very rich time in which American culture was thinking about how to represent the black body.

Of course, at the turn of the century and beyond blackface minstrelsy is still happening and black comedians are blacking up and doing other approximations of blackface minstrelsy and there is a competition between white and black authors and producers over how the black body will be represented in the culture. I think that the reason why there is so much competition coming from so many different directions is because what they are debating is how American culture itself will be represented to itself and the world, and by this time the incorporation of American culture and Afro-American culture is pretty complete. That's why it's so important that the immigrants are coming, because they're going to be the new Americans. We blacks are already the old Americans.

I'm interested in the fact that the genealogy of black stereotypes is closely shadowed by the genealogy of any type of authentic black culture. It gets more and more difficult after this period to tell one from the other. So in other words when we as black people in the present discard black stereotypes from the turn of the century and before, we are literally throwing the baby out with the bathwater. And that's why I think it's so important that some black artists are resurrecting black stereotypes. I don't know if they understand why they're doing it or what it is they're looking for, but these stereotypes are objects of curiosity to black people. It's like a Pandora's box in which our past is contained. These are symbols . . . it's almost like when you send someone an e-mail and there's a program called Stuff-It which compresses the file to a tighter, more compact representation. That's what these stereotypes are like: they're tiny little microcosms, very tightly wound packages, containing lots of information. In a way black artists who are using them are doing something good, but I think we need more interpretation to understand what the use of it is.

To me the most interesting person doing this, the person who seems to know most what she is about is Suzan-Lori Parks. In particular I would direct you to her work, *The America Play*. Kara Walker's work is also stunning, although the focus in the black community in response to her has been on her masochism and self-hatred. I guess I do think young black women who take on the sexual objectification of their own bodies are implicated in a project of self-hatred but as a young black woman it is hard not to be drawn into this project. Your body, your youth and sexuality are all for the general use of the culture, if you put yourself out there. This is one of the things I like about being older and therefore less attractive to the meat market as a black woman.

The big thing that I've come to is that performativity in theater and music is visual. That's the big nexus in black culture.

THA: You obviously envision an increased role for the art critics and artists in the development of contemporary black culture. How do you see that role playing out going forwards?

MW: There is no established role for critical voices in black culture. Certainly not in the black press, which is largely celebratory and will remain so I suspect. I guess cultural criticism, at least in the black context, has become a mode of live performance, and in this sense underground, ephemeral, quixotic, and lost in the moment. You need to have been there when the criticism was launched. It is a transaction between critic and audience. Like this Bamboozled panel I was just on at NYU. My sense is that something important happened, but I don't even know how to talk about it.

Unfortunately I'm trying to figure out what's going on—we may be getting ready to have Bush for president. And that's probably going to be more important. I sense that we're moving in a more conservative direction, for the moment, and that people are not taking any chances. And that everybody is kind of pulling back. I must say that I think that what's going on with people at Harvard has a great deal to do with why that's happening because obviously they are in the leadership position and the leadership at this moment seems very conservative, in terms of pulling back and remaining inside the hallowed halls of privilege. There is not enough communication or interchange between different levels of the hierarchy of academia as far as black people are concerned, and I think everybody's afraid of being caught without a chair to sit in, you know like musical chairs. So some change is getting ready to happen right now and it's not clear whether the change is going to be for the better or for the worse or whether the status quo will simply remain. But nobody's taking any chances, including me.

Unpublished interview conducted by *The Harvard Advocate* (2000).

Note

1. I recently attended as a guest of my mother a conference called "Visualizing Blackness" at Cornell University, which was organized by Salah Hassan. It was a substantial beginning toward having a public discussion on black visual culture, although it focused largely upon the '70s black arts movement and those artists who were important in that context heavily dominated the proceedings (Amiri Baraka, Haki Madhabuti, Askia Mohammed Touré, Nelson Stevens, and so on).

II.

MASS CULTURE AND

POPULAR JOURNALISM

7.

Watching Arsenio

With a smile that says, "My middle name is pleasure," and a wardrobe that won't quit, Arsenio Hall is becoming young America's favorite late-night friend. In that nether region between prime time and Bryant Gumbel, television's need for sensuality is finally being met. Moreover, Hall, unlike Koppel, Sajak, Letterman, and Carson, constantly teeters on the edge of an outright multicultural transcendence and evinces a political conviction refreshingly left of center.

From *Julia* to *The Jeffersons*, from *I Spy* to *The Cosby Show*, the progress of African Americans on prime-time television, while sometimes fascinating to watch, rarely seems to make a critical difference in this society's understanding of blacks. Although we may now show our face in the place more than we did in the *Amos 'n' Andy* days of yore, the straitjacket of forms that degraded us or rendered us invisible remains intact.

But *The Arsenio Hall Show* changes the game, if not the rules. It is difficult to explain to the uninitiated the unmistakable appeal of this charming young man. Any one show you watch may even seem a little too silly to analyze—just so much raucous and raunchy fun as Hall laughs, jokes, and dances his way through the hour to the almost continuous musical accompaniment of his "posse," a five-piece band definitively inclined to funk. But watching him night after night, you realize that he is the guy you'd most like to party with because, unlike the stereotypically macho party animal, he has both his politics and his music together.

You can't imagine his being Fortune 500 paternalistic, like Daddy Cosby. Hipper about women and sex, he's neither kamikaze macho, like Pryor, nor buppie cool, like Money Murph. While he flirts outrageously with black women and white women alike, it is always the woman who takes the lead.

He seems just as comfortable cavorting in a house-rocking dance with the buxom, miniskirted Sally Kirkland as when calmly conversing with the statuesque Sigourney Weaver. Typically, Hall once described his relationship to show business with a line worthy of an Alberta Hunter blues: "I treat it like an intelligent woman. If you treat her right, she'll treat you right. If you don't, she'll be gone!"

While his show is not exactly black, it isn't exactly white, either. He books more Asian and Latino singers, actors, and comedians than I've ever seen in all my years of watching television. Hall seems to be molding his late-night hour into a combination *Sesame Street* and *Pee-Wee's Playhouse* for hip, postmodern, postfeminist adults who appreciate living in a multicultural society. There is educational value, for example, in how he nightly diffuses the social tension that exists around young black underclass males. Rappers such as Kool Moe Dee and L. L. Cool J are constant guests on the show. Hall himself is always donning the guise of the b-boy. One night, in a spectacular routine, he padded his stomach and thighs and performed a musical parody of the Fat Boys. The audience went crazy. Another night he came up behind his audience and stole a young black woman's purse, riffled through it—cataloging the contents for the camera—and then counted the cash, which came to eight dollars. "Yes," Hall cried ecstatically, pocketing the money as though he needed it.

But it is precisely this homeboy's present wealth and power—his expensive suits, his elegant set, his position as executive producer of the show, his no. 2 status behind Johnny (Carson) in the ratings—that make this all so right. White guests—from William Shatner and Betty White to Brooke Shields and Julian Lennon—seek his approval of their clothes and their politics and warmly endorse him on the air as though he were running for office on a third party ticket; while the black guests—from Angela Davis and Miles Davis to Magic Johnson and Natalie Cole—seem utterly at home and relaxed.

Finally, I suspect that the key to his popularity is not his guests or his humor, but his conviction that it's necessary to confront the problems of sexuality and race, poverty and drugs (as in Hall's antidrug TV spots) because "the real world" is here to stay. In the process, another kind of politics, beyond the Reagan-Bush-era malaise, actually seems entertaining, if not yet wholly viable.

Originally published as "Emergency Exit," *Emerge Magazine*. Premier issue, October 1989, 80.

8.

Black Stereotypes in Hollywood Films: "I Don't
Know Nothin' 'Bout Birthin' No Babies!"

Things haven't changed as much as you think since Stepin Fetchit stepped
and fetched, and since a handkerchief-headed Butterfly McQueen so provocatively announced in *Gone with the Wind*, "I don't know nothin' 'bout
birthin' no babies!" I know that over the years I've wanted to murder somebody much of the time when I've gone to the movies, and black stereotypes
have become only the most visible symptom of the problem—the easiest
thing to pick on.

The most aggravating thing about wide releases has been that the better
the film is, the more likely there is to be a total absence of black actors in
significant roles—not to mention their absence behind the camera. What
we're talking about here is simply another kind of stereotype, more difficult
to diagnose, more suitable to the sophisticated racism of the '80s and '90s:
invisibility.

Because of the restrictions that even including blacks automatically im-
poses on script, direction of actors, even camera angles, these movies generally risk dangerous levels of mediocrity. Sometimes it's as if, in sequences
with black characters, the film invariably drops down to the level of bad
TV drama or sitcom. Suffering from a structural inability to deal with black
images in other than flat, symbolic ways, the political unconscious just gets
out of control.

Which brings us to those recent pictures that consciously take on the task of providing black "role models"—the not-very-interesting but very commercial films apparently designed to capture the burgeoning market of black viewers. (According to Simmons Market Research Bureau [from 1986 data], 10 percent more black adult males than white adult males attend at least one movie weekly.) Although recent black stereotypes are neither obvious nor necessarily obnoxious, what they often have in common is their profamily and promilitaristic, violent bent. I think first of the two *Lethal Weapons*, with Danny Glover; *Die Hard*, with Reginald Vel Johnson in a supporting role; and the preglasnost *Little Nikita*, starring Sidney Poitier. Then there are *Mississippi Burning* and *Betrayed*, both of which pretend to be about racism, but employ black bodies only as abject decorative objects.

Interesting movies with either no blacks or scarcely any significant black presence (except as scenery) are still the rule. These include most of the films that I'd been dying to see in recent years, but which I went to see knowing that watching them would be like finding, once again, that black people don't really exist. To name but a few that were particular disappointments: *Kiss of the Spider Woman* (when I read the book, I imagined that the William Hurt character was mestizo); *The Untouchables* (just because the TV show was lily-white, did that also mean the flick had to repeat the error?); and *Broadcast News* (couldn't they have used one little skinny light-skinned researcher or something?).

Where would be the harm in one of the disciples in Scorsese's *The Last Temptation of Christ* being black, or at least not white? Instead, we had to float all our black Christian fantasies on the back of the anonymous Ethiopian hunk who screws Barbara Hershey's fat-lipped, heavily tattooed (does this mean she's not as white?) Mary Magdalene. The music does draw upon a fascinating third world mix, but colorizing The Last Supper would only deepen the fun.

As usual, women fare the worst. How will I ever forget Lisa Bonet's inarticulate mannequin, a slut voodoo priestess (this stereotype simultaneously slams the entire African diaspora and "women and blacks") who gets just what she deserves in *Angel Heart*? And what Billie Holiday would have called a "cute little maid" (played by Anna Maria Horsford in *Heartburn*) in the bad old days when black women got to play nothing else, is perhaps Nora Ephron's or Mike Nichols's idea of progress, but not mine.

There are apparent exceptions: fair movies with reasonably significant black roles. But this is also where we're most likely to meet some of the most compelling black stereotypes of the decade.

Forest Whitaker's oafish junkie in *Bird* follows in the footsteps of Dexter Gordon's childlike Bud Powell character in *'Round Midnight*. Both subjects are tragic primarily for their inability to find that entertaining white folks is sufficient justification for living. Morgan Freeman's drug counselor-cum-drillmaster in *Clean and Sober* represents an improvement—at least reducing the patriarchal claptrap—over a previous version of that kind of role, played by Louis Gossett Jr. in *An Officer and a Gentleman*—and yet both films feed upon the same neostereotypical notion that authority somehow cancels race.

The black good cop/bad cop couple in *Witness* (Brent Jennings and Danny Glover) is actually kind of fun, if you don't get too hung up on making the sociopolitical translation of this brand of either/or madness—which has our nation's white populace wishing Cosby would come to dinner one minute, and crying for the death penalty for the Willie Hortons of the world the next.

Moreover, it doesn't seem especially likely that the new movies will be much better, since the emphasis remains steadfastly on how black people are faring in a white man's world. There's Morgan Freeman and Esther Rolle playing chauffeur and maid in *Driving Miss Daisy*. There's the all-black regiment in the Civil War in *Glory*, whose cast includes Denzel Washington and Morgan Freeman. Of course, the focus of the film is on the white colonel who led them, played by Matthew Broderick. Then there's Washington as the ghost sidekick to Bob Hoskins in *Heart Condition*. You'll notice in all this, as well, a certain telling repetition of names. Yes, Washington and Freeman are the darkies of the moment, as were Glover and Gossett not too long ago. (Do I have to point out that there is no black female darkie of the moment?)[1]

Among the many troubles with the film version of Richard Wright's 1940 best-seller *Native Son* (which had a limited release in 1986) was that Bigger Thomas is the kind of character on whom the film industry, or, indeed, the mass media, has gained no distance whatsoever since the book came out. Movies that will cause Bigger's real-life counterpart to grow—or at least not shrink—or that would enrich the existence of the real-life counterpart of Bigger's even less-well understood black girlfriend, Bessie, still aren't being made, except in the few cases of black independent filmmaking. So it should come as no surprise that it was still impossible to make an honest picture about the likes of Bessie and Bigger.

But more to the point, what the growing young black film audience is doing can't be too far removed from what Bigger did at the movies: engage in escapist, self-contemptuous fantasies about how rich white folks live. Fantasies that, at least in the case of Bigger, led to murder.

Originally published in the *Village Voice*, 5 December 1989.

Note

1. Needless to say, this situation has changed remarkably since the original writing of this piece in 1986, with a whole new crop of black and/or female directors, as well as a new roster of A- and B-list actors in Hollywood and elsewhere. See some of the other pieces about movies in this volume.

9.

When Black Feminism Faces the Music,

and the Music Is Rap

Like many black feminists, I look on sexism in rap as a necessary evil. In a society plagued by poverty and illiteracy, where young black men are as likely to be in prison as in college, rap is a welcome articulation of the economic and social frustrations of black youth.

In response to disappointments faced by poor urban blacks negotiating their future, rap offers the release of creative expression and historical continuity: it draws on precedents as diverse as jazz, reggae, calypso, Afro-Cuban, African and heavy metal, and its lyrics include rudimentary forms of political, economic, and social analysis.

But with the failure of our urban public schools, rappers have taken education into their own hands; these are oral lessons (reading and writing being low priorities). And it should come as no surprise that the end result emphasizes innovations in style and rhythm over ethics and morality. Although there are exceptions, like raps advocating world peace (the W.I.S.E. Guyz's "Time for Peace") and opposing drug use (Ice-T's "I'm Your Pusher"), rap lyrics can be brutal, raw and, where women are the subject, glaringly sexist. Given the genre's current crossover popularity and success in the marketplace, including television commercials, rap's impact on young people is growing. A large part of the appeal of pop culture is that it can offer symbolic resolutions to life's contradictions. But when it comes to gender, rap has not resolved a thing.

Though styles vary—from that of the X-rated Ice-T to the sybaritic Kwa-nee to the hyperpolitics of Public Enemy—what seems universal is how little male rappers respect sexual intimacy and how little regard they have for the humanity of the black woman. Witness the striking contrast within rap videos: for men, standard attire is baggy, outsize pants; for women, spike heels and short skirts. Videos often feature the ostentatious and fetishistic display of women's bodies. In Kool Moe Dee's "How Ya Like Me Now," women gyrate in tight leather with large revealing holes. In Digital Underground's video "Doowutchyalike," set poolside at what looks like a fraternity house party, a rapper in a clown costume pretends to bite the backside of a woman in a bikini.

As one might put it, rap is basically a locker room with a beat.

The recent banning of the sale of 2 Live Crew's album "As Nasty as They Wanna Be" by local governments in Florida and elsewhere has publicized rap's treatment of women as sex objects, but it also made a hit of a record that contains some of the bawdiest lyrics in rap. Though such sexual explicitness in lyrics is rare, the assumptions about women—that they manipulate men with their bodies—are typical.

In an era when the idea that women want to be raped should be obsolete, rap lyrics and videos presuppose that women always desire sex, whether they know it or not. In Bell Biv DeVoe's rap-influenced pop hit single "Poison," for instance, a beautiful girl is considered poison because she does not respond affirmatively and automatically to a sexual proposition.

bell hooks, author of *Yearning: Race, Gender, and Cultural Politics* (South End Books, 1990), sees the roots of rap as a youth rebellion against all attempts to control black masculinity, both in the streets and in the home. "That rap would be anti-domesticity and in the process anti-female should come as no surprise," Ms. hooks says.

At present there is only a small platform for black women to address the problems of sexism in rap and in their community. Feminist criticism, like many other forms of social analysis, is widely considered part of a hostile white culture. For a black feminist to publicly chastise misogyny in rap would be viewed as divisive and counterproductive. There is a widespread perception in the black community that public criticism of black men constitutes collaborating with a racist society.

The charge is hardly new. Such a reaction greeted Ntozake Shange's play *For Colored Girls Who Have Considered Suicide/When the Rainbow Is Enuf*, my own essays in *Black Macho and the Myth of the Superwoman*, and Alice Walker's novel *The Color Purple*, all of which were perceived as critical of black men. After the release of the film version of *The Color Purple*, feminists were lambasted in the press for their supposed lack of support for black men; such critical analysis by black women has all but disappeared. In its place is *A Blackman's Guide to Understanding the Blackwoman*, a vanity-press book by Shaharazad Ali, which has sold more than 80,000 copies by insisting that black women are neurotic, insecure, and competitive with black men.

Though misogynist lyrics seem to represent the opposite of Ms. Ali's worldview, these are, in fact, just two extremes on the same theme: Ms. Ali's prescription for what ails the black community is that women should not question men about their sexual philandering and should be firmly slapped across the mouth when they do. Rap lyrics suggest just about the same: women should be silent and prone.

There are those who have wrongly advocated censorship of rap's more sexually explicit lyrics and those who have excused the misogyny because of its basis in black oral traditions.

Rap is rooted not only in the blaxploitation films of the '70s but also in an equally sexist tradition of black comedy. In the use of four-letter words and explicit sexual references, both Richard Pryor and Eddie Murphy, who themselves drew on the earlier examples of Redd Foxx, Pigmeat Markham, and Moms Mabley, are conscious reference points for the 2 Live Crew. Black comedy, in turn, draws on an oral tradition in which black men trade "toasts," stories in which dangerous bagmen and trickster figures like Stackolee and Dolomite sexually exploit women and promote violence among men. The popular rapper Ice Cube, in the album "AmeriKKKa's Most Wanted," is Stackolee come to life. In "The Nigga Ya Love to Hate," he projects an image of himself as a criminal as dangerous to women as to the straight white world.

Rap remains almost completely dominated by black males and this mindset. Although women have been involved in rap since at least the mid-80s, record companies have only recently begun to promote them. And as women rappers like Salt-N-Pepa, Monie Love, M. C. Lyte, L. A. Star, and Queen Latifah slowly gain more visibility, rap's sexism may emerge as a subject for scrutiny. Indeed, the answer may lie with women, expressing in lyrics and videos the tensions between the sexes in the black community.

Today's women rappers range from a high ground that doesn't challenge male rap on its own level (Queen Latifah) to those who subscribe to the same sexual high jinks as male rappers (Oaktown's 3.5.7). M. C. Hammer launched Oaktown's 3.5.7., made up of his former backup dancers. These female rappers manifest the worst-case scenario: their skimpy, skintight leopard costumes in the video of "Wild and Loose (We Like It)" suggest an exotic animalistic sexuality. Their clothes fall to their ankles. They take bubble baths. Clearly, their bodies are more important than rapping. And in a field in which writing one's own rap is crucial, their lyrics are written by their former boss, M. C. Hammer.

Most women rappers constitute the middle ground: they talk of romance, narcissism, and parties. On the other hand, Salt-N-Pepa on "Shake Your Thang" uses the structure of the 1969 Isley Brothers' song "It's Your Thing" to insert a protofeminist rap response: "Don't try to tell me how to party. It's my dance and it's my body." M. C. Lyte, in a dialogue with Positive K on "I'm Not Havin' It" comes down hard on the notion that women can't say no and criticizes the shallowness of the male rap.

Queen Latifah introduces her video, "Ladies First," performed with the English rapper Monie Love, with photographs of black political heroines like Winnie Mandela, Sojourner Truth, Harriet Tubman, and Angela Davis. With a sound that resembles scat as much as rap, Queen Latifah chants "Stereotypes they got to go" against a backdrop of newsreel footage of the apartheid struggle in South Africa. The politically sophisticated Queen Latifah seems worlds apart from the adolescent, buffoonish sex orientation of most rap. In general, women rappers seem so much more grown up. Can they inspire a more beneficent attitude toward sex in rap? What won't subvert rap's sexism are the actions of men; what will is women speaking in their own voice, not just in artificial female ghettos, but with and to men.

Originally published in the *New York Times*, 29 July 1990, Arts and Leisure section, p. 20.

10.

Storytellers: The Thomas–Hill Affair

Anita Hill is the black woman I've been waiting to see on TV all my life. In the eleventh hour of an otherwise depressing confirmation hearing of a right-wing black Republican for the Supreme Court, we find ourselves in the midst of an extended televised debate about sexual harassment, with Anita Hill at the center of it all.

It should be remembered that the Supreme Court didn't establish a hostile work environment as legally actionable until 1986. And yet the questions the senators kept asking Anita Hill's friends on Sunday afternoon were why they didn't advise her to speak out, to use the system and the law to protest the harassment that she says took place in the early '80s. But as her friend Ellen Wells confirmed in her testimony, it still isn't safe to tell.

"Being a black woman, you know you have to put up with a lot," Wells said, as she spoke movingly of her own experiences of sexual harassment, "so you grit your teeth and you do it." And how could any compassionate individual, especially someone who has had firsthand knowledge of such a situation, advise someone to disclose that experience before she is ready to weather what could be the devastating consequences?

It is gratifying to see such a display of courage and dignity on the part of any woman participating in the dominant discourse. Luckily, Hill's credibility is nearly beyond question because she is a Yale Law School graduate, a lawyer, and a tenured law professor. Furthermore, the issue Hill brought to the spotlight—sexual harassment in the workplace—is as omnipresent in society as it is legally elusive. As such, the Senate committee hearings, which have focused on whether or not Clarence Thomas sexually harassed her at the EEOC, have kept me and the rest of the nation glued to the TV screen for the entire weekend.

But there has been a long history of women recounting their stories, tales of abuse told by women not given credence by the public at large. This is especially true for black women, who are seldom believed when making public charges against men of sexual misconduct. And the Tawana Brawley case didn't help. The historical records go back to Harriet Jacobs and the early dismissal of her *Incidents in the Life of a Slave Girl.* More recently, charges of rape and sexual misconduct made against Mike Tyson and the St. John's rape case highlight that a woman's credibility is still under question. Some have suggested that it is Tyson who's being scapegoated by the press and that what really happened was that the St. John's victim was in the wrong place at the wrong time and was, therefore, asking for it.

Relevant here as well are the claims of La Toya Jackson of child abuse and sexual abuse by her father, and Roseanne Barr Arnold's accusations of sexual abuse by her father and mother. These women don't have a law degree or the kind of right-wing, Bible-belt credibility that Hill can claim. Barr (an overweight comedian) and Jackson (best known for being photographed in the nude and apparently having an excess of plastic surgery) have faced widespread skepticism as to the reliability of their accounts.

Barr and Jackson—although making more serious claims of incest and domestic violence against their victimizers—share with Hill the fact that they are disclosing abuses that happened to them years ago. For many on the Senate committee and, indeed, for many people in the United States, this makes their stories impossible to believe. But from a psychological point of view, it is well known that the ability to publicly disclose one's victimization is an act of great strength and fortitude. It doesn't happen until the victim is able to trust those around her and to believe that she has a receptive audience for her complaints.

In this case, it happens that Hill has not only the support of her friends and family, and of those who would like to see Thomas not confirmed, but she also has the support of what I would call a nation-within-a-nation. That is, a community or audience that understands and believes in her victimization and revels in her ability to publicly come to terms with it because her audience knows, firsthand, what she's been through. Once the victim has worked through her own victimization and chooses to reject it, she may have no choice but to disclose. What remains is for the rest of us to deal with it.

Originally published in the *Village Voice*, 22 October 1991, pp. 29–30.

11.

Talking about the Gulf

FEBRUARY 5, TUESDAY EVENING, at B. Smith's. The occasion is a Doubleday party for three new books (by Mary Helen Washington, Gerald Early, and C. California Cooper) in Anchor's Black Voices, Black Heritage series. The bar is open. Waiters in white ties serve hot hors d'oeuvres, and the place is packed with the up-and-coming niggerati fashionably dressed in dignified shades of silk, velvet, jersey, and leather.

Present are Lionel Hampton, Arthur and Jean Ashe, Gordon Parks, Stanley Crouch, Marie Brown, Lisa Jones, Nelson George, Marie Evans, Paula Giddings, Susan Taylor, Beatrice Nivens, Stephanie Stokes-Oliver, Bernice Steinbaum, Audrey Edwards. Heavy with potential profitability, the aura might best be described as perfumy.

Talking with different people, it is hard to slip the gulf in. Mostly we talk about other things, like the price of a meal at B. Smith's, Shaharazad Ali, *Mulebone*. But the elegance of this party, in contrast to the condition of most black people in New York, haunts me. I have just come from the subway where many of the homeless reside; 50 percent of them, I'm told, are Vietnam veterans. Can the black veterans of the gulf expect better?

Mary Helen Washington, feminist and professor of literature at the University of Maryland, who, in fact, poses the salient question: "Do you know anybody in the gulf?" she asks.

"No," I say.

"Neither do I, and I have twelve nieces and nephews who are of draft age. They're all in college. This war will be fought by working-class blacks."

FEBRUARY 7, THURSDAY AFTERNOON, in World Humanities (the "great books" course) at CCNY in Harlem. My students are overwhelmingly black and Latino. Their tuition is about to be doubled and their tuition assistance cut by a governor who has proved to be an opponent of public higher education. Not surprisingly, the students would rather talk about the war than about *Pride and Prejudice*. Every student, without exception, knows somebody in the gulf.

When we talk about whether the war is justified, their emotions seem complicated by their sense of obligation to friends and family among the troops. No, the war isn't justified, but they remain preoccupied with the now academic question of whether or not reservists are truly obligated to serve in wartime. One black female student insists, "When they signed up, they took an oath to defend their country. If they didn't want to fight, they shouldn't have signed up!"

Angered by this remark, another black female student, who seems to speak for many in the class, says mournfully, "My brother is over there. He was in the military to get an education. He never expected to go to war. My mother is very upset. We don't know what is happening."

Other students, mostly male, whom I suspect of having even deeper feelings about the war, remain silent and grim but follow our conversation closely. Oddly, it is the women who do most of the talking.

Perhaps the most telling thing is their response to wartime censorship, which, as the generation that grew up between Watergate and Contragate, they regard as business as usual. When I point out that censorship is probably illegal and a violation of our First Amendment rights, one black male student insists, "They're going to do what they want to do anyway, and we'll hear about it after. Maybe." Others in the class nod in agreement.

Coming home on the subway during rush hour, I talk with the poet Ann Lauterbach, who also teaches at CCNY. We make jokes about our disappearing salaries (all state employees except the politicians are losing a week's wages due to the deficit) and the possibility of a "precision" bomb that could knock out the entire subway system even as it aimed for Gracie Mansion or Wall Street. Our fellow passengers, some of whom are wearing yellow ribbons, are visibly unamused.

After she gets off the subway, I read in the *New York Times* about how television advertisers don't want their upbeat commercials juxtaposed with the downbeat war news and that, as a result, the networks will be forced to further curtail war coverage.

FEBRUARY 8, EVENING. I read the *Amsterdam News*, in which reporter Don Rojas responds to charges that blacks are unpatriotic because so many of them refuse to wear yellow ribbons and put flags on their cars. Although blacks are much more likely to be opposed to the war than whites, they do not consider themselves less patriotic, according to a listeners' survey on WLIB. Perhaps because nearly 30 percent of the troops in the gulf are black, the survey found that many blacks in New York feel both "a patriotic duty to support the troops" and "pride in 'our men and women over there.'"

FEBRUARY 9, SATURDAY NIGHT, a long-distance telephone conversation with Beverly Guy-Sheftall, feminist literary critic and head of women's studies at Spelman, a black women's college in Atlanta. Antiwar efforts are not going all that well down there, she thinks. "Never have black folks been more confused about what to believe in," she says.

They are torn, Beverly explains, between pride in the accomplishments of Colin Powell and horror at the prospect that the black community will be devastated just as it was in the Vietnam War.

I repeat to her what Mary Helen Washington said, about only poor black folk being in the gulf. Beverly says that although many blacks believe this, she personally knows of several children of the black middle class who are in the gulf. "They dropped out of college and went into the military because they didn't know what else to do." Or "their parents wanted to save their college tuition," she says.

ANOTHER SATURDAY NIGHT long-distance telephone conversation with Faith, my mother, who teaches painting at UC San Diego to a generation that can't remember Vietnam. Yet they are all now painting war scenes. At the beginning of the term, she says they were painting an unusual number of flowers. "Enough with the flowers already," she told them.

Originally published in the *Village Voice*, February 1991.

12.

Beyond Assimilation

These days, if you read the *New York Times*, you may have already formed the correct impression that Afrocentricity is largely a question of history and pedagogy. What contributions, if any, have Afro-Americans made to U.S. culture? How will such contributions be recognized and acknowledged by curricular reform? How will such matters be predigested and served up as a list of tasty "facts" for public school instruction and SAT exams?

Nathan Glazer, a member of the Sobol Committee to review the social studies syllabi in New York's elementary and high schools, tells us in *The New Republic* that driving such reforms are the performance problems black children are experiencing in school. Afrocentric and multicultural educational reforms are designed to redress the high dropout rate and the low SAT scores and reading levels of black children. On the other hand, Glazer says, Afrocentrism and multiculturalism, by emphasizing "difference" and minority perspectives on national history, don't acknowledge that the immigrant experience has largely been one of assimilation. Most Americans couldn't care less where their ancestors came from. Moreover, he says, there is little evidence that recent Asian and Mexican immigrants want to do things any differently. That Afro-Americans and some Latinos want to emphasize "difference" reflects the fact that their attempts to assimilate have been frustrated.

I am not so sure about this word "assimilation." I suspect that the tendency for ethnic and postethnic populations around the United States to formulate endlessly minute hybrids and variations on The Man in the Gray Flannel Suit should be called something else that better reflects the fluidity and anarchy of the process. (Just think of the difference between folks in Buffalo, New York, and Amarillo, Texas, or Chimayo and Miami.) But I am sure of this: the resistance blacks and nonwhite Latinos have experienced to their upward mobility is called racism and thus far Afrocentrism and multiculturalism seem an inadequate response to it.

I am opposed to viewing "facts" as the major building blocks of education. Seventy-five percent of the time what goes on in school, when it is going well, is socialization. The integrated Lutheran elementary school I attended had more marks for manners and courtesy than it had for math or science. And with good reason. I was learning how to fit in. School was reinforcing the message I got from my family: bathe, wear clean clothes, speak when you're spoken to, and everything will be okay. This all-important process continues right through college. Consider, for example, those loathsome fraternities and sororities on every campus.

But the rest of the time, what makes pedagogy worthwhile is how the experience of education is structured, how the student learns to interrogate "fact," to challenge facticity. What we saw recently in the streets of Moscow and two years ago in Tiananmen Square—a population standing together to resist official "lies" and to fight for "democracy" and "freedom"—is also taught in school. So the very notion of an Afrocentric educational formula in which a list of appropriate "facts" would be disseminated strikes me as almost completely beside the point.

The problem that Afrocentrists and multiculturalists are facing is a breakdown in the socialization process, what Glazer calls "assimilation." My older Jewish colleagues at City College are fond of describing how they were successfully "assimilated" or socialized by arrogant, perhaps even anti-Semitic WASP teachers at Columbia University and elsewhere who knew nothing of their heritage or their struggles in Russia or Poland. But what they forget, again and again, is that they were white, or at least—as James Baldwin might say—about to become "white." Being white meant they didn't have to combat racism, as they swallowed the Eurocentric brew at the tea party of American education.

By "racism" I mean the idea that other races, especially black descendants of Africa, are inferior to the "white" race. The idea of black inferiority has a particular history in U.S. and European development and often an interesting relationship to other kinds of biases, such as misogyny and anti-

Semitism. This history of racism, unfortunately, is rarely taught by either Afrocentrists or Eurocentrists and this has always been and continues to be my problem with both programs.

Because the category of "race," itself, is both racist and mythological—and a symptom of what Fredric Jameson calls "the political unconscious" in that "we," as a culture and a civilization, find it almost impossible to describe it ethically or empirically—the mistake that both Eurocentrists and Afrocentrists make is to almost completely discount it.

In fact I think "race" is an embarrassment to everybody. But by ignoring it, we all, unconsciously, conspire to make it tick.

My "white" colleagues had the option to be good little boys and girls, politely imbibe Eurocentrism and unite with their WASP teachers under the banner of whiteness. People who are not only not white but are black are rarely faced with that option. This doesn't mean there aren't lots of exceptions, like Colin Powell and Clarence Thomas. What it means is that there are only exceptions, or "tokens." (In agony, I include myself in this group.) And the bulk of people of color, by which I mean those who are too black to become "white," will remain the unsocialized, unassimilated horde who don't do well in school because before you can do well in school you have to be accepted, and who don't do well in American society because before you can do well in American society, you have to be accepted. (See the Crown Heights riots.)

Of course, money helps. But there isn't much of that around, is there? As for the conspiracy theories and "fact" formulas of the Leonard Jeffrieses, need I tell you what grade he gets in courtesy?

Originally published in the *Village Voice*, 17 September 1991, pp. 41–42.

13.

"Why Women Won't Relate to 'Justice'":

Losing Her Voice

I had hoped that John Singleton's *Poetic Justice* would be the first black version of what feminist critic Molly Haskell once called a "women's film." A heady, ambiguous mixture of sentiment and feminist ideas, a women's film creates a universe in which women's thought and aspirations are at its center.

Certainly Singleton had an idea worthy of an Alice Walker or a Toni Morrison novel: A black woman named Justice writes poetry in order to mourn the death of her lover as well as the violence and dissension in the black community.

But he failed to look in the right places for role models. His job would have been a lot simpler if he had chosen to use, instead of the light lyrical verse of Maya Angelou, the work of one of the many black feminist poets—Lucille Clifton, Audre Lorde, Ntozake Shange, June Jordan—who focus on that painful intermingling of racism and unrequited love that makes the black woman blue.

As a consequence of his unwillingness to take this work or, indeed, black female thought seriously, his poet has no voice. He invents in Justice a character who seems capable of morality and intelligence, but then he gags her.

I suspect that Singleton researched the film by interviewing black women and that they told him what many black women continue to say even though it isn't true: that feminist ideas have nothing to do with black women, and that black women and white women don't share role models. In fact, though feminism has never been a mass movement in the black community, black female thinkers and writers have always figured significantly in the women's movement. And like all women, black women are deeply split along class and educational lines over women's issues.

It can be very confusing. So it isn't surprising that Singleton hasn't succeeded in forging the lessons of black feminist poetry and classic Hollywood women's films. But I hope he will try again. In the meantime, I also hope that *Poetic Justice* will stir further discussion of these matters in the black community.

Originally published in *Entertainment Weekly*, July 23, 1993, 43.

14.

For Whom the Bell Tolls: Why Americans Can't
Deal with Black Feminist Intellectuals

It's interesting to visit different bookstores in Manhattan just to see how they handle the dilemma posed by the existence of a black female author who is not a novelist or a poet but who has ten books in print. At the Barnes & Noble superstore uptown, they are getting perilously close to having to devote an entire shelf to bell hooks's studies, in the manner that there are presently multiple shelves on MLK and Malcolm X.

And yet she might prefer it if instead I compared her to the white male Olympians of critical theory—Barthes, Foucault, Freud, and Marx—and that it was only conformity to what she likes to call "white supremacist thinking" that prevents me from classing her with the founding fathers.

In the past fourteen years, as the author of ten books on black feminism, bell hooks has managed to corner the multicultural feminist advice market almost singlehandedly. bell hooks is the alias of Gloria Watkins, who is now Distinguished Professor of English at the City College of New York. Raised in the rural South in Hopkinsville, Kentucky, Watkins collected her B.A. at Stanford, going on to finish her Ph.D. in English at UC Santa Cruz over a decade ago. We've been hearing from hooks regularly ever since.

Much like her previous work, *Killing Rage: Ending Racism* consists of a collection of unconnected essays, some of them recycled from earlier books. As usual, the writing is leftist, dogmatic, repetitive, and dated. For instance, in the book's penultimate chapter, called "Moving from Pain to Power: Black

Self-Determination," Watkins offers the following turgid explanation of the failure of black struggle in the '60s:

> Revolutionary black liberation struggle in the United States was undermined by outmoded patriarchal emphasis on nationhood and masculine rule, the absence of a strategy for coalition building that would keep a place for non-black allies in struggle, and the lack of sustained programs for education for critical consciousness that would continually engage black folks of all classes in a process of radical politicization.

But then it was never in the expectation of beautiful writing or subtly nuanced analyis that we turned to bell hooks. With chapters bearing titles like "Healing Our Wounds: Liberatory Mental Health Care," "Where Is the Love?," and "Overcoming White Supremacy," we are being offered, simultaneously, a series of potentially contradictory solutions to what ails us.

hooks suggests that a black feminist analysis of "race and racism in America" is the essential missing component in current mainstream perspectives on race, at the same time that she offers a defense of black rage, in all its masculinist appeal, as inherently liberatory. ". . . I understand rage to be a necessary aspect of resistance struggle," she writes. Meanwhile, interspersed with the rage and the feminist analysis, she is also slipping us a kind of hit-or-miss guide to self-healing, self-recovery, and self-actualization.

THE NEW HOOKS began to emerge, like a butterfly from a chrysalis, about a year or two ago when Watkins abandoned the leftist rigors of the South End Press collective in Boston and her post as associate professor at Oberlin College, more or less at the same time, and moved to New York and CCNY, published *Outlaw Culture* and *Teaching to Transgress* with Routledge and *Art on My Mind* with the nonprofit New Press, only to turn around a few months later to publish *Killing Rage* with Holt, her first major mainstream publisher, this fall.

Using cultural analysis of popular culture, film, visual art, and pedagogy, with occasional outbursts of self-help rhetoric (to which hooks had already devoted an entire book—*Sisters of the Yam*), *Teaching to Transgress*, *Outlaw Culture*, and *Art on My Mind* all continue in the direction hooks's work has taken the past few years, as amply demonstrated in *Black Looks*; *Yearning: Race, Gender, and Cultural Politics*; and *Talking Back: Thinking Feminist, Thinking Black*. However, with *Killing Rage*, hooks is clearly trying to drive a wedge into the current white market for books on race and the recent upsurge in the black market for books on spirituality and self-recovery.

Given this onslaught of publication, accompanied by an alarming dearth of explanatory or analytic criticism about her work, either in mainstream or alternative venues, perhaps it should come as no surprise that the poorly researched cover story in *The Chronicle of Higher Education* (the *New York Times* of academics) on the hooks/Watkins phenomenon considers her not only the most viable voice of black feminism but also the only acceptable black female candidate for inclusion in the roster of the "new black intellectuals," whose emergence has been repeatedly announced in the pages of *The Atlantic Monthly*, *The New Republic*, the *New York Times*, *The New Yorker*, and even the *VLS*.

"When black feminism needed a voice, bell hooks was born," *The Chronicle* proclaimed a few months ago. Which makes her a candidate for the only black feminist who matters? Not. Perhaps the dominant discourse is given to these lapses of amnesia because some ideas are so repugnant to Western culture that they are forced to emerge, again and again, as if new.

There hasn't been much resistance lately to the idea of a mainstream feminist discourse or even to a left-wing alternative or to academic feminism. But what continues to boggle the minds of the powers that be is that black feminism has been around for a long time.

OUR VERSION OF the Second Wave of Women's Liberation (which was really just a continuation of the same wave that brought us here on the slave ship) began when black female civil rights activist Anna Arnold Hedgeman objected to the idea that no women had been asked to speak at the famous 1963 March on Washington. Throughout the '60s, there were numerous black women in the civil rights movement and the Black Power movement north and south who, though they may have shirked the label at the time, should be considered honorary members in the black feminist hall of fame because of the contribution they made to human rights: for instance, Rosa Parks; Ella Baker, who helped found both SNCC and Southern Christian Leadership Conference; Ruby Doris Smith, executive secretary of Student Nonviolent Coordinating Committee who died prematurely at twenty-six; and so many others.

But it was in 1970 that black feminism really began to emerge as an autonomous discourse with the publication of the anthology *The Black Woman*, edited by noted black feminist author Toni Cade Bambara, and the organization of such groups as Third World Women's Alliance, led by Frances Beale. In 1971, *The Black Scholar* published an article called "Reflections on the Black Woman's Role in the Community of Slaves," which was written by

Angela Davis in her prison cell, kicking off the black feminist critique in the social sciences (later revised and expanded for her collection *Women, Race, and Class*).

And 1972 was the year that Shirley Chisholm became the first black woman ever to run for president, despite the lack of adequate support from either white feminists or Black Power advocates. In her autobiography *The Good Fight*, the openly feminist Chisholm concluded that the failure of her campaign had more to do with sexism than racism.

Although the author was white, the publication of feminist historian Gerda Lerner's *Black Women in White America: A Documentary History* in 1972 was crucial to subsequent intellectual developments in black women's history in that it raised many more questions than it answered. A great deal of promising research (i.e., the work of Paula Giddings, Elizabeth Fox-Genovese, Jacqueline Jones, Hazel Carby, Barbara Smith, Deborah McDowell, Deborah Gray White, et al.) was among the results.

Also in 1973 the National Black Feminist Organization (NBFO) was founded at a meeting called by black feminists in New York, at which I was present. Both Chisholm and Eleanor Holmes Norton spoke to a packed house at the first national convention of NBFO in 1974 at Barnard. The NBFO subsequently became a nationwide organization with thousands of members before it petered out, some say for lack of support from the white feminist establishment. Meanwhile, a more informal discussion group of black women writers called The Sisterhood began meeting at Alice Walker's house in Brooklyn. Attendees included me, Toni Morrison, June Jordan, as well as virtually every significant black female writer of the next decade.

When Ntozake Shange swept New York with her theatrical production of *For Colored Girls* in 1976, first at the Henry Street Settlement House, then at the Public, and then on Broadway, you might say we were ready and waiting. Black lesbian activist and publisher Barbara Smith had already written or was about to write her *Toward a Black Feminist Criticism*, which would first circulate as a handbook throughout the Northeast corridor in 1977, kicking off a literary critique, to parallel the one already launched in the social sciences by Lerner and Davis, that would resonate throughout the humanities.

Smith's article only served to confirm what a lot of black feminists already knew, which was that the steady flow of novels and poetry by black female authors—Maya Angelou's *I Know Why the Caged Bird Sings*; Toni Morrison's *The Bluest Eye* and *Sula*; Alice Walker's *The Third Life of Grange Copeland, In Love and Trouble, Once*, and *The Color Purple*; Toni Cade Bambara's *Gorilla, My Love*, and *The Salt Eaters*; as well as the poetry of Nikki Giovanni, Audre Lorde, Sonia Sanchez, June Jordan, Lucille Clifton, Sherley Anne Williams, and others too numerous to name—represented a momentous paradigm shift not only in black feminism but in the women's movement overall.

Certainly literary criticism would never be the same, as the Modern Language Association soon began to realize. In the mid '70s, celebrated black feminist lesbian poet Audre Lorde and her white comrade poet Adrienne Rich, who had been since her days as a SEEK instructor in the late '70s at CCNY a committed third worldist, helped launch a multicultural feminist intervention, spearheaded by Lorde's subversive and visionary aphorism in *Sister Outsider* within and beyond the ranks of the MLA, which has resulted in a profound shift in academic tolerance, in general, for both feminist and multicultural-inflected discourses. Such trends in academia have served to bring down the wrath of the Jessie Helmses and the Gertrude Himmelfarbs as surely as Robert Mapplethorpe's *Black Book*.

Although the humanities tend to get all the credit for the fireworks, in fact, without the black feminist response to Senator Moynihan (i.e., Joyce Ladner and Inez Reid, et al.) as well as Davis's critique of the then-prestigious new historiography on slavery (Eugene Genovese, Herbert Gutman, et al.) from which the subsequent interest in the "lost voices" and the "narratives" of black women came, I am not sure where we would be.

Inspired, enthralled, and overwhelmed by all these developments, in 1979 I published my first book, *Black Macho and the Myth of the Superwoman*, still considered by some to be the first self-conscious polemic salvo of the new black feminism. I was torn limb from limb for being too young, for being bourgeois, for not being scholarly, for having ill intentions, and for not having solidarity with black men, in these very pages by both Stanley Crouch and Darryl Pinckney.

Surely all the anthologies, publications, conferences, discussion groups, dialogues, and debates that followed on black feminism and black male-female relations are not an illusion. From 1979 to 1981, I spoke on more college campuses than I care to remember, and I wasn't the only black feminist out there. In those days, it was black feminist lawyer Flo Kennedy, not hooks, who was pulling down the megalecture fees.

ALL OF THIS black feminist activity preceded the publication of bell hooks's first book, *Ain't I a Woman: Black Women and Feminism*, in 1981, as Gloria Watkins well knows. Indeed, Watkins begins the book she now claims to have actually written years before by chastising Gloria Steinem for her blurb on the jacket of *Black Macho*.

"Steinem makes such a narrowminded, and racist, assumption when she suggests that Wallace's book has a similar scope as Kate Millett's *Sexual Poli-*

tics . . . One can only assume that Steinem believes that the American public can be informed about the sexual politics of black people by merely reading a discussion of the '60's black movement, a cursory examination of the role of black women during slavery, and Michele Wallace's life."

I wouldn't go so far as to suggest that hooks is deliberately and maliciously attempting to obliterate the vast and subversive history of black feminist discourse. In *Ain't I a Woman*, hooks does a fine job of providing the historical overview of black feminist thought. But progressively her analysis has become more and more self-centered, narcissistic, and even hostile to the idea of countervailing perspectives. Given more to the passive-aggressive approach in dealing with black women, she is never direct.

For instance, in an essay called "Black Intellectuals" in *Killing Rage*, while she claims for herself an exemplary humility, simplicity, open-mindedness, and commitment to revolutionary struggle, she also distances herself from the rank and file of black intellectuals with comments like "Most academics (like their white and non-white counterparts) are not intellectuals" and "Empowered to be hostile towards and policing of one another, black female academics and/or intellectuals often work to censor and silence one another."

In *Black Looks*, hooks repeatedly rails against those pseudoprogressive whites who would "eat the other" in their perpetual attempt to appropriate the transgressive energies of artists, writers, and theorists of color. But then hooks is also capable of writing, "When patriarchal support of competition between women is coupled with competitive academic longing for status and influence, black women are not empowered to bond on the basis of shared commitment to intellectual life or open-minded exchange of ideas. . . . Since many women in the academy are conservative or liberal in their politics, tensions arise between those groups and individuals like myself, who advocate revolutionary politics."

What hooks is doing here is what I call eating the other. Yes, people of color can eat each other, too.

Those of us who first became black feminists in the early '70s knew so little about the black women—the artists, intellectuals, and feminist activists—who had come before us. It took a long time to find the record they had left. However, this wasn't because the record didn't exist. Rather, the documentation was either destroyed or mouldering in dusty attics and rare-book collections, and it was no simple matter to retrieve them. It no longer surprises me that Zora Neale Hurston, Nella Larsen, and Jesie Faucett all had to be rediscovered.

And it should come as no surprise to anyone that, not only was there a black feminism before bell hooks, there was a black feminism long before most of us were born. There were black feminist abolitionists before the Civil War and there were black women suffragettes, whose works are now preserved and annotated by the Schomburg Collection of nineteenth-century black women writers, as well as by other publishing efforts such as Florence Howe's Feminist Press.

But when I was a kid, the only one I knew was Sojourner, and I didn't know much about her.

The black feminist historian Nell Painter, professor of history at Princeton, is currently working on a biography of Sojourner Truth and has already published several excerpts from her research in which she suggests that the famous "Ain't I a Woman" speech, which so many feminists have clung to over the years, might have been a historical conflation of a number of different events and speeches, none of them anything like the speech we've come to know and love. Since Truth was illiterate and unread, not an intellectual but a charismatic itinerant preacher who wandered about the countryside expecting strangers to provide her next meal and her next place to sleep, she wasn't exactly into knowledge production.

Moreover, Painter suggests that part of the legacy of the racisms of the period comes down to us in the willful misreading of the iconography of Sojourner Truth photographs. When we study her portraits, we see that they were carefully composed by her to counter the self-perpetuating myth of her as unlettered and crude ex-slave. Painter argues that Truth's efforts in this vein reveal her to be wiser and more calculated in her understanding of the forces of racism unfolding around her in the abolitionist movement and during Reconstruction.[1]

Meanwhile, Truth's "Ain't I a Woman" speech has been institutionalized as the originary moment of black feminist discourse. Many works — hooks's first book, as well as Deborah Gray White's history of slave women, *Ar'n't I a Woman*, and even *Black Macho* — bear witness to her presumed power as a black feminist foremother. But suppose Painter has uncovered a nasty little paradigmatic secret about black feminism: that the iconic status of Truth is much like the iconic status of Hurston, or indeed any single black female figure, in that it is meant to stand in for the whole. Its primary function is to distract us from the actual debate and dilemma with which black feminist intellectuals, artists, and activists are really engaged.

In fact, I would even go so far as to say that the media success of *Black Macho* placed me in possible danger of the same instant iconic status. But I was twenty-seven, naive, inexperienced, and had no concept of the subtleties that Painter is describing. Whereas hooks has had a long, steady climb, from the publication of her first book to her present position, poised to enter the mainstream. Is she being manipulated by the structural racism and misogyny of the mainstream media or is she an opportunist trying to turn a fast buck? I think perhaps a little of both. Frankly, she can't begin to make a dent in this structural thing by herself. As for the opportunism, how do you suppose revolutionaries will occupy themselves in these reactionary times? And the timing is perfect.

IN CASE YOU hadn't noticed, there's a black book boom. It has many dimensions, from the apartheid of the publishing industry itself, to the phenomenon of the black public intellectual, to *Time* magazine's construction (with Henry Louis Gates Jr.'s help) of a new black cultural renaissance. But one aspect of the boom that is grossly underreported is the accelerating interest in a New Age kind of spiritualism and the rhetoric of self-recovery. When this tendency is combined with a public black intellectual component—such as in the case of the works of bell hooks, Cornel West, and a host of others—it can be unfortunate indeed.

Watkins is openly and proudly religious, or what she would call spiritual, which is a euphemism for religious. Nobody has ever accused black folk of not being religious enough. But it may be precisely this religiosity that not only serves to fuel the overreported anti-Semitism but also the much more prevalent anti-intellectualism that is fast becoming the only thing that most dark peoples splattered around the tristate area have in common.

Watkins's *Killing Rage* suggests that we bury the racial hatchet in places like New York through spiritual growth. But in the title essay, hooks still has a long way to go. Her story begins with the words, "I am writing this essay sitting beside an anonymous white male that I long to murder." She and her traveling companion had sought first-class upgrades in exchange for their coach airline seats at a New York airport, but when they got on the plane, there was a white man sitting in the friend's first-class seat. Watkins immediately reads this situation as deliberate racist sabotage on the part of the airline representative at the counter.

A stewardess was called to clear up the dilemma of whose seat it was, but anybody who flies on airplanes with any regularity knows who won. If there are two people with the same seat assignment, the butt in the seat has the right of way.

But not without Watkins going ballistic. "I stared him down with rage," she writes, "tell him that I do not want to hear his liberal apologies . . . In no uncertain terms I let him know that he had an opportunity to not be complicit with the racism and sexism that is so all-pervasive in this society" by voluntarily giving up his cushy seat in first class to her black friend now condemned to the cramped conditions of coach.

I guess I'm just hard-hearted Hannah, but somehow I'm not weeping for Watkins here. I can remember the insanity that began to grip me in the midst of the whirlwind of publicity around *Black Macho* when, all of a sudden, it became desperately important to me whether or not I traveled first class or coach. I am quite familiar with this illness. I call it first class-itis, or, more simply, celebrity-itis. Given the symptoms, you shouldn't be surprised at all that there is no hint in Watkins's narrative of the seemingly obvious antibourgeois alternative of having joined her friend, in solidarity, in coach.

Black feminist intellectuals generally kowtow to hooks and dutifully quote her numerous books, but they don't like her and they don't trust her. She doesn't represent the views of black feminist academics (most of whom she would dismiss, in any case, as privileged members of the bourgeois academic elite), and yet we go on mumbling under our breath.

Released in her last books from the rigor of the South End Press collective—where editorial decisions are made jointly—what was once merely typically bad leftist writing has become self-indulgent and undigested drivel that careens madly from outrageous self-pity, poetic and elliptical, to playful exhibitionism, to dogmatic, righteous sermonizing. Sometimes as I read some of this stuff, I can't believe that I am reading what I'm reading.

For instance, in *Outlaw Culture* hooks sets an *Esquire* reporter straight about the notion that the women's movement was prudish in the '70s. "We had all girl parties, grownup sleepovers," she told him. "We slept together. We had sex. We did it with girls and boys. We did it across race, class, nationality. We did it in groups. We watched each other doing it." Or, hooks will say, ". . . the vast majority of black women in academe are not in revolt— they seem to be as conservative as the other conservatizing forces there! . . . I've been rereading Simon Watney's *Policing Desire*, and thinking a lot about how I often feel more policed by other black women who say to me: 'How can you be out there on the edge? How can you do certain things, like be wild, inappropriate? You're making it harder for the rest of us. . . .'" Watkins knocks everybody. She has done everything and known everything, long before it was fashionable to do so. Yet she is rarely specific or precise about her experiences or her references.

She can also be a chameleon, taking on camouflage colors in different environments, as in her interview with the rapper Ice Cube. In talking with him about *Boyz N the Hood*, she says of the lead character Tre, falling into the vernacular: "You don't want to be him 'cause he didn't have no humor hardly, he didn't have much. Part of what I try to do as a teacher, a professor, is to show people just 'cause you're a professor and you got a Ph.D., you don't have to be all tired, with no style and with no presence." Constantly citing her experience of child abuse at the hands of her family, physical abuse by her former lover, black poet and scholar Nathaniel Mackey, as well as the "racist" and "sexist" reaction of the "white feminist" and "black male" and "white supremacist patriarchal" establishment, she epitomizes the cult of victimization that Shelby Steele, Stanley Crouch, and Jerry Watts have written about so persuasively.

While I have no desire to play into the hands of the Right, everybody knows that p.c. rhetoric has become a problem, and hooks has made herself queen of p.c. rhetoric. Without the unlovely p.c. code phrases, "white supremacy," "patriarchal domination," and "self-recovery," hooks couldn't write a sentence.

hooks reminds me of the young people in my youth who would come from the suburbs, dress up like bohos, and hang around in the Village for the weekend. You just sprinkle these words around and you're an automatic academic leftist.

In *The Manufacture of Consent*, Noam Chomsky reminds us that the principal function of mass culture is to distract most Americans, perhaps as many as 80 percent, from issues of real power, domination, and control. The other 20 percent, whom Chomsky identifies as the educational and intellectual elite, votes, runs the media and academia, and, as such, is actively, although probably not consciously, engaged in manufacturing consent. Although it's not all that important how the 80 percent chooses its poison, the predilections of the 20 percent elite can be crucial. According to Chomsky's vision, the correct information is almost always out there, but it is literally buried under the continuous and overwhelming flow and bombardment of mass cultural noise and distraction.

In an imperceptible shift from automatic leftism to cultural studies, most of what hooks chooses to write about—Madonna, *The Crying Game*, *The Bodyguard*, Camille Paglia, shopping, and so forth—is noise. Part of the distraction of mass culture, and now the most popular mass cultural commentary (sometimes called cultural critique or cultural studies) as well, is that its function is increasingly continuous with that of its object of study. At best, it is becoming mind-fuck candy for the intellectually overendowed. In other words, much of it has become just highfalutin noise.

As for what there ever was to value about hooks's work, I am not the ideal person to say because I have never felt comfortable with the world according to bell hooks. Yet it should be said that hooks/Watkins has a saucy, mischievous, and playful side, which is fascinating. It emerges occasionally in her affect and intonation as a public speaker but rarely makes it to the page. Although that edge peeks out in some of the riskier moments in *Outlaw Culture*—when she is dissing Camille Paglia, or in some of her speculations about rap—for the most part, hooks grossly underestimates the willingness of her reader to comprehend her particular journey.

IN BLACK FEMINISM, two clearly divergent paths are emerging: Either one travels the high road, the intellectual-creative route, out of which such women as Walker, Morrison, and Bambara have carved their path—every step earned and copiously contextualized so that you know exactly where you are all the time—or one travels the low road, the gospel according to bell hooks firmly in hand, the path etched in the vertiginous stone of rhetoric, hyperbole, generalizations, platitudes, bad faith, phony prophetism, and blanket condemnation.

Inspired though we may be by the Morrisons, the Walkers, the Fannie Lou Hamers, the June Jordans, most of us don't have it in us to be them. And you can't really follow them because they're not leaders. I don't mean this as criticism. They don't present themselves as leaders. Whereas hooks is all too happy to present herself as your leader, if you just have to have one.

But, in fact, black feminists don't have any leaders, if you mean by leaders people who will stand up and say that they are leading black women down one, independent and autonomous path because black women—whether they are lesbian, intellectual, married to white men, or considered atypical in any other way—have no desire to put more distance between themselves and black men, either individually or collectively. It has to do not only with romance but with a political commitment to black identity, black struggle, and the painful lessons of black history.

On the other hand, if one stops looking for leaders who claim to know the direction black women should follow and looks instead for black female role models, for lack of a better term, who know their stuff and who have spent their lives conquering a particular field, there are tons of potential "leaders" all over the place.

If you think of an ideology as a religion, then the church of black feminists is not one that you have to attend or even declare yourself a member of. In fact, it is better if you don't. Like the Quakers, black feminists don't proselytize or seek converts. The history of organized women's movements and their symbiotic relationship to the dominant discourse is nasty indeed: see the work of Davis, Giddings, or any feminist historian worth her salt for details.

Also, it is precisely the point of black feminism, or any feminism on behalf of the dispossessed, to empower the disenfranchised — both women and men — what Gayatri Spivak has called the subaltern. Subalterns are not necessarily defined by race (although their skins are usually dark), gender, sexuality, or geography (although they are concentrated in certain parts of the world) but by their relationship to global issues of class, poverty, and power.

Their problem is their lack of symbolic power and agency in the dominant discourse. The subaltern speaks but she doesn't speak to us. hooks is not the link. The subaltern doesn't write books. As for whether or not Ice Cube can speak for the subaltern, I'll leave it to you to figure that out.

Originally published in the *Voice Literary Supplement*, 7 November 1995, p. 19.

Note

1. Herein I am making a correction in the original copy in order to more accurately reflect Painter's thesis in her book on Sojourner Truth. Since writing this essay, I have taught the book several times. I don't entirely agree with Painter's interpretation of Truth's use of photos or her reading of Truth's personality, but it is a subtle and wondrous reading indeed.

15.

Miracle in East New York

Being a lapsed Baptist isn't the only reason I hate Christmas. The best thing about it is that it gives me an excuse to play my *Christmas with Mahalia* CD again. Jackson's evocative baritone on bluesy, gospel versions of tired classics like "What Child Is This?" and "O Holy Night" is slamming in any season.

When I was a kid in the '50s growing up in an Edgecombe Avenue tenement in Harlem, I wondered how anybody could dislike Christmas. Although the black community was still segregated and economically depressed, the adults I knew were joyful, gregarious, and hopeful about the future. My grandmother, Momma Jones, was really into all the trappings: the holly and ivy, the special tablecloths, the china and silver. When the blessed morning finally arrived and my sister and I were allowed to get up, what greeted us in the living room was a fantasy vision worthy of the *Nutcracker Suite*.

But now that I am in my mid-forties, and still childless, everything that could change has. At Christmas, instead of anticipating the presents I'll get or even give, inevitably I think, as do millions of other adults I'm sure, of the people I loved who are no longer here, of my own mortality, of the sometimes life-threatening holiday depressions. The splendor of Christmas in New York along Fifth Avenue, Park Avenue, and Broadway is beginning to feel like a bad joke perpetrated by the Trumps and Lloyd Webbers, the Patakis and Giulianis, to distract us from the fucking bleak New Year that is sure to follow. Wouldn't a moratorium on shopping and a candlelight vigil for the death of human decency feel more appropriate about now?

I guess you could say I needed a Christmas miracle, and not on 34th Street. Another screening of *It's a Wonderful Life* just wouldn't do it. Two weeks ago when I scanned the *New York Times* for holiday entertainment, the many midtown shopping-district versions of the *Messiah*, the *Nutcracker Suite*, and *A Christmas Carol* were not for me either. What I needed was a return to Christmases past. I needed a colored, uncommodified Christmas, what Stanley Crouch would call a "Negro" Christmas, an urban, working-class Christmas like the ones I used to know growing up in Adam Clayton Powell's Abyssinian Baptist Church in Harlem. Not a white Christmas, as in "The Great White Way," or Radio City Music Hall's Rockettes, or Bing Crosby dreaming of a white Christmas, but a "God Bless the Child That's Got Its Own" kind of Christmas, the sort of Christmas that Mahalia and Momma Jones might have relished.

I found it on Hendrix Street in East New York, Brooklyn, where the St. Paul Community Baptist Church was staging *Black Nativity*, a gospel play by poet Langston Hughes. Hughes wasn't into religion much either, but as one of the great architects of the cultural legacy of the African diaspora, he worshiped all its genres, gospel included. In *Black Nativity*, currently out of print but increasingly becoming the darling of black community theater (with other productions this year in Philadelphia, Washington, D.C., and at the Apollo Theater), Hughes gave us black folk a chance to thumb our noses at Christmas's godforsaken whitewash of capitalism.

St. Paul's adaptation reinvents the birth of Christ in a contemporary African American context, specifically, in the East New York neighborhood around the church. Narrated by Senior Pastor Johnny Ray Youngblood, this elaborate extravaganza, including professionals and parishioners, men and women, children and the elderly, was directed brilliantly by Jesse Wooden Jr. for the fourth year in a row. With nine hundred seats sold out for every performance of its four-night run, St. Paul's *Black Nativity* has already become an East New York institution.

I know I will be back, front and center, next year. Everything was sheer perfection: the foot-stomping musical direction by veteran arranger and conductor Mario E. Sprouse, choreography by James Gaines, costumes by Loyce Arthur, sound design by Charles Young, lighting by William H. Grant III. The set by Felix E. Cochren, which surrounded the altar in the main sanctuary, featured an A&P grocery with sales posted, a Field of Dreams bookstore, beauty parlors, and chicken joints.

Mary Jackson (played on alternative nights by dancers Robin Gray-

Bishop and Jauquette Greene) is an unwed mother-to-be; Joseph Jackson (dancer LaKai Worrell) marries her although he doesn't know who the father is. Mary is approaching term, and they have no place to stay. The story proceeds from Mary and Joseph's unsuccessful search for shelter to the delivery of the baby by a circle of homeless women to the dance of the so-called night people (druggies, prostitutes, and so forth) who are turned around by the birth of Christ. In the grand finale—which unfolds around the tableau of Mary, Joseph, and baby Jesus—the orchestra, the Ghanaian Drummers, the soulful choir, and the cast of one hundred—now dressed in shimmering Africanesque finery—erupt into a jazzy rendition of "O Come All Ye Faithful." When the handsome Reverend Youngblood leads a chorus of "Amen," with the entire audience on its feet clapping and joining in, I remember how good it feels to be submerged in the rhythms of a thousand voices.

The story of Christ's birth was hardly the point, even though I did appreciate the production's blasting the prejudices and narrow-mindedness of a black community unsupportive of its single mothers. St. Paul's Mary wasn't an exalted, pristine figure placed on a pedestal as though she might break. Rather, she was a strong woman struggling to survive in a harsh and unfeeling world.

The point for this lapsed Baptist was the Alvin Ailey-esque dance (didn't you know that what church had always been missing was dancing?); the divine music; the myriad voices of soloists such as William Keitt Jr. (the postman), who stopped the show with his rendition of "No Room"; Natalie Dawn Oliver as the homeless Sister Inez; Michael Portee, who sang "Sweet Little Jesus Boy" in the smoothest bass since Robeson; and Crystal Henderson, whose pipes equaled those of Aretha, Whitney, and Anita on both nights I saw her.

The performance was as carnivalesque as the West Indian Day Parade but with more discipline, focus, and creative intensity. The action of the players, singers, and dancers frequently spilled into the pews and throughout the house, massaging and assaulting our senses. A riveting combination of Brechtian surrealism, African ritual, West Indian Pentacostalism, and Colored Museum-like vignettes, St. Paul's *Black Nativity* was more than theater, more than spectacle, more than Christmas—just what I needed.

Originally published in the *Village Voice*, 2 January 1996, p. 16.

III.

NEW YORK

POSTMODERNISM

AND BLACK CULTURAL

STUDIES

16.

The Politics of Location:

Cinema/Theory/Literature/Ethnicity/Sexuality/Me

[There is an important] need to examine not only racial and ethnic identity but *location* in the United States of North America. As a feminist in the United States it seemed necessary to examine how we participate in mainstream . . . cultural chauvinism, the sometimes unconscious belief that white North Americans possess a superior right to judge, select and ransack other cultures, that we are more "advanced" than other people of this hemisphere . . . It was not enough to say "As a woman I have no country, as a woman my country is the whole world." Magnificent as that may be, we can't explode into its breadth without a conscious grasp on the particular and concrete meaning of our location here and now.
—ADRIENNE RICH, *Blood, Bread and Poetry: Selected Essays, 1979–1985*

First I must begin by speaking of the title of this program: A Third Scenario—Theory and the Politics of Location, which was proposed to me and the other participants in terms of what was called "the impossible rubric of cinema/theory/literature."

It was important to arrive in England before I could take seriously the problem of trying to make a statement in this context. I have never spoken outside of the U.S. It occurs to me now that I needed to be outside of the U.S. in order to know whether or not the intuitions I was having about the relationship of various kinds of cultural activity to women of color, and to black women in particular, were at all reliable. When Cassie McFarlane, a British filmmaker and a black woman, picked me up at Gatwick Airport, I began to explain to her in some detail what I planned to talk about. "What about the politics of location?" she interrupted me. I hadn't really thought about the question although the phrase comes from the name of an essay by Adrienne Rich that I had read very carefully because it was included in her book *Blood, Bread and Poetry*, which I had reviewed for the *New York Times Book Review*. I said to Cassie then, "What about it?" And it was only at that moment that I began to really think about a "politics of location" from the perspective of a cultural criticism informed by black feminism. So I am grateful to Cassie for putting me on notice.

I hadn't allowed myself to think about the question of a "politics of location" because, as I now realize, I was angry that I had been asked to speak within a framework defined by a white feminist who has probably exercised more power than any other in the U.S. in determining the essential reading list for Afro-American and Third World feminist literature, a list which neither includes nor mentions my work. When I say reading list, that's a euphemistic way of referring to book contracts, book sales, teaching jobs, tenure, publication in anthologies and journals, without which it is now impossible to be a writer, much less a black feminist writer. I used to wonder who else was not getting mentioned, who else was being buried alive. But what *my* "politics of location" has taught me is that, if it is ever going to stop, the question must not be who is being buried, but how does it continue.

Nevertheless, and not without usefulness, the Adrienne Rich quote above was proposed by the architects of this forum (John Akomfrah and Pervaiz Khan) as a way of grappling with the problem of reading cinema/theory/literature in the context of ethnicity/sexuality. While it was presented by them as a quote from the essay "Notes Towards a Politics of Location" (1984), in fact it is from another essay in the Rich book called "North American Tunnel Vision" (1983). Both essays reflect upon a quote from Virginia Woolf's *Three Guineas*, which says, "As a woman I have no country. As a woman I want no country. As a woman my country is the whole world." But whereas "North American Tunnel Vision" draws upon a talk given at a radical feminist meeting in New York, "Notes Towards a Politics of Location" derives from a talk at the First Summer School of Critical Semiotics, Conference on Women, Feminist Identity and Society in the 1980s, held in Utrecht, Holland. Herein, perhaps by the accident of the use of a quote from a political meeting in New York, which is presented to us as a quote from a meeting on critical semiotics in Europe, we approach the crucial nexus, which Rich sought to engage in both essays: that of critical theory, aesthetic practice, and political consciousness.

Yet the use of Rich's formulation remains problematic for me because

Rich may be appropriating black feminist analysis even as she seems to be sponsoring and defending it. On the other hand, a "politics of location," as Rich describes and defines it, speaks *to* the problem of white feminist appropriation of women of color in an extremely useful and essential manner.

Also, participants were sent a series of questions. Two in particular struck me as suggestive:

1. What does it mean to enjoy reading *Beloved*, admire *School Daze*, and have a theoretical interest in poststructuralist theory?
2. How does one begin to theorize a politics of location? Namely the locating of theory in cinema, of cinema in literature, and vice-versa?

These are crucial questions, I suppose, because of the way in which Afro-American film, in particular, seems to rely upon Afro-American literature, and also because Afro-American culture and poststructuralist theory are considered by so many to be clearly incapable of intersecting or overlapping.

Finally, I would like to invoke, by way of broadening or deepening our perspective, three additional cultural texts, two of which are from American mass or pop culture and the last of which is from Rich again.

The first is a cover of the *New York Post*, which features a large photograph of a fifteen-year-old black girl named Tawana Brawley. It is alleged that she was raped by a band of white men in Poughkeepsie, New York (racist slurs were written on her body with feces, it is also reported). But it seems it will never be known for sure what really happened to her because she was advised not to speak by Reverend Al Sharpton, a black political activist who claims to be carrying on the tradition of the civil rights movement, although what he's best known for is the community-based (Brooklyn) organization he administers and for having a great many press conferences. I would emphasize, however, that everything I know about Sharpton and about Brawley's case comes to me through the mass media (the Left media tends to ignore the case out of embarrassment, I suspect).

Meanwhile, it becomes impossible for black people in his community to definitively reject him merely on the basis of the information that comes to them through the media since they know all too well that the media systematically distorts their image and their words. They are bound to distrust it, rather than him. The only other information they may get is from Sharpton, himself. And when he speaks, neither rape nor sexuality are an issue; the facts and the case are clear; either you believe him or you don't. He says he speaks for Tawana because it is not safe for Tawana to speak.

In any case, a few days before I left the U.S. after having not spoken to the media over a period of a year since the case was first reported, Brawley, together with Sharpton, held a press conference, during which she read a prepared press release, and one of the things she said was, "I'm not a liar and I'm not crazy," which is what the *New York Post* used as their banner headline along with a large photograph of her on the cover. This is the first statement that seems to be coming directly from the lips of this fifteen-year-old black female, who as a teenager and a woman of color is a member of perhaps the most silenced population in the world. Directly beneath her statement and picture, in much smaller print, white male expertise announces its verdict. Columnist Pete Hamill (who used to be left) writes "After Tawana who will believe the next black woman who says she was raped by white men?" Columnist Jerry Nachman writes, "Tawana and the Rev. Al have become the Bonnie & Clyde of the 80s."

But if at all possible, what I would like you to remember is Brawley's statement, which may or may not be in words of her own choice, but words, nevertheless, which directly address the impact of the mass media campaign against her: "I'm not a liar and I'm not crazy."

My second cultural text involves a cover story in *Ebony* on the famous black female talk show host Oprah Winfrey. Besides having been a lead actress in the films *Native Son* and *The Color Purple*, she is becoming very active as a "feminist" television and film producer, with an emphasis on buying and promoting black literary properties. Some of you may know *Women of Brewster Place* by Gloria Naylor. Winfrey bought the rights to it and has done it as a television production, which features herself in one of the leading roles. Her enormous success as a black talk show host, which has made her millions of dollars, has made it possible for her to have a control unprecedented among black women over film and television production. That she has become known to most of the public first through her prominent role as Harpo's wife Sofia in the movie version of black feminist Alice Walker's novel *The Color Purple*, that she seems to be focusing on black women writers — or "good roles" for black women — in literary properties she's choosing to buy, and that her production company is named "Harpo," which spells Oprah backwards (also the name of her husband in *The Color Purple*), all suggests to me that what we are witnessing is a black feminist version of an ambitious, acquisitive mainstream "liberal" feminism.

The story about her in *Ebony* focuses upon the lavishness and wealth of Winfrey's home. She lives in a huge white-on-white-on-chrome condo on the 57th floor of a building complex in Chicago. What she says in this story, which really stood out to me, and which I've chosen to invoke in this forum is, "It is the height of bad taste to talk about what something costs." Of course, *Ebony* is the most widely circulated black magazine in the U.S. It is, they say, rigidly controlled by one of the richest black families in the U.S. As a rule, *Ebony* does not report bad news, or engage in any kind of criticism of anything whatsoever. It is fairly safe to venture that Tawana Brawley and Al Sharpton will never darken *Ebony*'s fair pages.

TAWANA BRAWLEY: "I'm not a liar and I'm not crazy." Oprah Winfrey: "It is the height of bad taste to talk about what something costs." And the final reference actually comes from the Adrienne Rich essay, "Notes Towards a Politics of Location": "We who are not the same, we who are many and do not want to be the same." Here, it seems to me Rich speaks simultaneously as a poet, theorist, and political thinker.

To address a "politics of location" introduced by the words of the American poet and lesbian feminist Adrienne Rich is especially painful to me for many reasons. It is not because Rich is a lesbian feminist which, on the contrary, draws me to her work with fascination. And it is not because she is a very famous white American poet, although such an identity as a writer seems extremely alien to me. Rather my discomfort is caused by the fact that the proper name "Adrienne Rich" signifies to me a place in American feminism that I've been locked out of. It is a critical juncture at the crossroads of a white mainstream academic feminism, which is well paid, abundantly sponsored, and self-consciously articulate, and a marginalized, activist-oriented black feminism, which is not well paid, virtually unsubsidized, and generally inarticulate, unwritten, unpublished, unread. For those of you who may not be familiar with the role Rich has played in black feminism, I'd like to quote from my review of *Blood, Bread and Poetry*: "In the midst of an increasingly visible American feminist literary criticism that rarely includes black women writers in its canon, Ms. Rich has for some years performed a unique service of mediation. For instance, when she won a National Book Award for poetry in 1974, she insisted on sharing her honor with her co-nominees Alice Walker and Audre Lorde." Rich, who means well I'm sure, pretends to sponsor that which it is not in her power to sponsor, that which she can only silence: a black feminist voice and theory. Yet there is another location, beyond the cloak of relative silence which Rich has thrown over the black feminists who are embraced by her—the Barbara Smiths, the Gloria Josephs, the Audrey Lordes, who are not published by the Nortons or the Viragos as Rich is, and who hardly seem able to bring themselves to mention "theory" much less write it. I find my own work in that third place—"other" to Adrienne Rich's "other" and yet still fully engaged by their positions.

The pain has to do with being denied and rendered invisible by an increasingly official history, by the side you thought you were fighting for once.

Throughout *Blood, Bread and Poetry*, there are extensive book lists and foot-notes. Neither bell hooks, if I'm not mistaken, nor I make it to even those footnotes. To me, Rich is the gatekeeper then, somebody who defines the in-side, thus keeping me out. (Did I only imagine myself there?) For me, these are my "politics of location" — writing in silence, writing which is not read or read seriously, writing that is disavowed and disallowed. Still I have always read Rich with great pleasure and self-recognition. So it breaks my heart, although no more than it breaks my heart to read any text produced by the West.

I STILL PONDER the book I wrote, *Black Macho and the Myth of the Super-woman*, and the disturbance it caused: how black women are not allowed to establish their own intellectual terrain, to make their own mistakes, to invent their own birthplace in writing. I still ponder my book's rightness and wrongness and how its reception almost destroyed me so that I vowed never to write political or theoretical statements about feminism again. I ponder the years in which I tried to fictionalize in a novel the story of my publication and of my madness and the rejection by many including my family. I ponder as well that even as I gingerly and carefully proceed to try to recognize and acknowledge all the preexisting intellectual and territorial boundaries — which never recognize me in turn, my own black feminism — my homeland, which I helped to create, which still sees me as out of order because I understood that to publish is to communicate willingly and force-fully with whites who, after all, still control the publishing industry and the global production of knowledge in which mainstream and left publishing participates.

Part of the politics of location for a black woman writer who insists upon writing less than novels and more than personality profiles for women's magazines, which I have done, is that there is no pre-ordained location, be-cause there is no power. So a "politics of location" is entirely a process for me, unlocated. Or perhaps it is because I haven't found the connections yet. Per-haps this is the level at which my work can be in dialogue with itself without superimposing a premature closure or a false unity.

In a week's time I may observe that the young black female folk singer Tracy Chapman has a hit album (which features a song called "Talkin' 'bout a Revolution") and is on the cover of *Rolling Stone*; Florence Griffith Joyner, "the fastest woman on earth," is on the cover of *Newsweek*; Geraldo Rivera (once known as Puerto Rican) and Oprah Winfrey both emphasize inter-views with convicted mass murderers on their extremely successful talk shows, during which they ritualistically berate the "murderers" while the audience cheers them on; neither Bush nor Dukakis makes any reference at all to "race" in a two-hour televised presidential nominee debate, although they both confirm repeatedly that they are "tough on crime"; while the Congress considers stiffer penalties for drug traffickers, including the death penalty, and a national workfare program for people, or rather women, on welfare. Ben Johnson, the black Canadian gold medallist, is banished from the Olympics in Seoul for using a drug that may be quite widely used by Olympic medalists, and again "race" is never mentioned.

In any case, these and other now seemingly superfluous matters will crop up in Hollywood films — just as Oliver North cropped up as Tom Cruise in *Top Gun*. Then they'll crop up in literature, then in journals that publish theory. Feminists may or may not help to demystify the process. Blacks may or may not help because everybody who writes has a stake in the process itself. Neither, as they are presently organized (or as I am presently organized) will include me. So my process, or my location, is necessarily schizophrenic and dialogical in that it originates from multiple positions which are not my own, which cannot be reconciled or contained by another.

First there was journalism, then the book *Black Macho and the Myth of the Superwoman*, then the fields of history, literature and critical theory, and, finally, a return to film and television as a field. The background, the years before *Black Macho*, is not especially important except to say that I was a black feminist. It seemed vastly urgent to communicate to black women that feminism was relevant to their lives, that we were in need of precisely the kind of liberation that white women were then proposing. We were repressed as well as oppressed. I know I was. Our desire had been thwarted and perverted just as surely as our labor was alienated and our bodies were exploited and commodified. But then when it came to writing, it turned out to be very much a problem of spanning several locations at once, none of which I was able to call home.

Journalism was my medium, mostly because no other writing space seemed available to me financially or educationally. Yet journalism was not *Black Macho*'s final location. Rather it was claimed by black sociology, even as black sociology cast it out. Then there was mainstream, left-liberal American feminism, which orbits around the privileged existence of the middle-class American woman, who reads a lot, may write, and who calls herself a feminist. Most such women are white although a critical number, who formed a crucial part of the audience for my book, are black. Finally, there were the under-privileged, unwritten, unread masses, most of whom are black. Although they are not generally the readers of black feminism, they are almost always the object of black feminist speculation. My book was continuous with that tradition, although it tried to discuss a black "middle-class" woman as well. I had no feeling for the politics of location then, or rather the politics of no choice. I did not then know that I needed to insist upon occupying these and more positions simultaneously. Until I did insist upon occupying several positions at once, I would never speak to anything but silence, even as Tawana and Oprah do now, for all their publicity.

After the fury *Black Macho* unleashed upon me for making what I thought were the obvious criticisms about black male leadership, I sought the answer to this one question: "Why was it that the moment of my greatest publicity, when *Black Macho* was a best-seller and I was frequently on television, why was that highly public moment also the moment of my profoundest silence and powerlessness? From which came a series of questions: Why couldn't I write? Why when I tried to write, was I rejected? Was I a "successful author"? Was I a "bad writer"? Did race have nothing to do with it? Did gender have everything to do with it? Where does writing come from? Where does it go? Not, what is a writer? A writer isn't anything at all but what gets published, but where does a writer write? And to whom?

First I sought the answers to these questions in Afro-American intellectual history until I realized that history is always already written. Which means that Afro-American history is largely written by the very culture that defaces and disappears it. Then I sought my answers in Afro-American literature, which proved a better frame for these questions in such works as Zora Neale Hurston's *Their Eyes Were Watching God* and *Mules and Men*, Ralph Ellison's *Invisible Man*, James Baldwin's *Go Tell It on the Mountain*, Toni Morrison's *The Bluest Eye*, Ntozake Shange's *A Daughter's Geography* and *For Colored Girls Who Have Considered Suicide/When the Rainbow Is Enuf*. The frame was no longer merely the problem of history (what actually happened) or the problem of intellect (what black people had written about themselves) but rather the problem of "reality" itself, as the proprietary domain of those who would produce and, therefore, reproduce the primary and central "knowledge of the world," which appropriates blacks, the poor, certain kinds of women — which is most women — anybody who can't or won't organize their words, or their color, or their bodies to conform to that which manifests "reason" in the phallocentric sense.

In Afro-American literature, I found location in its unrelenting interrogation of the premise that "white is, therefore black is." Ellison's "invisibility"; Orlando Patterson's "social death" (Patterson is the one historian included here); Hurston's, Morrison's, and Shange's "variations on negation," or what are more commonly called "negative images," all deny race or ethnicity as a simplistic opposition, as well as denying race as autonomous essence. The assertion of "race" is negated. The negation of "race" is asserted. To be "black" is to be "crazy," these writers seem to say: a nomadic process, not a location but multiple locations, not a homeland but a temporary and provisional resting place.

Yet I quickly realized that the literature was not enough for it was continually being appropriated by a critical discourse which (1) disallowed its potentially radical vision regarding black existence, and which (2) most importantly, disallowed the continuation and proliferation of black writing, the bringing forth of new Ellisons and Morrisons. As the accumulation of distinguished chairs, magazine covers, and literary awards accrue to the proper names, these cultural icons become devoid of history and content — wordless — like those black models prominently featured in all the fashion magazines. Perhaps even now Ellison has become, even before his death, little more than a leather-bound book on a shelf in a fancy apartment at an all-white party. Traffic (or culture) will bear it, absorb it, forget it, remain unaltered by it. Even Ellison, himself, can now imagine only the most conservative cultural agenda.

So I became concerned about the critical context that shapes the reception and definition of literature. Then, through realizing that contemporary Afro-American literature is not "literature" yet, certainly not in the sense that Milton, or Blake, or Wordsworth are literature, I began to be concerned about the cultural context in which literature exists, or the cultural compact in which the novel or the poem participates, much as that in which the Pepsi commercial or the rock music video or the exhibition at The Museum of Modern Art exists. Not through any obvious or necessarily intentional calculation or correspondence, together they form a cultural compact that also floats the multinational corporation–totalitarian regime on the other side of the world; the CIA's secret government in the U.S. and the "homeless" who drift not only from one street corner to another but in some parts of the world, from one country to another.

Literary criticism and critical theory were, of course, crucial in getting me to acknowledge and recognize such connections — first Antonio Gramsci, Walter Benjamin, Raymond Williams, Terry Eagleton, Fredric Jameson, Henry Louis Gates Jr., and Houston Baker. Then Roland Barthes, Jacques Lacan, and Jacques Derrida. Then feminist film criticism from E. Ann Kaplan to Jaqueline Rose and Teresa de Laurentis. Then Michel Foucault, Julia Kristeva, Claude Lévi-Strauss, Hal Foster, Edward Said, Gayatri Chakravorty Spivak, bell hooks, and Stuart Hall, although not necessarily in that order, and not exclusively. This is no official reading list but obviously the reading I'll admit to. Feminism, which perhaps provides the theory that is closest to my intentions is also extremely problematic, as most theory is, for its unconscious acceptance of the politics of the major versus the minor, or the center versus the margin, as bell hooks called it once.

But then, as Julia Kristeva suggests in her essay "Women's Time, WOMEN's TIME," there are at least three feminisms occurring simultaneously in the West: the feminism that seeks female "equality"; the feminism that seeks female autonomy; and the feminism that attempts to deconstruct its own basis in binary oppositions of gender, ethnicity, and class. It is difficult for me to accept the idea that the debate that each entails may not be particularly relevant to the average black woman's life, for I am an average black woman, too. Yet I am groping for a semiotics of criticism that will guide me through the pleasure I experience in reading Fredric Jameson despite the realization that, while black women may eventually become interesting to Jameson as an object or speculation, our "theory" will never participate in his critical "bricolage."

In any case, the usefulness of theory, for me, has ceased to be about finding the right one or the right combination even, but rather it is about, as a reader of it, the mobility of multiple theoretical positions. What's helped to make this clearer to me—that it is all right to feel at home nowhere—are recent developments in film and television and recent theories of postmodernism and poststructuralism. Reading then, particularly the kind of reading that involves filling in the gaps, or spanning them, is key to understanding, or understanding that which is not yet understandable: theory or speculation that is no longer religious. Without theory or criticism, film and TV are perhaps incomplete, perhaps inclined to fascism: no more and no less fascist than we are without criticism. The eye sees, then feels, but never finishes the thought. Rather it is seduced into a shallow, preemptive understanding. There is only pleasure, without self-recognition, or reorganization. That pleasure (the other side of which is always pain) may have grave political consequences. Or to put it another way (for I do not wish to be prescriptive), I suspect that unless one is interested in interrogating the relationship of one's pleasure to ethnicity, to sexuality, to issues of race, gender, and class, then one's viewing becomes out of balance and incomplete.

"Mechanical reproduction" has been responsible for profoundly reorienting our view of the world, our sense of the world as a unified and coherent place that reflects the reliability of key master narratives. Meanwhile, there is the suspicion that I've had for some time, and which critics of color are corroborating now, that the postmodern critique mirrors the outsider's or the migrant's or the nomad's sense of being in the world. Stuart Hall refers to this as "the centering of marginality" in his essay "Minimal Selves." These matters may be much of what is really being talked about when one hears talk of a film or a TV show as an event significant in a way entirely different from the eventfulness of Michelangelo's painting on the ceiling of the Sistine Chapel at the Vatican. That is to say, perhaps, reproduction's dispersal of "art" had the effect of decentering "mastery," just as production's dispersal, or "deterritorialization," of people of color has had the effect of decentering "the West."

In front of the TV set. Buying or not buying the *New York Post* or *Ebony* or the *New York Times* and reading or not reading them. What are the politics of that location? How much does it matter what color or what sex you are then? Aren't we all, finally, in the same place in that sense, as paralyzed subjects, unless we theorize otherwise? Or imagine otherwise? Connected, although not equally responsible or in power?

It seems to me that Afro-American literature functions in an extremely intricate relationship to black film. That relationship is important because it involves audience consumption at different levels of culture: the novel and the film are designed for and aimed at different class and race audiences. So in this progression from literature to film, something more is being said to an audience which is being reformed by a new cultural opportunity. Clearly in the case of *Native Son*, *Go Tell It On the Mountain*, and *For Colored Girls*, literature provides these films with a major source of narrative. But perhaps more interestingly, in work such as Spike Lee's *She's Gotta Have It* and *School Daze*, the sense of black literature as a coherent sequence of great authors, or a so-called canon, is there feeding the film's politics of location. I am referring to the scene in *School Daze* in particular, of the black college campus that seems to draw upon Jean Toomer's *Cane*, James Weldon Johnson's *Autobiography of an Ex-Colored Man*, Ralph Ellison's *Invisible Man*, Alice Walker's *Meridian*, as well as the Du Bois vs. Booker T. Washington vs. Marcus Garvey vs. Zora Neale Hurston debates about assimilation, acculturation, and education. In *She's Gotta Have It*, the three scenarios that Janie goes through with her three husbands in *Their Eyes Were Watching God* are reformulated, although both Lee's film and Hurston's book are about whether or not a black woman will be able to control her own narrative. Whereas Janie may have seemed successful, Nola Darling seems defeated in the end when she is raped.

But even more interesting to me is the idea that a large African diasporic cultural context or paradigm is feeding this and other work in Afro-American film and Afro-British film, so that, for instance, the debate about black male leadership, which I describe as encumbered by the myth of black masculinity in *Black Macho*, is actually an ongoing cultural problematic, which intersects in both Claude Lévi-Strauss's and Roland Barthes's notions of "myth," as both true and false, both "primitive" and "modern." The usefulness of Lévi-Strauss and Barthes to all of this is that their theories reveal structuralism's racism, or rather its blindness to "race," a blind spot that we inherit when we attempt to come back to this theory at the core of poststructuralism, which may then claim to be open-ended and indeterminate. It is open-ended and indeterminate about everything except "race." The problematic of black male sexuality re-emerges then at multiple levels of cultural participation as fragments in a discussion about "race" as that which is never mentioned and "gender" as that which is always mentioned (although these criteria are usually reversed in black discourses). When it finally takes apparent form it is as race/(gender), the combination that is almost always present in any compelling American cultural event, yet which is never talked about: we might best describe it as an absent presence or a present absence.

We see this, for instance, in all the passion that mass media brings to reporting the Al Sharpton/Roy Innis conflict over the Tawana Brawley case. We see it in the network's fascination for Jesse Jackson's concession speech at the Democratic Convention, in which his unwed teenage mother—particularly her quilt-making—is proposed as the model for political participation, yet none of the media coverage mentions it as a race/(gender) nexus.

It is apparent again in the character of Dap as a student leader in *School Daze*. His phallic linearity competes unsuccessfully for attention against a foregrounded plethora of entertaining spectacle that frantically piles up race/(gender) conjunctions without commentary or analysis. And we see it again and again, in the character of the black militant leader in Isaac Julien's *A Passion of Remembrance*, this time openly ridiculed by the carnivalesque dance and the dialogic desire of black male homosexuality and black female lesbianism. In each of these films, there may be a common center in the black global politics of 1968, even as the location of the film practice is elsewhere in a postmodern politics of sexuality. The idea is that the problematic of "the myth of black masculinity" should not simply be pursued as an issue of chronology, influence, or intentions but rather as one ongoing paradigm of black political style, and therefore a critique, particularly in regard to sexuality, whose time has arrived.

Originally published as "The Politics of Location: Cinema/Theory/Literature/Ethnicity/Sexuality/Me" in *Frameworks* and presented at the conference *Theory and the Politics of Location* in Birmingham, England, in 1989.

17.

Black Feminist Criticism:

A Politics of Location and *Beloved*

I would like to use Toni Morrison's *Beloved* as a springboard for a proposal that I hope you will find both provocative and useful.

Beloved seems to me our preeminent example, in an African American feminist context, of what I think of as a critical fiction, because it remakes, demystifies, and transforms the character of history as the master narrative. It problematizes and pluralizes how we think of what the West calls "myth." *Beloved* fundamentally restructures and challenges the prefabrication of the West, or at least that small portion of Western history known to us as slavery in the antebellum South. Most importantly, it focuses on the lost, irretrievable portion of that history—the voice and the imagination of the black female slave who could neither read nor write nor even bear to remember.

Myth, *Beloved* seems to propose, is not only a viable alternative to the narrative of mastery called history, it is an essential corrective to the way in which the vision of mastery in the past continues to hamstring the applications of history in the present. It is true that the category of "myth" has served as a convenient vessel for trivializing non- and anti-Western discourses. But it would be a great mistake, I would argue, to throw out the term, for it describes as well a crucial historical reality.

To recall our history, it is not enough that we recall our loss; we must recall the *process* of loss. For African Americans, who can turn to no unviolated homeland in culture or history, it is too late to correct the discarding and discounting of Afrocentric myth, magic, or spirituality that attended our brutalization and domination by simply re-including it. Much of what has been discarded and discounted has been lost forever. Instead, *Beloved* tells us, and as African American literature by women has been helping us to understand, we must choose to recount and recollect the negativity, the discount, the loss. In the process, we may ultimately make a new kind of history, a kind of history that first recalls how its own disciplinary discourse was made in brutality and exclusion, and second, a history that selects as its starting point the heterogeneity of the present.

For the time being, we are forced to turn to such critical fictions. Black women in the United States are already making a new kind of literature. What we need desperately as well is a new kind of black feminist literary and cultural criticism, the boundaries of which will reach beyond strictly academic audiences. It is essential that this cultural criticism engage with the dominant discourse. By dominant discourse, I'm talking not only about the rhetoric of ultra-right think tanks like the Heritage Foundation but, equally important, about the various knowledge productions of the art world and other cultural avant-gardes of the Left. I am talking about becoming visible and audible in institutions like the Dia Center for the Arts and the New Museum and publications like *The Nation* and the *Village Voice*. We must do this, quite simply, because the racism and sexism of this and other cities are threatening to kill us if we do not speak against them. We cannot settle for any ghettoization, however attractive that ghetto may be, of black women's writing, the boundaries of which will reach beyond strictly academic audiences.

The purpose of this critical activity will be, in addition to direct political engagement, (1) to diagnose and describe our exclusion from past and contemporary creative, intellectual, and academic life in the United States; and (2) to precipitate our inclusion in critical discourse, not only in the humanities and the arts but also ultimately in the sciences, medicine, technology, politics, law. I don't fool myself, on the basis of any essentialist naïveté, that the mere inclusion of phenotypically black, biologically female persons will serve to correct all our woes. Rather, the guiding principle here is that the project and process of seeking inclusion will raise consciousness and provide alternative strategies in revising intellectual, artistic, political, and economic agendas in the United States.

So the necessity for black feminist critical engagement has become my primary concern and has led me to be very interested in developments in African American literary criticism, for that is the academic and disciplinary home in which much black feminist critical engagement finds itself. This is so precisely because, since the emancipation of blacks from slavery in the 1860s — which made it no longer illegal for most blacks to read and write — the bulk of a black female intellectual or discursive contribution has been made in literature-fiction, poetry, plays, autobiography, essays, and, to a lesser extent, journalism.

Of course, the shortcomings of such a disciplinary home are of precisely the same character, as Cornel West points out, as those that plague African American political leadership when it focuses its energies entirely on electoral politics. Just as there are specific limits on the degree to which problems that beset the black community can be addressed or corrected at the electoral level, there are specific limits on the degree to which the problems that plague black women can be addressed at the level of academic African American literary criticism, African American Studies, or women's studies. Nevertheless, the tenor of recent press coverage of issues related to this problem (especially in the *New York Times*, as usual) suggests that it would be entirely incautious to dismiss at this stage the continued necessity for the most basic kind of equality discourse, affirmative action, and clarification of goals in regard to women of color in academia.

Therefore, rather than suggesting that feminist or even identity politics have become a bad project in the neo-imperialist, neocolonialist, appropriating West, I would agree with art critic Griselda Pollock that not only feminist but also identity or minority politics mark out three fluid horizons in the West, each of which, when critically engaged, can create what Pollock calls new knowledges. These three horizons I will tentatively call equality, difference, and the deconstruction and demystification of the dichotomizing of equality and difference. I know the unwieldiness of the name offends, but part of the solution lies, in fact, in the accurate naming of it. The importance of mobilizing on these three basic horizons simultaneously is best indicated by recognizing the fact that the basic assumptions of equality and difference are constantly being challenged and eroded in the dominant discourse and on the Left. When this happens, one is forced to drop back to square one and to reassess the most basic kinds of claims to equality and difference.

The first level of struggle, for equality, asserts the notion that black women and black men are just as good as white women and white men in producing literary texts, fiction, poetry, plays, and literary criticism. This is the simplest and most uninteresting strategy of feminist minority identity politics and yet, as I have said, must necessarily be the foundation for all further theoretical, speculative, and interventionist cultural operations and processes. Because it is constantly being challenged, equality continues to be something that we need to argue about and for. But it becomes a hegemonic barrier to all other discourses if it is seen as an end in itself. On the other hand, to exclude equality claims from a black feminist critical practice would be playing political and economic Russian roulette.

On the second horizon of struggle is difference. Blacks, women, gays, lesbians are different, special, unique, and not to be collapsed into other categories; not to be subsumed, invisible-ized, appropriated, or otherwise discarded in favor of other priorities. Every category has its own priorities that must be taken into account in any discussion and forging of coalitions. Difference should be celebrated for its own sake and on its own terms. This level of critical discourse is not to be taken for granted as self-evident or already safely achieved. It is essential that we keep acknowledging difference as a process rather than as a fait accompli. We must, at the same time, diligently stand guard against any institutionalized definitions of difference. An example: a black studies department such as the one at City College in New York City, in which the chair of the department maintains, against the notion of white philosopher Michael Levin that blacks are different and therefore inferior, the notion that blacks are different and therefore superior. The reason that arguments of superiority have to be fought against as diligently as arguments of inferiority is that the two positions cannot be extricated from one another. Each argument makes the other inevitable, so much so that they can even be taken to be precisely the same argument. It's worth noting that I'm willing to make this argument from the politics of my position as a black feminist madwoman in the attic who is struggling to come down from the attic. It seems to me that only those who have never been required to question their "membership" in a group feel entitled to make claims of superiority for that group.

Of course, the level of struggle that interests me the most is ultimately the deconstruction of the binary opposition of equality versus difference, for this is the level on which language wreaks the havoc of indeterminacy versus premature closure. Anti-essentialism is one of the philosophical responses to this problem. But in the absence of a profound critique of dichotomizing practices in general, it is, at many junctures, structurally and institutionally impossible to wage struggle at that level. In other words, it is not always possible to insist that as we speak about the problems that plague us, we call into question the language we speak. Of course, this is where critical fictions come in to save the day. The question for me, and I suppose this has always been the question for cultural critics, is how this energy can be tapped for all critical and political enterprises.

Originally published in Philomena Mariani, ed., *Critical Fictions: Discussions in Contemporary Culture* (Seattle: Bay Press, 1991).

18.

Why Are There No Great Black Artists? The Problem
of Visuality in African American Culture

From the outset, the Black Popular Culture conference exceeded my wildest
expectations. During the three days of the conference, I was stunned, awed,
and amazed by the output of such a fascinating array of minds. But perhaps the most surprising and welcome gift of all was Manning Marable's discussion of the political content of the conference poster, which juxtaposed
images of now Supreme Court Justice Clarence Thomas and University of
Oklahoma Professor Anita Hill. Because the poster had initially been viewed
as problematic by the staff of the Studio Museum in Harlem, it had not been
displayed during the first evening of the conference, which was held there.

From the earliest planning stages, it had always been my hope that the
conference poster would refer to recent popular cultural events. But there
was no way I could have anticipated such a mass cultural event as the Hill–
Thomas hearings. For weeks, images of Thomas and Hill flooded our newspapers, magazines, and television screens. Moreover, for many feminists,
myself included, the Hill–Thomas confrontation became a watershed event
for its conjunction of issues of politics, race, and gender.

When Anita Hill accused Clarence Thomas, Supreme Court judge nominee and former head of the Equal Employment Opportunity Commission,
of sexual harassment, Thomas responded by accusing the United States Senate and the press of engaging in the high-tech lynching of an uppity black.
The newsprint, news magazine, and video representations of the faces of

either Hill or Thomas, or both in combination, rapidly came to signify a complicated nexus of the histories of slavery, lynching, sexual harassment and sexual abuse, the Supreme Court and Senate, black conservatism and black politics in general, and African American culture in the public imagination.

Hill and Thomas are conservatives, and as such, the hearings featured a long line of their conservative supporters, demonstrating the resourcefulness and strength of middle-class blacks on the Right.[1] Because both Hill and Thomas are from poor, rural backgrounds, are dark-skinned, and have obviously black facial features, there were no grounds upon which to accuse either of being less than authentically black. Yet their graphic and highly publicized argument with one another immediately caused a crisis of interpretation in the black community; the threat of a woman who had broken the unwritten law of gender was seen as more of a problem than Thomas's right-wing politics on the Supreme Court. Hill was automatically interpreted by an alarming number of black women as scheming and conniving for no other reason than that she was a black middle-class woman with an education and a career and because she had complained of sexual harassment on the job.

It was my suggestion to the designer of the poster, Bethany Johns, that we juxtapose newspaper images of Hill and Thomas in the poster because of the way in which their confrontation had come to represent multiple issues having to do with the hybridity of black popular culture. Featuring the two of them together was meant to pose symbolically the various contested narratives of black culture/popular culture/U.S. mass culture the conference was designed to explore: the debates of black feminist discourses versus black male authority in black struggles, black republicanism and conservatism versus blacks on the Left, black nationalism versus black popular culture, black crossover appeal in mass culture versus black-centered popular culture. Also, I was fascinated by the automatic volatility of situations in which race collides with gender in visual representation.

I would suggest that some of the anger the Hill–Thomas hearings aroused had to do with many viewers feeling overwhelmed by the visualizations of TV. Although the most sensitive matters discussed were not visualized— such as the pubic hair on the Coke can—the threat that they might be was perhaps looming, given the presence of the medium of television. To picture Hill and Thomas in our conference poster would indeed be a picture that would invoke a thousand (million?) words.

In fact, since the conference I've been imagining the image in the context of Barbara Kruger's work, which has never featured a black image. The text would read, "Mommy and Daddy are fighting"—speaking to another set of psychological tensions provoked in the black community (perhaps the very thing the Studio Museum was uneasy about) in response to Anita Hill's charge of sexual harassment. According to the official version in black political thought, black males and females are not supposed to disagree, even, or perhaps, especially in the context of the family. This is partly why the myth of the Huxtable family in *The Cosby Show* has so much power for black television audiences. The psychoanalytic paradigm in which the family romance describes the struggle within the family for sexual identity is supposed to have little or no relevance in a black context, and yet the very denial of it gives it an added explosive power.

That the juxtaposition of Hill and Thomas in the poster proved to be a problem reveals something about the problem of visuality in African American culture. I would like to propose that vision, visuality, and visibility are part of a problematic in African American discourse, and that problematic has much to do with related issues of gender, sexuality, postmodernism, and popular culture. The problem takes many forms—from the resistance to using Hill and Thomas as an image for a black popular culture conference to the problem of a white-dominated art world that does not usually conceptualize blacks as visual producers.

In the context of mass culture, the image of the black is larger than life. Historically, the body and the face of the black have posed no obstacle whatsoever to an unrelenting and generally contemptuous objectification. And yet, until recently, there has been no position within or outside American visual culture from which one could conceptualize the African American as a subject. The prominence of black directors in film finally threatens to change that picture. But the difficulty of the project for black film has to do precisely with the history of a mostly invisible black visuality.

In 1971, art historian Linda Nochlin wrote an essay titled "Why Are There No Great Women Artists?"[2] thus founding, in one extraordinary stroke, the discourse (dare I call it a movement?) of feminist art history. Of course, we are immediately suspicious of this simplistic narrative. There were, in fact, a lot of other struggles going on, including the political struggles among women and blacks; and within those struggles, there were a lot of art historians and critics, and, most of all, there were a lot of artists. Such moments as Nochlin's article are anchored in multiple historical conjunctions and cultural formations. For instance, Lucy Lippard, who was and continues to be a major agent for feminist activism in the art world, was also writing art criticism at the same time. But what really fascinates me about the Nochlin article, to which I expect to return again and again in the work I am doing on visuality in African American culture, is the profoundly positive and constructive effect of what many unbelievers then perceived as a negative gesture.

Indeed, I have already seen the fruits of my own negative gesture in naming this paper "Why Are There No Great Black Artists?" In her review of the conference, Daniela Salvioni remarked that she couldn't figure out why I would want to entitle my closing remarks "Why Are There No *Famous* Black Artists?" (mistakenly getting the title of my closing remarks wrong),[3] especially given the recent surge of black visual artists in the mainstream art world—among others, Adrian Piper, David Hammons, Cheri Samba, and Renee Green—at a time when the art world appears to be committed to recasting, extending, and developing the networks and principles by which it has always defined its parameters."[4]

Salvioni's article appears in an issue of *Parkett* devoted to David Hammons and Mike Kelly. That Hammons, who is black, recently won a MacArthur and was included in the exhibition "Dislocations" at the Museum of Modern Art (MoMA) is perhaps what Salvioni means by suggesting that the art world is demonstrating a new commitment to extending its parameters. But Kirk Varnedoe, director of painting and sculpture at MoMA still feels the works of female and/or black artists are of insufficient quality. The principal engineer of the "High & Low" exhibition at the MoMA, he managed to refer extensively to American popular culture without ever mentioning or invoking the image of blacks, much less referring to blacks as visual producers.

And do we need to be reminded of the records of the Guggenheim, the Whitney, even Dia, and the figures Howardena Pindell compiled in "Art (World) & Racism," in regard to exhibiting and collecting the works of black artists?[5]

Even a short list of names—Piper, Hammons, Martin Puryear, Jean-Michel Basquiat—appears to Salvioni to be redefining the parameters of white world acceptance, although it would be futile to attempt a list of white male artists (who continue to epitomize what constitutes the center) that wouldn't cover several pages. Indeed, Salvioni's substitution of "famous" for "great" in her recapitulation of my talk's title is a telling mistake. "Famous" suggests the judgments and trends of the moment—which have always been promiscuous in their instrumentalization of black artists—whereas "great" usually refers to everlasting cultural processes as they have been codified in art history and museums for centuries. Fame may or may not lead to greatness. If you're black, and you're not a musician (music is the one area in which blacks are allowed "greatness"), it almost certainly will not.

When the article by Nochlin first came out, I, too, was among the un-believers, one of those who were profoundly suspicious of the negativity of Nochlin's proposition. I was nineteen years old and a student at the City College of New York. I was taking art history courses and already occasion-ally writing art criticism. Under the influence of my mother—who was an artist involved with the Art Workers Coalition, Art Strike, and an organi-zation she founded called WSABAL (Women Students and Artists for Black Art Liberation)—I was participating in the art world Left as a black feminist activist. At the time, it never occurred to me even to think about being an art historian. I was going to be an art critic, a black Lucy Lippard who could affect the here and the now as I saw it, the situation in the streets. But first, I had to get through these art history courses.

These were my identities: feminist, black, art critic, writer, left activist. Although I insisted at the time that all these things were connected, they were not—not in or through me and not in the world. And because of that, I couldn't deal with those art history courses. It has taken me decades to understand how difficult it would have been to do what I was trying to do then—become an art critic.

For me, the purpose of this conference was to nurture critical practice among African American intellectuals. As an African American intellectual, I know how difficult it has been and continues to be to engage in critical cultural practices. The purpose of this conference was to move the center of African American cultural discourse beyond literary criticism into other politically significant precincts such as popular culture. In the process of planning this conference, I anticipated the black visual art, art criticism, and artists would be neglected (even though the conference would be given by fine art institutions). And so, I named my talk "Why Are There No Great Black Artists?" to address this lack and to specifically challenge the wisdom of excluding regimes of visuality from discussions of black popular culture.

Now, as I said, I was one of the unbelievers in response to Nochlin's article. What the hell did she mean there were no great women artists? For starters, my mother was a great woman artist and, moreover, there were lots of other great women artists I knew about. That there were more great men than great women had to do with how women had been unfairly disadvantaged his-torically. It was wrong, I thought, to rub salt in the wounds. But, as I was to subsequently discover over a period of twenty years, Nochlin was engaging in an institutional critique. She was addressing the problem of the institu-tionalization of rock-solid (as solid as the statue of Teddy Roosevelt with his Indian and his African in front of the Museum of Natural History) social, cultural, and economic boundaries around Western conceptions of genius, individual talent, art, creativity, the artist, the master, culture. Nochlin's article was about women letting go of an old, defeatist, masochistic, soul-killing paradigm.

Her article shared a parallel conceptual framework with other initiatives taking place around gender issues across a variety of discourses in the social sciences, the humanities, and the other arts. This moment founded a new kind of feminist scholarship and criticism and, indeed, a new "kind of woman." Feminist scholars went from chasing windmills to modeling the kinds of foundations of thought upon which alternative institutions and alternative critical practices are built.

Now the problem with all of this, as we all know, was that it proved to be a very white middle-class affair; and even for those who were white and middle class, this feminist scholarship was and is still experienced as alienating and too abstract (although, if you return to Nochlin's article, it is devastatingly clear). A lot of people had a problem with the careerism of those who followed in the footsteps of such innovators of feminist criticism as Nochlin. But the most radical elements of that very institutionalization have not managed to graduate from their rather tenuous foothold on the margins of the art world and the academic establishment.

But I wish to retrieve a moment from Nochlin's article for further use. Throughout, as Nochlin grapples with the historical problem of the woman artist and, even more importantly, the visual problem of the representation of women in art, she adds to her formulation again and again the words, "and black artists, too."

Of course, the key problem among feminist theorists of color in our debates around identity and "otherness" has been this notion of "and blacks, too." The insight of the most recent generation of feminists of color has been that blacks (or black women or women of color or black men) cannot be tacked onto formulations about gender without engaging in a form of conceptual violence. In no theoretically useful way whatsoever are blacks *like* women.

However, what Nochlin writes about the inaccessibility of the institutionalization and construction of greatness is absolutely and frighteningly true for black artists, too. Indeed, black artists in the U.S. context have been subject to an even more absolute and devastating restriction upon their right to genius, individual talent, and Matthew Arnold's celebrated "sweetness and light."

One of the major focuses of Nochlin's article is the status of the female body in the proliferation of the nude in Western art. As is well known, the white woman is objectified with great frequency and loving and lavish attention. But as Judith Wilson discussed at the conference, black nudes are virtually nonexistent in the work of black artists of the nineteenth century, and in the twentieth century, they continue to be rare. Black artists were, no doubt, responding to the extraordinary contempt and loathing surrounding the black body in European and American eighteenth- and nineteenth-century thought and visual culture. The question of the black nude is, then, one of the subjects for which the formulation "and blacks, too" would be totally inappropriate.

The problem here has to do with the always volatile combination of race, gender, and sexuality. Whereas the sensuous white female nude, painstakingly objectified for the pleasure of the white male spectator, is not only a commonplace but, indeed, a cliché of white Western imagery in fine art, the black female nude is disproportionately rare, especially in the conceptualizations of black artists.[6] White artists rarely depicted black nudes because of their lack of faith in black humanity, and black artists, in their turn, did the same, perhaps in response to the stereotypical emphasis on an allegedly animalistic hypersexuality.

"There are no women equivalents for Michelangelo or Rembrandt, Delacroix or Cezanne, Picasso or Matisse, or even, in very recent times, for de Kooning or Warhol, any more than there are black American equivalents for the same," Nochlin wrote.[7] The question most characteristic of hegemonic discourse — if you are just as good, where is your Beethoven, your Bach, your Titian, your Rembrandt? — is also the characteristic question in a black context. According to Paul Gilroy, long before "scientific racism gained its intellectual grip," Hegel "denied blacks the ability to appreciate the necessary mystery involved in the creation of truly symbolic art."[8]

Interestingly enough, however, the "Why are there no great black artists" mindset (and I mean in regard to visual artists) has not really been formally challenged by critical practices. And herein, I am expanding the category of visual art to include a much greater array of the visual work in a technological society: advertising, as well as commercial photography, design, architecture, fashion, film, and TV, in addition to the more elevated forms of fine art — painting, sculpture, and conceptual art. There has not been nearly the focus on reconceptualizing aesthetic criteria that there has been on refuting scientific rationalizations of racism. Basically, this means what we've tried to do is tie down one of two fists (science and aesthetics) in a combination punch. It should come as no surprise that racism succeeds again and again in freeing the other fist.

For those who can't fathom the relationship between the judgments and practices of the art world and the art market, I am here to tell you that the relationship of this formation in corporate capitalism, which has global manifestations, is that of two peas in a pod. Coming back for a moment to the issue of the institutionalization of visual regimes, I see "Why are there no great black artists?" as a crucial question. It is key, first of all, to providing the support to artists—in so-called black communities, outside of black communities, and around the world—that they need to continue their very critical work of disproving the lie of black invisibility, on the one hand, and lack of vision, on the other. I do not mean this self-indulgently. This is not merely about entertainment or pleasure, although these concerns are crucial as well.

From what I heard said at times about the visual arts during the conference, I think many black intellectuals don't know who black artists are. I sensed a contempt for the visual art institutions in which the conference was held, especially the Studio Museum, where the audience was forced to share the space with current exhibitions. This was so because the Studio Museum is a black institution; unlike Dia, it doesn't have enough money to have a separate auditorium. Quite a lot of black visual artists were present at the conference; I recognized Camille Billops, Mel Edwards, Lorraine O'Grady, Renee Green, Faith Ringgold, and Seitu Jones, to name a few. Black artists can be very quiet. I learned a new respect for the quiet ones; it is precisely the ones who are most quiet that we need to pay attention to.

These people—black visual artists—make things and make visions. Their job, their goal is to re-envision vision. What have they ever done to deserve our contempt? I think we need to begin to understand how regimes of visuality enforce racism, how they literally hold it in place.

In black communities and in white communities and in all the colored communities in between, I am interested in the potential for a revolution in vision. The relationship of the problem of visuality (who produces and reproduces vision) to popular culture and material culture and, ultimately, history is vital. We are in danger of getting wasted by ghosts, by what the black film historian Thomas Cripps calls "black shadows on the silver screen,"[9] by effusions and visual traces that haunt us because we refuse to study them, to look them in the eye. Many of us who come out of a black analytical tradition are in a world of darkness in regard to these matters.

Parallel to the visual void in black discourse, and intersecting with it, is the gap around the psychoanalytic. Besides Frantz Fanon, another African American interpreter of Freud and the psychoanalytic is Ralph Ellison in *Invisible Man*. We need to look for others. This gap brings us to the verge of another crisis, a crisis of mind. As we all know, the mind, even the black mind, is not made up of just literacy and intellect. It has not finished its work or fulfilled itself even if it can sing like Mahalia Jackson or dance like John Bubbles. It goes on fucking us up and throwing us back, and it must be listened to. For me, the crucial aspect of African American nihilism that can be concretely addressed is that which we might identify as psychoanalytically derived, if such a dimension were conceivable in a black context.

Take, for instance, the very compelling scenario that unfolded at the conference, in which Houston Baker provocatively began his presentation by stating that he was not gay. Ostensibly he was responding to Henry Louis Gates's remarks about viewing *Looking for Langston*, remarks in which Gates suggested that he and Baker experienced homoerotic pleasure.

More to the point for me, when Baker, who could be described as the dean of African American literary criticism, announced that he was not gay, it was as if the entire conference reformulated itself around him. In emotional terms, I would describe it as the moment the father said he was not gay, which every son in the room had to challenge. His remarks caused an extraordinary amount of consternation. The debate that ensued between him and young male members of the audience proceeded to completely preoccupy this panel, which was ostensibly about gender *and* sexuality and, as such, would have ordinarily been expected to focus on matters having to do with black women as well.

One of the goals of this conference was to achieve a gender balance in which the black feminist voice would be at least as strong as the male voice, but that didn't quite come off. Usefully, Lisa Kennedy suggested the discussion had gotten bogged down in Oedipal reenactments and that such reenactments were characteristic in African American cultural discourse.[10] Paul Gilroy went on to rebuke African American theorists for their presumably wrongheaded preoccupation with the family paradigm. But I don't think we have a chance of comprehending our own irrationality outside of the framework of the family romance.

One more thing. There is by now too vast an array of compelling narratives in which African American music is the founding discourse of the African American experience. Indeed, African music is the founding discourse of the diaspora, and that is probably as it should be. But, for my part, I am at war with music, to the extent that it completely defines the parameters of intellectual discourse in the African American community. For me, the self-limiting paradigm is not the family but musical production.

The morning of the final day of the conference, Gene, my husband, flicked on the television just in time to hear the words of a Cable News Network commentator announcing Kimberly Bergalis's death: "Kimberly Bergalis, who gave AIDS a human face." This seemed to me an extraordinary visual formulation: a white middle-class woman infected with HIV by her dentist. And, of course, it implied that all the faces of people of color and gays with AIDS are not human.

Throughout this conference, the specter of AIDS and the threat it poses to all constructive intellectual activity on the Left haunted us. Despite the emotions this problem arouses, I think we owe it to ourselves to analyze the visual constructions of AIDS that render our visions both invisible and impossible. Mourning the dead, while deeply necessary (and I do mean to suggest that the hoopla over Baker's announcement was a kind of mourning), doesn't rid us of the necessity for analyzing the past, doing something to shape the present, and anticipating the future.

I would like especially to thank Phil Mariani for the initial idea of giving this conference at Dia and for her absolutely crucial contribution, as co-organizer, to its execution. I've always suspected that she was a heroic individual, but this conference proved it beyond a doubt. I would like to thank David Sternbach, Brian Wallis, Maud Lavin, Cornel West, Stuart Hall, bell hooks, and Lisa Kennedy for their encouragement and support and for their help in the formulation of black popular culture as a discourse. Most of all, I would like to thank Coco Fusco who first introduced me to Ada Gay Griffin, Isaac Julien, and black film circles in general, and who recommended me for inclusion in the 1988 Birmingham Film Festival where I first met Stuart Hall. And, finally, I would like to thank Gina Dent, who made this volume possible.

Originally published in Gina Dent, ed., *Black Popular Culture: A Project by Michele Wallace* (Seattle: Bay Press, 1991; reprint, New York: New Press, 2000), 333–346.

Notes

1. Since the revision of this essay, Toni Morrison's excellent collection *Race-ing Justice, Engendering Power: Essays on Anita Hill, Clarence Thomas and the Construction of Social Reality* has appeared and provides a provocative and informative addendum to our discussion of Anita Hill. This volume accounts, in part, for the shift in our conception of Anita Hill as conservative, a shift which is also confirmed by her recent organization of and participation in a conference entitled Race, Gender and Power in America, held at Georgetown University Law Center, October 16, 1992. Other engaging work on these topics includes bell hooks's "A Feminist Challenge: Must We Call Every Woman Sister," in *Black Looks: Race and Representation*; The Black Scholar's *Court of Appeal: The Black Community Speaks Out on the Racial and Sexual Politics of Thomas vs. Hill*; and the depiction of Anita Hill by black artist Willie Birch in his recent exhibition in SoHo, New York.

2. Linda Nochlin, "Why Are There No Great Women Artists?" *ARTnews* 69 (January

1971); reprinted in Linda Nochlin, *Women, Art, and Power* (New York: Harper and Row, 1988), 145–178.

3. Daniela Salvioni, "Black Popular Culture," *Parkett* 31 (1992): 136–139, emphasis added.

4. Ibid., 139.

5. Howardena Pindell, "Art (World) & Racism," *Third Text* (spring-summer 1988): 157–190.

6. See Lorraine O'Grady, "Olympia's Maid: Reclaiming Black Female Subjectivity," *Afterimage* 20, no. 1 (1992): 14, 15, 19.

7. Nochlin, "Why Are There No Great Women Artists?," 150.

8. Paul Gilroy, "Art of Darkness: Black Art and the Problems of Belonging to England," *Third Text* 10 (1990): 47.

9. Thomas Cripps, *Black Shadows on the Silver Screen*. Documentary, 55 min. 1976. Produced by Post Newsweek Stations. Distributed by Lucerne Media.

10. This refers to unpublished remarks.

19.

High Mass

Most critical analyses of modernism and postmodernism conventionally preclude any discussion of "race," gender, and race/gender conjunctions. Taken from the modernist canon, examples of these conjunctions would be Manet's *Olympia* or Picasso's *Les Demoiselles d'Avignon*, both of which feature either a black or a racialized female figure. Postmodern examples might include Ishmael Reed's iconic use of Josephine Baker in *Mumbo Jumbo*, feminist conceptual artist Rénee Green's appropriation of the *Hottentot Venus*, or even the omnipresent whiteness of Barbara Kruger's images. I'm interested in moments and events in which (race)/gender constructions are inscribed—especially in the nineteenth- and twentieth-century France, Germany, England, and the United States—because I find existing concepts of modernism and postmodernism (I can't separate them) unacceptably unilateral and exclusive.

We're overly familiar with the complaints against modernism and modernist critical practices. Such complaints regarding the cult status of the art object, the depoliticization of the "avant-garde," and the reification of art—together with calls for the death of the subject, "realism," and/or liberal humanism—often exhibit a circular logic and white-male narcissism that's hard to take; the complaint one rarely hears has to do with modernism's racism and its attendant objectification of women of color. And despite its harping on modernism's failures, postmodern criticism similarly falls short in challenging the race and gender hierarchies in most contemporary "high" cultural or mass cultural work.

From a certain point of view, postmodernism might even seem like a pretty ridiculous word that only white Ph.D.s (or wanna-bes) feel comfortable using, but the now-conventional critical analyses of postmodernism (i.e., Hal Foster, Brian Wallis, Craig Owens, Fredric Jameson, Jean Baudrillard, Andreas Huyssen) map out a terrain that I find impossible to forfeit to the "white boys." Their challenge to modernism's low/high schemata offers an opportunity to look at Afro-American cultural production from a fuller perspective. Black feminist scholars such as Hazel Carby have already begun (by substituting cultural description and analysis for canon formation) to recast the Harlem Renaissance as one in which the music of Bessie Smith, Ma Rainey, and Victoria Spivey (as well as the writing of Zora Neale Hurston and Nella Larsen) are as significant as the writings of W. E. B. Du Bois, Langston Hughes, and Alain Locke.

The demystification of mass culture's impact on high culture speaks to my current preoccupation with the visual in Afro-Am culture. The construction of the black face, figure, and form has been and remains deeply problematic. It doesn't get any less complicated, or easier, to "do the right thing" just because the cultural producer in visual media (painter, sculptor, or illustrator; photographer, film- or videomaker; fashion designer or model) is black or not-white, and therefore the durability of these (race)/gender conjunctions (see either *Boyz N the Hood* or *Jungle Fever*) remains intriguing.

Originally published in the *Village Voice* Literary Supplement, October 1991, p. 24.

20.

Symposium on Political Correctness

I find "political correctness" a difficult term to get a handle on as a black feminist cultural critic. Questions having to do with intersections of gender, sexuality, and race that concern me are highly marginal to the upper strata of academia, and are almost always peripheral to the most important debates among white intellectuals and academics. The determining criterion here is not just "race," but the fact that I view "race" (along with sexuality, gender, and class) as a crucial term in interpretation.

Therefore, I think that the "political correctness" rubric is not usually designed to address me or other marginal types, such as Afrocentrists. Rather it is directly aimed at the hegemonic center or the strongest white male and female academics, along with a few token blacks in the liberal humanist and Marxist tradition(s). As such, its swipe at me is unintentional and thus not altogether effective or even threatening. From this perspective the question about whether or not popular culture can be politically correct is nearly an impossible one for me to answer. I guess it really depends on how it is being employed.

As Andrew Ross has pointed out, the Right is now placing "popular culture" on the laundry list of "politically correct" topics; whereas not too long ago the Left viewed a serious locus on popular culture as highly politically incorrect. Neither of these two bookends of the knowledge industry has much affect on me now. Moreover, the point to me is that the expanding territory of popular culture studies and even an emerging black popular culture studies is, itself, already a minefield of potential political incorrectness. Herein, I am using the term "political correctness" or "incorrectness" to relate to a set of spoken or unspoken rules operating in regard to how you are supposed to name and pursue this topic.

As the person who organized the Black Popular Culture conference in 1991 at the Studio Museum in Harlem and the Dia Center for the Arts in Soho (along with Phil Mariani) and as a participant in the subsequent anthology edited by Gina Dent, which has just been published by Bay Press (in collaboration with Dia), I have positioned myself, you might say, as one of the creators or initiators of a new field of study in black popular culture.

When I first started to think about doing the conference, it seemed to me that the leading black intellectuals were entirely too focused on making all or most of their pedagogical and theoretical points in the context of a moribund literary criticism. The biggest fight, as exemplified by the series of charges and countercharges by Joyce Joyce, Henry Louis Gates Jr., and Houston Baker Jr., in 1987 in *New Literary History*, was framed in terms of whether black literary criticism should take a deconstructive/theoretical or a new critical/a-theoretical approach. Much of the subsequent African American literary criticism has been written with that debate in mind. Meanwhile, the key texts in the United States that were being produced by blacks, and that were commenting upon the present status of blacks, were almost exclusively in the realm of popular culture. Even the recent success of black women writers had begun to transcend the high art category and had crossed over into popular culture via film and TV talk shows.

I hoped that the conference would encourage black intellectuals in and outside of academia to reformulate their pedagogical revolution using something other than remote historical literary texts and to go beyond their exclusive reliance upon a literary critical tradition never designed to deal with the present vitality or the cultures of the African diaspora. I wanted to promote the realization that in other places, especially in Britain, blacks have employed critical theory to multiple and variegated ends in examining the relationship of cultural texts to contemporary political and economic conditions. In this goal I believe I was successful. Many conference participants were already addressing questions of popular culture. In any event, most now employ popular culture in major ways in their various acts of interpretation. My own interest in black popular culture has always been as a corollary to my interest in high culture and the way in which in a modern/postmodern historical context, popular or mass culture and high culture really function in dichotomous relationship to one another. In other words, in the larger scheme of things, you can't have one without the other, nor is it really possible to explain one outside of the context of the other. For those who would prefer to simply discount the importance and influence of high culture, a hierarchical arrangement in which high culture is viewed as superior to popular culture continues to play a decisive although frequently invisible role in some crucial cultural formations.

To provide a quick illustration, look, for example, at the ambivalent critical reception of the Jean-Michel Basquiat retrospective at the Whitney Museum. Despite the awesome brilliance of Basquiat's work, the reviews have been mixed and the Whitney has found it impossible to travel the exhibition to other major museums. Why? Because of the perception that Basquiat's life and work tipped the scale too much in favor of popular culture. Although the hypercanonical Andy Warhol was his buddy and mentor, and although Basquiat is dead and therefore no longer has an ongoing lifestyle problem, he is still perceived as the notorious graffiti artist and enfant terrible. The fact that his painting incorporates mass cultural codes from a variety of sources (lots of modernist and postmodern company here) — music, product design, medical encyclopedias, etc. — enables the problem to continue. Rather the trouble is that he was culturally black and therefore, does not really fit comfortably anywhere in our present high/low and black/white cultural hierarchies.

But to talk about popular culture as though it weren't also mass culture, as though it isn't always operating in competition with high culture, is to forget that popular culture is also a by-product of a process of exclusion. Perhaps as much as high culture, it is a symbolic resolution of profound patterns of commodification, reification, and stratification. As such, popular/mass culture needs to be mourned as well as celebrated for there is no such thing as doing "the right thing" in popular culture. There is no such thing as a pure popular culture of and for "the people" any more than any state or any collectivity can be completely of and for "the people." This is true not only of black popular culture. Cultural production of any kind is always filled with somebody's pain, regardless of how much we may like a particular cultural product or whether we may view it as "politically correct."

As such, my focus has always been on examining visuality in popular culture, not only for autobiographical reasons (my mother and grandmother were visual artists) but also because it has been a key factor in both European high culture and African traditional culture. Despite its prominence within popular culture, visuality is strangely contained or underemphasized in black diasporic cultures, and especially in African American cultural interpretation. The relative powerlessness of blacks in high culture, especially

in the visual arts, complements the scarcity of black producers in visual production in popular culture and the usually loathsome instrumentalization
of blacks as objects in the visual discourse of popular culture.

Of course, there have been interesting recent alterations in this situation.
For instance, the recent fanfare over a few carefully selected black fine artists,
(which is not to say they don't deserve it). And, in the context of Hollywood
film, the emergence of a few carefully selected black filmmakers. One immediate drawback of ignoring the relationship between "high" and "low"
here is that one might miss the opportunity to see these two developments
as related to one another.

Quite frankly, I am also interested in how black producers unconsciously
reproduce black self-hatred and contempt, how they can sometimes take for
granted in the most amazing ways that white is "right" or more "beautiful," especially in regard to images of women. While black popular culture
producers may draw a larger black audience than black fine artists, it is the
producers who are most adept at visualizing these kinds of automatic assumptions, and it is the artists who are more inclined to problematize these
and related issues. In the dominant culture certain practices in fine art trickle
down to popular culture on a continuous basis, but most of the flow is in
the opposite direction, with fine art appropriating the strategies of popular
culture at a much quicker rate. But because the black artist is held in such
slight regard by most black, colored, and white intellectuals, not to mention most blacks who form the audience for black popular culture, there is
virtually no trickle down in this. Meanwhile, I would really like everybody,
perhaps especially the black artists and filmmakers in question, to pay more
attention to one another. Many artists of color are already paying close attention to black filmmakers and black popular culture in general and, of
course, it is reflected in their work (I am thinking of such artists as Loma
Simpson, Adrian Piper, David Hammons, Carrie Mae Weems, Glen Ligon,
Lyle Harris, Fred Wilson, Pat Ward Williams, Danny Tisdale, Corinne Simpson, Guillermo Gomez-Pena, Coco Fusco, Felix Gonzalez Torres, Andres
Serrano, Renee Green, Houston Conwill). Whereas I don't think the most
popular filmmakers are paying much attention to the work of artists, even
though that work is engaging with mass cultural codes, as actively as black
film itself.

It was in order to prompt others to pay attention to such matters that I got
involved in black popular culture studies in the first place. What I found was
that there is still a heavy aura of political incorrectness associated with black
"fine" art in the context of black popular culture discourses, even as there
continue to be some remnants of political incorrectness about black popu-

lar culture among far too many black artists and art administrators. What happened at the Dia/Studio museum conference is a case in point. From the outset my priority was to focus on, and emphasize, cultural production, particularly in film and video, which either transcended the dichotomy of high/low — such as Isaac Julien's *Young Soul Rebels* and his *Looking for Langston*, Greg Tate's excerpt from a forthcoming novel — or which gave high culture new depth, such as Marlon Riggs's *Tongues Untied*, Julie Dash's *Daughters of the Dust*, and the documentary film that Michele Parkinson and Ada Gay Griffin were making on Audre Lorde. What I am getting at is that when we were talking about "high" cultural, we should have been talking about the high/low dialectic as a possible corrective for what ails popular culture. But my problem with the process was that it didn't go far enough to encompass the forms of high cultural production, as well. The necessity (read this as "political correctness?) for viewing all black cultural production as a reflection of a perceived authenticity in the realm of black music, and our general unwillingness to deal with visuality on its own terms, were powerful deterrents in this regard.

Originally published in *Social Text* 36, fall 1993.

21.

The Culture War within the Culture Wars

Everyone knows war means the situation is pretty negative. A war is a fight or a series of battles over something about which people have agreed to disagree; at least temporarily, peace is out of the question. Since I first heard the terminology "culture wars," sometime around when I first discovered Robert Mapplethorpe's stunning photographic nudes, I wondered what it meant for black people, or even for people like myself—black cultural workers, intellectuals, artists, and academics. Just exactly who was at war over what, and how many sides were there? Were we participants and, if so, whose side were we on?

According to then (and still) current usage, the definition of culture wars was limited to the immediate ramifications of the successful effort in the late 1980s and early 1990s by the Christian Right and conservative forces in the federal government to censure and decimate the National Endowment for the Arts. Culture wars, as in the title of the book edited by Richard Bolton (New Press, 1992), referred specifically to a series of attacks on instances of "high culture," which included what the Right considered either salacious or religiously blasphemous content—for instance, most famously, Andres Serrano's photograph *Piss Christ*, which Senator Alfonse D'Amato denounced from the floor of Congress in the spring of 1989, and Robert Mapplethorpe's photographs of gay black and white men engaging in sexual acts, which led to fifty senators and one hundred and fifty representatives threatening to curtail NEA funding if it continued to support such allegedly "offensive" and "indecent" work.

What was happening in these specifically targeted campaigns aimed at the heart of the National Endowment for the Arts seemed all of a piece with an unprecedented strengthening of the right wing, as evidenced by its well-calibrated attacks on similarly objectionable kinds of materials (which were denounced as either anti-Christian or "pornographic") in public school textbooks and libraries, as well as in magazines, film, and TV. The year before, the American Family Association, led by its executive director Rev. Donald Wildmon, had sharpened its teeth with an attack on Martin Scorsese's film *The Last Temptation of Christ*, complaining that it was "immoral" and "anti-Christian" because Christ was portrayed by Willem Dafoe as an imperfect and sexual human being.

The Right's ongoing battles, often on a local level, against liberal "victories," such as the right to abortion, bilingual education, and Aid to Families with Dependent Children (AFDC), seemed not unrelated. The consistent theme of such policies was that the Right wasn't feeling in a generous mood. It was unwilling at the moment to tolerate some of the more nihilistic impulses of modern art, or to share the vast wealth of the United States with the poor or with Mexican immigrants from just across the border or with teenage mothers.

In her 1989 article "The War on Culture," anthropologist Carole S. Vance suggested a possible explanation of the timing of the attack on fine art. As she pointed out, both legislative houses were then under Democratic control and Reaganomics had peaked, a political situation that left the conservative Right casting around for more vulnerable chinks in the armor of public opinion. Because "high culture" seemed so central to white liberal hegemony, edgy work such as that of Mapplethorpe and Serrano was perfect for their purposes.

But what, if anything, had this to do with the ongoing and bloody struggles of the race wars in which this country had been engaged since the first Africans stepped off the boat onto the coast of Virginia in 1619? In a sense, it seemed too obvious to recall that artists of color had always been particularly dependent on public funding, such as that provided by the NEA, because they continued to lack the kind of private sector support that even moderately successful white artists might take for granted. In every conceivable sector of the arts, "successful black artists" either earned proportionately less (as musicians or actors) or had substantially fewer success stories (as painters, dancers, photographers, and sculptors) or both (as architects, film and theater directors, as well as in other kinds of management positions, such as museum directors and curators, related to the arts).

Nevertheless, the culture wars as defined by Bolton and Vance were perceived as having little relative consequence in the so-called black community, or even among black artists and cultural workers generally. The reason is not that such battles were trivial or unimportant and therefore beneath the radar of more serious racial problems. Rather the trouble was that in the cultural realm black artists rarely (never actually) occupied the star status of a Robert Mapplethorpe or a Martin Scorsese. The Corcoran, The Museum of Modern Art, or the Walter Reade Theater are still relatively new spaces in terms of the exhibition of black works. The fact is that the culture wars represent a pitched battle among hegemonic insiders only: the liberal bourgeoisie against conservative right-wing wanna-bes, with the laissez-faire of the former pitted against the good ole fashioned American intolerance and xenophobia of the latter. Between the two contenders on the playing field, the question is, who will dominate the dominant discourse?

Because blacks rarely get to be contenders, except comparatively recently in sports (e.g., Michael Jordan, Inc.) and entertainment (e.g., Michael Jackson, Bill Cosby, and Oprah Winfrey), we have little input in this discursive arena, and most of us seem to know it. In particular, when it comes to the black visual artist, her paramount problem seems to be, no matter how successful she is, too much public neglect and too little fame, not too much controversy and too much censure.

It is not intended as a negative criticism to point out that most black artists tend to operate effortlessly within the well-worn perimeters of conventional dominant (white) morality. I guess they figure they have already violated a central tenet of conventional morality just by virtue of being black, so why exacerbate one's outsider status? For the black artist, controversy of a sexual or blasphemous nature doesn't ensure fame or even attention; rather, it tends to equal silence or even death and is generally to be avoided. Even in the case of black artists who have found themselves subject to censorship, or whose work might even be said to court censorious responses, épater les bourgeois is more likely to be aimed at the black bourgeoisie than at the white.

Certain black artists come to mind immediately in this context. In painter Robert Colescott's deliberately stereotypical images or Lyle Ashton Harris's nude photos of himself and his brother Thomas Harris in whiteface, their sardonic barbs don't mock the pretensions of whites (who more than likely will dominate the small numbers of potential purchasers of the work) but of blacks. Colescott's appropriation of the stereotypical iconography of turn-of-the-century caricature and illustration challenges the black, not the white, suppression of such images. Harris's use of male nudity in juxtaposition with whiteface turns blackface on its head and poses a double threat to conventional blacks who don't want to come to terms with either sexuality or the deep-seated desires of some blacks to be white.

The multicultural era in the art world was launched in 1990 by the exhibition "The Decade Show," which was organized collaboratively by the New Museum of Contemporary Art, the Studio Museum in Harlem, and the Museum of Contemporary Hispanic Art. In a dialogue among the three museums' directors featured in the exhibit's catalogue, Studio Museum director Kinshasha Conwill openly concedes that her institution could not display some of the work selected for the show. Although the museums agreed on gender, sexuality, and identity as the exhibition's three main themes, Conwill stated, the Studio Museum could not house the sexuality component. Though such work, with its explicit sexuality, overt nudity, and pointed references to AIDS might not raise an eyebrow downtown, according to Conwill, it was intolerable on 125th Street. When the performance artist Robbie McCauley, whose event was inadvertently scheduled for the Studio Museum, proceeded to take her clothes off in a re-enactment of the ordeal of a black woman slave on the auction block, Conwill was reportedly outraged. In black communities, among mixed-gender audiences, censorship of explicit displays of sexuality, or even of simple nudity, goes without saying.

But in the black community, it is important to know, there is a great deal more than explicit sexuality that is censored as a matter of course. As organizer of the 1991 Black Popular Culture Conference, hosted jointly by the Dia Center for the Arts and the Studio Museum, I was told that it would be impossible to display the conference poster on 125th Street and, indeed, at the Studio Museum itself. The poster had no apparent or explicit sexual content. It featured photographic images of Clarence Thomas and Anita Hill in frontal medium close-ups in the act of testifying at Thomas's Senate confirmation hearing. The photomontage composition was arranged so that Thomas and Hill appeared to be confronting one another directly. What was offensive about the image was never fully articulated by Studio Museum officials, though, on a gut level, I understood their response and even expected it. In the end, they tried to suppress the poster by claiming that since the conference was already sold out, the poster would constitute false advertising.

IN THE INSTANCE of the painter Jean-Michel Basquiat, his life has always been much more controversial than his art. The nature and content of Basquiat's paintings have attracted some vociferous nay-saying, most notably from the likes of Morley Safer on *60 Minutes*, who turned himself into an art critic for the purpose. The Western tradition of painting on canvas is so well established and thoroughly explored in all its conceivable facets — from the empty, unpainted canvas to the cut up and draped canvas to action painting with house paint — that it is no longer possible to do an aesthetically controversial painting, as in the kind of controversy that Jesse Helms, Al D'Amato, and Donald Wildmon were able to generate about the photographs of Mapplethorpe and Serrano; in these times, controversial painting has become an oxymoron.

When all is said and done, and despite the drug addiction and the origins of his career in graffiti art, the most controversial aspect of Basquiat's life was his race rather than his lifestyle. Black people just aren't supposed to aspire to become masters of fine art (which he obviously did, judging from the extraordinary volume of his work). They just aren't. What is more, the notion that blacks aren't supposed to aspire to be master painters is as true now as it was in 1900 or the 1920s or the 1960s. Perhaps even more so, since the canon of modern art in the later half of the twentieth century really has more member (white) painters in good standing than it can possibly ever use. Nevertheless, if Basquiat had been white, for all his neuroses and instability, his work, which was brilliant, would have been heralded as a critical turning point in high culture. Indeed, it is, in fact, heralded as such by the few of us in the art world who are able to bracket issues of race when making aesthetic judgments. Nonetheless, because he was black (even though he is no longer alive, which actually helps), he has to be constantly and ritualistically discredited by the likes of Morley Safer. As late as 1992, his Whitney Retrospective could not find any other museums to tour.

Contemporary black women photographers, such as Carrie Mae Weems, Lorna Simpson, Deborah Willis, and Pat Ward Williams tend to make works that interrogate the invisible predictability of black female images. Simpson is well known for her figures showing only the backs of their heads, and Weems's work dramatizes black women's working-class lives as heroic and exceptional. While Simpson and Weems include texts, both Willis and Williams work with photomontage. None use much nudity, except in the case in which Weems reconfigures the frontal nudity of Louis Agassiz's daguerreotypes of black female slaves, or when Willis and Renee Green redeploy the nudity of the eighteenth-century *Hottentot Venus*, Saartjie Baartman.

In the case of Kara Walker's sexually explicit and sadomasochistic silhouettes portraying masters and slaves almost attacking one another's bodies, again the controversy is basically among black artists. In this instance, two older black female artists, Howardena Pindell and Betye Saar, whose wonderful works have been unjustly neglected, felt the need to send around a petition protesting the fact that Walker's work had won an award from the MacArthur Foundation. They argued that she was only twenty-eight, that she was still at an early stage in her career, and that her depiction of black women could be perceived as demeaning. The very fact that the work demeaned black women, Pindell and Saar claimed, clinched the prize. Although I could never agree with censorship, particularly of work as delightful and diverting as Walker's, I have some sense of what Pindell and Saar are complaining about. As one woman artist suggested to me, if Walker's work were more preoccupied with demeaning sexual relations between black men and white women, the art world might not be so enamored of her product.

I know Pindell better by her art world activism, although her career stems back to the early '70s when she graduated from Yale, worked at the Museum of Modern Art, and was inactive politically. At some point, Pindell began to grow outraged by the traditional neglect of black artists by the major museums and began to publish statistical studies of their performance in this regard. I only became aware of her meticulously expressive paintings and performances recently when I got to see them in a video documentary done about her by Linda Goodman. What sticks in my mind is Pindell done up in white face and a blonde wig playing to the hilt a white girl who can't comprehend why blacks are always complaining about racism since she has never noticed it. The funniest thing about it is that she is so convincing in the role.

Like Pindell, Betye Saar was one of the few black women artists to get attention in the '70s, becoming one of the two black women (the other was Barbara Chase-Riboud) who helped to integrate the Sculpture Biennial at the Whitney in 1972 as a result of the efforts of Lucy Lippard's Ad Hoc Women and WSABAL. She was known for Joseph Cornell–like boxes, which contained such figures as Aunt Jemima holding a rifle. Saar is also the mother of the younger artist Alison Saar, who has enjoyed a great deal of recent attention and whose work has been included in the last two Whitney Biennials. The daughter publicly dissented from the position of the mother in regard to Kara Walker and stated that she thought her mother was committing "career suicide." Sparked by her anger at Walker's work, after a long period of inactivity in her own career, Saar did a series of Aunt Jemimas, as if to demonstrate to Walker how a stereotype should be treated. These were then shown at Michael Rosenfeld's on 57th Street.

In those rare instances in which a black artist is positioned precisely in relation to the dominant in the manner of a Karen Finley or a Robert Mapple-thorpe, such as Marlon Riggs as director of the controversial documentary/autobiography *Tongues Untied*, or such as Cheryl Dunye as director and star of her first feature, *Watermelon Woman*, not fame and fortune but near total invisibility can be the consequence. Although both films were denounced on the floor of the Senate and in the *Washington Times* for their homosexual or lesbian content, and *Tongues Untied* couldn't even be aired in a number of PBS markets, Dunye's film flopped in New York and never got a commercial release, while Marlon Riggs is hardly a household word, even though he is widely revered in queer circles. Both can be rented in reasonably hip video stores yet most blacks have never seen or heard of either of these films, and wouldn't like them if they had.

I will never forget the occasion in 1988 when I was lucky enough to be with black British filmmaker Isaac Julien as his *Passion of Remembrance* was screened for a black Brooklyn audience. As I recall, there was no male nudity at all in this highly political indictment of Margaret Thatcher's racial poli-cies. Yet in the one scene in which two men briefly kiss, there were loud ejaculations from members of the audience, who then proceeded to walk out.

Although current interpretations of the culture wars often make a con-nection between the specific struggle over censorship and an overall liberal-ization in civil society around issues of sexual preference, gender, race, and ethnicity, culture wars nevertheless is most often interpreted as an attempt to limit the individual artist's aesthetic vision to the perimeters of alleged cul-tural norms: no explicit sex, no antisocial behavior, no "immoral" views or scenarios. When we try to compare such repression of the artist to the kind of intolerance of multiculturalism and diversity that is so common among conservatives in this society, the comparison quickly becomes thin because there really isn't a lot of comparison. Whereas the wars over multicultural-ism are more about whether former outsiders will be assigned a new status either closer to the inside, or actually inside, the culture wars are the battles the dominant stages with itself, over which strain of the mainstream, the lib-eral bourgeoisie or the conservative yahoo working class, will achieve hege-mony over contemporary values and mores. The impeachment proceedings against President Clinton provide the latest scenes in this ongoing cannibal-istic feeding frenzy.

The comparison I am tempted to make is that the danger of prohibiting the artist free expression poses precisely the same threat to the bourgeoisie that religious blasphemy poses to religious fundamentalism and conservatism. Modern art and high culture long ago became the dominant religion among the bourgeoisie, the sacred sphere in which the most exalted values are trotted out. To tamper with it, to artificially limit its aspirations to the incommensurable is to invite the ultimate immorality. Bourgeois liberalism provides this demilitarized zone, in effect, in which it is possible to evoke all kinds of otherwise reprehensible behavior without judgment or censure. Liberalism's politics of representation takes for granted a limbo between thoughts and fantasy on the one hand, and intentions and actualities, on the other.

But the larger issue for me is not this particular culture war between bourgeois liberalism and the yahoos, but another, longer and more protracted culture war over race. The culture war of race has been going on, without interruption, pretty much since blacks first arrived as slaves and indentured servants on American shores. This war can be divided into various periods over the centuries: the precolonial; the Revolutionary War through the Civil War; Reconstruction through World War I; the '30s through World War II; the civil rights movement and the Black Power movement; and the present stage, which began in the mid '70s after everyone had pretty much conceded that the Black Power movement was over, thanks to efforts above and beyond the call of duty by the FBI and J. Edgar Hoover.

From at least the period of the Revolutionary War, the institution of slavery, itself, necessitated a complex set of relations between slaveholders internationally in which slaveholders and slave traders freely traveled from place to place in order to avoid compliance with local mandates of gradual emancipation or liberalizations of slave law. For instance, when the Haitian Revolution occurred at the turn of the nineteenth century, Haitian slaveholders fled with their slaves to Louisiana or Florida or South Carolina where the institution was more stable. When the United States emancipated their slaves nationally in 1865, there were slave owners who had already anticipated such a development by fleeing with their slaves to places such as Brazil or Cuba, where slavery hadn't yet ended.

During the Spanish American War at the turn of the twentieth century, the struggle of still-enslaved Cubans was a central precipitating factor. When the United States liberated the Philippines, Puerto Rico, and the Dominican Republic from the Spanish, inhabitants of these places hoped this meant that they would now be free citizens as was true, presumably, of the former slaves of the South. Yet they might have known that their hopes were not to be realized if they had been aware that at the very same time, the South was undergoing a brutal struggle to deny former slaves their civil rights, including the vote. This struggle included gruesome spectacle lynchings in which black men and some women were disemboweled and burned alive in broad daylight before huge, celebratory audiences of men, women, and children.

In retrospect, European and U.S. imperialism seamlessly took the place of slavery in the continuous exploitation of native and diasporic populations in Asia, Africa, and the Americas. Europeans and Americans, such as Theodore Roosevelt, William McKinley, and Woodrow Wilson, told themselves that they were carving up Africa in order to stop the slave trade internal to the continent, and yet forced labor, torture, murder, and even genocide became their modus operandi in ravaging African peoples and resources. Whereas the slave trade had once linked the Eurocentric world in its relation to the African Diaspora, now the new Darwinian concept of "race," as commodity and artifact, provided the common thread of moral ideology. The tabula rasa of Africa needed inscription, King Leopold, H. M. Stanley, and other imperialist adventurers thought, by those who were wiser, more civilized, and more advanced.

Little, or close to nothing, is remembered about such events and alignments by Americans today, yet we continue to live the moral, spiritual, economic, and psychological consequences of these policies regarding Africans and their descendants in the culture war of race. To begin with, Afro-Americans have never had any kind of a chance to recover from the traumatic wounds of slavery, and the African continent has not even begun to recover from imperialism. Psychological trauma that remains unaddressed and is forgotten by the conscious mind doesn't just go away. It hangs around, continually fucking up lives. Witness the thousands of black youth packing the prisons, even as they know close to nothing about all this history. How do I know they know close to nothing? Because almost no one, except aficionados of American historiography, is in a position to know much about slavery and its aftermath. Such topics have no place in the curricula of our schools or colleges. I respectfully submit that the problem here continues to be "race," that shadowy, nebulous concept that has so little empirical meaning and yet whose symbolism continues to tower over representation in the West.

In a vague way, most arguments about the "culture wars" involve race. After all, it probably isn't an accident that Andre Serrano is racially mixed and Latino in ethnic origin, and that Mapplethorpe's most famous photographs are of black men. The Right seems as agonized over the changing demographics of the U.S. population to include more people of color as it is about the shift in sexual mores away from patriarchal heterosexuality. But issues of "race" are further complicated by the fact that while conservatives are generally unified on race issues, progressives aren't.

The liberal Left features a range of hostile hot points on issues around race and identity. Just to name a few: the militant antimulticulturalism of Todd Gitlin, the fence-sitting bourgeois liberalism of the *New Republic* crowd, which accommodates both "hanging judge" Stanley Crouch occasionally snapping at such black cultural icons as Spike Lee and Toni Morrison and the misguided theater guru Robert Brustein's long-standing vendetta against August Wilson's opus; the otherwise noteworthy progressive activism of Noam Chomsky, who insists, nevertheless, that the civil rights movement is not one of the paradigmatic movements of the '60s; the not-so-progressive phenomenon in the Left liberal cohort of Ivy League chauvinism, which takes a variety of subtle forms: besides the black Yale mafia, there's the if-you-didn't-go-to-Harvard-whatever-else-you-did-do-doesn't-matter school of '60s historiography.

I became aware of the modern phase of a protracted "culture war of race" in the process of the Anita Hill–Clarence Thomas confirmation hearings in the fall of 1991. A key defining event was provided by the point at which Clarence Thomas described himself as having been subjected to a "high tech lynching." It was as if he had pushed the "culture wars" button for the media, for all the various socioeconomic divisions among blacks themselves, for ideological divisions between progressives, between left, right, and liberal feminists, between people of color of various hues and classes. Somehow it was suddenly clear that progressives everywhere were pitted against one another in an endless series of irresolvable quandaries. From the standpoint of a coherent progressive agenda, everything was thrown out of sync, and has been so pretty much ever since.

Although the real deal is that the shift didn't all happen on that day when Clarence Thomas made his famous declaration about the "high tech lynching," but it had been happening gradually all along, perhaps consistently since the demise of Black Power and the unfolding of myriad social and cultural consequences of the Reagan revolution in economics politics. It is just that it was only then, in the midst of the Thomas hearings and Anita Hill's protracted testimony before the Senate, that I began to see something of a pattern.

There have been a number of other events both before and after Thomas's confirmation on the Supreme Court that featured a similar kind of cannibalism, in which progressives of different stripes and colors attacked one another, leaving the Right to have a field day. In New York, one of these was the Crown Heights riot, with the sequel of a murder trial juxtaposed with Giuliani's successful campaign for mayor, casting David Dinkins out of office for being soft on anti-Semitism in the black community. Another event that played as big in New York as in California was the release of the Rodney King videotape. The televised trial in which the police were acquitted by a nearly all-white Simi Valley jury was followed closely by the first major multicultural riot in L.A. Rodney King finally got more justice in civil court. Performance artist Anna Deavere Smith wrote and performed *Twilight* at the Shakespeare Festival Public Theatre and on Broadway in an attempt to air the medley of perspectives coming out of the riot.

Of course, the super event in this category was the O.J. debacle, starting with the car chase, followed by the doctored (darkened) mug shot of O.J. on the cover of *Time* magazine, extending through the televised trial and the transformation of the various lawyers on both sides into celebrity commentators on COURT TV, and the soon to follow proliferation of news format networks. One of the penultimate moments for me was the release of the photos and videotapes of black women celebrating over O.J.'s acquittal juxtaposed with the tears of white women. On such occasions, the dominant discourse of the mass media suffers greatly from the absence of a cadre of official and approved black female voices. Rarely did one hear from anyone who could represent the thousands of prominent black women who weren't overjoyed over O.J.'s acquittal, or who were deeply distressed over O.J.'s possible guilt.

Such women, a fair number of them academics and intellectuals, had hastily organized themselves back in 1991 into a group called Black Women in Defense of Ourselves in order to take an ad in the *New York Times* supporting Anita Hill's right to publicly declaim her harassment by Clarence Thomas and in order to let it be known that large numbers of black women were not supportive of Clarence Thomas's nomination. Such groups have had little success in making their positions known in the dominant discourse. That was made transparently clear on the occasion of Louis Farrakhan's Million Man March on Washington in 1995.

Much to the surprise of many of the women associated with Black Women in Defense of Ourselves, such as law professors Kimberly Crenshaw and Patricia Williams; One Hundred Black Women leader Jewel Jackson McCabe; Angela Davis, head of Women's Studies at Spelman College; Beverly Guy-Sheftall; historian Paula Giddings; and others (including myself), the project of black male atonement for the sins of the black community (drugs, unemployment, and the financial abandonment of their families) and the implicit exclusion of black women from the march, was supported by previously more progressive black leaders such as Cornel West of the Socialist Democratic Party and Ben Chavis, who was then the president of the NAACP. Despite a press conference at the Hilton Hotel and a well publicized teach-in at Columbia University on the night of the march, the group failed to differentiate their positions in the eyes of the media from the masses of black women, who were simply pleased to hear that black men wanted to apologize for neglecting them and their children, even if it did take Farrakhan to finally make them do it.

At the center of each of these conflicts was debate about the nature of "race," whether or not it exists, and if so, what its essential meaning or significance might be. In fact, there isn't anything about "race" whatsoever, in the context of a progressive agenda, that isn't open to debate and interrogation. The televised trial with interracial cast and a love/sex interest has become the defining event of such debate, along with persistent demonstrations of the incommensurability of various once conventional legal, moral, and aesthetic codes.

All such occasions invariably link up with cultural production frequently ranging beyond the hallowed precincts of the art world into popular cinema, TV, music, theater, literature. At the same time, the art world serves a particularly important function within this constellation, which is why it has so often been, and will probably continue to be, a favorite target of the conservative and religious Right. The claim to the absolute right of freedom of expression, which underwrites the authority of the entire mainstream of cultural production in the United States, obviously sticks in the Right's craw as a defining feature of bourgeois liberalism and as a sign of the Right's lack of hegemony. No one should ever be entirely free to do or to say anything, the racist Right appears to believe.

As for the ability to constrain expressions of bourgeois liberalism, market forces can be manipulated much more effectively and seamlessly to perform this function in keeping artists of color in line. But when it comes to public or government funding for fine art, the Right is trapped in the losing battle of having to publicly articulate its obsolete notions concerning aesthetic quality, which rely on limitations such as "realism" and "common sense" and "decency" and which are no longer subscribed to by any segment of the art world.

The Right apparently continues to view art as pedagogical and instrumental, a mode of instruction, while the liberal/Left views it as more of a process of enlightenment, a mode of catharsis and consciousness raising, even to the point where some of the most esteemed (by audiences, not collectors) art of the day, such as conceptualism and performance art, enshrines the process and the installation, not the object.

The object isn't the primary focus anymore, even in the most substantial and concrete art work today. Louise Bourgeois's magnificent and psychologically engaging sculpture is not designed to aestheticize your living room, any more than David Wojnarawicz's paintings, Serrano or Mapplethorpe's photos, or David Hammons and Adrian Piper's installations are. At the same time, the Right's struggle over the object is deployed not only as an article of faith but cynically, as a means to an end. Their goal is to discredit progressive reform on all fronts and shore up a hopelessly obsolete white patriarchal status quo against the tide of the continuous waves of demographic changes in U.S. populations. Whereas those of us who think of ourselves as progressive are stuck on process because, unlike the Right, we aren't sure yet where we would like to end up.

Originally published in Brian Wallis, Phillip Yenawine, and Marianne Weems, eds., *Art Matters: How the Culture Wars Changed America* (New York: New York University Press, 1999), 166–81.

22.

Boyz N the Hood and *Jungle Fever*

The first time I saw John Singleton's *Boyz N the Hood*, I was completely swept away by the drama and the tragedy. It was like watching the last act of *Hamlet* or *Titus Andronicus* for the first time. When I left the theater, I was crying for all the dead black men in my family.

In the neighborhood in Brooklyn where I live, I began to see *Boyz N the Hood* T-shirts instead of "Stop the Violence" T-shirts of the months before. Unlike *New Jack City*, which celebrated violence with all the abandon of the old cowboy movies, *Boyz N the Hood* really seemed to try to take a critical stance toward violence. It could even be seen as a valid symbolic response to the then-recent beating of Rodney King by the Los Angeles Police Department. Moreover, through the popularity of the film, space for the acknowledgment of the alarming rates of black male homicide and incarceration grew in the dominant discourse.

But then, a black single mother brought the demonization of black single mothers in the film to my attention. In a second viewing of *Boyz N the Hood*, what made me most uneasy about the portrayal of these single black mothers was how little we're told about them, how we, as viewers, are encouraged, on the basis of crucial visual cues, to come to stereotypical conclusions about these women. We never find out what Tre's mother does for a living, whether or not Doughboy's mother works, is on welfare, or has ever been married, or anything whatsoever about the single black mother whose babies run in the street.

Before *Boyz N the Hood*, there were two kinds of black female characters in films—whores and the good girls. Following "race" film conventions set in the days of *Cabin in the Sky* and *Stormy Weather*, these women were all portrayed as lightweight (and more often than not, light-skinned) cartoon characters. The peak of this trend is Robin Givens's recent performance in *A Rage in Harlem*, where she plays the ebony femme fatale.

In *Boyz N the Hood*, however, a third kind of black female character appears. I call her the Shaharazad Ali nightmare: single black mothers who are white-identified and drink espresso (the buppie version), or who call their sons "fat fucks" and allow their children to run in the streets while they offer blow jobs in exchange for drugs (the underclass version).

Shaharazad Ali, in case you've forgotten, was the big hit of the summer of 1990 with her book, *The Blackman's Guide to Understanding the Blackwoman*. For 180 pages, she insists upon the shortcomings of the black woman by the sheer force of argument. Her judgment of the black woman in a nutshell: "nearly psychotic."

If mistaken for "real life" instead of symbolic representation, I am afraid that a movie like *Boyz N the Hood* engages in the same brand of opaque cultural analysis. Its formula is simple and straightforward. The boys who don't have fathers fail. The boys who do have fathers succeed. And the success of such a movie at the box office reflects its power to confirm hegemonic family values.

Spike Lee's *Jungle Fever*, although a much more complicated film, worried me as well. In the context of representation, gender and race have no irreducible meanings, only the ones we assign them. But neither Singleton nor Lee seems aware of social constructions of race and gender. Whereas Singleton is highly effective in naturalizing his black postnationalist essentialisms in *Boyz N the Hood*, Lee is less successful at the same project when he takes on interracial sex.

Jungle Fever is not as easy to decode as *Boyz N the Hood*. At the narrative level, the film tells three interrelated stories. In the first and the most important of these, a black male architect, Flipper Purify (Wesley Snipes) is married to Drew (Lonette McKee), a buyer at Bloomingdale's. Their preadolescent daughter attends a public school in Harlem, and the family lives in a brownstone on Strivers Row, one of two middle-class blocks in the middle of the worst section of Harlem.

At the architectural firm where he works, Flipper becomes sexually involved with Angie Tucci (Annabella Sciorra), a white temporary secretary who lives with her father and brothers in Bensonhurst. Working late evenings, in a series of extremely brief scenes — one never gets the impression that they either know or really like each other — Angie and Flipper end up having sex on Flipper's drawing board.

In the outdoor night scene that follows, Flipper tells his best friend, Cyrus (Spike Lee), a high school teacher, that he is "cheating on Drew" with a white woman. "You got the fever — the both of yous!" Cyrus responds, meaning "jungle fever." Jungle fever turns out to be a condition in which blacks and whites (Asians, Native Americans, and Latinos appear to be both immune to the disease and irrelevant to the narrative) become intimately involved because of their curiosity about racial difference (perish the thought) rather than for love.

From this moment on, the film treats Angie's and Flipper's jungle fever much like a crime. In two dramatic parallel scenes, Drew evicts Flipper from their Harlem apartment, and Angie's father beats her up and throws her out of the house in Bensonhurst. Flipper is even forced out of his white architectural firm. Self-described "outcasts" in their own communities, Angie and Flipper take an apartment together. When it doesn't work out (and there was never any possibility that it would), Flipper goes back to Drew, and Angie goes back to her family.

The film's second story concerns Flipper's crack-addict brother, Gator (Sam Jackson), and his relationship to their mother, a housewife, and father, The Good Doctor Reverend Purify, a fanatical born-again Christian who forbids Gator to enter the house. Yet, Gator is always at the door seeking money for crack from his mother (played brilliantly by Ruby Dee). The eerie mise-en-scène of the parents' home — the mausoleum decor, the constant playing of Mahalia Jackson records, even the frightened, sexually repressed demeanor of the reverend's wife — hint strongly that Gator's addiction was caused by the reverend's criminally bad fathering.

The third story revolves around Paulie (John Turturro), Angie's boyfriend, who lives with his father (Anthony Quinn) and runs a candy store in Bensonhurst that also serves as a hangout for a group of Italian American men. These men are extremely vocal about their racial attitudes.

They hate blacks, we come to understand, partly because of their own fear that as Italians they don't look as white as they should. Their envy of whiteness and blondeness is viewed as an integral part of their loathing of blackness. But their hatred of blackness doesn't preclude their sexual interest in black women.

From the beginning, it is clear that Paulie is uncomfortable with the virulent, expressive racism of his clientele and is interested in Orin Goode (Tyra

Ferrell, who played the welfare mother in *Boyz N the Hood*), a black woman who comes into the store to ask him to order the *New York Times* and to encourage him to apply to Brooklyn College. Paulie receives a beating from his friends while on his way to visit Orin. When he arrives at Orin's door, the implication is that he's finally been successful in throwing off the burden of his father's restrictive view of marriage and family.

But what this film is really about is the threat of a female or aberrant sexuality to traditional family values. Reminiscent of the more impressive opening shot of *Psycho*, an opening shot takes us directly into Drew's and Flipper's bedroom where they are having sexual intercourse. Drew's screams get progressively louder as she begins to shout, "Don't wake the baby!" The camera cuts to their daughter Ming's bedroom, where Ming sits up in bed, her eyes wide open, and slowly smiles.

Later, when father, mother, and daughter are having breakfast together, Ming asks, "Why is Daddy always hurting Mommy?" When Drew explains that they were making love, Ming says she was only testing to see whether or not they would tell the truth. Flipper then walks Ming to school amid the drug addicts and abandoned buildings.

This short sequence of shots, which goes from Drew's and Flipper's bedroom to Ming's bedroom to the kitchen and then to the streets of Harlem, can be viewed as a preview of the film's double agenda on race and sexuality. On the one hand, we are supposed to read Drew's cries during sexual intercourse as idiosyncratic, Ming's mock curiosity about it as cute, and Drew's forthrightness in her explanation as progressive. But, on the other hand, there is a problem being subtly delineated: the little black girl who already knows too much through her premature entry into the mysteries of adult sexuality.

In another walk to school later in the film, Flipper and Ming run head-on into Vivian (Halle Berry), Gator's crack addict girlfriend who tells Flipper, "I'll suck your dick good for $5 . . . $3!" A startled Flipper turns to Ming and shakes her, shouting, "Don't you ever do anything like that!"

Not only is Flipper deeply threatened by the prospect of dominant female sexuality—Angie's as well as Drew's, Vivian's, and his daughter Ming's—but the yawning threat of female sexuality somehow becomes, within the film's larger narrative, responsible for the devastation and insularity of ghettos, both Italian and black American. Later in the film, when Flipper finds Gator in the dark, teeming Taj Mahal—a mythical crack factory supposedly located in Harlem on 145th Street and Convent Avenue (actually there's a very old and famous Baptist church on that corner)—Flipper calls Vivian a whore. Vivian responds by yelling, "Eat my pussy!" This confrontation becomes yet another pretext for Flipper to be afraid his daughter will grow up to be like Vivian. After all, Ming already knows too much about sex.

Meanwhile, a crucial visual strategy in the film, undergirding the theme of uncontrolled female sexuality, is Lee's instrumentalization of skin color and lighting effects. In a technique borrowed from the noir tradition, many scenes were filmed at night, the strong lighting increasing the play of light and dark. As the film progresses, the shadows around both Flipper and Angie grow more and more dense and obfuscating.

Annabella Sciorra, Lonette McKee, and Wesley Snipes, despite their marvelous individual talents, were all apparently cast for hair color and complexion: Sciorra because she's a dark-skinned white woman; McKee because she's a light-skinned black woman (visually, the racial difference between Sciorra and McKee is nil); and Snipes because he is dark. The striking visual contrast of dark and light skin is worthy of a Benetton ad.

In the film itself, Snipes is often dressed in strong bright colors — persimmon, red, or purple (an unusual palette for a man represented as middle class and dull) — whereas almost everybody else who appears with him, especially the women, wears black, presumably to further heighten the color contrasts. As Flipper's relationship with Angie progresses, its deterioration is signaled not so much through dialogue as by the way his face grows darker and is increasingly cast in menacing shadows. In some of their later scenes together, only his teeth and the whites of his eyes are visible. And sometimes, he is merely a black silhouette.

Lee's meticulous attention to visual effects isn't supported by correspondences in plot, dialogue, or characterization. As the film progresses, Drew, Flipper, and Angie become slick aestheticized surfaces, too slippery to get a handle on. The strongest characters in this film are Vivian, who epitomizes the negative threat of out-of-control sexuality and passion, and Gator, the crack addict who, nevertheless, comes across as straightforward and successful in his manipulation of the entire family system.

When Reverend Purify murders Gator in a veritable oedipalfest, the patriarchy is the loser. *Boyz N the Hood* and *Jungle Fever* demonize black female sexuality as a threat to black male heterosexual identity, and yet I find both films visually irresistible. Why and how this is the case is a question I plan to continue to pursue.

Originally published in Gina Dent, ed., *Black Popular Culture: A Project by Michele Wallace* (Seattle: Bay Press, 1991; reprint, New York: New Press, 2000).

IV.

MULTICULTURALISM

IN THE ARTS

23.

Race, Gender, and Psychoanalysis in Forties Films

To be human is to be subjected to a law which decenters and divides: sexuality is created in a division, the subject is split; but an ideological world conceals this from the conscious subject who is supposed to feel whole and certain of sexual identity. Psychoanalysis should aim at a destruction of this concealment and a reconstruction of the subject's construction in all its splits. — JULIET MITCHELL, *Feminine Sexuality: Jacques Lacan and the Ecole freudienne*

It is not entirely true that no one from the world I knew had yet made an appearance on the American screen: there were, for example, Stepin Fetchit and Willie Best and Mantan Moreland, all of whom, rightly or wrongly, I loathed. It seemed to me that they lied about the world I knew, and debased it, and certainly I did not know anybody like them — as far as I could tell: for it is also possible that their comic, bug-eyed terror contained the truth concerning a terror by which I never hoped to be engulfed. — JAMES BALDWIN, *The Devil Finds Work: An Essay*

Whereas oral representations of Afro-American culture,[1] as epitomized by black participation in the record industry and in some aspects of popular theater, demonstrate a cycle of invention, appropriation, and reinvention,[2] in the realm of visual representations of blacks, it often appears as though only one predatory kind of figuration dominated. That figuration can be summed up as what Boskin calls the Sambo figure.[3] His first appearance occurs on the stage in the minstrel dramas that manufactured white su-premacist versions of black culture, in which white actors played all the roles in blackface. This figure was quickly adapted to a set of conventional stereo-types in illustrations, photography, and advertising. The filmic counterparts were in evidence most strikingly in the early film *The Birth of a Nation*, which set the racial agenda for the film industry.[4]

But there was mounting evidence that film has been a chief player in race relations, or lack thereof, since the release of *The Birth of a Nation*. Up until the release of *Guess Who's Coming to Dinner?*, there is an interesting corre-lation between national governmental policies regarding race and film por-trayals of racial subjects, especially in regard to the military, for instance.[5] While there was a period of about a decade, after the blaxploitation era, dur-ing which characterizations of blacks were virtually nonexistent in Ameri-can films, since 1986 and the release of *The Color Purple*, film has gradu-ally emerged as the principal arena in which the problem of the visual in Afro-American culture is being interrogated and reformulated. Regrettably, in both cases—that is, in the case of civil rights interventions in the Holly-wood film industry in the forties, fifties, and sixties, and in the case of the recent emergence of black film—the construction of gender relations has been sadly predictable, conventional, and even retrograde.[6]

Gender is as important as race to understanding how invisibility has worked historically in all fields of visual production.[7] A great deal of impor-tant work has been done on how constructions of gender have impacted on visual media. In particular in film studies, there has been an impressive out-pouring of academic feminist film criticism in the United States. Grounded in what I will call a post-Marxist preoccupation with the subversive capabili-ties of cultural practice (also called cultural studies), much of this film criti-cism has also been heavily influenced by the cross-fertilization of psycho-analysis and semiotics. The content generally circulates around questions of female spectatorship and whether or not the gaze is "male."[8] Most such debates stem from the influence of Laura Mulvey's groundbreaking article "Visual Pleasure and Narrative Cinema," first published in *Screen* in 1975.[9]

Lately, however, when posed in psychoanalytic terms in which the forma-tion of the subject is not historicized, the problem of the gaze has become a source of irritation to those who wish to propose alternative subjectivities on the grounds of race, ethnicity, sexuality, or class. While various practition-ers of feminist psychoanalytic film criticism are attempting to incorporate this challenge into their methodologies, much of their earlier work, which relies so heavily on Lacan, makes it all too clear that sexual difference has absolute priority as the bedrock of the formation of subjectivity.

Alternatively, the question of spectatorship, when detached from its psychoanalytic moorings, has shown itself more adaptable to other approaches, most prominently one in which an ethnographic focus on audience reception is substituted for the psychoanalytic reading of how subjectivity is challenged and reconstituted by a particular filmic practice.[10] Unfortunately, however, I think such approaches, while useful, also serve to reconsolidate the present consensus regarding the raceless ahistoricity of sexual difference and the unconscious. In the end, you're still left with the impression that you have to be middle class, white, and American or European in order to have experienced gender differentiation as a crisis of signification and in order to have an unconscious.[11] I regard this as a potentially dangerous idea.

First, the exclusion of the black subject from discussions of psychoanalysis, as well as other prominent academic discourses, has meant that race has been largely excluded from consideration in many of the various fields of the humanities. As such patterns of exclusion quite naturally carry over into the interdisciplinary fields of postmodernism, critical theory, cultural studies, and women's studies, it has meant that theoretical formulations in these fields don't ever have to encompass or account for women of color or black women. Even emergent analyses of new identities and subjectivities of postcoloniality, race, and sexualities don't have to add up in terms of providing a better understanding of the subjectivity of women of color, particularly minority or black women in the United States.[12] Rather, the result of adding all these debates and discourses together is quite the opposite: the subjectivity of the woman of color or the minority woman is placed under further erasure.

My delineation of the cultural phenomenon of invisibility, both racial and gendered, in the case of the black woman, and forays into the various realms of the problem of the visual in Afro-American culture, are attempts to find out why this is so and whether or not anything can be done to reverse this trend. My intention is first, if possible, to theorize *this* problem as the *real* problem of the visual. Second, failing to adequately theorize this problem (which seems almost inevitable in any individual attempt), my goal is rather to open a space or an aporia in which such theorization (or practice) will ultimately have to take place. While the practice of such theorization is not confined to the biological woman of color — I am not a vulgar essentialist — women of color should feel welcome to engage in such theorization and practice.[13] "The difficult I'll do right now," as Billy Holiday used to sing and my mother always likes to remind me, "but the impossible will take a little while."

My emerging convictions regarding these matters has led me to adapt a

radically deconstructive posture vis-à-vis the problem of a corrective interpretation. The purpose of the deconstruction is neither nihilistic nor aimless
(although I enjoy thinking of myself as an anarchist) but the pursuit of an inexorable third term or category in which both race and gender can be taken
into account.

In the following essay — my first in-depth essay on film — my intention is
to engage in a preliminary examination into conjunctions of race and gender
in feminist film theory and criticism. First, I will discuss some of the basic
characteristics of race in classic film history as they have been delineated by
Afro-American film historians. Then, moving on to a discussion of forties
classic films, I will focus on suggesting how this conception of race might
be considered in relationship to gender concerns in feminist psychoanalytic
film criticism. In the discussion of the "problem" films of the 1940s — *Lost
Boundaries, Home of the Brave,* and *The Quiet One* — I will take on issues
bearing upon the psychoanalysis of race. Unfortunately, such discussion will
remain introductory and rudimentary because of space.

According to Donald Bogle, there were five basic stereotypes essential
to the characterization of blacks in American films from the very beginning. The first four were drawn from the case of black characters in Harriet
Beecher Stowe's *Uncle Tom's Cabin* (which was made into film on several
occasions): Toms, coons, mulattoes, and mammies.[14] The last and most marginal of the stereotypes, "the big black buck," dates back only to the appearance of D.W. Griffith's *The Birth of a Nation* in 1915. In this film seeking to
justify the rebirth of the Ku Klux Klan, in which key black characters are
portrayed by whites in blackface, brutal black bucks assault white men and
threaten to "rape" white women in scenes pretending to recreate Reconstruction's impact on the South.

The Birth of a Nation detailed the South-should-have-won-the-war positions that would dominate representations of blacks in a wide range of fields
(politics, history, literature, film, popular illustrations, ephemera, and advertisements) for the better part of the century.[15] But Bogle says the film's
most important contribution was epitomized in the figure of the brutal black
buck, who provides a kind of key to the subsequent concerns in black film.
He credits *The Birth of a Nation* with having made the screen appearance of
violent, sexual black men so controversial that for a long time blacks were
cast "almost exclusively in comic roles."[16] Although he explains that type-
casting plagued all minorities in U.S. films, "no minority was so relentlessly
or fiercely typed as the black man." The subsequent appearance of the bad
black man on screen is interpreted as a strategic triumph. "Not until more
than half a century later," after *The Birth of a Nation*, "when Melvin Van

Peebles' *Sweet Sweetback's Baadasssss Song* (1971) appeared, did sexually assertive black males make their way back to the screen," Bogle writes.[17]

The fantastically misogynistic *Sweet Sweetback's Baadasssss Song* is still being celebrated by young black filmmakers and hailed as the fatherwork of black independent film.[18] It goes without saying, however, that practices of resistance are always deeply compromised by their willingness to make major concessions to other hegemonic conventions. Also *Sweet Sweetback's* canonization seems an explicit call for some manner of psychological reading of its scenario. It might be a good idea to begin with the failed oedipal scene that begins the film, in which director Melvin Van Peeble's son, Mario, is shown nestled between the thighs of a full-grown black woman (old enough to be his mother) having sexual intercourse, her legs spread-eagled as she cries "sweet sweetback!"

Although Bogle doesn't really focus on sexual difference, it is clear within his system which stereotypes are male and which are female. Mammies and tragic mulattoes are females. Mammies are generally "overweight, middle-aged, and so dark, so thoroughly black, that it is preposterous to suggest that she be a sex object." Whereas the tragic mulattoes are the forebears of the part black woman — the light-skinned Negress who is "given a chance at lead parts" and is "graced with a modicum of sex appeal."[19] Coons can be female, as in the case of Topsy — a female child coon — but gender in coons is viewed as arbitrary and insignificant. Of course, bucks are always male and highly sexed. Thomas Cripps also emphasizes the centrality of *The Birth of a Nation*, not as a source of black stereotypes but as a focal point for racial responses to Hollywood practices, among which he includes the "struggles of a weak minority for a protective censorship . . . a century long campaign to affect Hollywood movies at their source, and finally, a parallel line of race movies."[20]

It was *The Birth of a Nation*, more than any other cultural event, Cripps says, that propelled blacks to unite in a coalition with other ethnic groups and galvanized the membership of the NAACP to protest Hollywood practices. Blacks lobbied for laws banning racial slander and made direct appeals to Griffith, who insisted right up until his death that his film was not racist. Finally, various factions, including the NAACP; Booker T. Washington; Elaine Sterne; Carl Laemmle; Julius Rosenwald, vice president of Sears and Roebuck; and vaudeville promoters and stockbrokers organized to make their own rebuttal film called *Birth of a Race*. The film, unlike *The Birth of a Nation*, did poorly at the box office. It featured an odd assortment of racially uplifting scenes — "Simon the Cyrene helping Jesus to bear the cross, head shots of the races of the world, Lincoln and emancipation." In the last reel,

Cripps says, "a black and white farmer are working in the field when they hear the nation's call to arms, whereupon they dissolve from overalls into military uniforms and march off toward the camera and out of the frame."[21]

In Hollywood in the forties, this drama played out on a larger scale than ever before. The demands of World War II coincided with the peak of the film industry's influence in the United States. The war itself had a profound impact on women's roles and on perceptions of the status of race in general, and black in particular. The film industry was a full participant in the dissemination of these issues.

During the war, while the men were abroad in the military, women were encouraged to work in factories and to replace men on the job in general. One of the results in the film industry was the consolidation of the importance of the "women's film." There had always been films in which female characters dominated. In the forties, gender became a field of polarization in film, as though in response to a rising anxiety over sexual difference. The conventions of sexual difference were concretized precisely in a system in which there were predominantly films about men and then smaller numbers of films about women aimed at female audiences.

After the war such conventions were further made problematic by the appearance of a series of interesting filmic effects later called film noir in the sixties. In such films, the polarization of gender was often accompanied by an implicit racial polarization. For instance, in *Mildred Pierce*, as in many of the women's films and in film noir, the cast is all white. The presence of the black Butterfly McQueen as a comedic assistant, cook, waitress, and finally maid (her downward mobility is part of her hegemonic appeal) only serves to pepper the stew, to further corroborate the unquestionable whiteness of Mildred's and Vida's world. When Butterfly first comments on Joan Crawford's obvious industry and ambition, "I don't know how you get up so early in the mornin.' I sleeps till noon," she identifies herself as consistent with a long line of coon characters.

From the vantage point of individual talent or from the perspective of the limitations of the "star" system, despite the obvious stereotyping, Butterfly McQueen obviously made a unique contribution to American film. In fact, she belonged, as well, to a complex tradition of feisty maids and housekeepers (most of them white working-class types) in film noir that deserves further study.

But I would also argue that in McQueen's scenes with Joan Crawford, Butterfly provides a "study in black and white." A recurrent feature of visual racial stereotypes, this "study in black and white" provides not only the shadow/light visual juxtaposition so effective in Manet's *Olympia* but also, from the perspective of genre, the bumbling, lazy, black, asexual, and child-like female provides further emphasis on the sexual appeal, businesslike maturity, and competence of the white female by her structural location as a binary opposition.[22]

Interestingly enough, some feminist film critics have pointed out how the fetishizing of the female figure in classical Hollywood film, because it doesn't function to further the plot, may threaten to subvert the dominance of a phallocentric narrative and, as such, the status quo. In this context, Butterfly's role might be interpreted as a further generic means of minimizing such dangers or, on the other hand, as a further incorporation of fetishizing. Both Butterfly's lines and her visualization are decorative aspects of mise-en-scene. She has even less to do with the plot than the various settings of lower-middle-class home, waterfront café, roadside restaurant, beach house, and fabulous mansion. It is possible to describe the film in many ways without ever including her, as I would imagine feminist film criticism has repeatedly done.

In such a context, how does one introduce questions of identification and female spectatorship in regard to the black female viewer? I am proposing that it is important to so do in thinking about dominant film practices in the forties, because blacks formed substantial audiences for such films. According to Jacqueline Bobo, by 1942, there were 430 black movie theaters (90 percent white owned or managed) in thirty-one states, and about 200 more white theaters with black sections. By 1943, blacks were spending about $150 million annually on movies.[23]

In the fifties, I grew up in Harlem as a member of a family that had lived in Harlem for three generations. There were still large movie theaters in and around Harlem then. My mother and grandmother constantly took my sister and me to the movies downtown as well as uptown. Radio City Music Hall at Rockefeller Plaza (along with the Central Public Library on 42nd Street and The Museum of Modern Art on 53rd Street) were cultural fixtures in my growing up, institutions to which we repeatedly turned for pleasure as well as confirmation of our understanding of the status quo. My mother and my grandmother often laughed about how my sister and I had been taken to see *The Wizard of Oz* at Radio City Music Hall when we were two and three (1955) and had ended up under the seats because we were so frightened by the dazzling lights and sound. It was reluctantly agreed that perhaps we were a little too young for such a large school, but just barely.

Much as it was for women and gays in Manuel Puig's novels (*Betrayed by Rita Hayworth*, *Heartbreak Tango*, *Kiss of the Spider Woman*), the "stories" and "stars" (their costumes, hairstyles, and affectations) of the Hollywood films of the thirties, forties, and fifties formed an intensely important cultural currency between the women in my family. As movies such as *The Maltese Falcon* (1941), *Double Indemnity* (1944), *Laura* (1944), *Mildred Pierce* (1945), *The Dark Mirror* (1946), *Gilda* (1946), *The Postman Always Rings Twice* (1946), *Caught* (1949), *Sunset Boulevard* (1950), and *The Big Heat* (1953) were shown and reshown on television, my grandmother and mother taught me to know and love Lana Turner, Rita Hayworth, Gloria Swanson, Joan Crawford, Ingrid Bergman, Gloria Grahame, Barbara Bel Geddes, and Barbara Stanwyck, not because they were "white" but because they were "stars."

It was always said among black women that Joan Crawford was black, and as I watch these films again today, looking at Rita Hayworth in *Gilda* or Lana Turner in *The Postman Always Rings Twice*, I keep thinking "she's so beautiful, she looks black." Such a statement makes no sense in current feminist film criticism. What I am trying to suggest is that there was a way in which these films were possessed by black female viewers. The process may have been about making problematic and expanding one's racial identity instead of abandoning it. It seems crucial here to view spectatorship not only as potentially bisexual but also multicultural and multiethnic. Even as the "Law of the Father" may impose its premature closure on the filmic "gaze" in the coordination of suture and classic narrative, disparate factions in the audience, not all equally well indoctrinated in the dominant discourse, may have their own way, now and then, with interpretation.

But the question remains of how black female viewers regarded the Butterfly McQueens and Hattie McDaniels that occasionally and awkwardly (veritable flies in buttermilk) appeared in these films. As a child, I suppose I rebelled against identification with McDaniel and McQueen, but as an adult I came to know Butterfly McQueen as a woman who owned a brownstone on Convent Avenue in Harlem, along the route I took to City College every day when I was an undergraduate there. I learned that her career had been greatly diminished by her unwillingness to continue to play such roles as Prissy in *Gone with the Wind* (1939).

Later, I learned that Hattie McDaniel was the first black person to win an Oscar (and the only black woman until Whoopi Goldberg in 1991) for Best Supporting Actress in *Gone with the Wind*.[24] Given the narrow restrictions on the roles that black actresses could play in the thirties and forties (either maids or entertainers), McDaniel excelled at her craft. She was so perversely commanding in the "Mammy" role that Jamaica Kincaid was moved to write in the *Village Voice* in 1977 that she had always wanted a Mammy.

As an adult, as a woman, as a black woman and a feminist, I strongly identify with both the restrictions McDaniel and McQueen faced and their efforts to surmount them. I've seen such little improvement in the film roles for black women (especially dark-skinned black women) in my lifetime. As a desiring subject, my coterminous and simultaneous identification with Joan Crawford *and* Butterfly McQueen in *Mildred Pierce* helped to form the complicated and multifaceted "me" that "I" have become. This process of identification, I would submit, has never had a comfortable resting place, given dominant film practices, so as I've grown older and wiser, it is ever more constantly in motion.

Yet I find myself irresistibly drawn to many of the concerns that psychoanalytic feminist film criticism raises. When Kaja Silverman writes in a description of how suture works to corroborate sexual difference, "The spectacle of classic cinema promotes a constant re-enactment of the primal 'discovery' of the female subject's lack,"[25] this strikes me as an apt way to describe one of the agendas of *Mildred Pierce*. But it is also important to remember that this conception of "the female subject's lack" has a particular history and socioeconomic trajectory and that within that system of "lack" there is also inscribed a racial hierarchy in which white women are privileged. It boils down to the following: White feminists have a hard time imagining themselves as agents of racism but feminists of color don't have a hard time with this at all.

As for other kinds of black participation in the films of the forties, what Cripps calls "race" films had all but died out by 1941. Whereas the production of what Bobo calls "independent Black-cast films," many of which were financed by whites, reached their third and last peak in the mid-1940s.[26] Often mirroring Hollywood generic conventions, some of the actors who specialized in stereotypical roles in white films, such as Mantan Moreland, Stepin Fetchit, and Bill Robinson, also starred in black-cast films such as *Tall, Tan, and Terrific* (1946 — Moreland), *Big Timers* (1946 — Stepin Fetchit), and *Harlem Is Heaven* (1947 — Robinson).[27]

Also in forties Hollywood films, there were often a lot of black entertainers singing, dancing, or playing instruments in musical interludes that functioned as self-contained segments. Bogle calls this "the Negro Entertainment Syndrome" that was designed to use blacks in films without having to integrate them into the plot. These segments could be cut out of the film when showing it in the South.[28] The performances of both Hazel Scott and Lena Horne were circumscribed by such conventions. Scott, a child prodigy and concert pianist, refused to appear in films as anybody but herself seated at the piano. As she told *Ebony* in 1944, "black women were too often cast as whores or maids."[29]

Like Scott clinging to her piano, Lena Horne clung to her role as a chanteuse in "a long line of movies where she was pasted to a pillar." Bogle quotes Horne saying, "They didn't make me into a maid, but they didn't make me anything else either. I became a butterfly pinned to a column singing away in Movieland."[30] Where she probably got to stretch out the most was in the black-cast musicals *Cabin in the Sky* (1942) and *Stormy Weather* (1943), although neither film did that well at the box office.[31]

What did do well at the box office, however, were the "problem" films of 1949. *Home of the Brave*, *Lost Boundaries*, and *Pinky*, Bobo tells us, were the highest grossing films of 1949 for their respective studios: United Artists, Film Classics, and Twentieth Century Fox."[32] Both *Pinky*, directed by Elia Kazan, and *Lost Boundaries*, directed by Alfred Werker, tell stories about passing. In *Pinky*, Jeanne Crain, a white actress who plays the daughter of Ethel Waters, revisits her mother in the South after having passed for white in the North.

Lost Boundaries is about a black male doctor, Scott Carter, and his wife Marcia (played by white actors Mel Ferrer and Beatrice Pearson) who pass for white in a small New Hampshire town called Keenham and raise two children, a boy, Howard and a girl, Shelley, (also played by white actors — Richard Hylton and Susan Douglas) without telling them that they have black blood. When World War II begins, the fierce patriotism of father and son forces both to enlist. Dr. Carter is given a post as a doctor and an officer in the navy until his black blood is discovered. The navy then rejects him entirely.

In the film's climax, Dr. Carter tells Howard that he has black blood. Howard is driven half mad by the realization that he is a "Negro." He runs off to Harlem (which includes a close-up of street signs for 135th Street and Lenox Avenue as documentary-type footage of Harlem street scenes) to find out what it means to be black. In a dingy rooming house, while he sleeps, tossing and turning, we watch images over his head of his father, mother, and sister dissolve into visibly black images.

In a dark hallway of a rooming house he gets drawn into a fight. When the police come, he is found standing over a dead body with a knife in his hand. He is arrested and interrogated by a friendly black police lieutenant played by Canada Lee, who explains why his father didn't want him to be black. If you can be "white," why would you ever want to be "black," all the visibly black characters say, again and again, in the film. In the end, he is happily reunited with his father and they with the town, in a final scene in church in which the minister delivers a sermon preaching racial tolerance.

In this film, "passing" as a psychological dilemma is gendered male. The parallel scene of the mother telling the daughter is never shown. All the evidence would suggest that the daughter took the news rather calmly. In fact, the *Reader's Digest* story on which this "true story" was based completely focuses on the psychological traumas of the son, which were much more complicated than in the film. In *Reader's Digest*, Howard (named Albert Johnston), who already had a close black friend at college, thinks of himself as liberal and seems pleased when he first learns that he is black.

But then his grades begin to fall, he contemplates suicide, and his father sends him to a "well-known Negro psychiatrist." While in the navy, he is sent to a mental hospital. After discharge from the navy, he begins to travel around the country looking up relatives, trying to figure out which way is up. The tale goes on and on, with a series of interesting ethnographic details about Negro society and "passing" in the forties.[33]

In *Home of the Brave* (directed by Mark Robson), a black soldier (James Edwards) named Peter Moss suffers from paralysis because his best friend, a white man (Lloyd Bridges), begins to call him a nigger and then gets killed immediately afterward. Under the supervision of a psychiatrist, who becomes the tiresome superego of the narrative, we are told that Peter is paralyzed because he feels responsible for his friend's death; he wanted his friend to die. His psychiatrist says he wanted his friend to die not because he called Peter a nigger but because everybody in battle wants the person next to him to die instead of himself.

Your problem has nothing to do with being a Negro, the psychiatrist yells at Peter. You have to get this chip off your shoulder and realize you're like everybody else! A cured Peter, able to walk again, ends up going off with a white one-armed soldier named Mingo, to start a restaurant.

In *The Devil Finds Work*, a book he wrote on film in 1976, James Baldwin says of this scenario:

> But why is the price of what should, after all, be simple human connection so high? Is it really necessary to lose a woman, an arm, or one's mind, in order to say hello? . . . A man can fall in love with a man: incarceration, torture, fire, and death, and still more, the threat of these, have not been able to prevent it, and never will. It became a grave, a tragic matter, on the North American continent, where white power became indistinguishable from the question of sexual dominance. But the question of sexual dominance can only exist in the nightmare of that soul which has armed itself, totally, against the possibility of the changing notion of conquest and surrender, which is love.[34]

Two documentaries, *The Quiet One* (1948), written by James Agee and directed by Sidney Meyers, and *Let There Be Light* (1946), directed by John

Huston, both focused on a universal male psyche from a psychiatric point of view, both of which also suggest that racial categories simply don't exist. These two documentaries help to further clarify the nature of the dilemma Baldwin elucidates. In *Let There Be Light*, three black soldiers are included among a random sample of psychologically impaired World War II veterans. Although one black soldier says, in a group therapy session, that he didn't speak until he was seven, and another — who has repeated crying spells — says he was raised to look down on children whose families had less, race is never mentioned in the highly psychoanalytic narration of the voice-over. Sponsored by the military, *Let There Be Light* was never actually released because of its transgressive honesty regarding the extent of psychological problems (about 20 percent of casualties) among World War II veterans.

In *The Quiet One*, a little black boy who has been abandoned by his parents and now lives in the Wiltwyck School for Boys in upstate New York, must deal with his feelings of self-hatred and alienation. Scripted by James Agee, *The Quiet One* juxtaposes documentary footage and staged dramatic scenes with a psychiatrist narrator. In flashbacks, we see the little boy's environment of poverty and deprivation as he is beaten and tormented by a mean old grandmother in the ghetto.

The unfolding drama, which never allows him to speak in his own voice (rather the psychiatrist paraphrases his remarks from their psychoanalytic sessions), shows him learning to negotiate his feelings of love for a black male counselor. Again, throughout this film, race is never mentioned.

Even a brief perusal of these materials suggests to me how specifically calibrated were issues of race, especially race in relation to gender, in films made in the forties. In the aftermath of the Jewish Holocaust, Hiroshima, Nagasaki, the Japanese internment, the integration of the military, and the early stages of the McCarthy era and the Cold War, the particular political environment of the late forties made the range of safe discussions of such topics a narrow one.

What is fascinating to me, and deserves more examination, is the question of how the increasing prominence of a psychiatric and psychoanalytic discourse impacted on definitions and criteria of race as a national "problem" within dominant film practices. Obviously, none of these films is really about women. There are no women at all in *Home of the Brave*. In *Lost Boundaries*, the women are among the most conventional and limp I've ever seen in film. The positive-image mandate means these women have to be dreadfully dull. In *The Quiet One*, the women are nothing more than lifeless shadows. But what fascinated me about all of these films is the superimposition of a narrowly psychoanalytic oedipal drama on the otherwise reckless vagaries of race.

The institutionalization in the forties of a psychoanalytic/psychiatric discourse in the United States was central to the formation of conventional notions of masculinity, sexual difference, family, and personality in dominant film practice.[35] What is more, the ways in which these conventions were translated into plot, suture, and mise-en-scène continue to inform contemporary perceptions of film that is pleasurable to watch. Particularly suggestive here is that further examination of these matters might reveal unanticipated insight into the gendering of race, the problem of the visual in Afro-American culture, and "the changing motion of conquest and surrender."

Originally published in Manthia Diawara, ed., *Black American Cinema* (New York: Routledge, 1993.

Notes

1. I realize that the problem of defining Afro-American culture in any cohesive way is insuperable. See Paul Gilroy, "It Ain't Where You're From, It's Where You're At: The Dialectics of Diasporic Identification," *Third Text*, no. 13 (winter 1990/91): 3–16. By the term I don't mean anything more heady than whenever and wherever blacks attempt to grapple with issues of identity and self-representation. The agent might be considered anybody, from a lone black actor working in a project entirely produced by whites (such as Courtney Vance in John Guare's Lincoln Center production of *Six Degrees of Separation*) to an institutional framework such as Spike Lee and his company, Forty Acres and A Mule.

2. LeRoi Jones, *Blues People: Negro Music in White America* (New York: Morrow, 1963); Charles Keil, *Urban Blues* (Chicago: University of Chicago Press, 1966); Lawrence Levine, *Black Culture and Black Consciousness: Afro-American Folk Thought from Slavery to Freedom* (New York: Oxford University Press, 1977); Robert Palmer, *Deep Blues* (New York: Viking, 1981); Nelson George, *The Death of Rhythm and Blues* (New York: Pantheon, 1988).

3. Joseph Boskin, *Sambo: The Rise and Demise of an American Jester* (New York: Oxford University Press, 1986), 13. Boskin suggests that this figure, who was widespread in Britain (perhaps even conceived there) as well as in the United States, was usually male, and perhaps constitutionally "male" in gender. See my "De-Facing History," *Art-in-America* 78, no. 12 (1991): 120–29 (also chapter 36 in this volume) for further details on how Sambo images functioned in the visual arts in the nineteenth and early twentieth centuries.

4. Donald Bogle, *Toms, Coons, Mulattoes, Mammies, and Bucks: An Interpretive History of Blacks in American Film* (New York: Viking Press, 1973); Thomas Cripps, *Slow Fade to Black: The Negro in American Film, 1900–1942* (New York: Oxford University Press, 1977).

5. Thomas Cripps, "Film" in Jannette L. Dates and William Barlow, eds., *Split Image: African Americans in the Mass Media* (Washington, D.C.: Howard University Press, 1990), 124–172.

6. Karen Grigsby Bates, "'They've Gotta Have Us': Hollywood's Black Directors," *New York Times Magazine*, 14 July 1991, pp. 14–19, 38–40, 44, including cover.

7. I take my concept of "invisibility" from Ralph Ellison's use of the term to describe the condition of blacks in the United States mid–twentieth century in relation to historiography and the production of culture in *Invisible Man*. References to "invisibility" range over most of the essays in *Invisibility Blues: From Pop to Theory* (New York:Verso/ Routledge, 1990). In my earlier *Black Macho and the Myth of the Superwoman* (reissued by Verso/Routledge in 1990 with a critical introduction), I suggested that gender was as important as "race" to understanding the plight of the woman of color.

8. There are important exceptions to these generalizations about feminist film theory. For instance, in *Camera Obscura* 22 (1989): 20–21 ("The Spectatrix" issue), Constance Penley describes herself as having "studiously avoided or even resisted the idea of the female spectator" in favor of a more heterogeneous concept of identification. Also, in regard to the constant making problematic of these issues, see the range of essays in E. Ann Kaplan, ed., *Women in Film Noir* (London: British Film Institute, 1978); E. Ann Kaplan, ed., *Psychoanalysis and Cinema* (New York: Routledge, 1990); and Jane Gaines and Charlotte Herzog, eds., *Fabrications: Costume and the Female Body* (New York: Routledge, 1990).

9. Laura Mulvey, "Visual Pleasure and Narrative Cinema," *Screen* 6, no. 3 (1975): 6–18, 11. There are many examples. Some notable ones are Jacqueline Bobo, "*The Color Purple*: Black Women as Cultural Readers," in E. Deidre Pribram, ed., *Female Spectators Looking at Film and Television* (New York: Verso/Routledge, 1988), 90–109; Manthia Diawara, "The Nature of Mother in *Dreaming Rivers*," *Third Text* 13 (winter 1991): 73–84; Trinh T. Minh-ha, *When the Moon Waxes Red: Representation, Gender and Cultural Politics* (New York: Routledge, 1991); Jackie Byars, *All That Hollywood Allows: Re-Reading Gender in 1950s Melodrama* (Chapel Hill: University of North Carolina Press, 1991); bell hooks, "Is Paris Burning?" *Zeta Magazine*, June 1991, 60–64; Jane Gaines, "White Privilege and Looking Relations: Race and Gender in Feminist Film Theory," *Screen* 29, no. 4 (fall 1988), 12–27.

10. Janice Radway (in *Reading the Romance: Women, Patriarchy, and Popular Literature* [Chapel Hill: University of North Carolina Press, 1984]) and Stuart Hall ("Encoding/ Decoding" in *Culture, Media, Language: Working Papers in Cultural Studies, 1972–79* [London: Hutchinson, 1981]) have been highly influential in this context. Good examples of this approach abound; for instance, most of the essays in the Pribram anthology cited above, and the essays in the "Popular Culture and Reception Studies" issue of *Camera Obscura* 23, May 1990.

11. See my essay "Multiculturalism and Oppositionality" (chapter 25 in this volume).

12. Happily, there are wonderful exceptions to this generalization in the works of Hazel Carby, bell hooks, Gayatri Spivak, Trinh T. Minh-ha, and Kobena Mercer.

13. See my "Modernism, Postmodernism, and the Problem of the Visual in Afro-American Culture," (chapter 39 in this volume); "De-Facing History," (chapter 36 in this volume): 121–128, 184–186; "Multiculturalism and Oppositionality" (chapter 25 in this volume).

14. Bogle, *Toms, Coons, Mulattoes, and Bucks*, 3–6.

15. See my subsequent writings on silent film: "Uncle Tom's Cabin: Before and After the Jim Crow Era," *Drama Review* 44 (2000): 137–56; "The Good Lynching and *The Birth of a Nation*: Discourses and Aesthetics of Jim Crow," *Cinema Journal* 43, no. 1 (2003):

85–104; "Oscar Micheaux's *Within Our Gates*: The Possibilities for Alternative Visions," in Pearl Bowser, Jane Gaines, and Charlie Musser, eds., *Oscar Micheaux and His Circle: African American Filmmaking and Race Cinema in the Silent Era* (Bloomington: Indiana University Press, 2001).

16. Ibid., 16.

17. Ibid., 16–17.

18. *New York Times*, 31 March 1991, p. 9.

19. Bogle, *Toms, Coons, Mulattoes, and Bucks*, 14–15.

20. Cripps "Film," 131.

21. Ibid., 134–136. Also, see Manthia Diawara's "Black Spectatorship: Problems of Identification and Resistance," in *Screen* 29, no. 4 (fall 1988): 66–76, for a sensitive reading of crucial "Gus chase" sequence in *The Birth of a Nation*, which takes into account contemporary issues in psychoanalytic film interpretation.

22. I would say that comedy is never incidental or unimportant in a drama.

23. Jacqueline Bobo, "'The Subject Is Money': Reconsidering the Black Film Audience as Theoretical Paradigm," *Black American Literature Forum* 25, no. 2 (summer 1991): 424.

24. Halle Berry became the first black woman to win an Oscar for Best Actress for her role in *Monster's Ball* in 2002.

25. Kaja Silverman, *The Subject of Semiotics* (New York: Oxford University Press, 1983), 223.

26. Cripps, "Film," 145; Bobo, "*The Color Purple*": 423. Bobo defines independent black-cast films as "films made by Black people or white-backed organizations which featured Black actors and actresses."

27. Bogle, *Toms, Coons, Mulattoes, and Bucks*, 108.

28. Ibid., 121.

29. Ibid., 122. Scott appeared in *Something to Shout About* (1943), *I Dood It* (1943), *The Heat's On* (1943), *Broadway Rhythm* (1944), *Rhapsody in Blue* (1945).

30. Bogle, *Toms, Coons, Mulattoes, and Bucks*, 127.

31. Lena Horne, *the* black female film star of the forties (the first black woman ever to appear on the cover of a film magazine), was closely aligned with Walter White of the NAACP and Paul Robeson and was extremely political. In fact, her political positions led her to being blacklisted and banned from film roles. Horne was listed in *Red Channels* in June of 1950 for her support of the Hollywood Independent Citizens Committee, the Joint Anti-Fascist Committee, and W. E. B. Du Bois and Paul Robeson's Council on African Affairs. Gail Lumet Buckley, *The Hornes: An American Family* (New York: Knopf, 1986), 203–213.

32. Bobo, "*The Color Purple*," 424.

33. W. L. White, "Lost Boundaries," *Reader's Digest*, December 1947, 135–154.

34. James Baldwin, *The Devil Finds Work* (New York: Dial Press, 1976), 68.

35. Krin Gabbard and Glen O. Gabbard, *Psychiatry and the Cinema* (University of Chicago Press, 1987), xv. While recent discussions of Frantz Fanon (*Black Skins, White Masks* [New York: Grove Press, 1967]) are relevant here, they are beyond the scope of this present essay. Briefly, however, it seems to me that Fanon is not especially useful to a black feminist film criticism because of the way in which he succumbs to, and conflates, the confusion of the "woman" and the "primitive" or the "uncivilized" (not white) in Freud.

24.

Multicultural Blues:

An Interview with Michele Wallace

The following interview was conducted by Jim Drobnick in 1990, at Michele Wallace's home in Brooklyn.

DROBNICK: Do you see an emerging acceptance of multiculturalist aesthetics? Is it fair to call multicultural theories and writings an "ism"?

WALLACE: I suspect that when we evaluate "multiculturalism" as an "ism," it will be a lot like "primitivism." Multiculturalism is a by-product of conflating differences between a wide variety of cultures. Primitivism, as you know, was the outcome of Europeans looking at nonwhite, non-Western cultures and deciding to characterize them as the opposite of "civilization." The West considered its civilization in a period of decline and, in order to rejuvenate itself, adopted isolated aesthetic features from tremendously complex, diverse, and heterogeneous cultural matrices. It randomly selected elements from whole histories and cultures and languages. I suspect multiculturalism will serve the same function as a lifeline to the West.

There are also political ramifications. When the West finally recognizes the demands of its tremendous minority presence, it will perhaps reveal "multiculturalism" as its response. "Minority" voices (which, in the world, are not minorities but, in fact, majorities) will say, "We want a fair share of the wealth we produce, we want to see and create images that reflect our reality, we want to read and write a history that includes us, we want a share in running and defining this government's institutions, we want a share in directing the production of knowledge, and so on," and the West will answer, "Multiculturalism means we already have that. Come to us, you diverse, heterogeneous people, and we will explain to you once again how multiculturalism reflects you."

DROBNICK: Do you consider multiculturalism to be a bourgeois, academic phenomenon?

WALLACE: I do. It would have to be. For the most part, anything originating from a white perspective that uses the same kind of knowledge to look at African Americans, as well as Koreans or Puerto Ricans in this country, without an acknowledgment of class, gender, how long they have been here, whether their immigration was illegal or legal, I have to call profoundly antihistorical and antimaterialist, and probably racist to boot. I'm not opposed to theorizing multiculturalism. It just can't be a program like primitivism. If mostly white people talk about it, as when mostly white people talked about primitivism, it will subjugate rather than benefit the people inscribed within that framework. If it's a program that museums and institutions use to appropriate the vitality of the nonwhite world, then it's bad news. It can only be useful if it is an opportunity to theorize the multiple theoretical positions of minorities in first world countries and the problems of third world peoples in third world countries.

DROBNICK: I agree that remembering the abuses of primitivism is useful to check the claims of multiculturalism. My perception, though, is that multiculturalism originates from marginalized, minority, and third world artists and writers. Could what you be referring to actually be post-structuralism or postmodernism? Something which I consider multiculturalism to critique?

WALLACE: My feeling is that when you get to the position of multiculturalism you have already put together a lot of other critiques. And generally the people who make the critiques don't put them together. Let me point out that there is incredible separatism among the ethnic minorities in this country. Native Americans feel no desire to be lumped together with black Americans, black Americans with Asian Americans, etc. These people don't know anything more about each other than white people know about each of us. A potential struggle exists between these minorities because we have different disabilities and different problems.

There is a critique of postmodernism coming from minority cultures and third world cultures. There's also a postcolonial critique of postmodernism, which I wouldn't attempt to summarize. The minority/ethnic critique, which is not really formalized as a critique, says, "You leave us out, therefore we leave you out." On the other hand, poststructuralism is disturbing in its failure to integrate postcolonial, minority, and multicultural perspectives and issues. As a white, male, academic discourse, it fails simply because it speaks in a major voice while the essence of these issues is minor.

Fredric Jameson could very well deal with so-called minor culture, except he doesn't do minor things. He does major things. Gayatri Spivak chose to do "a minor Indian woman writer" precisely because she is a postcolonial, nonwhite woman. She understands the importance of speaking not for but about the silenced and the voiceless in the world despite her project as a poststructuralist to explode the myth of being able to speak for the other. Postmodernism has the potential to create a very important space, one that cultivates a wide range of political, theoretical, and cultural development. But it has not so far realized that potential except in the work of such post-colonial, postmodern critics as Gayatri Spivak, Homi Bhabha, and Trinh T. Minh-ha.

We're beginning to see postmodernism in terms of its critiques: whether or not it is a side effect of television, or late capitalism, and so forth. The temptation now is to use it to pinpoint the bad guys, like literary critics who romanticize the aesthetic power of postmodernism. They simply reinscribe modernism in high culture under another name. The good guys use postmodernism to make political critiques of the media and trends in international economics. As I understand it, postmodernism describes a development in late capitalism, technology, and communication. It permeates culture, even that portion of culture that says, "I deliberately set myself outside of you." However, the number of people writing about postmodernism is very limited.

DROBNICK: Postmodern theory is felt by some to be a new form of cultural hegemony. By arguing for the rejection of individual subjectivity and the impossibility of meaning, the liberating power of art is rendered inconsequential. This seems to leave an ethnic culture with no tools to assert itself.

WALLACE: The postmodernism I am interested in focuses on how peoples of color have been treated by these developments. The tools minority cultures work with are the same tools everyone else works with. I don't believe peoples of color can withdraw themselves from postmodern theories and postmodern processes and postmodern effects. Their lives are still touched by television. To retreat is to put oneself in tremendous danger. For instance, one project of the Black Nationalism Movement in the '60s was to retreat into the ghetto and make it a homeland. Come on. It's a ghetto. It was created by a specific set of social and economic conditions. It's a space of ignorance, poverty, disease, and terrible conditions for women and children. You can try to valorize it as some wonderful, romantic motherland, but it's a ghetto and that's what it will remain. It's a space of powerlessness.

DROBNICK: Since minorities in the U.S. do not control separate territory, the cartographic press that Frantz Fanon, Edward Said, and Jameson describe, the process of recovering one's own territory (if at first only in the imagination) and purging it of occupiers, is not physically possible. Does this make multiculturalism difficult in the U.S.?

WALLACE: It's not an option in the U.S. or anywhere in the world. Subjugated peoples are not pure. Quite the opposite. We bear all the negative impulses of repressive cultural processes. Because our culture is a response to subjugation and domination, we can theorize about cultural processes that take into account domination and subjection, instead of forgetting or ignoring it. If we argue for a separatist "Give us a few states" proposal, where black people will live without white people, we repeat the conquer/colonialist paradigm. There are so many ways of replaying apartheid.

DROBNICK: One feminist writer, Nancy Hartsock, is quite suspicious of the motives of postmodernism. She asks, "Why is it, exactly at the moment when so many of us who have been silenced begin to demand the right to name ourselves, to act as subjects rather than objects of history, that just then the concept of subjecthood becomes 'problematic'? Just when we are forming our own theories about the world, uncertainty emerges about whether the world can be adequately theorized? Just when we are talking about the changes we want, ideas of progress and the possibility of 'meaningfully' organizing human society become suspect?" She concludes that, for any marginalized group seeking a redefinition of themselves according to their own form of nationalism, or nationalisms, postmodern theories are dangerous to adopt.

WALLACE: I agree and disagree with her. This call for feminist forms of nationalism, even when considered in the most positive sense, gives me a very negative feeling. They always impose prescriptive standards of behavior. Their failure is to think that we can start from the beginning with a new nation. The questions postmodern theory raises are the very questions that create the opportunity to theorize another kind of subjectivity, one not as dependent upon the dominance inherent in nationalism or of history as a linear narrative or of a unified subjectivity that overrides difference. It's no accident that both postmodernism and multiculturalism happened when peoples of color and women began to move out of their allotted place to say, "I don't accept the fact that I am supposed to belong here. I belong wherever I want to go." Its power emanates from the fact that the crises emerge from a variety of cultural locations simultaneously, including the location of critiques of ethnicity such as are being made by black, British, and Marxist approaches. Maybe postmodern theory is the white male way of contending with this crisis.

I don't see postmodernism as a threat. Feminists, African Americanists, and postcolonialists seeking to fill academic positions of authority make this kind of argument. Once there, they can be very successful at retrenching institutional academic practice.

DROBNICK: Multiculturalism seems to be a more activist project than postmodernism. Instead of merely describing the world, it seeks to intervene and change it.

WALLACE: To intervene in the world, multiculturalism has become "theory." It aspired to be an international language that transcends the usual differences already inscribed in language. It wants to transcend the space between the people who have ideas and the people who do things in the world. That is a joke, of course. "Theory" doesn't transcend anything. The true problem is that, generally, "people of color" don't participate in theorizing at this level and the "people of color" who do so act as symbolic white males or as the by now equally unilateral and symbolic "other."

Trinh Minh-ha, whom I like, subverts her own authority. Her practice is poetic. I'm afraid, though, it misses an important opportunity to teach and empower people who are disempowered within the dominant structure. I feel that the more poetic we are, the more inaccessible the crucial information becomes. To me, every idea is connected to questions of "How do you teach it to people who feel they don't know it? What do they already know that we can know together?" I would like to teach people to make wild stabs at either postmodern or multicultural theory and to maintain a healthy skepticism toward it all.

DROBNICK: It's also a question of motivating people instead of bludgeoning them with intimidating theory.

WALLACE: But you can also bludgeon them with poetry. Once again the romantic conception of poetry being closer to reality obfuscates the fact that, for some people, mathematical propositions are more understandable than poetry.

DROBNICK: My understanding of Trinh and her concept of "theory as non-theory" is to avoid what you've already criticized: the totalizing tendency of theory.

WALLACE: But sometimes it is important to totalize. In the translation from theoretical propositions to practice, there is a necessity for some totalizing concepts.

DROBNICK: Do you see the possibility that multiculturalism could fall into the trap of relativism or pluralism? In an article where W. J. T. Mitchell calls pluralism a strategy of "repressive toleration," he cites a conversation between George McGovern and William F. Buckley in which both cry for pluralism in Latin America: McGovern meaning self-determination, Buckley meaning acceptance of U.S. military intervention and freedom for U.S. corporate interests.

WALLACE: To me, the trap is this: there are many people in the world and most of them are not white. White male culture dominates all the others. That dominance includes theory and epistemology, as well as culture. Multiculturalism rebuts that by saying everything once thought to have only one version now has many different versions. There is no one location for the truth. But multiculturalism still suggests that there is one way of providing an overview of all the "Others." It has yet to deconstruct itself as a category. It has yet to be a process that undermines its own authority.

The distinction between relativism and pluralism, to me, is pretty useless. From what I understand about international politics, nobody is going to leave Latin America alone, or any other country in the world. On the other hand, Buckley's position is indefensible. The real problem involves a denial of the economic and political interdependence of all countries in the world. McGovern's policy to let Latin American countries decide their own form of government is simply the mirror version of Buckley's: we should still intervene to make sure they're democratic. In practice, neither position significantly alters foreign policy because what's truly generating the relationship is global capitalism, which is not even being acknowledged.

There is always a need to ask economic and material questions of one's multicultural ideas. Obviously, we all came to the U.S. because of economic considerations. Particularly blacks, because we were brought here as slaves. Not many others had options, either. The notion of people choosing to come here is a lot of romantic ideology. I don't believe that the Chinese or the Russians or the Germans had much of a choice. How many options do you have if you're starving in your country? If you're subject to political oppression?

DROBNICK: How is an ethnicity defined? Is the political community different from the cultural community?

WALLACE: Absolutely. One of the things that define political and economic as well as cultural issues is the relationship to the immigration experience and how far removed it is. People still struggling with citizenship or with the language have a different relationship to these issues than people who can speak the language, for whatever it's worth, and those for whom citizenship is not a question.

I think we can draw together around some issues and we should. But I don't believe that people of color are automatically politically correct. There is strong inclination to be just the opposite. You're trying to prove you're not disenfranchised, you're trying to uplift yourself. You want to succeed and don't want to take chances. If you feel there are better chances to succeed by becoming a doctor or lawyer rather than writing multicultural theory, you'll do it.

In the past, black intellectuals have been placed in a peculiar situation: in order to survive they were inclined to take a conservative direction. To refuse brought trouble to oneself. I suspect that Zora Neale Hurston was not necessarily a reactionary in that she was actively going out of her way to thwart the black struggle, but she was in a way that many black intellectuals had to compromise themselves. It was years before Langston Hughes could shake off the curse of publicly declaring himself a leftist. He recovered by overcompensating to the right. While it was very impractical for black intellectuals to be on the left in the '30s, '40s, and '50s, now it seems impossible to be anything else.

I don't see any context for hounding black intellectuals today, but it can always come back. We're living in one of the few spaces in the world, in one of the few times in history, in which severe punishment is not the consequence for asking hard, political questions. I have no confidence that this will continue forever. Somebody may be compiling a McCarthy-like list right now. In a sense, black artists and intellectuals have always gotten blacklisted. I don't know how else to describe the systematic exclusion of blacks from the highest levels of cultural success. This has a great impact on whether or not we are able to be interesting as intellectuals or artists. When we look back upon their work, that process may seem invisible. Although recently some important work has been published emphasizing such problems: for instance, the biographies of Langston Hughes (by Arnold Rampersad), Paul Robeson (by Martin Duberman), and W. E. B. Du Bois (by Manning Marable).

The impulse to organize around the issue of being a "minority" can also be a conservative position. Nevertheless, African Americans, because we've been here for so long, and because we've attempted to integrate and were repelled, have forged a unique model of cultural development. One not based upon a homeland or a home language or racial or cultural purity but upon mixing different cultural approaches. Henry Louis Gates calls this "critical signification": reading the dominant cultural critically, and then reversing its trends, making a joke about it, parodying it, deconstructing it. Black culture becomes then a process rather than an essence to be reified.

DROBNICK: Critical signification prioritizes the hybrid. Yet, is it useful for forming a community of shared concerns, for establishing a culture that is beyond being reactive?

WALLACE: It describes what African American culture is. Most previous descriptions of our culture have defined it as a failure. Yet, we were doing this other, unnamed cultural process, which may be in fact more characteristic of what people actually do. How many people in the world live in their historical homeland? These nomadic principles offer a new paradigm of cultural tolerance and incorporation and accommodation. It may be "reactive," as you call it, but it has allowed black people in this culture to feed off the dominant culture and produce more culture. Like in terms of our music and our fashion. We are big culture producers despite the most profound discouragement.

Blacks have always been deprived in terms of our access to the production of culture. To some degree, this deprivation has produced an extraordinary resourcefulness. If blacks had the access to film and television and photography and architecture that they now have in music and dance and religion and sports, there is no reason why they wouldn't produce the same extraordinary results.

DROBNICK: Why do you think that celebrating a culture different from the mainstream is so threatening to that mainstream?

WALLACE: Cultural diversity threatens those who control the production of knowledge — a certain category of white males. Supremacy and mastery is the definition of "intellectual" in this culture. In academia, mastery of one's subject generally means that you've withdrawn all kinds of messy material and sexual considerations from your field of specialization. If your subject is history, you've killed off the people and turned it into a thing so you can possess objective knowledge. In the process of claiming it, you have disowned the peoples to whom it belongs.

Then you teach it to others, which means they submit to your mastery. It's like a religious conversion. You admit to not having known anything before and then take on a new knowing and being from this omniscient person. When you're completely denuded of everything you had before, then you too become eligible for this mastery. Becoming knowledgeable means indoctrination by that process. Artists go for it, too. Sometimes in a bigger way than scholars.

Then you go around protecting your territory. We scholars don't have nations or land, but we have our territory, the specialization we protect from people who would invade and destroy the rigor. To the ignorant people who don't know, we have to teach. I think this kind of attitude works counter to actually teaching the process of being knowledgeable. The end result is knowledge as a thing: "I know this and now I will give it to you and then you will know it." Teaching is not that. Teaching is showing you what I did in encountering the object of knowledge. It is teaching the process rather than teaching the thing. Educators refrain from that because they would create critically conscious people, people who would then go on to decide, "I want to change the government." And all that, which a certain class of white males now consider under their control, would be open to a diverse, heterogeneous population, those who are deemed unqualified, and who are kept from ever being qualified.

The educational deprivation of the black community is extreme. If you've read Paolo Freire, you know it's not accidental, it is absolutely necessary. Education is politics. You don't educate someone you intend to disenfranchise. How to educate black children is a mystery to many people because the model of education is so imbued with notions of dominance and mastery. When you encounter the situation of educating someone different from yourself, in order not to enslave them, but to free them, you have to train them to question and eventually supersede your authority. This is unheard of.

DROBNICK: As a professor of literature, you've had to do some thinking about revising the literary canon. Would opening up the canon to minority literatures work for or against the teaching of critical consciousness?

WALLACE: I think something inherent in the formation of canons stifles critical consciousness. Canons and traditions work against radical pedagogical views. Not only should a more diversified range of literature be taught but literature itself should be taught as a problematic category, to counteract the perception of it as self-evident and naturally constituted.

It doesn't really matter whether you teach canonical or noncanonical literature or some mixture of the two. More important is teaching debate about the canon, about literary tradition, how standards of quality are invented, on whether literature is a concept with redeeming social value. This way minority students, in particular, can understand some of the ideological history behind the formation of canons. For them, the use of literature as a soft way to redo a person's cultural perspective is very loaded by colonial histories of domination and subjugation.

DROBNICK: Literature in that sense is the arbiter of civilization. Did not literary canons and colonialism develop contemporaneously, with literature used as an index of civilization, justifying the subjugation of those without writing?

WALLACE: Yes. The history of civilization was formulated to be a unilinear development, with cultures arranged hierarchically along a timeline. To then appreciate or have respect for cultures in which writing was not the centerpiece of knowledge was absolutely impossible. Remnants of this continue to operate even after we recognize such things as cultural diversity and the contingent linking of writing and intellect. Our assumptions still privilege writing as the seat of knowledge and the epitome of human development.

DROBNICK: Are there rights pertaining to cultures? I'm thinking of Native American protests about museum practices: warehousing human skeletons and representing their cultures as dead and artifactual. Is there still a problem of who can speak for these cultures, whose voice carries legitimacy for the rest?

WALLACE: Yes, Native Americans ought to have a say about their representations but I think that it is problematic to assume they will be in agreement. Again, talk about minorities and their ability to represent themselves leads me to a concern about their education. Education should be raising questions about these issues of representation, which have to be raised in any confrontation with "reality." You're more likely to be educated about these issues at Harvard than you are at a state university or certainly at any public high school. There is an unequal access to the means of representation, but there is an even more unequal access to the interpretation of representation.

I'm very concerned about that for Native Americans. What I often find in encounters with them, usually men, is that they are pretty romantic about these issues. These men have not begun to question their ability, for example, to speak for the women of the tribe. In valorizing the preliterate or the nonliterate, there is often a silencing of diverse points of view. When I hear someone saying there is a Native American or a Cherokee point of view, it worries me. Behind that point of view is a lot of domestic pain for the people who have to live with it. They surrender to it out of a sense of obligation or loyalty. When you come from a people who are not doing well, it's hard to feel a right to rebel against their authority.

There is silence in our culture, especially vis-à-vis the dominant culture. A not telling, a resisting of public representation, a feeling of "My words are not me." The public space is also the white space, so it didn't matter that I was their teacher. They knew I represented that authority. Think of the hundreds of things they would say if they were talking to a friend. This is but a small instance of the tremendous silencing of women of color even within the space of their own culture.

DROBNICK: In *Black Macho*, you've spoken of the limited space white women and black men have made for black women in the feminist and civil rights movements. Women of color are "the other of the other."

WALLACE: The other of the other is the totally untheorized space that such women occupy, the people who are not speaking. Their history is unwritten, their voices are not heard and their images are uncorroborated.

It's like the position theorized by Julia Kristeva, the "abject." It's a third position of silence in the discourse of the other: the unspeakable, the repulsive. When the other tries to speak within the dominant discourse, it usually assumes a dominant role. But what of the people who are left? There is always a silenced, unspeakable space. I think of it as a doubling up of a person, of being, for instance, black and female, or gay and poor. When you get two or three layers of this, the silence is just reconsolidated.

Originally published in *Attitude: The Dance Magazine* 6, no. 3 (1990): 2–6.

25.

Multiculturalism and Oppositionality

Many individual events on the current cultural landscape conspire to make me obsessed with contemporary debates over multiculturalism in both the art world and the culture at large. My concern is grounded first and foremost, however, in my observation of the impact of present material conditions on an increasing sector of the population. These material conditions, which include widespread homelessness, joblessness, illiteracy, crime, disease (including AIDS), hunger, poverty, drug addiction, alcoholism, the various habits of ill health, and the destruction of the environment are (let's face it) the myriad social effects of late multinational capitalism.

In New York City, where I live, the population most affected by these conditions consists largely of people of African, Latino, or Asian descent, some of whom are gay; blacks either from, or one or two generations removed from, the South, the Caribbean, or Africa; or Latinos of mixed race from the Caribbean or Central or South America; or Asians from Korea, the Philippines, or China. In other parts of the country, the ethnic composition of the population that is most economically and politically disenfranchised may vary to include more poor whites, women and children of all races and ethnicities, gays, Native Americans, and Chicanos. In New York City this population, which accounts for more than half the population of the city, is menaced in very specific ways by inadequate and formidably expensive housing and medical care; by extremely shoddy and bureaucracy-ridden systems of social services and public education; by an inefficient, militaristic police force; and by increasing street violence and crime promoted by drug trafficking and high rates of drug addiction.

One of the immediate consequences of this system is that except for those people who are rich, white, and male (and therefore virtually never leave the Upper East Side), people live in fear in New York City. And contrary to the impression that one might get based on the overreporting of those incidents that involve black-on-white crime, it is women, children, old people, and especially young men of color who live under the greatest and most constant threat. In the spring and summer of 1991, even as multicultural- ism was being debated in the cultural pages of the Sunday *New York Times* and celebrated by a variety of cultural events in the art world, New York City's nonwhite community was doubly menaced by a series of events. Their symbolic and political weight tended to endow these events with a certain quality of hyperreality, however fleeting.

These events were (1) the black boycott of the Korean fruit market in Flat- bush, held in response to high prices and the alleged ill-treatment of a Hai- tian woman; (2) the trials of the murderers of Yusef Hawkins; (3) the trials of the Central Park rapists; and (4) the story of producer Cameron MacKin- tosh's resistance to the Actors Equity Association's decision that the white, British actor Jonathan Pryce should be replaced by an Asian as the lead in the Broadway version of the musical *Miss Saigon*. Perhaps the media rep- resentation of each of these events deserves its own analysis at some point, although I am not sure that any one of them significantly departs from well- established media patterns in racializing various kinds of "news" stories, especially those stories that include underlying gender issues.[1] Rather in this instance I wish to invoke them, and their extraordinary coverage in the mainstream media, as a background to the present discussion of multicul- turalism.

The character of the response—in the media and in the streets—to the trials of the Central Park rapists and the murder of Yusef Hawkins, to the *Miss Saigon* debate and the Korean store boycott begins to give us some idea of the complex and contradictory attitudes in the dominant culture toward events that take place at the interstices of racial and social difference. The Central Park rape incident was first portrayed as "wilding" by New York City newspapers—a term apparently relevant only to the gang violence of black male youths, for it was not used to describe the attack by white male youths on Hawkins in Bensonhurst.

As for the black boycott of the Korean store in Flatbush and MacKintosh's refusal to bring *Miss Saigon* to Broadway, given the insistence on the part of

Actors Equity that Pryce be replaced by an Asian, the New York City press handled the former event as though it were a transparent case of black-on-Asian racism, whereas the latter event was reported as a blow for "artistic freedom," "freedom of expression," and even "multiculturalism." In the process a mockery was made of the history of Asians in the American theater: Yul Brynner in *The King and I*, as well as the white actor who played Charlie Chan, were paraded as positive examples of "nontraditional casting."

Although it is not surprising to encounter these contradictory attitudes in the mainstream, it is interesting to note how related ideological conflicts are played out in the programming and attitudes of the art world and the cultural Left. Thus far this particular arena of multicultural discourse has centered around attempts by writers, artists, and others to establish relationships or kinships between issues of gender, sexuality, and ethnicity. In the past the problem for cultural activists has been how to theorize links between and establish commonalities among diverse constituencies. The current cultural-Left and art-world versions of multiculturalism respond to this problem by circumventing theoretical discourse altogether in favor of a virtually unrestricted inclusiveness. I suspect that the link multiculturalism is trying to establish between discourses on feminism, sexual preference, and ethnicity could be more usefully viewed as a pragmatic political coalition: the cultural Left version of Jesse Jackson's Rainbow Coalition against the rising tide of the conservative Right.

While multiculturalism's inclination toward unrestricted inclusiveness as opposed to hierarchical exclusiveness doesn't automatically lead to significant structural changes in existing aesthetic and critical priorities and institutional discourses of power, it could offer and thus far has offered more opportunities for critical discussion outside the dominant discourse, and dissent and debate within, than its present aesthetic and critical alternatives. These alternatives I see as (1) a "color-blind" cultural homogeneity that originates in liberal humanist ideology; (2) separatist aesthetics and politics such as "Afrocentrism"; and (3) racist/sexist aesthetics, which range from the cultural fascism of a Hilton Kramer in *The New Criterion* to the social fascism of such right-wing vigilantes as the Ku Klux Klan and the youth gangs that attacked Hawkins in Bensonhurst and the female jogger in Central Park. Thus, despite my reservations about multiculturalism, I have become a reluctant supporter of it. At the same time it is crucial to its usefulness that we view multiculturalism not as an obdurate and unchanging ideological position but as an opportunity for ongoing critical debate.[2]

In an essay on "Endangered: Art and Performance by Men of Color" (a series of performances and exhibitions at Intermedia Arts Minnesota in

1990 that included work by Marlon Riggs and Essex Hemphill and Japanese-American sansei cultural critic and poet David Mura [1990]), the exemplary multiculturalism of this series is juxtaposed with *New York Times* critic Richard Bernstein's remarks on the threat of multiculturalism in an article entitled "The Arts Catch Up with a Society in Disarray" (Bernstein, 1990). Reading Mura's essay, I am reminded that my remarks about multiculturalism are designed to invert Bernstein's. Mura summarizes Bernstein, who characterizes multiculturalism as "the new tribalism," in this way:

> Bernstein quotes Arthur Schlesinger's remark that the melting pot has yielded to the "Tower of Babel." In a seeming effort to complicate Schlesinger's observation, Bernstein admits there is a necessary connection between "artistic matters and the harsh world of the streets, where things seem to be getting conspicuously worse."
>
> What follows is a litany of the recent racial cases that have rocked New York—the rape and assault of the Central Park Jogger; the incident in Bensonhurst; Tawana Brawley; the picketing of Korean grocers; Washington, D.C., Mayor Barry's drug trial. Through such a listing, Bernstein creates an unspoken association in the reader's mind: Minority artists find their sources in the violence of the streets; this is the main difference between minority artists and mainstream tradition. A further implication: minority artists represent the anger and violence of the barbarians at the gate, figures of chaos and dissolution (1990).

While Mura goes on to talk about other issues surrounding multiculturalism, I would like to reclaim here Bernstein's image of social chaos as the basis for any successful multiculturalism. The politicization of art against which he rails is precisely what is absolutely necessary. As for a society in disarray: when has American society ever been in order for people of color and people of sensitivity, for those who are visibly and invisibly other? For the poor, the gay, the women, the children, the disabled, the elderly, the not white? "Society" is now in disarray for Bernstein only because he, and those of his cast of mind, has been forced to recognize that he is not the only one on this planet, that he is, in fact, a distinct although not yet endangered "minority."

In the following remarks I want to analyze three contemporary instances of multicultural programming and artwork: the panel and film series "Sexism, Colonialism, Representation: A Corrective Film Series" (1988) held at the Dia Art Foundation and the Collective for Living Cinema in New York City and organized by feminist film critic Berenice Reynaud and filmmaker Yvonne Rainer; "The Decade Show" (1990), a joint exhibition of the New

Museum of Contemporary Art and the Museum of Contemporary Hispanic Art and the Studio Museum in Harlem; and Rainer's film *Privilege* (1990). These events exemplify an interrelated set of issues relevant to current multicultural practice in the art world: the problematic elision of race within dominant psychoanalytic models of criticism, the accompanying lack of work by people of color that theorizes the relation of race to issues of class and gender, and finally, the tendency in multicultural programming to rely on artists and writers of color as the "subject matter" whose experience is then reconstituted through the theoretical elaboration of white intellectuals.

I want to begin by considering the controversy surrounding the coverage in the pages of *Afterimage* and *Screen* (1988) of the conference "Sexism, Colonialism, Misrepresentation" by the Cuban American critic and curator Coco Fusco. The event consisted of a series of three panels and the screening of forty films from Africa, Australia, the Middle and Far East, Latin America, and Europe. These films included, in addition to many films by people of color, films by white feminists and even one film by a white male on the French Left. Instead of addressing the films—a possibly endless discussion given the range of aesthetic and critical issues arising from any series of independent films—or even all three of the panels, I would like to focus on Fusco's criticism of one of the panels, "The Visual Construction of Sexual Difference."

Before going any further, I should say that not only was I involved in the "Sexism, Colonialism, Misrepresentation" conference but I am acquainted and friendly with Reynaud and Rainer and a close friend of Fusco. As such, it would be both impossible and ill-advised for me to attempt to engage in a thorough critique of their works or their intentions, especially since I am wholly sympathetic to their various endeavors. It is my assumption that Coco, Berenice, Yvonne, and I are on the same side in matters having to do with gender, culture, and the mythologies and realities of "race."

Fusco begins her discussion by reminding us that "the blossoming of multicultural media events" is a response to the "perceived need to redress the effective ethnic segregation of the art world" (1988, 6). The particular division of labor that she describes is one in which white, "avant-garde" intellectuals "theorize about racism while ethnic film and video producers supply 'experiential' materials in the form of testimony and documentation, or in which the white intelligentsia solicits token third world intellectuals to theorize about the question—that is, the problem of the Other—for the white intelligentsia" (7).

Much more insidious to me than the problem of white intellectuals theorizing nativist "data" is the problem of "whiteness" itself as an unmarked term in such conferences and discussions. This was particularly noticeable in the discussions that followed the panel on "The Visual Construction of Sexual Difference." A large portion of time was given over to arguing about what could be expected of psychoanalysis in terms of cultural resistance, whether or not psychoanalysis could be historicized, and whether it could be made to do political readings of cultural production. For the most part the participants seemed thoroughly convinced that such a combination would be unthinkable.

What Fusco says about the problem of this panel is that, first, "to ignore white ethnicity is to redouble its hegemony by naturalizing it. Without specifically addressing white ethnicity there can be no critical evaluation of the construction of the other" (1988, 9). Second, she says, "it did not officially include any interrogation of the Eurocentric prioritization of sexual difference" (9). Of the conference overall, she further says, "there operated a Eurocentric presumption that sexual difference could be separated from other forms of difference and that the theoretical models that privilege gender based sexual difference could be used to understand other difference" (9).

My view, however, is that the challenge of multicultural criticism cannot be met simply by prioritizing other kinds of difference to the exclusion of gender but rather by theorizing sexuality, the body, and gender from other cultural perspectives. The solution is not to reject Freudian, Lacanian, and Foucauldian discourses about sexual difference out-of-hand in order to return to the pragmatics of race and class, for then we confront the old problem of a reductive "social realism" hamstringing critical analysis. Moreover, we don't want to neglect the contribution that feminist thought on the Left (in both cultural studies and psychoanalytic film criticism) has made to thinking about cultural responsibility—specifically the idea that gender and sexuality are socially and culturally constructed, yet individual desire is never fully described or subsumed or determined by such constructions.

It is true that the Left feminist avant-garde has had a rocky and uneven history (which needs to be recorded) in dealing with its own tendencies toward racism, elitism, and cultural apartheid. But it is also true that this sector, unlike any other, has been instrumental in foregrounding a political discourse on art and culture, thus fostering a climate in which it becomes at least hypothetically possible to publicly review and interrogate that very history of exclusion and racism.

The problem remains, however, that within the various progressive political and cultural positions there is an almost total lack of theoretical discourse that relates "race" to gender and sexuality. It is not often recognized that bodies and psyches of color have trajectories in excess of their socially

or culturally constructed identities. What is needed to achieve effective social change is some intervention in the present deployment of these bodies
and psyches, an intervention that demands a sophisticated level of theorization of racial and social identity. This is where the extraordinary, thus far
almost insuperable, difficulty arises in effecting concrete social transformation through discussions of cultural interpretation. In the rush to analyze,
many of us not only reinscribe Eurocentric dominance and hegemony but
also stifle the possibility of more pragmatic interpretations based on the belief that psychoanalytic and other forms of theory simply can't deal with
racial differences.

For me the most interesting thing said in the panel was Joan Copjec's
commentary, drawing from the work of African psychoanalyst Frantz
Fanon, *Black Skins, White Masks* (1967). "The most insidious effect of the
colonizing enterprise is that it constructs the *very desires* of the colonizing
subject. The danger lies in the implied assumption that the content of desire
is defined by the apparatuses of domination," Copjec argued, paraphrasing
Fanon. "Psychoanalysis has never claimed that the subject is totally mastered by the social order. Psychoanalysis is the discourse which obliges us
to think the *subversion of mastery—not* only of the subject by itself, but also
the subject by the social" (Benamou et al., 1990, 46; my emphasis).

Such ideas seem crucial to reconceptualizing the black female subject,
black feminist cultural resistance, and a multicultural consciousness. And
yet the discussion that followed Copjec's remarks seemed extremely uneasy
about the relevance of such a discourse to other than middle-class, white,
feminist women, as though a culturally relativist perspective would preclude
any attempt at psychoanalytic interpretations of subjectivity.

The problem arises in conversations such as this from a basic misunder-
standing. Despite the general critique of essentialism in many feminist discussions, when Reynaud asked the panelists and the audience, "So which
father are we talking about? Are we talking about the heterosexual repressive
father, about the white father, about the master of language, about the colo-
nialist father, the capitalist father? We are constructing these fathers, and we
are constructed by them. When we talk about patriarchy, what are we talking about? Who is the enemy?" (42), she implicitly identified herself and
other white feminists on the Left with the "colonized." Yet neither bell hooks
nor Isaac Julien nor Kobena Mercer, in their subsequent comments, felt as
though they could afford to confuse the position of white women in discourse with the position of the racially and ethnically colonized. "How does
the canon of psychoanalytic discourse deal with the absence of black women
in these new forms [TV, film] of representation?" Julien asked. "I think the

Law of the Father is different from the Law of the Land," Julien further proposed, "and this is an inseparable identity for black subjectivity" (45).

In such exchanges everyone is far too polite to come out and say the thing that needs to be said first — women are not to be trusted just because they're women, any more than blacks are to be trusted because they're black, or gays because they're gay, and so on. Unfortunately, what proves this position, besides the glaring examples of women, blacks, or gays who are profoundly reactionary, is precisely such superficially progressive discourses as feminist psychoanalytic film criticism, which one can read for days on end without coming across any lucid reference to, or critique of, "race."

How am I to understand this discourse as oppositional if it seems to do even less than the classic film tradition it reflects upon to challenge or interrogate racial/cultural apartheid? If racism (racial stereotyping or the confinement of black characters to the margins of the plot) is one of the most fundamental features of the Hollywood classic film tradition, and moreover, if the way in which such racism was imposed upon black female characters is eminently describable, how are we to regard the exclusion of such material altogether from what purports to be an ideological critique?

When Constance Penley suggests in a discussion that "we have to accept psychoanalysis in terms of its quite modest claim. It is a theory of sexual difference. It may not be easily articulable to the other kinds of differences discussed today" (Benamou et al., 1990, 43), I can only respond that I am unwilling to cede sexual difference to white women. Sexual difference is something that women of color, poor women, and gay women share with white, middle-class, heterosexual women. How am I supposed to regard a theory of sexual difference that doesn't apply to women of color? To my mind such theoretical discourses, in which "race" is marginalized, trivialized, and excluded, provide the component parts for the structure of racism in the dominant discourse. This has meant and continues to mean that as you turn to the cultural left you are greeted by the emphatic symbolic representation of your own invisibility. At least "race" is real to the reactionary right.

I'd like to suggest that there may be opportunities for control and theorizing that are not being adequately seized by people of color. People of color need to be engaged in critical and theorizing practices around multiculturalism as it is currently being developed in cultural institutions, in universities, and in public schools. Where I see the most intensive theorizing going on among African American critics, for example, is in academia and in response to *texts*, particularly historical literary texts. Although such activity is important and necessary, I also think that given the political/economic context in which we're living we have a responsibility to reach a broader audience by making connections between the interpretation of canonical texts, tradition building, and what has been happening in the Supreme Court and the Middle East in recent years.

Rainer's film *Privilege* (1990) is a laudable effort on the part of a white, feminist avant-garde filmmaker to integrate issues of race and ethnicity into her work. Yet however intriguing the result is, the film is still depressing for its inability to take seriously the subjectivities of women of color. Again, I want to emphasize that what is at issue here is not whether or not bodies of color are included on the set or in the film (or on the panel). In this case the shortcoming of multiculturalism is a structural dilemma. In order to believe that the subjectivities of women of color have been taken seriously, I have to see a structural change in the ways in which their voices are incorporated into the cultural discourse.

I am also disturbed by the feeling that I need to do this kind of post-mortem on a work of art because, right or wrong, I still believe that artists are special and that the cult status of the work of art is not all bullshit. And I definitely don't believe in censorship. To the contrary, I wish more white feminist cultural producers and artists would foreground "race" in their work. On the other hand, if I haven't the right as a black feminist to critique what they've done, then the positive effects of the effort are canceled.

Although *Privilege* is in an entirely different league from such mainstream filmic attempts to deal with race as *The Long Walk Home* (1990), *Cry Freedom* (1987), *Betrayed* (1988), *Mississippi Burning* (1988), *Round Midnight* (1986), or *Bird* (1988) in that Rainer allows women of color to speak from a variety of positions, the filmmaker still shows no concrete interest in having the women of color themselves theorize race, or class, or gender. The positions from which women of color speak in the film are qualitatively different from, and inferior to, the positions from which white women, white men, and men of color speak.

The ideological positions from which white men speak in the film are the least complex and interesting. Although the lawyer who works in the district attorney's office is portrayed as a humane character, he's still a racist and a sexist. The "white male" medical authorities (some of whom are women) that pervade the film's documentary sections are almost comic in their inflexible pathologizing and palpable ignorance of female sexuality. Nevertheless and needless to say, white men come across with as much authority as ever.

The white women—from the character Jenny whose storytelling structures the film's plot to the former anarchists who are interviewed about their experience of menopause—are repeatedly humanized through close-ups, point-of-view shots, and dialogue. As viewers we are encouraged to identify with Jenny's anxiety about aging, her fantasies about men, her guilty admission that she lied under oath in order to get the Latino Carlos convicted of rape. The interviews with the former anarchists, in which they weave aspects of their political lives into their reflections on menopause, are equally fascinating. The women emerge completely triumphant over the symptoms the white male doctors describe.

The men of color, much like the white men, are highly inflexible and one-dimensional. Almost everything they say is quoted from a text by a male author of color — Piri Thomas, Eldridge Cleaver, Fanon, etc. — selected precisely for their authors' inability to conceptualize black female subjectivity. Moreover, the film dwells on the issue of whether black men or Latino men want to rape white women, a question that I find both irritating and uninteresting. Rainer's film attempts to deal with issues of race and gender but ignores the historical rape of the black woman — which literally founded the African American race and the African Diaspora. What interests me is the larger issue of how dominant ideologies and discourses of power continue to structure desire. This is particularly true for men, black, white, and brown, but it is also true for women.

Which brings us to the women of color in the film. The film begins with a documentary-style interview with a nameless black woman, a "native," about menopause. That woman is my mother, Faith Ringgold. Ringgold is an important African American artist and one of the key early black feminist voices in antiwar, antiracist, and feminist art-world activism. Yet she isn't asked to talk about the impact of race on menopause, or race in the art world or the film world, or anything that might identify her as who and what she is — a highly opinionated and influential black female subject. Three other interviews with black women, at least two of whom were recommended by Ringgold, are interspersed within the main narrative. Ringgold's statement that "Getting older is a bitch" opens the film because it foreshadows the main character Jenny's perspective on aging, not because it makes problematic racial privileges. Rainer admits in a recent interview to having "missed an opportunity to ask the women of color in the film how they felt race impinged on their aging and on their treatment by the medical establishment" (Easterwood, Fairfax, and Poitras, 1990, 9).

Novella Nelson plays the black character Yvonne Washington, whom we are supposed to conceive of as a kind of alter ego of the white Yvonne Rainer. The black Yvonne, we are told, is the "author" of the documentary on menopause for which Ringgold and other black women are interviewed but not asked about race. But despite the apparent combination of a fully developed alternative subjectivity, or alternative position in discourse, Yvonne serves largely as a foil or straight man for Jenny's narcissistic reveries. In interviews Rainer has credited Nelson with having influenced the final form of the film by improvising lines, which she chose to leave in. Nelson's desire to intervene in the script doesn't surprise me at all, given the film's equation, at one point, of racial and gender difference with feces and blood, as an explanation for why white men find "blacks and women" equally contemptible. As far as I'm concerned, this theory of racism, which Rainer borrows from Joel Kovel (1970), is thoroughly inadequate because it discounts the historical accomplishments of African American culture and other cultures of the African Diaspora. For the most part, the alternative subjectivities of women of color are a product of precisely such cultures.

Finally, the representation of Digna (Gabriella Farrar), the Latina who is beaten up by Carlos and subsequently incarcerated in Bellevue mental hospital, is perhaps the most deeply problematic. The antithesis of madness to "voice" is not sufficiently interrogated. Digna "speaks" from Bellevue in a straitjacket about how Latinas are more likely than white women to be diagnosed as schizophrenic. But not only is the viewer never told where this information comes from, there is also no suggestion that this woman might be able to resist or subvert such a deadly cultural hegemony. More to the point: women of color don't generally speak from madhouses. Is the voice and visualization of Digna, a Latina, so deeply problematic for Rainer that she can only be figured "speaking" under the profound erasure of a straitjacket and incarceration in a mental hospital?

Does this mean that Digna is the most oppressed? Is she meant to represent a kind of extreme antithesis to "privilege": the subject who is completely without privilege? Rainer establishes a hierarchical continuum along which the individual's potential capacity for racial and gendered privilege and victimization is carefully calibrated. According to this view, white men can't be victims any more than a Latina can have privilege. In summation, my point is that while women of color were ostensibly allowed to "speak in their own voices" in *Privilege*, they were not empowered to structure the discourse of the film. Nor will women viewers of color be empowered to imagine themselves as structuring subjects of the film discourse. Or if they are (and this would be the best scenario), it will be to rebel against Rainer's invisible but nevertheless real authority as a preeminent feminist filmmaker, as well as that of other well-meaning artists, theorists, and academic intellectuals.

If we move from Rainer's film to the exhibition "The Decade Show: Frameworks of Identity in the 1980s," we encounter an instance of "multicultural" programming that seems intensely engaged by issues of authority, authenticity, who speaks for whom, and how discourses that flatten and trivialize difference are constructed. But there is a level of failure in this exhibition that, again, demonstrates the failure of the present potential for multicultural discourses as processed by white feminists.

"The Decade Show" is an example of programming and theorizing by white feminists. When I speak of white feminists I mean Marcia Tucker, the director of the New Museum, whose background in the art-world left goes back to the 1960s, and Laura Trippi and Gary Sangster, who were the New Museum's curators for this exhibition. Although curators and personnel were involved at the other two institutions, in their catalogue statements they made clear that what they hoped to achieve is distinctly pragmatic (Herzberg, 1990; Patton, 1990). In contrast, the New Museum's conception of the show is self-consciously theoretical. Sharon F. Patton, the Studio Museum's curator for "The Decade Show," begins by writing:

> For the Studio Museum in Harlem, The Decade Show is a curatorial endeavor to insert artists of color, especially African American artists, into the history of contemporary art in the United States. The institutional agendas were clear: first, to pluralism within the theater of the art world. The exhibition is a response, albeit not unique nor the first, to the exclusion of many African American artists from the critical art literature, art history, and exhibitions on American art. Many of the represented artists have been denied, or have had limited access to "mainstream" modernist and postmodernist documentation in terms of professional recognition (other than peers) and legitimization. (1990, 77)

In the context of "socially conscious art," which Patton says is the "agenda of the eighties" (77), she is talking about African American artists getting their piece of the economic pie, sharing in the enormous wealth of the art world. Except with regard to her critique of racial exclusion, Patton is not advocating any profound alteration in the structure of the mainstream.

The same is true of the essay by the curator from the Museum of Contemporary Hispanic Art. While Julia P. Herzberg invokes the necessity for "meaningful cross-cultural dialogue" and "comprehensive inclusion" (1990, 37), her essay, even more than Patton's, provides an inventory of artists of the minority group in question that focuses intensively on the value and originality of their art; in other words, on their ability to produce the transcendent art object upon which the cult value and the market value of art are based.

It is Trippi and Sangster, curators at the New Museum, who take on the task of providing the theoretical overview, the context for interpreting the conjunction of cultural practices, cultural production, and economic, political, and social realities.

A cornerstone of modern Western aesthetics—with its impressionisms and expressionisms, on the one hand, and its ideal of disinterested, universal judgment on the other—is the idea that the autonomous self helped provide a base for the larger edifice of modernity, an edifice built for the benefit of a largely white, largely male few, at the expense of the many. The application of dialogic models to considerations of identity suggested that the self be understood not as an entity but as a provisional construction, a weave of differing dialogic, or discursive, threads (Herzberg, 1990, 64–65).

This exhibition, Trippi and Sangster argue, whether the artist is gay, or feminist, or a person of color, or some combination, is not really about "identity" as a unified, monological field but about "identities." They quote from and rely heavily upon Stuart Hall for this observation. As Hall wrote in *ICA Documents 6* in an essay called "Minimal Selves,"

> It may be true that the self is always, in a sense, a fiction, just as the kinds of "closures" which are required to create communities of identification—nation, ethnic group, families, sexualities, etc.—are arbitrary closures; and the forms of political action, whether movement, parties, or classes, those too, are temporary, partial, arbitrary. It is an immensely important gain when one recognizes that all identity is constructed across difference. (Hall, 1987, 45; quoted in Trippi and Sangster, 1990, 65)

The extraordinary and ironic thing about the authority of Hall's remarks in this context is that although the ideas come from poststructuralist thought, they are filtered through the imagination of a very committed political activist who happens also to be black and originally from the Caribbean. Needless to say, he is not identified as such by Trippi and Sangster's essay. So Hall speaks here not only about ideas but also about material realities. In a very concrete and specific sense, the so-called "identity" of the diasporic subject is constructed from a plurality of "wheres" and "whats," as well as where and what one is not. As Stuart Hall, Gayatri Spivak, Cornel West, Hortense Spillers, bell hooks, Trinh T. Minh-ha, and so many other people of color who are interested in what is vaguely called "theory" might remind us, the nature of the overview changes depending upon the politics of location of the author. For instance, in Trippi and Sangster's essay, the reality of the art world in the 1980s is described in terms of the metaphor of a board game called Trivial Pursuit, and the art of making a deal is discussed in the sense that Donald Trump might use the word "deal." How real is this picture for artists of color or for critics or museum administrators of color? Where is the overview of artists and cultural critics of color on the Left emanating from marginal theories and practices themselves? Don't we need one? Who will write it?

Originally published in *Afterimage* 19, no. 3 (October 1991): 6–9.

Notes

1. In each case gender provides an underlying impetus for an explicitly racial story: in the Korean fruit market boycott a black woman was allegedly struck by an Asian male; in the Central Park rape a white woman was raped by black and Puerto Rican boys and men; in the Yusef Hawkins murder, we were told the initial provocation had to do with the suspicion that a white Bensonhurst girl was dating a black boy. In the case of the Cameron Mackintosh/ *Miss Saigon* debacle, the part that Jonathan Pryce played was a pimp who sells sex with Vietnamese women to mostly white American GIS. See Joan Didion's interesting article in the *New York Review of Books* (1991) on why the rape or murder victim in nationally reported crime cases is always a "young, white attractive female" (45).

2. As the 1990 debates on culture in the mainstream press tended to center on censorship, the following year's round of debates centered on the notion of "political correctness." Interestingly enough, if one sees the censorship debate and the political correctness debate as stages in a larger, ongoing multiculturalism debate, then one will also see that the continuous underlying motivation of the dominant discourse is to delay or forgo the validation of alternative subjectivities and discourses as long as possible in favor of re-consolidating the center as one in which all debates are between "the Left" and "the Right," both of which are viewed as white (they have no ethnicity or "race"). Of course, racial issues are continually subsumed by the so-called larger debates of censorship or political correctness, and in the process, blacks are neatly objectified (from the naked, black male bodies in Robert Mapplethorpe's photographs to Jules Feiffer's cartoon about political correctness in which a black female college student gloats over having been able to function as a racist for a semester).

Works Cited

Benamou, C., J. Copjec, M. Gever, b. hooks, and G. Koch. 1990. The visual construction of sexual difference. *Motion Picture* 3, nos. 3–4 (special issue documenting the proceedings of the conference "Sexism, Colonialism, Misrepresentation"): 34–48.

Bernstein, R. 1990. The arts catch up with a society in disarray. *New York Times*, 2 September, sec. 2, pp. 1, 12–13.

Didion, J. 1991. New York: Sentimental journeys. *New York Review of Books*, 17 January, pp. 45–51.

Easterwood, K., S. Fairfax, and L. Poitras. 1990. Interview with Yvonne Rainer. In *Yvonne Rainer: Declaring Stakes*. San Francisco: San Francisco Cinematheque.

Fanon, F. 1967. *Black Skin, White Masks*. New York: Grove.

Fusco, C. 1988. Fantasies of oppositionality: Reflections on recent conferences in Boston and New York. *Afterimage* 16, no. 5 (1988): 6–9; *Screen* 29, no. 4 (1988) ("The Last 'Special Issue' on Race?").

Hall, S. 1987. Minimal selves. In L. Appignanesi, ed., *ICA Documents 6*. London: Institute of Contemporary Art.

Herzberg, I. P. 1990. Re-membering identity: Visions of connections. In *The Decade Show: Frameworks of Identity in the 1980s*. New York: New Museum of Contemporary Art.

Kovel, J. 1970. *White Racism: A Psychohistory*. New York: Pantheon.

Mura, D. 1990. The minority artist and the nature of difference: or, Caliban speaks. *Public Art Review*.

Patton, S. F. 1990. The agenda in the eighties: Socially conscious art. In *The Decade Show: Frameworks of Identity in the 1980s*. New York: New Museum of Contemporary Art.

Trippi, L., and G. Sangster. 1990. From Trivial Pursuit to the art of the deal: Art making in the eighties. In *The Decade Show: Frameworks of Identity in the 1980s*. New York: New Museum of Contemporary Art.

26.

Black Women in Popular Culture:

From Stereotype to Heroine

I would like to begin by outlining the major touchstones of this talk. First, I believe that the most important questions to be asking in the study of popular culture are not whether any particular instance is good or bad, positive or negative, progressive or regressive. Despite the certainty and conviction with which we usually approach any occasion of popular culture production, without adequate contextualization, we really are not in a position to decide what is good and what is bad, or why.

Second, further historical investigation is crucial to formulating an adequate definition and delineation of the domain of popular culture. In particular, we have not yet arrived at this point in regard to the impact of peoples of color, or the impacts on them. My third point, which actually presents unprecedented obstacles to research, is that popular culture is inclined to be international rather than local, regional, or national in its formations. One of the things that we can say about popular culture is that it travels well, and we know that it was already traveling significantly from country to country, from continent to continent in the nineteenth century. The widespread reproduction of visual images almost immediately began to break through language barriers as well. For instance, cinema, which was silent in the beginning, traveled significantly from the very start.

My final point is to suggest that popular culture can provide the other side of modernism's high cultural narrative. While the focus of my current work is primarily North America, popular culture has always traveled so freely between the continents that one has to consider the iconography of popular culture as an international or global discourse, like modernism. Indeed, some scholars have begun to suggest that we should refer to a modernist popular culture, which paralleled the rise of modernism in fine art and high culture. While the ideology of high modernism, itself, implies a selection in which most cultural production is cast by the wayside as insufficiently rigorous or avant-garde, modernist popular culture recuperates the popular as politically influential and culturally revealing.

I would propose that a history of a modernist popular culture would be much more populous and inclusive, and that cultural production could then include those previously shunted aside categories and genres once and still so popular with the masses. When related to the relevant political narratives, as well, we begin to be able to make sense of that which seems to make no sense at all.

So the intention of these opening remarks is to tell you regretfully that I am not going to be presenting the hypothesis that the image of black women in popular culture has progressed from stereotype to heroine, although this is one of the many things that the image of the black woman can do, from time to time, but I would like to forestall considerations of structural progress until we understand a bit more about the conditions of production and reception. I am not prepared to say that there has been any progress in the images of black women in popular culture. Popular culture is really still such a new and young thing, I am not at all sure that any of us would be qualified to recognize progress even it were right under our nose. Progress relative to what? Where did we come from, with respect to popular culture? Where are we trying to go? Another way to pose the same questions is to ask, what is progress in popular culture? What is popular culture? Well it is culture, and it is popular. Beyond that, I am not so sure since popular culture has been constantly changing and expanding since its first appearances and continues to do so in our current historical moment.

Not only am I suggesting that images of black women in popular culture have not progressed or improved but also that perhaps this isn't the right question to be asking at all. The more important question concerns how images of black women are related to other cultural constructs. How do images of black women in popular culture influence other cultural constructs and how are they influenced by them? Or in other words, what is the relationship of images of black women in popular culture to everything else?

At this juncture in my investigation, I can't really answer very many of these questions. The kind of quantitative and empirical study, as well as the elaboration of the available primary sources, has not yet occurred. But the larger goal here is simply to disrupt the assumption that most of us automatically make in connection with popular culture, which is, first, that popular culture should or could be progressive, and second, that "heroines" are automatically superior to "stereotypes," that more is better than less, and most importantly, that visibility is automatically superior and more progressive than invisibility.

The point is also, I suppose, to get you to think seriously about how the visible world is constructed and of reproducible images in particular. Presumably, human beings used to live their entire lives almost completely without them. Now they are everywhere and it has almost become impossible to imagine life without the constant flow of imagery of one kind or another through the television, through the computer, through video, film, and advertising billboards and neon signs, through T-shirts and articles of clothing, and so forth. This situation did not come into existence in some organic way. It was constructed, and constructed fairly recently, over a period of the last two hundred years or so. It was constructed simultaneously with the rise of certain ideological assumptions regarding the immutability of certain categories of existence or identity, namely gender, sexuality, and race, and the relationship among them.

Needless to say, these ideological assumptions work best when we remain almost entirely unaware of how they function, although self-consciousness doesn't automatically negate them either.

So, in other words, we are receiving more and more of our ideas via this new universal or global or international language of images. The passive response, the usual response, is equivalent to affirming that the declarations this language makes are descriptively correct, in a process that may be something like "cultural hegemony" as described by Antonio Gramsci and Stuart Hall, or "ideology" as described by Roland Barthes.

Moreover, how one could or should properly make the active response, which might achieve an intervention or negation, is extremely unclear.

Having said all this, and thereby, I hope, given you some indication of the complexity of the crucial question, which is that we don't really know how to define popular culture, I want to go on to lay out some of the perimeters of the universe with respect to images of black women that I am exploring.

NOW, YOU MIGHT think that with such a topic, I would talk primarily about contemporary images. Everybody knows that popular culture is contemporary but, in fact, my view is that it is merely confusing to begin looking at popular culture by looking at contemporary popular culture. It is both too obvious and too opaque. I prefer to look at what some might call the roots of popular culture, and what others might call genealogies of various highly repeatable images, and the discourses that supported or produced them.

What were the original causes of popular culture? When did it start? Well, I am not at all sure what the answer to the first question is, but the answer to the second question might be the middle nineteenth century, or anywhere from fifty years earlier to fifty years later than that, depending, of course, upon how you ultimately define popular culture. The preconditions, rather than the causes, would be the invention and development of technologies of reproduction, such as printing presses, photography, film, image projection and light shows, dioramas and other popular forms of visualization, and the invention and development of technologies of communications, including most of the formerly mentioned phenomena as well as electricity, the steam engine, the automobile and the airplane engine—on the theory that faster travel facilitates and is ancillary to greater communication, such as the changes and expansion of mail services with the development of faster travel. I believe we can also say that thus far the evolution of popular culture has been largely a phenomenon under Western control but with highly significant interventions however coming from non-Western influences, and there is also an overall tendency for popular culture not to remain national or even hemispheric but rather to incline toward surmounting former ideological barriers to a formation that is global and international, following related trends in modern capitalism and structural economy.

A lot of people I know who are doing work in cinema studies are calling this field that looks at the proliferation of popular culture visual forms in the nineteenth century as precinematic. Sometimes these developments— performance trends such as blackface minstrelsy, variety shows, vaudeville, burlesque, and circuses that display genres such as freak shows, human exhibitions, natural history museums, colonial expositions and ethnographic museums; narrative genres, such as melodrama, gothic horror, farce; and pictorial genres such as Orientalism, primitivism or film noir, caricature, slapstick, and animated cartoons—evolve into popular or lower cultural forms. Sometimes they evolve into, or are subsumed by, high cultural forms, at least temporarily, such as cases in which a high modernism will incorporate popular cultural forms. An obvious example would be Dada or Pop Art. Or more often than not they are subsumed by that growing category of respectable but not cutting edge culture that you might call middle brow, often also thought of as somehow more feminine than masculine.

Within a scholarly context, up until relatively recently, all of American culture was thought of even by many Americans as, at best, middle brow, and at worst, vulgar and low. But these days it seems clearer and clearer that this kind of prejudice was a result of inadequate research, data collection, analysis, and knowledge production, not to mention also the exclusivity of that population that was able to participate in constructing the issues of investigation. Those who study popular culture have really just begun to achieve a fuller cultural picture of the past, which we can see, more and more, must include, in order to be precise, the integration of popular culture forms and their relationship to ongoing political discourses at the time. When you proceed in this manner, of course, you get an entirely different perspective on high culture as well.

We will begin with technologies of communication and reproduction but not because they are at the beginning. Indeed, many cultural critics, as diverse as Fredric Jameson and Jonathan Crary, have even suggested that these technologies emerge so forcefully at this time in Western cultures precisely in order to do certain kinds of ideological work such as the observation, study, categorization, and specular control of that which is presumably non-Western, as a kind of follow up to ideas about race, gender, and sexuality generated by Enlightenment philosophies. Inadvertently, the focus is upon the Other, including the "decadent" civilizations of the Orient; the cultural inferiority of black, red, and yellow peoples; the primitives and the barbarians of the aboriginal populations of Oceania, Asia, Africa, and the Americas; the biologically and culturally feminine and nonheterosexual; the pathological, the insane, the criminal and the criminally insane; and even those more speculative categories of the invisible and the dead, which begin to completely disappear from the domain of the real in Western culture after this point with the rise of scientific, historical, and social science discourses.

I say inadvertently because there is always a great deal of cultural discourse in the West in which the "Other," particularly a racialized "Other" appears to be of no concern whatsoever. I would maintain that this is almost never really the case, and that absence, chasms, and lacunae are also susceptible to potential readings.

TO SPEAK SPECIFICALLY of the black woman in nineteenth-century visual representations, with respect, in particular, to those images that might have been carried over to cinema, I have identified three dominant figures and two lesser figures, which appear to be much less susceptible to popular repetition. The three principal images of the black woman that emerge in the nineteenth century are the mammy, the mulatta, and the female trickster figure. Lesser figures would include the strong, militant black woman, such as emerges in the image of a Harriet Tubman or a Sojourner Truth, sometimes an obvious variation on the Mammy, and the black woman idealized and romanticized within the context of an Orientalist imagery.

Of the three dominant images, I would suggest that even before slavery had ended, the mulatta had become the most important. I still have a lot more research to do regarding this figure in the broader international context. Sources of mulatto images are probably widespread, albeit still uncollected, wherever Africans were taken as slaves or as specular curiosities.

In the American context, one really prominent narrative source is *Uncle Tom's Cabin* (*UTC*), the novel written by Harriet Beecher Stowe and published in installments in a free soil journal in 1852. By the time the actual novel had appeared in full, it had already been adapted to the stage. At that time apparently copyright law was not what it is today so the fact that Stowe refused to have anything to do with stage adaptation left the field open to anyone and everyone who wanted to launch a version of her original text, as long as it was somewhat different. According to cultural historians, in the next fifty years or so, *Uncle Tom's Cabin* would become the most popular narrative ever, with reportedly five hundred *Tom* companies touring this country and abroad at the turn of the century. It should be mentioned, however, that the most popular versions were musical adaptations of variety revues.

With the widespread proliferation of versions of *Uncle Tom's Cabin*, you might guess that the versions ran the ideological gamut from virulently racist to benign, from proslavery to antislavery, from melodramatic or tragic to comedic and slapstick. Like so many iconic popular cultural texts, it was made to say both everything and nothing by virtue of sheer repetition and banality. But at the root, there were three highly compelling narratives subsumed under its title. Any one of the three, or all but one could and would be left out of any particular account, leaving the emphasis entirely on only one of the narratives, or the text might even be reduced to a series of tableaux, among which the most popular were the Death of Little Eva, the Death of Uncle Tom, the sale of Uncle Tom, Legree beating Uncle Tom, Eliza escaping barefoot across the ice, clutching her child in her arms, Topsy going through her characteristically somnambulistic routine, and Uncle Tom holding Little Eva on his lap.

To outline the three principle narratives in *Uncle Tom's Cabin* and to compare them with subsequent interpretations and variations is important because the structural variations in the uses of this text in relationship to concurrent political developments and the progress of racial discourse has much to reveal about the character of popular culture. Stowe interweaves the three, not necessarily in this order, for those of you who don't know or have forgotten this once popular text: the first narrative concerns Uncle Tom's plight, from the time he discovers that he has been sold, along with Eliza's little boy George, by his gentle but weak-willed master, Mr. Shelby. In preference to selling a lot of the other slaves, and disrupting a variety of the slave families, Shelby opts for selling his favorite slave. Extraordinarily strong, trustworthy, useful, and at the peak of maturity is how Stowe describes Uncle Tom.

In the beginning of the novel, Tom is a god-fearing, religious man whose ethical seriousness and courage are unquestioned by all who know him. He is also completely nonviolent, even saintly and quite deliberately constructed as a Christ figure. In the course of the book, Tom has three masters: Mr. Shelby, St. Claire, and the evil Simon Legree.

Included in the St. Claire episodes, Uncle Tom is adopted by Little Eva, St. Claire's daughter, after he rescues her from drowning. Her premature death from consumption has always figured as a popular cultural high point in most versions of *UTC* because of her saintliness. In contrast to the purity of Little Eva, the dirty, unkempt, wild and chaotic figure of Topsy, the female trickster figure in Stowe's text, is always juxtaposed with Little Eva, along with Eva's spinsterly Northern aunt, Ms. Ophelia. Topsy is presented by Stowe as the abused child, unloved, parentless, and immoral, a direct reflection upon the weaknesses of the institution of slavery. St. Claire teases Ophelia that despite her Northern liberalism, she can't even touch Topsy without cringing. Very soon after their first meeting, Ophelia gives Topsy a good bath, cleaning her up, dressing her appropriately for age and gender and instructing her personally. Ultimately, after Little Eva and St. Claire have died, Ophelia takes Topsy North to be educated. Curiously, however, Topsy is always presented theatrically as she initially appears, an uncontrollable and filthy sprite who steals Aunt Ophelia's ribbons in pure acts of indecipherable spite.

Tom's final master is the evil and dissolute Simon Legree. Legree tries to train him to beat other slaves, to be a slave driver. Of course, Tom refuses and in an attempt to break him, Legree whips Tom nearly to death. Tom's story is the best known, the best remembered, and the most reproducible of the three narratives.

The second narrative configuration centers on the affairs of the mulatta Eliza, her mulatto husband George, and their son, all of who can pass for white, the only kind of mulattos who seem to matter much in literature of the nineteenth century. At the beginning of the novel, George is already running away because his master is unbearably mean and George is quite politically militant. Eliza decides to run away when she discovers that her child is about to be sold along with Uncle Tom. Eliza successfully escapes to the North with her son, rendezvous with her husband, and they subsequently are forced by the pursuit of fugitive slaves in the North to retreat to Canada where George continues to be quite politically outspoken and active. Aspects of this story have become highly popular and others have not. For instance, Eliza's relationship to her child and their escape is often represented but not George's politics and militancy.

The third narrative figuration, which is the least popular of the three but the most interesting to me, finally unites the other two. It is the story of Cassy, also a mulatta, Simon Legree's degraded housekeeper and personal concubine. She intercedes on behalf of Uncle Tom when Legree beats him. When Legree subsequently demotes her to field work and takes a younger mulatta girl Emmaline for his housekeeper and mistress, Cassy conspires to fool Legree into thinking the house is haunted and manages to rescue the younger girl from a fate truly worse than death by escaping with her. Uncle Tom is finally beaten to death because he refuses to disclose to Legree where Cassy and the girl have gone. Cassy and the younger girl end up in Canada where they are united with Eliza and George, and they all turn out to be related. As I recall, Cassy, who is an extremely heroic figure by any calculation, turns out to be Eliza's long-lost mother.

In 1903, the first film version of *UTC* was made by Edwin Porter. Most of the black parts were played in blackface, including Uncle Tom played by Porter himself. I suspect that part of the rationale for this is that physical contact between whites and blacks was really not permissible after the turn of the century because of Jim Crow laws, as well as state censorship boards. It runs about twenty minutes and consists of a series of tableaux with intertitles. The presentation of both Uncle Tom and Topsy are completely conventionalized in the 1903 film. The one thing that is an innovation of the period is that a cakewalk segment by an actual black corps of entertainers is inserted into the sequence celebrating Little Eva's return home.

THIS REPRESENTATION OF black entertainment history simultaneously with the most extraordinarily repressive conditions for blacks and other racial and ethnic minorities is an interesting feature. Black entertainers extended upon and reinterpreted the conventions of blackface minstrelsy, in some ways subverting its deadly hegemony at the same time that their rebellion against white norms was not apparent since they traveled freely throughout the South, performing for both white and black audiences. The particulars of segregation are not fully understood.

This particular sequence in the 1903 performance is representative of stage productions of *Tom* companies at the turn of the century, in which a variety of entertainment interludes employing huge companies of black singers and dancers were employed interspersed with the flow of a series of iconographic representations of *Uncle Tom's Cabin*. As you can see, they represent the interjection of an urban sophistication, ragtime and post-slavery performance practices and discourses into this nostalgically Southern, rural antebellum scenario.

In the seventh version, which was made in 1914 and directed by William Robert Daly, for the World Film Corporation, for the first time Uncle Tom was played by a famous black actor named Sam Lucas who had been a famous blackface minstrelsy performer and a songwriter. Indeed, he had been one of the pioneers in the black entertainment industry of the previous era. At the same time, he was most famous for his portrayal of Uncle Tom on the stage.

The film was made in the final years of his career when he was in his sixties so his Uncle Tom was necessarily an elderly man. He died soon after, having contracted pneumonia, the story goes, during the film by actually jumping in the water to rescue Little Eva. There are several advances over previous versions, aside from the fact that Uncle Tom is played by a black person. All of the obviously black people are played by actually black people with one exception: Topsy.

While there are several indications that this is a very politically advanced and even subversive version of *UTC*, the presentation of Topsy is almost indistinguishable from her presentation in the 1903 version. It is played in blackface by a white female actor famous for playing Topsy. She is a flat, farcical, and stereotypically ridiculous character. Despite the obvious need to dignify the presentation of Uncle Tom and all the other themes Stowe's novel pursued, nevertheless, Topsy was still used as comic relief in an entirely uncomedic version of *UTC*. I think it is interesting that this is a black female stereotype. And, indeed, Topsy is representative of what you might call the impact of popular entertainment values on the text. By 1914, she continues to echo the performance standards of the period in a manner incommensurate with the other features of the text. Why? I don't really know, but it would seem to suggest that images of black women did not progress in the same direction or in the same manner as images of black men. I will return to that subject later.

WHEREAS THE REBELLIOUSNESS of Cassy, her heroism and courage are presented more strongly than perhaps any other of the film versions of *UTC*, of which there were more than ten, from what I am able to tell by reading about them. Also, quite surprisingly, a black male slave shoots Legree fatally at the end, which is not what happens in the novel. So in this instance, the film version actually goes beyond the novel in its militancy.

Friday evening I will be introducing *Birth of a Nation* at the Brooklyn Museum. There is no convention of black film history more taken for granted than the idea so emphasized in Donald Bogle's history that the first appearance of the black buck stereotype was in the form of Gus in D. W. Griffith's *Birth of a Nation*. Gus, who pursues a young white girl, forcing her to jump off a cliff, is lynched and castrated (depending upon the version) by the Klan in *Birth*. Gus is played by an obviously and ostentatiously white actor who grimaces horribly under his black cork. He is just about the most thoroughly unconvincing imitation of a black man I've ever seen. But in the seventh version of *UTC*, which was released one year before *Birth*, an actual, phenotypically black man actually shoots Legree on camera. Of course, he shows no obvious interest in white women and perhaps that is more the key than militancy to the essential features of the black buck. This is a controversy well placed in the early part of the century in American history, a controversy over which a lot of unnecessary black blood was spilled.

Obviously this issue of the image of black men has direct bearing upon images of black women, since the two are somehow presumably complementary. Yet at this time, the variety of black male images historically available are much broader than those usually discussed—first, this image of the black male who murders Legree in this version of *UTC*; also the images of Jack Johnson's fights, which were widely circulated on film earlier in the century were deeply influential and impacted negatively on the notion of permissible representations of black men in which both *UTC* and *Birth* were made. Also, I would suggest as well that we look at images of other men of color during the period and juxtapose them with historical events: the representations of Native Americans, say in the Wild West show, versus the extermination and containment policies being employed by the military in the West at the same time; the genocide of the Asian male and females in the Philippines versus the presentation of Asians in such films as D. W. Griffith's *Broken Blossoms* and Cecil B. DeMille's *The Cheat*—all of which reflected the evolving perceptions of race under the pressures of continental expansion and imperialism.

Two things are interesting to me—this is occurring at the same time that there is a great deal of tension around issues of lynching, prompting Ida B. Wells's celebrated rebuttals, as well as the developments of the Niagara Movement and the emergence of the NAACP, which were partially born in the struggle against the early exhibition of *Birth*. Also, there is no comparable flow of images of black women. The males are the irrefutably dominant figure.

Second, nevertheless, the dominant image of women, the mulatta and the trickster figure, i.e., Topsy, are both complementary to the pressures being exerted on the male figures. The mulatta, a figure of great consternation, because she is the product of the dreaded and forbidden union of black and white, reappears as the despicable and sinisterly insane Lydia in *Birth*, Senator Stoneman's conniving mulatta housekeeper. Not accidentally. One of Dixon's and Griffith's purposes in writing *Birth* was to refute *UTC*. Whereas Topsy completely reverses the threat of the nameless, faceless black threat of a subversive masculinity. Unsexed, primeval and inchoate, Topsy nevertheless is completely transformed by Stowe into a potential model citizen, a development that cinema cannot accommodate to the screen even seventy years after the publication of the novel.

Originally presented as a talk at Rutgers University in 1997.

Works Cited

Bernardi, Daniel, ed. 1996. *The Birth of Whiteness: Race and the Emergence of U.S. Cinema*. New Brunswick, N.J.: Rutgers University Press.

Clifford, James. 1991. *The Predicament of Culture: Twentieth-Century Ethnography, Literature, and Art*. Cambridge, Mass.: Harvard University Press.

Coombes, Annie E. 1996. *Reinventing Africa: Museums, Material Culture, and the Popular Imagination in Late Victorian and Edwardian England*. New Haven, Conn.: Yale University Press.

Dower, John W. 1986. *War without Mercy: Race and Power in the Pacific War*. New York: Pantheon Books.

Duncan, Carol. 1995. *Civilizing Rituals: Inside Public Art Museums*. London: Routledge.

Haraway, Donna. 1989. *Primate Visions: Gender, Race, and Nature in the World of Modern Science*. New York: Routledge.

Kaplan, Amy, and Donald Pease, eds. 1993. *Cultures of United States Imperialism*. Durham, N.C.: Duke University Press.

Morton, Patricia. 1991. *Disfigured Images: The Historical Assault on Afro-American Women*. New York: Greenwood Press.

Nederveen Pieterse, Jan. 1992. *White on Black: Images of Africa and Blacks in Western Popular Culture*. New Haven, Conn.: Yale University Press.

Shohat, Ella, and Robert Stam. 1994. *Unthinking Eurocentrism: Multiculturalism and the Media*. London: Routledge.

27.

The Search for the Good Enough
Mammy: Multiculturalism, Popular
Culture, and Psychoanalysis

By now I suppose everybody knows on the Right, Left, and in the middle that multiculturalism is not the promised land. As employed by universities, museums, and advertising companies, the utopian idealism of a multicultural philosophy becomes a pragmatic institutional technique for neutralizing the myriad economic, political, and social demands of diversity. As we can readily see in such institutional practices from the Whitney Biennial to a Benetton ad campaign, multiculturalism doesn't necessarily redistribute power or resources. Although a few individual people of color may achieve employment, or rise higher in the ranks than they might have otherwise, collectively, people of color aren't necessarily empowered by multiculturalism. Rather, an ambiance of cultural diversity (a subaltern mise-en-scene, if you will) can serve to obscure the fact that nothing at all has changed for the diverse populations in question. More importantly, there may be little alteration in how the dominant group—or the oppressed groups, for that matter—conceptualizes diversity.

And yet while we're slapping the wrists of the Whitney Museums or the Benettons (mostly for being pretentious and holier than thou), let us not forget that the Whitney is doing better than the Museum of Modem Art and that Benetton's ads led the way for the recent increase in the use of models of color in ads for Oil of Olay, Ralph Lauren, the Gap, and other companies;[1] which is to say that, even at its most cynical and pragmatic, there is something about multiculturalism that continues to be worth pursuing. For all sorts of reasons—in order to save the planet and live at peace—we do need to find many ways of publicly manifesting the significance of cultural diversity, of integrating the contributions of people of color into the fabric of our society.

But the problem with multiculturalism, in general, is that it tends to lump people of color together. People of color don't think of themselves as people of color, for the most part. Perhaps we should (for global reasons), but most of us don't. Most of our problems seem, at least to us, very specific and very local. So perhaps the real problem is that unified, monological identities such as people of color or whiteness are always unrepresentative fictions, just as globalizing, totalizing theories never work. Because we conceptualize our problems in terms of unworkable fictions (that is, whiteness, people of color), is it inevitable that our solutions will also be ultimately unworkable (from multiculturalisms to Rainbow Coalitions)? I'm not sure.

A year or so ago when I put together the Black Popular Culture Conference at the Dia Center for the Arts, I thought that a focus on popular culture in cultural analysis would help cultural critics to deal with the material, historical, and emotional specificity of populations of color. I also thought that using popular culture as primary cultural texts would help to draw African American cultural analysis, in general, to a higher level of engagement with contemporary social, political, and economic issues. I suspect that's been true, perhaps because African American cultural analysis is always inclined in this direction in any case, but there were some unanticipated limitations to this approach as well.

First, popular culture is not some obscure subsidiary of contemporary cultural production. Given the global revolution that's taking place in telecommunications and computer technology, popular culture is *the* main event on the world stage. As such, it is not a cohesive or singular entity nor can it be effectively described at this point because it is still, I suspect, in a relatively early stage of development. The point about popular culture, or mass culture, or the overlap of the two, is that it is overwhelming, drowning out, and subsuming other forms of cultural production. In particular, so-called fine art—from opera to painting and sculpture—is being irreversibly affected by contact with popular culture.

But what I've come to realize is that the way in which one regards (or disregards) such issues is symptomatic of one's approach to cultural analysis in general. Without taking the global cultural and economic revolution of telecommunications and computer technology into account, we can simply read black popular culture, or indeed any popular culture, precisely the same way we've always read Shakespeare or Milton—not in its social or cultural context. Popular culture isn't inherently a subversive text. We needn't necessarily read it as a living, unfolding drama. It is just as subject to slaughter through analysis as Shakespeare is, or, indeed, precisely because we imagine that it encompasses only the desires of the "low," we can allow ourselves to take shortcuts and liberties in analysis that we could scarcely imagine in dealing with so-called high culture.

I've gotten really interested in the possibility of a creative use of psychoanalysis in combination with multiculturalism and popular culture to think about issues of race conjoining gender and sexuality in the relationship of culture to society. This area of potential study seems to me particularly suggestive because feelings about race, and the relationship of race to gender and sexuality, tend to work so unconsciously in cultural representation and social relations in the West.

I am well aware that a lot of people feel as though psychoanalysis of any kind is utterly useless in social analysis because of its developmental ahistoricism, but what continues to draw me back to it, after all, is the idea of the "unconscious" as a generalizable repository of all those social and psychological impulses that don't fall comfortably under the heading of the intentional. When I suggest the "unconscious" should be generalizable, it is not because I think there is only one kind of unconscious and that it can only function in a single way. In fact, I think it more than likely that if there is an unconscious, it is plural, variegated, and probably somewhat alterable by historical time and geographical space, although not at the rate of history or culture themselves.

For example, when we suggest that an Oedipus complex might have made more sense for the nineteenth-century Viennese bourgeoisie Freud described than for twentieth-century Vietnamese youth, we are taking into account that the psychological operations described by the Oedipus complex, indeed, are altered by context, environment, culture, and history. This doesn't mean, however, that the identity formation accounted for by an Oedipus complex shifts with each permutation of context, environment, culture, and history. In other words, psychological functions may alter in time although not necessarily in precise synchronization with history, culture, and environment. Crosscutting the other systems, the unconscious, nevertheless, is less sensitive to change.

Because the idea of an unconscious is still fairly controversial in most circles, there hasn't been a lot of work done on diversifying notions of the unconscious. But so many processes in culture and society operate at the unconscious level—the economy, social change, individual and collective psy-

chology, gender, race, sexuality, hegemony, our knowledge of grammar—
that the reality of some kind of unconscious realm seems to me fairly certain.

Of course, the problems in psychoanalysis arise in terms of the specific descriptions of how the unconscious is constructed and how it functions, particularly in terms of gender, sexuality, and race formation. Although there is a great deal of debate in regard to most of the major tenets of psychoanalytic thought, all of the approaches still flaunt their color blindness. I think that the general failure to take into account the impact of "race" or cultural diversity is not necessarily owing to anything intrinsic to psychoanalysis but, rather, has to do with who uses psychoanalysis and what it is generally used for. It is very rare for anybody of color to write about psychoanalysis. The most prominent exception has been Frantz Fanon. (Because of his sexism, misogyny, and his misguided ideas about revolution, Fanon's work seems to me extremely limited in its present-day application.) Also, because white psychoanalysis hasn't been interested in people of color, in general, or thought that "race" played an important role in identity formation, certain kinds of questions having to do with race never get posed.

Let's face it: "Race" isn't taken seriously as a category by most academic or intellectual discourse in the West, so why should psychoanalysis be any different? Furthermore, because people of color, when perceived as mentally ill, are generally thought to fall into the category of those who are too sick to be reached by psychoanalysis, what would be the point of trying to think through ways of describing "race" in psychoanalytic terms? In order to communicate with whom?

But there are already lots of different kinds of psychoanalysis and there could be a lot more. There is the feminist psychology of Phyllis Chesler and Dorothy Dinnerstein and the feminist psychoanalysis of Nancy Chodorow and Carol Gilligan and, embedded in such practices, a reconsideration of issues having to do with the failure of Freudian psychoanalysis to deal with the reality of his patients' stories of incest and sexual abuse. There's the object relations theories of Melanie Klein and W. D. Winnicott and others and the very important question of whether or not the mother-child dyad, as formulated by Adrienne Rich and other feminists, is actually the cite of primary identity formation in men and women instead of the Oedipus complex. Further, did Freud really scrap the Seduction Theory because he couldn't deal with history, social reality, and the reality of trauma?

Moreover, in current practices of psychoanalysis and in radical theories of psychoanalysis, the question often asked is how accurate are victims in reporting their experience of trauma? At what age do we become accurate witnesses? What is the role of fantasy and the unconscious in the experience, recollection, or memory of trauma? Moreover, what kind of psychological damage does trauma cause and can such victims be reached by psychoanalysis? If one thinks about Toni Morrison's novels *The Bluest Eye* or *Beloved* or Alice Walker's *Meridian* or Toni Cade Bambara's *The Salteaters*, such questions take on an even greater resonance.

Who can be reached by psychoanalysis? Perhaps even more to the point, what causes mental illness? Can talk therapy reach people who are mentally ill? Can psychoanalysis be used as a means of social revolution, as some radicals have suggested? Are the mentally ill being unfairly oppressed by our categorization of them as mentally ill?

Is psychoanalysis accurately understood, itself, as a form of repression? Or is it just that we've been paralyzed much too long by the mistaken assumption that psychoanalysis designates a limited and narrow bourgeois Eurocentric problematic? Is it possible that, instead, psychoanalysis simply stands in for an entire, unconscious level of experience most of us have barely begun to explore?

Moreover, there is the way in which cultural analysis has appropriated various forms of psychoanalysis. In particular, I have been interested in feminist literary and film criticism and the use of feminist readings of Lacan's readings of Freud to reconsider the role of fantasy and the unconscious in cultural texts. Also, more to the point, Michel Foucault's description of psychoanalysis as the definitive context for the development of the human sciences in the late nineteenth century in *The Order of Things*[2] is highly compelling.

Such questions and observations to me seem to be highly suggestive for thinking about problems of African American cultural and social analysis. Large numbers of African Americans (as well as other peoples of color) continue to be traumatized by the American experience. Moreover, a great deal of discussion about the African American aptitude for progress continues to circulate around speculation regarding the structure of our families, the frequency of female-headed households, teenage pregnancy, and drug-addicted babies in our communities.

In *Disfigured Images: The Historical Assault of Afro-American Women*, historian Patricia Morton traces this preoccupation with African American family structure back to the myth of the black female slave as invented by American historians. The deviance of the black woman in the slave quarters (her physical strength, her sexual promiscuity, her propensity for dominance in the household, and her emotional callousness toward her children and her mate) became the linchpin of theories of black inferiority first in the historical accounts of white and black historians and then in sociological accounts.[3]

Not only did sociological accounts become social policy in the form of the *Moynihan Report*, when we turn to the "Mammy" specifically, the most prominent and long-lasting of "disfigured images" of the black female, we begin to see how social policy and analysis converge with popular culture production. From *Birth of a Nation* in 1915 to *Gone with the Wind* in 1939 to *Raisin in the Sun*, the most important myth of the black woman—the Mammy—configures and thus delimits black female cultural participation.

On the other hand, as Morton suggests, Mammy is not just a myth. Or rather, the power of her mythology is that she is both real and unreal. There is no question that there has always been and there continues to be a strong black woman who provided profoundly crucial services to the black community and the black family. There can be little question that she also provided myriad essential services to the white community. Useful people tend to be useful to all those with whom they come in contact.

The point for me, however, is that there is a great deal of self-destructive, masochistic hostility for the myth of Mammy in the black community as a stereotype, hostility which quite commonly overflows to embrace most contemporary black women, black mothers, and perhaps teenage mothers in particular. In reading Morton's account of the stereotype and how it rests upon presumptions of black male inferiority and the dysfunction of the black family, one can understand the hostility. Nevertheless, aiming the hostility at contemporary black women constitutes an attack upon the "body" of the self or the race.

Feminist psychoanalytic conceptions of the "mother" could prove useful in exploring this phenomenon because general cultural trends of simultaneously loathing and worshiping the mother are not only at play in African American self-perception but also in the way in which African American culture is regarded by the dominant culture. First, one might want to think about what psychological role the mother actually plays in the black family. Does race make a difference in the identity formation of the child and to whether or not a mother is "good enough?" What difference does race make? What, for instance, is the psychological future of the children who are raising themselves in the Sudan and in Ethiopia? What are the long-range costs of such crisis management? What are the long-range costs of what is happening to many black children today in poor black communities?

The way feminist cultural analysis uses psychoanalysis could provide ways of reading cultural stereotypes of black women more fully, or against the grain. I'll admit it is still hard for me to imagine how current feminist uses of Lacan might come into play, but there is no question that textual representations of black women, particularly of Mammy, could benefit from deconstruction and analysis. Current feminist uses of Lacan seem to me too fashion-bound, too divorced from problems of social policy, and too accepting of the structures of white domination and male supremacy.

Since I, myself, am neither a psychologist or a psychoanalyst, I am not prepared to work through all the implications of psychoanalysis taking race seriously, although I hope somebody will someday. I would like to propose that psychoanalysis might prove quite useful to a multicultural black popular-culture analysis. The goal for me in such cultural analysis is to combine, or at least to establish a connection between, social analysis and cultural interpretation simply because this is what oppressed minorities need cultural analysis to do. I can provide three examples of how this can be done.

My first example is taken from history: the construction of race and gender in Hollywood films in the 1940s and 1950s such as *Gone with the Wind*, *Pinky*, and *Imitation of Life*. Such matters are inherently difficult for analysis because black producers (such as Oscar Micheaux) were generally so powerless and peripheral to the mainstream that black performers were made to play such marginal roles. Current practices of social segregation, economic disenfranchisement, and conventions of stereotypical images all serve to further trivialize our attempt to focus on race. And yet it is crucial to analyze the relationship of race to gender in this period of film history precisely because it sets the standard for everything that was to follow. Ideals of imagery and narrative were established then.

The question a psychoanalytic approach allows one to ask is how was the virtual "invisibility" of blacks then central to the function of American hegemony expressed through the classic Hollywood cinema of this period? If you look at *Gone with the Wind*, for example, obviously, in a very real sense, this film is not about blacks at all but about a fantasy notion white Americans had of the antebellum South. It was about the screen chemistry of Vivian Leigh and Clark Cable, the film's innovative set design and lighting techniques, and David Merrick's megalomania. On the other hand, a psychoanalytic approach allows us to suggest, as well, that this film is also about slavery, about a certain kind of historical narrative, and the social and economic status of blacks in the antebellum South. Most importantly, the film reflects directly upon the status of blacks at that moment in 1939 in the United States and projections for their future. Also, a psychoanalytic approach might lead us to reflect upon the subliminal effects of constructions of race on black and white spectators, as well as spectators of color.

Now these may seem like obvious observations for many of you, but you would be hard pressed to find much film analysis to corroborate it. As a child I remember viewing *Gone with the Wind* and being really taken aback by the realization that it had something to do with race at the same time that none of the discussions of the film, in books or in the press, seemed to take its racial content seriously. The most that might ever be said, reluctantly, if you brought it up was that the racial stereotypes were rather unfortunate. It reminds me of how American democracy was explained in my introduction to a U.S. politics course—it was an otherwise perfect system except for the negligible flaw of slavery. Thanks to Freud, Derrida, and Foucault, we know now that systems don't really work that way. As likely as not, the negligible flaw provides the crucial clue to what's up.

In particular, extending upon Morton's work, one might look at the successful attempt to trivialize Mammy's role in comic terms in *Gone with the Wind*. Where were blacks then? Where were they going? How does this aspect of the film, the Mammy stereotype, reject our focus, and subvert our thinking about race or about any of the historical realities of the period?

My second example proposes a possible reading of the contemporary black film scene. There are many novel and new ways in which a psychoanalytic reading of the unconscious might be employed here, in terms of texts, audiences, authors, or institutional practices. It's all still pretty much virgin territory. For instance, if one looks at the representation of black female protagonists in such films as *Just Another Girl on the IRT*, *Poetic Justice*, and *What's Love Got to Do with It*, one might dismiss such representations as insignificant, either on the grounds that these weren't such great films or on the grounds that black women were relatively powerless to determine their content. Although *Just Another Girl on the IRT* was written, directed, and produced by Leslie Harris, a black woman, it would also appear that her struggle to get the film produced forced her to make commercial compromises that rendered the film not a reliable indication of what she might have done if she'd had more control. But a psychoanalytic approach to such matters might take all of this and more into account. How was her compromise staged?

In *Just Another Girl on the IRT*, the protagonist is a foul-mouthed teenager from black Brooklyn who wants to finish high school in three years and become a doctor but she accidentally gets pregnant. Unable to make up her mind about whether or not to have an abortion, she uses the $500 her boyfriend offers her to pay for it to go on a shopping spree with her girlfriend. Yet when she goes into labor early and the baby is accidentally born in the boyfriend's house, she commands him to dispose of the baby in the trash. Fortunately, he fails to do so and the picture ends with boyfriend, protagonist, and baby happily reunited.

There are many confusing aspects to the portrayal of this young woman, but the key one for me is why she refuses to consider getting rid of the baby (legally, in the form of an abortion before it is born) and yet so readily disposes of it (illegally, in the form of murder) once it is born. On the other hand, this representation fits well with Morton's stereotype of the black Mammy or mother. And the formal criterion of the maternal melodrama, in regard to the protagonist's antagonistic relationship with her mother, comes into play as well.

I saw this film on a Sunday afternoon in a ghetto movie theater in Louisville, Kentucky. The sparse audience consisted of mostly black teenage girls (a number of whom were accompanied by their own infant children) who laughed uncontrollably during the protagonist's painful and bloody labor scene, yet grew silent when she commanded her boyfriend to throw the baby away. I suspect these inconsistencies in plot and in audience response reflect profound ambivalences in the views of the director and the Louisville, Kentucky, black female teenager audience about abortion and motherhood, ambivalences which it might be fascinating to pursue and connect.

On the other hand, neither *Poetic Justice* nor *What's Love Got to Do with It* were written or directed by black women and yet texts by black women (poetry by Maya Angelou and an autobiography by Tina Turner) were, to some degree, influential. How are *Poetic Justice* and *What's Love Got to Do with It* not black women's films? How do these films reflect upon the status of black women in our society?

The protagonist in *Poetic Justice*, Justice, as played by Janet Jackson, is supposed to be a hairdresser poet yet we never see her write or recite poetry. As a character she is sketchy and ill formed and seems to have no ideas whatsoever. Moreover, why did John Singleton choose the mostly lyrical, upbeat poetry of Maya Angelou over the work of one of the more profound black feminist poets such as June Jordon, Lucille Clifton, Audre Lorde, or Alice Walker? In the end, this film is quite disturbing because of what Singleton is trying to say about violence and dissension in the black community and in the black family. How can he raise such issues without taking black women more seriously? Moreover, what does his treatment of this matter in *Poetic Justice* (as well as the commercial success of the film) tell us about the ongoing success of black boyz/gangster films?

Of course, *What's Love Got to Do with It* is a much more satisfying film for women primarily because of the compelling performances of Laurence Fishburne as Ike and Angela Bassett as Tina and because of the endlessly fascinating voice of Tina Turner, herself, on the soundtrack. Although the story of Turner's physical abuse would seem to provide an opportunity to publicly deal for the first time in film with the identity formation of a black woman, in fact, we have instead a narrative that frolics carelessly from bravura performance to musical number to bravura performance. The narrative dimension of this film never really takes off and, as in most musicals (although the film is not a musical), there is no sustained drama. Of course, part of the problem is that Tina Turner is still alive and seems not in favor of any kind of intensive public thoughtfulness about her experiences.

My final example of using psychoanalysis in cultural analysis would be to use it to consider contemporary events such as the dissemination of the videotape of the beating of Rodney King, the court trial in Simi Valley of the police who beat him in Simi Valley, the subsequent response to the verdict in the form of a riot and/or rebellion in the streets of Los Angeles, and so forth. First, I'd like to point out the way in which the revolution in telecommunications irreversibly impacts on all the events connected with the LA rebellion and all the texts resulting from it. It seems to me impossible and useless to consider King's beating independent of issues of representation.

The major point to be made about the whole Rodney King matter is that the videotape changed everything about how we discuss police brutality. The fascinating thing, however, was the resistance of the courts and the jury to the videotape as reliable documentary evidence and the manner in which mostly conservative forces in the society began to behave as though they had always taken for granted that video imagery could be subject to an endless series of interpretations. Of course, in fact, this hasn't been the case at all in the past. The lesson for me here is that interpretation itself is always ideologically motivated.

There's no end to how psychoanalytic approaches might be used to examine the impact of race and gender on contemporary events for unconscious motivations, ambivalent impulses, repression, and possibly contradictory truth content. For example, consider King's question, "Why can't we all get along?" Why was this innocuous question immediately taken up by everybody far and wide, as though it had never before occurred to anyone, or as though it were precisely the question that had been on everybody's mind all along? Why was a society that ordinarily would have had no interest in anything a Rodney King had to say be suddenly convulsed by his rather simple question? What does all this mean? What can it tell us about race, about popular culture, about the possibilities for multiculturalism, and about ourselves?

A probing psychoanalysis, which took its natural link between the humanities and the social sciences more seriously in general, might allow African American cultural analysis to become more sophisticated, to respond more directly to social policy. Cultural shame over black women as mothers is a cultural construction older than we realize. And the problem can be addressed at myriad levels through an adaptive psychoanalytic approach: through individual and group therapy and counseling addressing personal and psychological issues; through financial and educational relief;[4] through deconstruction of stereotypes at the cultural level by means of direct cultural production, as well as through cultural analysis, criticism, and pedagogy.

Originally published in David Theo Goldberg, ed., *Multiculturalism: A Critical Reader*. Cambridge, Mass.: Blackwell, 1994.

Notes

1. In a recent (September 1993) article called "The Ugly Side of the Modeling Business" in *Essence* magazine, Deborah Gregory and Patricia Jacobs write about the first press conference of The Black Girls Coalition, a protest group consisting of some of the top black models who complain that they are grossly underrepresented in fashion advertising, designer shows, and the editorial pages of consumer magazines. "A paltry 3.4 per cent of all consumer-magazine advertisements depicted African-Americans," Gregory and Jacobs write, "despite the fact that we comprise approximately 11.3 per cent of the readership of all consumer magazines and 12.5 per cent of the US population." Jacobs and Gregory take their statistics from a City of New York Department of Consumer Affairs report on the use of people of color in magazine and catalog advertising called "Invisible People" and issued in 1991. Of course, there are those who think that having blacks in ads is worse than not having them, that their presence serves to obscure the pernicious character of economic power. To this I would counter: while we're waiting for the ultimate socialist revolution, what's wrong with spreading the wealth around? Is it better that only whites work in advertising? If so, why is it okay for blacks to teach in universities or work in government and not okay for blacks to work in advertising? Universities, governments, and advertising are linked by the same money, the same power, and the same system of domination. It seems foolish, impractical, and naive to me to participate in one and not the other.

2. Michel Foucault, *The Order of Things* (New York: Random House, 1970).

3. Patricia Morton, *Disfigured Images: The Historical Assault on Afro-American Women*, (Westport, Conn.: Greenwood Press, 1991).

4. The idea that the goal of life for all black teenagers, and all black people, should be lifelong work seems to me not to take into account the limited capacities of the planet. I'd agree that a work-based identity can be socially useful and psychologically fulfilling, but there may not be enough useful work for all of us. As such, we may need to consider other constructive avenues for our energies, and current workfare policies are misguided, at best. On the other hand, financial relief and educational support seem essential.

V.

HENRY LOUIS GATES AND AFRICAN AMERICAN POSTSTRUCTURALISM

28.

Henry Louis Gates: A Race Man and a Scholar

The success of *The Color Purple* in movie theaters and *The Women of Brewster Place* on TV is a popular reflection of the gradual shift in Afro-American studies from an emphasis on the history of men to the literature of women. And it speaks well, perhaps, for the healing of rifts between black feminists and male critics—in evidence since the controversy over Ntozake Shange's 1976 choreopoem *For Colored Girls Who Have Considered Suicide/ When the Rainbow Is Enuf*—that the single most influential player behind the scenes in this unfolding drama is not a woman but a man. Henry Louis Gates Jr., preeminent African American literary critic, scholar, and author, winner of numerous awards and fellowships, including the prestigious MacArthur Fellowship (the so-called "genius" award) in 1981, picks up where the excitement in black studies about the history of slavery left off over a decade ago. His question is, What happens when the slaves learn to read?

On sabbatical from Cornell University, the 39-year-old Gates has moved down to the National Humanities Center in Research Triangle Park, N.C. A talkative and friendly man whose voice bears no trace of the cultivated British accent one might expect from a Ph.D. in English Literature from Cambridge University, Gates acknowledges his debt to history. "When I was an undergraduate at Yale in the late 1960s," Gates says, "Afro-American studies for me was history, as I think it was for most of us." He has paid and continues to pay his dues as a historian, but significantly, he promotes history that includes a great many more women's voices than it did before.

As general editor of the thirty-volume *Schomburg Library of Nineteenth-Century Black Women Writers* (Oxford University Press) — to which ten new volumes will be added in the fall — Gates is trying to republish everything black women wrote and published in the nineteenth century. Black women writers have often suffered from a notion that clearly originated in white Victorianism: that anonymity, like chastity, is to be preferred in women. It was Gates who helped to make this crucial point — along with an emergent informed feminist literary criticism — when, in 1983, he resurrected from obscurity Harriet Wilson's extraordinary 1859 novel *Our Nig*, the story of a black female indentured servant in the North and the first novel by a black woman to be published in the United States. (It was republished by Random House.)

Gates is also the general editor of the forthcoming (January 1992) *Norton Anthology of Afro-American Literature*, which will be definitive, widely accessible, and as fat as the Manhattan telephone book. This is the first time African American literature will be afforded a volume all its own in the distinguished Norton series, so Gates is involved in canon building — the selection of an African American literary Talented Tenth. "A canon is to a tradition," Gates explains, "as marrow is to bone." He defines this canon to include more women, which also means, not coincidentally, that the literature of poor people and oral literature will be taken more seriously. Zora Neale Hurston and other black female Harlem Renaissance writers — once disparagingly criticized by such black studies luminaries as W. E. B. Du Bois, Sterling Brown, and Richard Wright — now provide the peak experience in the canon, as Gates describes it. Gates believes that his anthology can help change the fact that of the fifty writers most taught in U.S. high schools, only two are black, Richard Wright and Lorraine Hansberry.

Nor is Gates's influence confined to stuffy, scarcely read academic journals. Wearing his journalistic and cultural entrepreneur's hat, Gates frequently contributes literary and cultural commentary to the *New York Times* and the *Village Voice* and has also persuaded Lincoln Center's Gregory Mosher to revive the musical *Mule Bone*, co-authored by Langston Hughes and Zora Neale Hurston, this spring.

We've come a long way since 1975, when both academia and the publishing industry were predicting the death of black studies because of the loss of students and readers and the political clout to reproduce either. The excitement generated by the Black Power and civil rights movements in the

'60s and early '70s led to an increasing interest in who the slaves were and what they thought, resulting in the publication of such books as *The Slave Community* by John Blassingame (Oxford University Press, 1972), *Roll, Jordan, Roll: The World the Slaves Made* by Eugene Genovese (Pantheon, 1974), and *The Black Family in Slavery and Freedom* (Pantheon, 1976) by Herbert Gutman.

But while white scholars always managed to dominate the field in history, a cultural nationalism movement spearheaded by the poet, playwright, and essayist Amiri Baraka led to the emergence of the black aesthetic, which pursued a pure black essence in literature and literary criticism by examining everything from the blues to the black church in terms of the question, What is the nature of blackness?

In his *Figures in Black: Words, Signs, and the "Racial" Self* (Oxford University Press, 1987) and *The Signifying Monkey: A Theory of African-American Literary Criticism* (Oxford, 1988), Gates describes this kind of thinking as "essentialism" and disagrees with it. He argues that blackness is not about a particular content but is a particular style, which he calls "signifyin'." His theory of "critical signification" takes its name from a black folk figure, the Signifying Monkey, and Gates himself likes to emphasize his theory's dependence on black vernacular oral tradition. But there are others—black feminist critics in particular—who disapprove of its affinity with the so-called Yale School of Deconstruction, which is grounded in postmodern and poststructuralist developments in Continental Philosophy.

Gates's emphasis on blackness as a cultural style has been endorsed by the black writers Trey Ellis and Greg Tate as the basis for a neoblack aesthetic. The point is, black people have managed to produce a distinct culture despite the fact that we were brought to these shores as slaves and forced to adopt a European religion, a European language, and European names. What matters, Gates reasons, is not whose language is spoken or whose religion is practiced but, rather, that those practices are systematically imbued, through "imitation and reversal," with an African style—race, after all, being only a metaphor.

WALLACE: Why was the work of historian John Blassingame so pivotal to the course of Afro-American studies in the late '60s and early '70s?

GATES: One of the curious facts of African American intellectual history is that until John Blassingame's *The Slave Community* (1972), no black scholar had dealt with slavery in a full and adequate way. People like John Hope Franklin had talked about slavery, but mostly as the story of its abolition. Blassingame went back to try to re-create the life and heart and mind of something he called "the slave community" — a brilliant phrase, one of the great phrases in the history of Afro-American studies. He went to the writings and the testimony, oral and written, of the slaves themselves and used what they had to say about slavery as the basis to create a portrait of 350 years of our oppression in the New World. Blassingame's great work was to wipe out that whole racist strain in American historiography, or slave historiography, and put in its place a new set of standards based on this testimony.

Then Blassingame decided to take an exemplary black figure, a former slave who wrote and spoke eloquently, Frederick Douglass, and put into a fourteen-volume edition essentially everything that he said and thought. This gave birth to a slew of books about the slave experience. Then it kind of played out.

By 1975, people were predicting the imminent death of black studies, a political fad in the late 1960s, so they said, created in response to demands of students who took over university buildings, not a valid area of intellectual inquiry on its own. The best thing that could happen, many argued, was for Afro-American studies to be integrated into traditional disciplines.

WALLACE: One of the places where the myth of this death of black studies was really having a strong impact was in publishing. And people like Toni Morrison, who was an editor at Random House in the 1970s, were fighting it.

GATES: That's right. I'll give you an example. When I was an undergraduate, one of my mentors was John Morton Blum, the great American political historian. He said, "Look, I think you have writing talent." So I got this agent. She was white and vice-president of her literary agency. And I went off to Cambridge in 1973 on a Mellon Fellowship.

Wole Soyinka was there, in exile from Nigeria. He'd been let out of prison and had come to Cambridge for a year. So I started working with him and eventually became the American editor for his journal, *Transition*.

Meanwhile, I got this exclusive interview with Eldridge Cleaver, who was living underground in Paris. I came back to England all excited and sent my agent a telegram. Two weeks later my agent hadn't contacted me. I sent another cable and finally called her, which is a big deal for a student in England. It was very expensive. She said, "Well, I didn't write you because there is no market for this story and no market for black studies. I've been thinking that what you need to do is start writing about white people."

There are moments in relationships when somebody does or says something, and the relationship is over at that second. I hung up, and I wrote her shortly after and said it was best for me to find another agent, that if I couldn't write about black people, I wasn't going to be a writer. That was January of 1974.

WALLACE: How did the transition in Afro-American studies from an emphasis on history to literature occur?

GATES: The foundations for the black women's movement had been laid with the publication in 1970 of *The Bluest Eye* by Toni Morrison, *The Third Life of Grange Copeland* by Alice Walker, *The Black Woman: An Anthology* by Toni Cade Bambara, and *I Know Why the Caged Bird Sings* by Maya Angelou. And, again, with Morrison's entrepreneurial editorial energy, all these factors were in the air and began to reach their full development by the late 1970s, and a whole new energy center was produced. The reason that the black women's movement is so important to black studies is that it expanded our potential readership, the potential "market" for black studies, consisting as it did of black women, black men, and white women. And now, of course, white men. Black studies and women's studies met on the common terrain of black women's studies. And I think that that, more than any other single element—and I'm sure of this—saved black studies from its demise.

WALLACE: Why is it important to talk about literature? I mean, black people understand in a very organic way why it is important to study one's own history. They understand it as identity and know the cliché: You don't know who you are if you don't know where you came from.

GATES: For well over 150 years, many black scholars and autodidacts have felt it important to chart the intellectual achievements of black people. The attempt was to make catalogs, an encyclopedic collection of the black people who succeeded, as armament against the attacks of white racists. Intellectual history has always been important to our people because white Western society, in order to justify slavery, declared that we lacked intellect. It was used against us in the same way that our SAT, MCAT, and LSAT scores are used against us today—our dropout rates, our illiteracy rates, etc. I think that many white people in this society, more than half, think that we are innately inferior by intellect.

Just as history is a representation and socially produced—an intellectually produced fiction of what reality might have been one hundred years before—so, too, literature gives us an immediate version of the representation of experience and identity. It's almost as if there is a time warp between the two. History is concerned with the past, literature with the present. But they both are concerned with the re-creation and representation of identity and experience. So I see the two as naturally linked.

I think it's important for the young executive class, the generation of black professionals who are now working in business, investment banking, and law, to be acutely aware of their culture, because you cannot stand in American society as a lone black individual or as any other kind of ethnic individual. You have to stand on a foundation of group ethnic culture and identity. It's going to be a long time before that aspect of the power make-up of American society changes. Our tragedy is that often the most sensitive and intelligent among our people feel so estranged, for various reasons, from the group. They believe that they can be successful only if they distance themselves from our group, and so they don't take the time to read our literature and our history. They think that they are driven as special individuals who are somehow making it because they are different from the larger mass of black people who are not making it.

WALLACE: Don't you think they also sometimes don't know where to begin?

GATES: There is no excuse for any intelligent person not to know where to begin. There are too many of us doing too much. You could look in *Books in Print* under black and just begin, start anywhere.

WALLACE: Let's talk about the *Schomburg Library of Nineteenth-Century Black Women Writers*. You said that part of what you are doing is documenting the history of African American literature and reconstructing the archive. What prompted all this?

GATES: I like to think of myself as having a theoretical hat and a historical hat. Or maybe they're two heads—that's a better metaphor. Because of my historical training, I'm interested in archival work. And, really, archival work is the glamour area of black studies.

The success of *Our Nig* blew my mind. I think it sold about 50,000 copies. For a nineteenth-century black woman's novel, that's extraordinary. And I had a lot of satisfaction out of that. It satisfied my Columbus complex to discover something. Secondly, here was a black woman who was downtrodden, who had no hope. And this black woman, finally, is having her say. That's great, if you ask me, really great.

But I was thinking, if *Our Nig* was back there, there must be other stuff too. There's more than one book remaining to be discovered. So I began a National Endowment for the Humanities and Ford Foundation-funded project called The Black Periodical Literature Project. The staff and I started putting together bibliographies. We started going through other people's bibliographies, writing down all the books published by black women. I soon came to realize that there were quite a lot, maybe as many as fifty individual titles that were pretty much out of print, and that they were an incredible treasure house of knowledge about black women's experiences, to which nobody but a handful of scholars had access. You couldn't even find them all at the Schomburg or the Moorland-Spingarn at Howard.

I put together a list of forty-five titles that would fit into thirty volumes, and I began a long and discouraging process of trying to persuade various publishers to do this series. Forget the big commercial houses; I decided to go to reprint companies and even they weren't very particularly interested in the project. Two years of pounding the streets of New York led to a lunch at Oxford University Press. Another year later, I got a call saying that they'd decided to do it, with two caveats. The first was that they publish all the books at once. The second was that I had proposed to them that I would try to get thirty other scholars to do introductions, and I would write a general overview. I wanted to bring a lot of people in. This was in the fall. Everything had to be in by July 1st. I remember the sense of exhilaration that I had, because it was just such a mind-boggling thing.

WALLACE: What's the current project you're doing?

GATES: Right now I'm working on a book called *Black Letters and the Enlightenment: Race and Reason* [not yet published]. Its purpose is to help us understand why literature has always had a prime role in our politics. You see, we produced a literary tradition because people said we couldn't produce one. We produced it because Europeans said until we produced one, we were fit to be nothing but slaves. It's a back-ass way of producing literature. We didn't produce it because of a primal motivation to talk about love and death and all the things that writers write about; we produced it to make a larger statement about the worth of our group. Our literature has always been committed, political, and social in the West, from the very beginning.

WALLACE: Could you explain why black women writers have become such an important part of your work?

GATES: It's ridiculous to me that black men would protest the success of black women, because to a large extent I think what black women did was introduce new conventions of representation, new ways of seeing, new ways of telling a story. Some black male writers, the sons of Richard Wright and of Ralph Ellison, were tending to tell the same stories over and over. Who among black male writers was talking about children, about intimacy, about sexual love? It's not there. More often in the black male tradition there is the concern with white men and white racism.

What the daughters of Zora Neale Hurston have done is to tell a new tale and tell it in a new way, not only with new content but with new voices, new music, new lyrics. That's exciting. In part, I think the success of the black women's movement is a critique of the black male tradition and the way that it played itself out. Convention in literature can harden and be part of a social problem even more than its critique or its liberation. And these new writers have shown us that by showing us different ways to tell the story.

Originally published as "An *Emerge* Interview: A Race Man and a Scholar," *Emerge Magazine*, February 1990, 56–61.

29.

If You Can't Join 'Em, Beat 'Em:

Stanley Crouch and Shaharazad Ali

What you should notice first about *Notes of a Hanging Judge* is its back cover. In place of the usual congratulatory blurbs, we are offered Stanley Crouch's own provocative sound bites on such cultural icons as Democratic presidential candidate Jesse Jackson ("a man besmirched by his own conduct, his ambition, his willingness to make pretzels of the truth"); novelist Toni Morrison ("*Beloved*, above all else, is a blackface holocaust novel"); and filmmaker Spike Lee ("It is precisely because Lee can make audiences laugh that the fascist aesthetic he follows with such irresponsible deliberation slips the critical noose").

What does this capsule presentation mean? These past eleven years, we have known Crouch as the lone black naysayer; the contentious jazz and cultural critic for the *Village Voice* and *New Republic*; the rowdy opponent of feminism, black women writers, gay rights, rap music, Prince, and anything culturally subversive and progressive. His job was also always fundamentally shaped by his opposition to the frequent rigid black nationalism of the local black press, particularly the *Amsterdam News*, the *City Sun*, and WLIB.

Now this capsule presentation of Crouch's views on the back of his book serves to re-position him in relationship to a national mainstream (mostly white middle-class) audience. "We" (they?) are subtly being instructed to view him as the lone black critic, this time unbossed and unbought in a national and even a global context, braving yet unconquered frontiers of aesthetic cowardice and intellectual dishonesty.

When you add to this package Crouch's tricky introduction, in which he trots out a series of cryptically truncated positions on feminism, gay rights, and AIDS—although they are peculiarly irrelevant to the rest of the book— it becomes possible to diagnose a conventional sexual conservatism being palmed off as something new and improved.

The two reviews I've seen thus far bought the package. Gene Seymour in *The Nation* dismisses Crouch's "bilious sneering" at "cultural heroes like Toni Morrison and Spike Lee" in favor of observing that "informing all these essays, celebrations and putdowns alike, is a search for common ground and a reaffirmation of the social contract" and appreciating "the fact that, like any good jazz player, Crouch never repeats himself or does the predictable." Deidre English in the *New York Times Book Review*, after pointing out that Crouch's judgments are "strong and bitter stuff," goes on to pour it on: "Freedom from preconceived ideas opened up the world for fresh and honest reconsiderations; the essays that result defy neat characterization as liberal or conservative, for most share a more profound depth of feeling and breadth of thought than simplistic labels allow."

It's true that Crouch's work is often clever, interesting, and perhaps even right about the vagaries of contemporary black political figures such as Al Sharpton and Jesse Jackson. But more to the point, I find it impossible to ignore the particular cultural climate in which this book is gaining popularity (even making an appearance on the *Newsday* best-seller list). Why, the *New York Times Arts and Leisure* section wanted to know, is there all of a sudden a correspondence between "artistic matters and the harsh world of the streets?" From the point of view of the good old days of an unchallenged white male critical dominance, when the arts were high cultural and politics were low, Richard Bernstein recently diagnosed the flaw in our present situations as "the new tribalism, a heightened awareness of ethnic and racial separateness." He concluded that the myth of "permanent victimization" forms the basis of a pernicious "cult of otherness" which persists in debating and contesting Eurocentrism.

Meanwhile the background for this analysis is provided by a Supreme Court steadily edging toward overturning the right to abortion and further disarming key civil rights legislation. Using the works of Robert Mapplethorpe and Andres Serrano, Senator Jesse Helms argues against the NEA's use of public money for the arts. A suddenly censorious NEA then denies grants to four performance artists, three of whom are gay, and demands that all grant recipients sign a statement in which they agree not to use NEA money to do work that is "obscene" or "homoerotic."

From the perspective of cultural politics in the streets of New York, such events and race are linked by the AIDS crisis, which has served to connect the medical destinies of the heterogeneous populations who are particularly susceptible to HIV infection: poor black and Puerto Rican IV drug and crack users; their lovers and their offspring; gay men; and the mostly nonwhite populations of the Caribbean, Africa, and other parts of the third world, both gay and heterosexual.

Turning to even more racially loaded contexts, the Bensonhurst and the Central Park jogger cases in New York this summer served as occasions for print and electronic news media to drum home their message of the savagery of the black male underclass and the madness of its political leadership. The publicity around the obscenity charges against the rap group 2 Live Crew has played the same kind of role in media coverage of the cultural sphere. Meanwhile, Shelby Steele, the black English professor from San Jose, decries the very same cult of victimization in racial politics that Bernstein deplores in cultural politics. The controversy over replacing a white male, Jonathan Pryce, with an Asian male actor in the Broadway version of *Miss Saigon* provided a perfect opportunity for ideologies of the liberal mainstream in the arts (would you believe actor Charlton Heston, talk show host Dick Cavett, and Broadway producer Cameron McKintosh?) to voice their absolute philosophical (and economic) opposition to affirmative action.

At the same time, on the home front among booksellers in the black community, Crouch's book often shares a table with Shaharazad Ali's self-published *The Blackman's Guide to Understanding the Blackwoman*, this summer's surprise best seller. At the recent West Indian Day parade on Labor Day in Brooklyn, every book table featured huge piles of the Ali book. Ali, a black woman herself, claims that "the Blackwoman is out of control" because "she does not submit to guidance by her God-given mate the Blackman," and "her disrespect for the Blackman is a direct cause of the destruction of the Black family."

While presenting no evidence of any kind except belligerent assertion, Ali titillates her grassroots audience by repetitively attacking black women on an extremely personal and sometimes pseudo-psychological basis. Poorly written and organized, the best way to get through the book is not cover to cover but by opening it to a page at random and reading aloud whatever your eye falls upon. For instance, on page 82 — "As a rule the Blackwoman cannot be fully trusted in money matters between she and the Blackman" —

or page 134—"He [the Blackman] is sick and tired of all that women's lib boldness and fed up with her aggressive actions"—or page 169—"There is never an excuse for ever hitting a Blackwoman anywhere but in the mouth. Because it is from that hole, in the lower part of her face, that all her rebellion culminates in words."

Ali has also turned out to have considerable crossover appeal on the dog and pony circuit, having sold over 200,000 copies in the black community, as well as having been featured on *The Sally Jessy Raphael Show* with a strange cast of characters including a black man with three wives, and in the *Daily News* and *Newsweek*. But the real basis of Ali's authority with a large black audience is not her attraction as a novelty act but the mythological force of her quasi–neonationalist Black Muslim perspective on the history of the black race and the plight of the black community, particularly the black family.

What is happening here is the same process that the cultural critic Joe Wood described in the *Village Voice* recently whereby Malcolm X becomes a cultural icon, a feature of black style among those who are otherwise un-familiar with his ideas. In the same manner, Louis Farrakhan/Al Sharpton–type black nationalism is, by default, reigning supreme in the black com-munity. The only real challenge to its hegemony thus far has been Jesse Jackson's Rainbow Coalition, but Jackson keeps losing, and elected black officials make a poor spectacle of classical integration as they characteristi-cally try to fit shrinking urban resources to burgeoning urban problems.

Yet in order to subscribe to the Farrakhan/Sharpton/Ali brand of black nationalist thinking, you must believe that male and female, black and white describe mutually exclusive categories, opposite ends of the conceptual uni-verse. This "natural" order regards the patriarchal family as the supreme so-cial organization and all other perspectives on race, gender, and sexuality as deviant. Unfortunately, white followers of Jesse Helms and black followers of Sharpton/Farrakhan are substantially in agreement about such matters.

In this light, Crouch's brand of cultural conservatism acquires new inter-est. The point is this: Where does he stand? It's actually impossible to tell from this book. Some may suspect that, like Ali, he is something of an op-portunist, on his own side and nobody else's, taking advantage of cultural upheavals of the moment to make a few extra bucks.

Even as he claims in the introduction to the book to be a traitor to the black nationalism of the '60s, unafraid of airing the dirty laundry of the black community and therefore somebody whom we can trust to give us the straight scoop on black culture, he pretends that his book is a critique of feminist and gay politics and culture, when it isn't. The introduction begins with the statement, "These essays, reviews, and columns are largely concerned with the struggles and fascinations surrounding racism, sexism, and sexual orientation." Only four of the essays in the book that follows, out of a total of thirty-seven, could be described as dealing with issues of sexism and sexual orientation. Much more consistent is the thread of homophobia, antifeminist bias, and cultural conservatism that runs through these four essays and seeps into others as well.

As the introduction goes on to indicate, his understanding of feminist and gay politics is completely instrumental. He sees the emergence of the women's movement and gay rights as a symptomatic demonstration of his obsession with the idea that black political development has deteriorated from the "complex vision of universal humanism that underlay the Civil Rights Movement" to the flight into the "xenophobic darkness," which has led to our still-lingering fascination with "embracing black power, black nationalism, black studies, the racist rants that were known as 'revolutionary black art.'"

While he claims that his tenure as a staff writer at the *Village Voice* made it possible for him "to come face to face with the feminist and homosexual liberation movements," it appears that quite the opposite has occurred when he says things like, "Much of what I read and heard from the paper's feminist ideologues and champions of homosexual liberation was quite familiar, reminiscent of what had been said when the Civil Rights Movement decayed into the mirror-licking of ethnic nationalism and condescending self-regard."

According to Crouch, the problem with feminist and homosexual activists was their mindless emulation of the separatism and self-righteousness of "black nationalism and armed black revolutionaries" and, in particular, the way that "homosexuals then advocated promiscuity and refused to be critical of the public sexual encounters that made parks off-limits to heterosexuals and children in places like San Francisco, where anything could go on at any time."

By making such comments, I suspect that Crouch is being deliberately provocative. His underlying aim is to appropriate the energies of contemporary feminist, gay, and Left struggles against the cultural conservatism of the Right without ever addressing the key issues in current debates. In his rhetoric about the gay movement, his crucial metaphor becomes the death sentence that AIDS has presumably inflicted upon homosexuals for their cavalier dismissal of "middle class morality" and the sin of sexual promiscuity. He employs AIDS as a stand-in for the kind of judgments that he considers to be his stock-in-trade.

In a mainstream conservative political environment in which the struggle over the death penalty seems emblematic of the recuperation of the Right, Crouch proudly proclaims himself to be a "hanging judge, much like Henry Morgan, who sent many of his former pirate buddies to the gallows." My question is, is a hanging judge what we really need in cultural criticism? Given the high rates of black infant mortality, the rising numbers of black crack babies, and the AIDS, tuberculosis, and mental illness that run rampant among the homeless population, are we really in need of more death sentences?

AIDS apparently designates an entire syndrome of opportunistic diseases afflicting large populations of gays and heterosexuals all over the world. Yet Crouch says in his idea of a tribute to gays, "As the plague set in and the doomed wore the emblems of purple welts, what had often seemed an essentially frivolous world took on a spiritual majesty that many besides myself probably thought beyond it. They embraced the dying and supplied them with extended families willing to clean their homes, take care of their correspondence, do their shopping, supply them with visits as regular as their health allowed, read to them, bring them flowers and recordings, and provide the human feeling that ennobles when morale is, finally, pointless."

Only the crisis of AIDS could force homosexuals into line, Crouch implies. "Like the armed black cadres of the late sixties who threatened and taunted the nation with what now seems suicidal intensity," he insists, "the cruising frenzy of homosexual life is over for the same reason: death." Yet again his remarks about AIDS enact a gratuitous appropriation of a timely and emotionally charged issue for what purpose? There is virtually nothing about AIDS in the rest of the book except his obituary for the black gay writer Lionel Mitchell, whom he claims as a friend. It is a rather clinical description of Mitchell's penniless and degrading death as a victim of AIDS.

In the second of the essays about homosexuality written in 1982, a discussion about "Gay Pride, Gay Prejudice" with novelist John Rechy and Lionel Mitchell, Crouch takes his usual opportunity to air his prejudices: "In friendships with white women, black homosexuals can easily take on the roles of male mammies, confidants, and exotics with both ethnic and sexual twists," and "since legend has it that a very famous Negro leader died from a caning he received when one of his white patrons discovered him in bed with his wife, it is also understandable why male patrons, whenever a choice has been available, have been partial to the talented young black homosexual."

Even when he praises gays, it is in order to reinforce his conception of an incontrovertible natural order in which heterosexual procreation, along with artistic genius, is at the pinnacle of social achievement. So many homosexuals are obsessed with "taste, art, style and minute detail," Crouch writes, because "in lieu of procreation, it allows association with the ageless greatness of human history."

Although Crouch uses the introduction to his book to take advantage of shifts in cultural values, particularly in regard to sexuality, in order to ply his wares, his own convictions about culture remain as solid as a rock. Even as he unquestioningly accepts the courtrooms' monolithic version of "justice" (the law of the Father), he is also thoroughly convinced of, along with the rest of the *New Republic* crew, the necessity for a high/low cultural divide beyond which chaos must surely lie. What complicates this perspective, however, is that Afro-Americans have always made an inordinate contribution to popular culture, either as producers (athletics, entertainment, and music) or, less fortunately, as objects of production (blackfaced minstrelsy, from the stage to film, and stereotypical Sambo images from paintings and postcards).

Crouch is incapable of admitting, or even seeing perhaps, that the source of the power of Afro-American blues, gospel, and jazz lay precisely in their origins in the popular and even the common. He wants to focus only on the transformation of jazz into classical jazz and fine art. Of course, there's nothing wrong with this project. It might even be regarded as crucial except that it tends to narrow Crouch's understanding of contemporary culture and blind him to other standards of cultural value besides genius, originality, and greatness. To him, almost anything new or popular is to be regarded with fear and loathing.

This is most blatantly clear in two essays that ostensibly deal with "sexism." The first was written in 1979, and its subject is me and my first book, *Black Macho and the Myth of the Superwoman*. The title of the piece, "Aunt Jemima Don't Like Uncle Ben," implies his familiar thesis, which is that black people he doesn't agree with are being manipulated as stereotypical minstrel figures in blackface in order to make fools out of other black people. He claims that it is an early draft "both technically and intellectually" for the much more interesting and disastrous essay "Aunt Medea," on Toni Morrison's novel *Beloved*, which is the second essay that deals with "sexism."

"Those whites within the media," Crouch writes, "who felt betrayed or affronted by the anti-white, anti-Semitic and violent tendencies of black nationalism during the '60s are promoting a gaggle of black female writers who pay lip service to the women's movement while supplying us with new stereotypes of black men and women."

Among the gaggle are the novelist Gayl Jones, who had then written *Corregidora* and *Eva's Man*; the playwright Ntozake Shange, who had written *For Colored Girls Who Have Considered Suicide* and *A Photograph*; and myself. Whereas the dominant culture had focused in the '60s upon publishing books and producing films which "would have been considered racist and would have been shouted down had they been written by whites," the focus now was on publishing black women, Crouch claims, as long as they write about "being brutalized by black men."

Such criticisms have become familiar by now in the mainstream press through such examples as Mel Watkins's critique of black women writers in the *New York Times Book Review* and Darryl Pinckney's critique of *The Color Purple* in the *New York Review of Books*. Black feminist literary critic Deborah McDowell diagnoses the problem for critics such as Crouch in an essay called "Reading Family Matters." Apparently, what is at issue is their attachment to a "family romance" in which "the Black Family cum Black Community headed by the Black Male . . . does battle with an oppressive White world." That this family romance is being "de-romanticized in writings by the great majority of black women writers" only serves to infuriate the still enchanted.

His discussion of *Beloved* stems from his view that the manufacture of self-pity has become a kind of cottage industry among black artists and intellectuals in the black community, which is ruining their ability to produce great art. *Beloved*, he says, continues the thesis of the work of James Baldwin, which is that "those who had suffered most knew life best," and "it seems to have been written in order to enter American slavery into the big-time martyr ratings contest, a contest usually won by references to, and works about, the experience of Jews at the hands of the Nazis."

When he calls *Beloved* a "black faced holocaust novel," he combines his two most wrongheaded attacks. First, the reference to blackface again trots out the question of whether black entertainers and artists are operating in their own best interests or according to white designs for them. Since black Americans are a people who continue to speak and write a language that was forced upon us at gunpoint and that, as slaves, we had to adapt, no black artist or intellectual can really protect herself from such a criticism. The legacy of a blackface minstrelsy that originally used white actors but which black performers ultimately adapted to purposes for which it was never intended, provides us with the crucial way of understanding Afro-American cultural development as necessarily always a doubling of contexts.

As for the question of holocaust, it seems fantastic to me that nobody has yet remarked upon the fact that Crouch is suggesting in his attack on Morrison that there is something wrong with a novel that focuses upon the Jewish Holocaust as well. This seems to me patently absurd; my view is that not too much but too little has been written about the plight of the body in human history. We might attend as well to the development of a recent cultural criticism focused on developments in art and literature in Weimar and Nazi Germany, which might serve as a model for black intellectuals and writers, and all other progressive intellectuals and writers, in our attempt to recover the stories of the black bodies of the African Diaspora, along with the stories of the white, brown, yellow, and red bodies that interacted with them.

Beloved is Toni Morrison's brilliant fourth novel, not only the linchpin of her oeuvre, but the ultimate accomplishment of black women's fiction and black feminist thought of these past twenty years since the publication in 1970 of the novels *The Bluest Eye* and Alice Walker's *The Third Life of Grange Copeland*, Maya Angelou's autobiography *I Know Why The Caged Bird Sings*, and Toni Cade Bambara's collection of essays, *The Black Woman*.

Morrison is hardly identifiable as an aggressive black feminist or cultural critic, and it always remains somewhat mysterious what she ever intends by any of her books. Yet *Beloved* seems to move deliberately and confidently beyond the scope of conventional historiographic limitations into a confrontation with a hypothetical world of ghosts, guilt, and "re-memory." In a book that conjoins major contemporary themes in Afro-American history, literary studies, women's studies, and cultural studies, *Beloved* provides the missing information that would make imaginable the social and cultural developments in our black and white "America" of the present.

As does no other work of Afro-American fiction in the twentieth century, *Beloved* speaks to the void of a black intellectual and cultural history which could explain the strength of the masses of poor black people, women as well as men. Instead of the usual parasitic relationship to the master narrative of "History" that one has come to expect in the historical novel, this "fiction" constructs an alternative historical narrative practice, which necessarily undercuts its own authority to finally even say what happened. *Beloved* may be the closest we'll ever get to the dream of a black feminist theory grounded in the historical experience of the black female body and black female desire.

Crouch is made uneasy by this novel's focus on the pain of the body, which he calls "self-pity." Consistent with patriarchal thought since the Crusades, he believes that pain is something you should leave behind you. As a consequence, any kind of feminist inquiry that acknowledged the body would be anathema to him.

It should come as no surprise, therefore, when he is infuriated by the following passage in James Baldwin's final essay in "Notes of Native Son" in which Baldwin, who visits a small Swiss village, seems to discover the very roots of Eurocentrism. Crouch repeats the entire quote in his essay on Baldwin and so shall I:

> These people cannot be, from the point of view of power, strangers anywhere in the world; they have made the modern world, in effect, even if they do not know it. The most illiterate among them is related, in a way that I am not, to Dante, Shakespeare, Michelangelo, Aeschylus, da Vinci, Rembrandt and Racine; the cathedral at Chartres says something to them which it cannot say to me, as indeed New York's Empire State Building, should anyone here ever see it. Out of their hymns and dances come Beethoven and Bach. Go back a few centuries and they are in their full glory—but I am in Africa, watching the conquerors arrive.

Baldwin thus makes the discovery that Eurocentrism and racism are part of a cultural paradigm in the West that need not be fully articulated or understood, either by its perpetuators or its victims, to work effectively. The dichotomizing of good and evil, in which the religious beliefs of the West are painted, is only the cover-up, or rather the language in which it becomes possible to safely explore (although it never changes anything) the woeful tale of conquest, imperialism, and domination.

In a fascinating essay called "Body and Soul," about a jazz festival in Italy, Crouch takes the opportunity to offer his reinterpretation of the cultural superiority of the West. His position boils down to the rather simplistic, ahistorical view that while Europe may have the advantage in producing great paintings, in the Italian Renaissance specifically, Afro-Americans have an advantage in having produced great music, in the form of blues, gospel, and jazz, specifically.

The implication is that Afro-American music is, metaphorically, rubbing noses with Italian Renaissance art by virtue of the fact of the jazz festival in Italy. Although this essay was written in 1983, he appears to be offering the ultimate challenge to Baldwin's argument about himself as interloper in the West. Because both Afro-American music and Italian Renaissance art, for him, tap the radical egalitarianism of Christianity as a major source of power, the problem of the lack of black visual representation in the West, which Baldwin so poignantly introduced, is collapsed into a naïve identification between black American and white European at the level of "genius."

But the great flaw in Crouch's conflation of Afro-American jazz and Western painting is his failure to take seriously the autonomy of the visual sphere in Western culture, without which the Italian Renaissance and, for that matter, the European conquest of Africa and the enslavement of blacks would, in a certain sense, have been unimaginable.

"Men on Art," a recurrent comedic sketch on the brilliant TV show "In Living Color" (produced by Keenan Ivory Wayans), draws our attention to this problem in the context of contemporary TV. In a spoof of TV film critics Siskel and Ebert, two ostentatiously gay black men, nearly but not quite transvestite, review some of the classics of Western visual art. Michelangelo's *David* gets two snaps with a circle because of its frontal male nudity (and also perhaps because Michelangelo was gay), whereas Botticelli's *The Birth of Venus* and Leonardo da Vinci's *Mona Lisa* are both disliked ("Hated it!" they cry in unison), presumably for their focus on the female body. Andy Warhol's *Marilyn Monroe* elicits a split vote as one of the pair says she was a whore, and one insists that she was the last of the truly great divas.

Ironically, their very process serves to emphasize the blatant heterosexism, by its negation, of most mainstream criticism. Also fascinating is that they have managed to inadvertently reveal the Eurocentrism usually only implicit in such practices. By choosing visual art as their subject matter, it goes without saying that the great masters, from Leonardo to Warhol, will be all white men and that the very notion of the classics is designed to justify the endless reiteration of a story of Western progress in which people of color did not participate.

Precisely because of this inexorable tendency to take for granted that aesthetic judgment is an expression of universal standards of "beauty" untainted by mundane political considerations, it is necessary for socially responsible cultural criticism to raise questions about its own methodology. To designate the right and the good, to tell people what they should accept and what they should reject—as is often the case with the monstrous hybridization of the critical faculty in American mainstream media, of which TV and film criticism is a perfect example—can only serve to further reinforce our current unsatisfactory and unequal cultural arrangements. A critic of this sort, if Afro-American, will merely find him- or herself explaining, justifying, and further consolidating the status quo. It goes without saying that Ali is such a critic. Unfortunately, Stanley Crouch is such a critic as well.

In Crouch's case, it is this blindness to the problem of the visual in Afro-American culture that leaves him totally unable to comprehend the profound importance of the work of the filmmaker Spike Lee. The legacy of the problem of the autonomy of the visual sphere in Afro-American culture is that Afro-Americans have never seen themselves except through the prism of racism. Crouch says of Lee, he "either lacks the intelligence, maturity, and the sensitivity necessary for drama, or hasn't the courage and the will to give racial confrontation true dramatic complexity." But film's universal appeal lies precisely in its moving images, what Maxim Gorky called its "kingdom of shadows."

The singular importance of Spike Lee's films has to do with the astounding uniqueness (given its context in the history of Hollywood films) of its vision of black people. *Do The Right Thing* or any other of Lee's films, or the films of those black filmmakers who begin to follow in his footsteps, are first and foremost about looking at black people before they are about anything else. Second, they are about black people finally seizing the means of imagining their own image.

The monumental importance of this endeavor makes the tendency on Lee's part, thus far, to trivialize and minimize the contributions—and bodies—of women particularly unfortunate. But to call Lee a fascist is ridiculous.

It would be just as ridiculous to label Crouch or Ali fascist, even as both seem extraordinarily hostile to black women. Rather, I am more struck by their contempt for the possibility of intellectual life within the black community. Of course Ali doesn't pretend to be an intellectual, or even interested in ideas, whereas Crouch's stunning facility with language leads one to expect more from him. Yet both books—the advocacy of Ali no less than the opposition of Crouch—confine us to the prison house of "Afrocentric" thought, now so fashionable in the black community. They both abandon us to the same inert pessimism, as though they thought they were shouting out into the darkness of an empty room where nobody was listening, as though the only thing that really mattered after all were selling books.

Originally published in *Transition*, no. 51 (1991): 214–225.

30.

Let's Get Serious: Marching with the Million

On the evening of the Million Man March, I attended an alternative teach-in sponsored by African American Agenda 2000 (AAA 2000), an ad hoc group of black, mostly feminist progressives opposed to the march. The two hundred people who gathered in a large, circular lecture hall at Columbia were youngish, intellectual, and academic. Nobody smiled or chatted. We were not happy.

I had just watched the revival meeting in Washington, live on C-SPAN. Farrakhan's tour de force was clever in its manipulation of African American iconography: Moses leading the Israelites through the Red Sea, Pilate tormenting a black Christ, the slaveowner Jefferson penning the Constitution. Moreover, the large barrier of bulletproof glass shielding the Minister and the taut Fruit of Islam bodyguards flexing their jaw muscles behind him, evoked the assassination scenario (King, Malcolm X, the Kennedys) and had a curious sadomasochistic resonance. It was fascist male bonding in spades, and I was disturbed by its apparent success.

AAA 2000's response to this madness featured an impressive list of Talented Tenth-ers including Kimberle Crenshaw and Kendall Thomas, both law professors at Columbia; Gina Dent, an English professor at Princeton; Cathy Powell, a lawyer from the NAACP Legal Defense Fund. I was invited to speak, too. Unfortunately, our session lacked the passion and momentum of the march. Speakers were careful not to attack the gathering itself or the men who attended, preferring instead to be calm and coolly pedagogic. It occurred to me that we Talented Tenth-ers were acting characteristically, as though enunciating clearly in the King's English and not raising one's voice might somehow carry the day.

The results, not surprisingly, were disappointing. An information packet made available to attendees provided a vast assortment of information about the black female's socioeconomic status, as well as articles on the intersections of racism and homophobia. But neither the packet nor the speeches even began to answer some important questions. First: What about the men at the march? Weren't they our brothers, our fathers, our kin? Where were the statistics on them? Second: How and when are we ever going to acknowledge the fear and desperation of the marchers? Last: Did the people who had bolted from their dinners and missed MacNeil/Lehrer in order to be at the teach-in really need empirical support for a progressive agenda? Shouldn't we have been focusing on what to do now?

No one "teaching" the teach-in was prepared to say. I think the principal reason is that the progressive coalition envisioned by AAA 2000 is more wish than fact. At the first meeting, everyone agreed that the organization would be open to all comers. But there had been a pitched battle among the inner core over the use of the word homophobia in the group's collective statement. Later, some people felt that news coverage of AAA 2000's press conference had focused too much on prominent individual members. Others didn't like the media's focus on Angela Davis, radical and ex-communist. In addition to this crabs-in-a-barrel sniping, I picked up a free-floating anxiety about sacrificing individual goals for the sake of sticking together.

Of course, some of that paranoia makes sense. Before the march, for example, several of us speculated that the event was staged primarily to promote Louis Farrakhan, Ben Chavis, Al Sharpton, and a range of others whose houses are not in order. When the march went over well with the masses, it wasn't anybody's job to say out loud that one million men had been duped. But the proceedings on the Mall made the paranoia of the Talented Tenth seem sadly prescient, leaving us in a familiar position: odd people out.

So, as I think about the teach-in now, I wonder how our bourgeois progressive resistance might make itself a little more relevant, and effective. Farrakhan isn't new to us; we all have Farrakhans among our families, our friends, our colleagues. Our dilemma is collective, and more than likely our solutions will be, too. Either we can have a big party and sell our books to one another, or we can get together and figure out whom we're going to vote for in the next election.

Originally published in the *Village Voice*, 31 October 1995.

31.

Out of Step with the Million Man March

For a feminist these days, the trick to feeling coherent is to quickly determine what is irrelevant so that you can ignore it and to keep a strategically flexible concept of what really matters. The more compelling the visual images, from an emotional standpoint, the more important it is to distinguish the real from the virtually real. I call it virtual reality when almost all you can find on the tube is O.J. Simpson or some other equally titillating subject, while Congress continues to decimate our future in the name of balancing the budget and extricating government from our lives.

A media event that promised the ultimate in virtual reality was the Million Man March, and my first, self-protective impulse was to ignore it. I call this useful, healing practice a "news moratorium," and I find it essential to survival in the age of virtual realities created by telecommunications. I knew the march would be the photo-op of the century precisely because it lacked a discernible political agenda, the ideal pseudo-event of race relations that hints at the coming of other more consequential events, which can never be delivered.

After all, it's just this variety of prepackaged folderol and ephemera that passes for real news on CNN, *Nightline*, and the network news, while much more pressing situations in the United Nations, Bosnia, Haiti, Mexico, and Liberia languish in the perpetual twilight of "international news." The nation had just come out of the interminable Simpson cycle, which climaxed with all those horrific pictures in *Newsweek* and *Time* of black women glee-fully celebrating O.J.'s acquittal, and now we were about to enter the season of the Million Man March. The march was not meant to celebrate or protest, but to atone.

To whom were black men supposed to apologize? To black women, ap-parently. And for what were they atoning? For their failure to be rigid, up-tight patriarchs and born-again family men. If you must atone, atone for violence against women and children, not for being vulnerable, imperfect, and human. And please don't atone in front of the Lincoln Memorial in Washington, D.C., where Congress is currently dismantling the Great So-ciety, and the Supreme Court is extracting the teeth from civil rights. The symbolism was positively creepy.

According to most black people, my people, the Million Man March was a huge success. But a success at achieving what? It alienated most white pro-gressives and many progressives of color, but what it achieved beyond that nobody seems to know or care. The brothers came together, bonded, and showed the country what? That they could come together and bond? It was a feel-good march. Feel good for fifteen minutes only to return to the impon-derables of joblessness, poverty, and despair in the black community. Mega-impressive in terms of imagery and melodramatic effect and low in political meaning, the Million Man March was tailor-made for the narcissistic mini-strations of a self-congratulatory white, male-dominated mainstream media concerned more with appearances than with substance.

The triumphant speeches by Betty Shabazz, Maya Angelou, and Queen Mother Moore obscured the real lessons. Farrakhan's two-and-a-half-hour filibuster went over the heads of the white media since it lacked obvious anti-Semitism, homophobia, and misogyny. Nevertheless, no amount of positive imagery can cause me to forget that if this version of a black Nazi coalition ever caught on with the Christian right, or the reactionary lunatic fringe that brought us the Oklahoma City bombing, I, and everybody I respect, could expect to be on the Class A purge list.

The Million Man March was just the latest in a long line of recent events in which issues of race, gender, and sexuality have been mobilized to critical mass by a profit-hungry media, the reactionary Right, and a black leader-ship chasm. Previous episodes include George Bush's campaign use of Willie Horton; Al Sharpton's manipulation of Tawana Brawley; the Central Park jogger rape scenario; the Anita Hill/Clarence Thomas debacle; the Mike Ty-son, Tupac Shakur, and Flavor Flav cases; and the O.J. Simpson trial and verdict.

As Noam Chomsky so rightly points out, the objective of virtual news is to keep potential progressives polarized over inconsequential differences of class, education, sexuality, and privilege. Meanwhile, Gingrich and company steal the gold at the end of the rainbow. Indeed, whatever the dominant media choose to focus on is almost always another version of the virtually real — absorbing but hardly the point.

Originally published in *Ms. Magazine*, January/February 1996, p. 22.

32.

Neither Fish nor Fowl: The Crisis of
African American Gender Relations

I think Orlando Patterson's essay "Blacklash" is a wonderful and important piece from the author of the groundbreaking study in comparative sociology, *Slavery and Social Death*.[1] It has always been among my dreams, as a black feminist, to get black scholars and intellectuals of Orlando Patterson's superb caliber to think seriously and write publicly about black gender relations. But I find it fascinating that he suggests that the effect of the Thomas-Hill hearings was "to bring to the forefront of national consciousness the critical issue of gender relations in modern America." For me, and for many other feminists like me, this issue has been at the fore of my life for almost as long as I can remember.

For the most part, I agree with the assertions that Patterson makes in this article, and it warms my heart to witness a prominent black male speaking on some of these issues. I have always been powerfully moved by his perspective on just about everything (excluding his contentious take on the Hill-Thomas confrontation on the Op-Ed page of the *New York Times*). Patterson writes that the civil rights movement was "a struggle for the final abolition of slavery, for the recognition of the black as a constituent member of his or her community. . . . These hearings were a powerful symbolic confirmation of the fact that race, while still important, is of radically changing significance. However unequally we may be treated, we are now very much a central part of this society."[2]

I couldn't agree more. In fact, I would really like to distribute copies of this article to the entire faculty of CUNY, where I teach, because the fairly subtle argument he is making about black families and gender relations is beyond most of them and because many of our students are trapped in the divisive, demoralizing structures he describes.

I have always considered the examination of black gender relations to be one of the definitive occupations of black feminism. Although I have never had a lot of company in this particular camp, it seems to me that while most feminists (mostly white but including a growing number of women of color) don't talk much about everyday empirical relations between men and women, there is a great deal of speculation about historical, cultural, and psychological constructions of gender and how they affect myths and realities of both masculinity and femininity. In contemporary feminist discourse in the circles I frequent, which is among cultural critics, legal scholars, art historians, anthropologists, sociologists, biologists, and film scholars, discussions of female gender and its construction rarely fail to take into account that constructions of female gender need to be thought in conjunction with constructions of masculinity.

Patterson does not concur when he observes that a problem in this kind of investigation has been "the tendency of black feminists, who dominate the discourse, to confine and confound, the problems of gender — which concerns both males and females in their relations with each other — with those of women's issues, or, when relational problems are considered, to privilege the standpoint of women, on the assumption that they are always the victims of the interaction. Black men have as much at stake. . . ."[3]

Well, my response to that is that I no longer see black feminism as the discourse of victimization. Indeed, I view feminism and victimization as somewhat antithetical, which may be exactly why black feminism today is such an odd and frail creature, not quite fish or fowl. Even I, a black feminist for twenty-four years, can't quite make it out. I certainly wouldn't attempt to define it in a monolithic way. Many black women who practice a brand of feminism can't even agree upon calling themselves feminists. At the MIT conference on black women in academia a year ago, and in most gatherings of black feminists, one rarely hears the word feminism. It is still a divisive word among black women. The fact that we don't generally use the word feminism to describe our meetings masks deep schisms in our ranks which we find impossible to discuss — along class lines, along cultural lines, along educational lines, and along lines of sexual preference.

A perfect example would be the preliminary response of black women to Anita Hill's claims at the hearing. Educated professionals and intellectuals overwhelmingly sided with Hill. Most working-class sisters and middle-class black women from working-class backgrounds sided with Thomas. I suspect that gay black women sided with Hill and that heterosexual black women were somewhat more inclined to side with Thomas. This difference in opinions among black women (like everything else having to do with black women) was never explored anywhere in the press, so far as I can tell.

On the other hand, it is true that black feminism often inadvertently privileges the standpoint of women, just as I would expect Patterson to privilege the standpoint of men. In "Blacklash" I was not disappointed in this regard. I don't want to quibble with most of his arguments, including the idea that black women have certain cultural advantages in the dominant society. What I am interested in is accounting for this situation, where some black women have a certain advantage (which results in their higher educational rate and the other indicators of success Patterson points out) at the same time that the plight of poor black women has become graver, and seemingly intractable. According to the black female historian Patricia Morton, in her book *Disfiguring Images: The Historical Assault on the Black Woman*, "Mammy," the dominant stereotype of the black woman since the late nineteenth century, conveys a cultural weight which is empirically real and, at the same time, mythologically pernicious.

Patterson is right, it seems to me, that poor black men find themselves in a soul-killing dilemma. My one caveat would be—and this should not be a competition—that young black girls are experiencing the death of the soul, as well. The suicide figures, the ones which suggest that black men have the highest rate of suicide and that black women have the lowest, are persuasive; but it seems to me there are other ways to kill the self besides deliberate suicide. Last fall the *New York Times* featured a series on 129th Street in Harlem, and the thing that struck me most about it was how interrelated gender definitions were in the destruction of that community. I mean for every father who won't marry and who is crippled or incarcerated as a result of his participation in the drug trade, there is also a mother who has no idea how she'll provide for the children she's having and who finds crack and alcohol a welcome relief from the realities of her existence.

I would also note that Patterson tends to view gender relations through a heterosexual lens. Using the work of cultural critic and literary theorist Eve Kosofsky Sedgwick in *The Epistemology of the Closet* and *Tendencies*, one comes to realize that the realities of individual subjectivity can involve a huge number of subtle differentiations and permutations of gender and sexuality, most of which we've barely begun to acknowledge or explore. As Sedgwick points out, everybody is different. Patterson needs to consider the psychological present more. Instead he seems preoccupied with the impact of the history of slavery. I would agree that slavery is still extremely important, but the reality is that when you're poor and black, male or female, it is still very hard to have *any* identity as an individual, psychologically. Not only doesn't the white dominant culture allow it, your family, your community, your political, intellectual, and cultural leaders don't usually allow it either. I don't want to argue with the specific hypotheses he makes about what is motivating the self-destruction of black men or how it works. Some of them seem a little far-fetched, while others seem brilliant and inspired to me, such as the idea that black macho "street culture acts as a belated, but savagely effective means of breaking with the mother."[4] The point is that he is proceeding in the right direction and that we need to be thinking along these lines. Granted, it came into my mind whether or not he had any real experience of black life in the streets, and it would have been helpful if he had filled in that blank; still, in general, I find the effort Patterson has made to understand black gender relations an entirely laudable and praiseworthy one. I hope this work will encourage others to take up the debate in the public sphere.

Originally published in *Transition* 5, no. 2 (summer 1995): 98–101.

Notes

1. Orlando Patterson, "Backlash: The Crisis of Gender Relations among African Americans," *Transition* 62 (1993): 4–26.
2. Patterson, "Backlash."
3. Ibid.
4. Ibid.

33.

The Problem with Black Masculinity and Celebrity

In the recent battles of the culture wars, the mantra of "political correctness" has had a chilling effect on multiculturalism and the prospect of progressive change of all sorts. As such, taking political correctness seriously as a form of critique was never anything I expected to do. In an article that analyzes the various mixed messages of the term, cultural critic Bob Stam asks: "Do we mean it in the original loftiest sense of a self-mocking apology for a politically indefensible taste, or in the right-wing sense of a broad brush attack on an incoherent array of ideological bogeymen?" (*Social Text*, no. 36: 30)

About two years ago, my response was to say that neither perspective had much to do with me, and that it was a fight between powerful men. But, at the time, I also suggested that a limited form of political correctness, or, as I defined it then, "a set of spoken or unspoken rules" plagued discussions of black popular culture. Now I would like to expand that critique to add that "political correctness" may be precisely the issue when it comes to the general inability of the dominant culture to take black people seriously and to see them as human beings.

Moreover, demonstrations of "political correctness" as the only visible alternative to wholesale denigration in the portrayal of blacks have had a devastating effect on black intellectual morale, in direct proportion to the degree that the black audience has assimilated the consumerist standards and values unrelentingly promoted by the media.

Let's face it, the world is in a hell of a mess, and nobody really knows how to fix it. Now that's a fact. And I do not know a single leftist I respect who will not admit that in private, if not in public. I will not go into detail about precisely what the problem is but I am sure you are familiar with the various hot spots: the post–Cold War impossibility of socialism; the immorality of global, postindustrial capitalism; too much meaningless and infuriating labor, red tape, and traffic; too much garbage, waste, and war; too much ethnic strife, starvation, and conspicuous consumption. Illiteracy and superstition, homelessness and disease are rampant throughout the world and seem increasingly incurable. Meanwhile, the rich just get richer, and so forth.

At the same time, I do not see much of a point in blaming our problems on masculinity or other binaries of gender, the heterosexual imperative, or even racialism, which is not to say that the heterosexual imperative or racialism is good. It is just to ask: If it is the fault of the heterosexual imperative or racialism that things are not going well, then exactly who am I supposed to target? I myself am said to be heterosexual, and I am definitely a racialist, but I never consented to a "heterosexual imperative." No one ever asked my permission about the race situation. I was born into it. We all were. The point is that it is not a simple matter to fix what is broken. The enemy is ourselves. We are all implicated, particularly those of us who have the wherewithal to debate the problems. Perhaps the multimillionaires are slightly more culpable than I am, but then, knowing that does not fix anything either.

So we are going to hell in a handbasket, but the thing that scares me the most is that pleasure might leave the world. The current interest in popular culture among leftist academics, intellectuals, and artists is largely motivated, I suspect, by the perception that popular culture — regardless of whose culture it may actually be — still seems able to maintain, against the onslaught of prudish utilitarianism and negativity, an intentional and deliberate space for fun and games, and damn the cost.

But the trouble I continue to have with black popular culture, perhaps especially the most vocal and prominent practitioners of rap, is not just a matter of a politically incorrect snobbism toward "renegade" forms of low culture. Granted, I am not especially enamored of the aggressive and belligerent stance often assumed in rap. I am getting to be too old, in any case, to kowtow to each new variation and twist in black youth culture. As an admitted outsider to many of the most highly contested forms of black popular culture, it still seems to me that the crucial problem for black intellectuals and cultural life is a problem we all share: the problem of celebrity. Within the dynamic of an increasingly technologized, computerized, and consumer-oriented dominant culture, the black body is frequently fetish-ized in disturbingly aggressive ways. This problem of how the procedures of celebrity are used to disenfranchise us all is not unknown in other communities and sectors of cultural production—among white rockers or high-priced actors in Hollywood films, for example. But it seems particularly unexamined and uncritiqued in African American cultural and intellectual production.

Visible black intellectuals and cultural producers are increasingly confined to the limited binary of those who are rich, famous, and narcissistic, or those who are poor, obscure, invisible. In fact, as the protagonist in Ralph Ellison's *Invisible Man* taught us, intellectual or cultural productivity among blacks requires that we seek out and explore complicated combinations of strategies of visibility and invisibility in order to survive. Black intellectuals and writers invariably teach us that the rich and famous treadmill is always a mixed blessing for any black person who is serious about his or her vocation, and whose vocation is other than self-promotion.

The way both O.J. Simpson and Mike Tyson fell from grace as black men has everything to do with the binary appeal of fetishization. What appalls me is not that Simpson and Tyson are seen as monsters for their alleged crimes but rather that they were idealized and worshipped to begin with. Only in the strangely parasitic black world spawned by the white dominant culture would a retired football star who was a sports commentator be a viable candidate for heroism.

As in any other community or culture, the best, brightest, and most productive people are rarely also the loudest, the crudest, the most duplicitous and hypocritical, the most calculating and aggressive, the most careerist, ambitious, shallow, and cutthroat. And yet, when it comes to the black world as projected through a white-dominated media, one quickly arrives at the impression that there are only two kinds of black people: the successful ones who do nothing but promote themselves and the underclass ones who spend all their time robbing, stealing, doing drugs, and killing. We are all aware of this double image. What I am trying to point out is that they are flip sides of the same coin, and neither of them has anything to do with who black people—black men or black women—really are.

This is why, invariably, most black intellectuals and artists always pray for more powerful black influence in media, but even there the situation seems hopeless, because black media exist under the financial thumb of dominant media and dominant advertising. When I recently considered the array of black magazines available in Barnes & Noble—*Ebony, Jet, Essence, Emerge,*

Upscale, *Vibe*, and about four or five hair magazines—I was discouraged. This is not to say *Essence*, *Emerge*, and *Vibe*, do not cover their ground well. It is just that invariably what these magazines emphasize and foreground is the success of the subject in terms of fame, wealth, and conspicuous consumption—in the *Ebony* profile of Terry McMillan, it is the car she drives, the house she lives in.

Just once I would like to see some focus on what thoughtful black people think about the issues: health, welfare, the economy, and so forth. Such commentary exists, but it is never highlighted. And thoughtful black people rarely become celebrities quoted in the *Times* on every topic from soup to nuts. Thoughtful black people are so generally unanticipated, their ability to earn a living can be seriously impeded. They are anachronisms in a black world in which black coverage in the daily newspapers, the TV newsmagazines, and *Vanity Fair* confines itself mostly to broadcasting either our fame and celebrity or our abjection.

Because black intellectuals and cultural producers have so little control over the designation of their heroes and "role models," invariably our representatives are chosen not on the basis of their intelligence or depth but rather on the basis of how much controversy they can stir up.

When you look at so-called black leadership as reflected by the mainstream media, what you see is a motley crew of the narcissistic, the vaguely ridiculous, and the inept. There is no actual lack of intellectuals, artists, and cultural workers in a wide array of fields. Rather, such people have always been there, continuing their work and making themselves useful in relationship to the *real* issues. Thoughtful and sensitive people have a tendency to find celebrity somewhat problematic. They may even deliberately avoid it; if, however, you are black and avoid celebrity, you will certainly be invisible. You might end up homeless as well.

Lately, I have been going quite often to use the research facilities at the Schomburg Center in Harlem on the corner of 135th Street and Lenox Avenue. The facility takes up an entire block. It is beautiful, calm, tranquil—an impeccably organized wealth of information, both in terms of staff and collections, which entirely contradicts the world of dominant black representations. Even the founder of the place, Arthur Schomburg—a black Puerto Rican—where does he fit among dominant racial stereotypes of black men? How many rappers mention him, or Carter G. Woodson, or W. E. B. Du Bois, or Ida B. Wells, in their rhyme schemes?

Outside on 135th Street is the vision of hell unfolding. On one corner is Harlem Hospital, where a corpse was found in the laundry chute a few years ago. On another corner are the shabby stores and greasy spoons of the ghetto. On another corner, a schoolyard. And on the fourth corner, the Schomburg, elegant and pristine, an oasis in the desert.

Inside, I am surrounded by the helpful assistance of an almost entirely black staff—from security guards to librarians and administrators. Not one person shouts "Black Power!" In fact, no one raises their voice at all. Despite the perpetual racket outside, there is a blissful peace within these walls.

In African American life and culture, it sometimes seems as though fame is everything, and that anybody who is not constantly in the media could not possibly be doing anything important. This is not to say that it is not nice to have famous black academics, writers, authors, artists, and athletes. It is both wonderful and necessary. I just think their value should be keyed to their substance.

For instance, Michael Jordan is famous for playing basketball perhaps better than anyone ever has on the planet, but the fact that he plays basketball so well does not make him a better human being than others in any way. In fact, it is likely that his personality is limited in some other way to compensate for his extraordinary abilities in this particular area. This is the way extraordinary abilities tend to work, which is precisely the reason that black artists and intellectuals should not be worshipped anymore than other kinds of people.

Worshipping them as heroes (O.J. Simpson) and saints (Martin Luther King Jr.) seems to me the flip side of the way in which black men in conflict with the establishment are demonized. Black men on welfare, homeless, with AIDS, in jail, and so forth are seen as disproportionately villainous, just as famous blacks are seen as disproportionately heroic. In both cases, blackness is fetishized. There is no middle ground. The idea that you could be good at something, in a quiet, self-confident way, becomes impossible to imagine, not only for the general American public but, more importantly, for young black people. They do not think it's possible because they rarely see it or hear about it.

Ultimately, the values that are held up to young people by the dominant society are all wrong, and it is not simply a matter of masculine values. Masculinity is not an inherently meaningful designation. Such qualities as courage, militancy, aggression, competitiveness, coolness, grace, elegance in battle, rigidity, and sexual promiscuity are not qualities that only men have. They are qualities that are exalted in our society, and women who have them are just as likely to rise to the top as men and perhaps just as likely to cause disaster in their personal relationships. The model of humanity such people employ is not real. It is a fantasy for men as well as women to think that you can be, in real life, a character in a movie.

Adults soon figure out that the price one must pay for recklessly flaunting such qualities may be death. The qualities that make it possible to grow old and endure the frustration and pain that are inevitable in life, whether one is male or female, are patience, kindness, reflectiveness, gentleness, thoughtfulness, strength, determination, playfulness, warmth, friendliness, a sense of humor, and a dash of honesty. Reckless daring and adventure are the spice of life, not the meat.

Because of this, nothing worries me more than the spectacle of Malcolm X's reification. Malcolm X died in the awful way he did because he discovered the lesson above too late to save his own life. He was not rich, but he was famous, and they killed him for it. In this sense, Malcolm X's life is a narrative much like the old, frightening Grimm's fairy tales, in which characters were burned up or torn asunder. The lesson of Malcolm X's life is not that one should live as he lived but rather to learn from the story of his death how to live.

Originally published in Maurice Berger, Brian Wallis, and Simon Watson, eds., *Constructing Masculinity* (New York: Routledge, 1995), this essay has been revised for this volume.

34.

The Fame Game

As I pondered my prospects as a writer in my early twenties, I began to notice that the common denominator among most successful black writers and intellectuals was that they had criticized other blacks in their work. Although the criticisms were often intended to precipitate constructive social change and never made solely for the edification of a white audience, they were generally how the black writer first came to public attention.

Whites, or at least their media moguls, didn't find it interesting when we applauded or praised one another's virtues. What was more interesting, even fascinating, was when we criticized each other. Booker T. Washington dubbed it the "crabs in the barrel" syndrome in his autobiography *Up from Slavery*, implying that backbiting was motivated principally by narrow-minded jealousy and competition. But the phenomenon of prominent blacks publicly castigating one another, or their race in general, went a good deal further than simple envy. Even after Black Power, the disturbing suspicion that the function of the black intellectual was confined to the performative continued to haunt me.

What you could say or do for the race itself had to be accomplished after you had satisfied this criteria of amusing, or titillating, the powers that be. The classic case is *Native Son*, the first black bestselling novel, which Richard Wright significantly altered to appease the scruples of the Book-of-the-Month Club. Nevertheless, in a lurid and suspenseful book, Wright portrays black women as dreadful, ignorant mothers and wretched, boozy girl-friends. The protagonist, Bigger, is himself an inarticulate psychopath. Yet, through his murderousness, we are told, he becomes a man. Then both James Baldwin and Ralph Ellison subsequently accuse Wright of crudely politiciz-ing the black experience, of ignoring its true human complexity. Neither of these gents, however, manages to evade black-on-black criticism either. Baldwin takes multiple hits for being too political and Ellison for not being political enough.

But not only did they endure black-on-black criticism, they engaged in it. In *Invisible Man*, Ellison lays waste to Booker T. Washington, the black nationalist, and the Harlem Communist schools of black leadership. In *Notes of a Native Son*, Baldwin critiques black culture for failing to produce a Michelangelo or Sistine Chapel. Through the '60s and '70s, the saga con-tinues unabated, as women writers Toni Morrison, Alice Walker, and Maya Angelou join the field. And those novelists, poets, playwrights, and intellec-tuals who have less negative intraracial commentary such as a Larry Neal or a Toni Cade Bambara also get less mainstream (white) attention.

In the '90s, the more things change, the more they stay the same. Black writers would appear to have more flexibility now that the publishing indus-try recognizes the existence of a black book-reading, book-buying public. Substantial numbers have developed loyal audiences that have made their taste for black heroics and accomplishments clear. Yet, despite the present proliferation of black writers in print, together with the various announce-ments of a black renaissance and a new, more resilient flock of black intel-lectuals with broader mass appeal, there is an aspect of this dilemma that remains unaltered.

Black intellectuals, cultural critics—whatever you want to call them—are still not free to speak their minds anywhere except in their living rooms. The secret of conquering the so-called public sphere, which is just another name for the white-dominated marketplace of ideas, continues to be having something critical to say about other blacks. This isn't to say that black intel-lectuals aren't doing something useful and necessary for black culture in their criticisms. But often it is at the risk of their intentions being seen as careerist and self-aggrandizing rather than philanthropic and salutary.

In recent times, the occasions that come to mind are Henry Louis Gates Jr.'s dissection of Afrocenric anti-Semitism on the Op-Ed page of the *New York Times*, the "Black Male" show at the Whitney, and my review of bell hooks's current books in the *Voice Literary Supplement*. As for my review of bell (I'll leave the other two matters for some future date), like most black cultural critics whose words may seem harsh, I was trying to make a constructive intervention. The point is, was, to say to white folks—and any other folks who didn't already know it—there are other black feminists besides bell, besides me. Ultimately, I made the decision that the particulars of how the *VLS* wrapped the package—the photos, the cover lines, so forth—was less important than the intervention itself.

Part of what you're always up against is the general plight of the progressive intellectual in these parts since forever, never more so than in our current historical moment. Another part of the problem is the present roster of extant publications. A cursory perusal of the newsstand will reveal these to be *The New Yorker*, *Esquire*, and *Ebony*, plus a shitstorm of computer, popular music, hair, and fashion magazines. The only decent forum for black intellectuals remains the obscure and difficult to find (try a good bookstore, not a newsstand) *Transition* and even more difficult to find *Renaissance Noire* and *Souls*. But perhaps the most important thing to remember, if you are going to survive in this "funnyhouse of the negro," is that the practice of critique, regardless of whose critique it is or what it is critiquing, should be taken with a grain of salt and a liberal dash of humor.

My first instruction in this school of thought came from poring over various texts in the wee hours of my blessed exile from being the *Black Macho* goddess of the Northeast Corridor. In Norman, Oklahoma, as a writing professor in the '80s, I'll admit I was pretty depressed about the situation of playing to a white audience, until I realized that numerous black authors— Douglass, Washington, Du Bois, Toomer, James Weldon Johnson—had already extensively debated the difficulties of writing intraracial critique in white America.

It was the new black literary criticism of Robert Stepto's *From Behind the Veil* and Gates's anthology *Black Literature and Literary Theory* that finally made me aware that these works were essential readings of the canon of Afro-Am lit. In this latter book's penultimate essay, "The Blackness of Blackness: A Critique of the Sign and the Signifying Monkey," Gates offers us a genealogy of African American culture in which a practice known as "signifying" provides the glue.

Du Bois had first spoken of this "double consciousness" in *The Souls of Black Folks* (1903); what it boiled down to, according to Stepto, Gates, and an increasing number of black intellectuals and critics (and despite the various theoretical differences), was that everything black writers wrote had a double voice. We were able to address the dominant white culture and black audiences—often in richer, denser, more complex terms—at the same time. As such, African American culture was not only a syncretic hybrid, as Ralph Ellison and Ishmael Reed had already made us aware of, but also much like a game of peekaboo that we black intellectuals and artists had uniquely fashioned in order to circumvent the full blow of white cultural hegemony. Reading Albert Murray's *Stomping the Blues* for the first time while in Norman also helped me understand the peculiar strategics of such movements.

Despite the seriousness of the issues involved (the political, economic, and cultural future of brown people on the planet), we can never afford to forget that being a black intellectual in the U.S. is still a game. Call it the fame game, or the culture game. While the stakes are quite serious, you must never take yourself too seriously because the game will continue whether or not you blow your top. As we've seen much too often lately, celebrity blacks are free to employ narcissism, nihilism, self-absorption, and social isolation defensively and in liberal portions just in order to stay in the game. But as long as they wish to remain cultural critics and not just hunger artists, black cultural critics cannot afford the luxury of declaring themselves incommunicado.

Originally published in the *Village Voice*, 5 March 1996, pp. 18–19.

35.

Skip Gates's Africa

Review Essay on *Africana: Encyclopedia of the African and African American Experience*, edited by Henry Louis Gates Jr. and Kwame Anthony Appiah (Basic Civitas Books, 1999); and *Wonders of the African World* by Henry Louis Gates Jr. (Knopf, 1999).

What is really at stake here is the corporatization of the African Diaspora. Gates seems to have cornered the market almost before anyone of any consequence had even figured out that it could be a market. Even more disturbing, and central to the controversy around the documentary, in particular, is that nobody can really figure out how much this pays. No one should expect the academic world to be happy about Professor Henry Louis Gates's recent success and bonanza in African diasporic products (there will be notecards, dolls, and calendars next). As for how to evaluate the products, I would say that the answer is this: the products are highly collaborative in nature, strange, and perhaps still too new and inchoate in their impact to judge.

It is as if Gates had somehow put himself up for office in academe, and he had failed to make full financial disclosure. The idea of a teacher, even a highfalutin Harvard professor and chair, growing rich from the practice of his vocation, and employing hundreds of other academics and independent scholars at minimal wages to do his grunt work, invites wild, virtually endless speculation. When I bring his name up among academics, I commonly find myself engaged in conversations in which the assumption is that Harvard pays him in perks and salary equivalent to at least $500,000 or even a million. He makes what CEOs of corporations make, academics say. They say he sits on sixty-five corporate boards and keeps a flock of proxies to attend the meetings for him. They say all kinds of wild things.

Even if some of this is true, and I vacillate on whether I believe any of it or not, is one man's paycheck what really matters here? Who doesn't know that these massive research projects aren't possible without hundreds of warm bodies to track down the footnotes? Should this encyclopedia be handled any differently from any of the other encyclopedias in the library?

But what people really have big trouble with is the BBC documentary *Wonders of the African World* hosted by Skip Gates Jr. himself in a Harvard T-shirt apparently looking for all the evidence he could find that an Afrocentric notion of black identity simply does not exist on the African continent. One of my Ph.D. students from the Cameroons who attended the so-called conference on the documentary at CUNY's Medgar Evers College in the heart of black Brooklyn said if Gates had been present, he might have been lynched. It is, no doubt, a scandal in the black intellectual world, albeit no scandal in America where corporate wealth is king: he is getting to be a fat cat, even fatter than the fattest cat of all, Booker T.

Gates's appropriation of the mantle of W. E. B. Du Bois makes everybody mighty nervous, too. Du Bois has only lately (last two to three decades) been retrieved from the dustbin of history owing to his leftist leanings during the Cold War. Such books as Adolph Reed's *W. E. B. Du Bois and American Political Thought* and Hazel Carby's *Race Men* suggest that Gates is appropriating the early, "liberal" Du Bois, even deliberately suppressing Du Bois's historical development toward a more radical political position. Meanwhile, hanging in the balance is the question of whether Booker T., the original author of the crabs-in-the-barrel hypothesis, was the sleazy operator he has often been made out to be, or the working man's last best chance under Jim Crow segregation. Is this one of those Right against Left battles, the old anti-communist rumbles stirring their eternal heads, the way the white leftists have always taught (and continue to teach) us, or are there more complicated loyalties and kinships here? Who are the bad guys and what are they about?

The salary situation for the average academic, the opportunities, and the gig have never been worse. In addition to a top tier, divided by a stratified hierarchy of city, state, and private colleges, Ivy Leagues and Top Ten, academe now features an entire second tier of fully trained, often even over-qualified, workers currently employed for no more than half of what the average one of us in the first tier is making. Hypothetically, they stand ready to replace us should we ever choose to act up the way the air controllers did all those years ago.

Sometime between when Nixon and Reagan got into presidential office, academics, students, and faculty who were leading antiwar resistance and other progressive causes, became a target of a conservative coalition of forces — corporate, religious, and god knows who else along for the ride — to stop academia from being a pivotal political force to swing the nation toward the liberalization of social policy. Herein we see a continuation of the culture wars thus begun, but this time academics, not artists such as Robert Mapplethorpe and Andres Serrano, are at the center. At the very point at which black academics are being impoverished and rendered helpless as never before, in strides the token successful black corporate academic of the world is simply doing it the way the white boys invented at Harvard, Princeton, and Yale. We can say it is crabs-in-the-barrel to complain, but that crab has been dining on filet mignon for years.

At this point not only have black academics turned on Gates but white academics and the rest of the left-leaning intelligentsia has as well. Of course, it comes too late to stop him by the usual means of notoriety and dismissal, which is why you don't hear a word about the problem in the mainstream press. People say we academics are afraid to speak against him but that is not it. We are not all junior professors seeking tenure, or adjuncts seeking permanence and security. There are surely many of us who owe our stature in part to his generosity but who are nevertheless beyond a point in our careers where we could not afford to risk saying whatever we were thinking about the matter.

Of course, there are some people who are paranoid enough to think that nothing about the schism appears in the press (read the *New York Times*) because Gates, supposedly like Booker T., has it all sewn up. But I think the reason we don't speak is because wiser heads know it isn't going to do any good, and it might hurt now that his production has crossed over into the corporate stratosphere. I would call it the *Eyes on the Prize* (the famous documentary series on the civil rights movement) syndrome, except that *Eyes on the Prize* was diplomatic and cautious enough not to feature the physical presence of its creator, Henry Hampton, who shaped it as surely as Gates shaped *Wonders*. You can expect, as was true with *Eyes on the Prize*, that the whole series of products will be loaded on every educational hard drive and featured in every reference section in every library in this country and a lot of other places in the world as well within the next five years. With Bill Gates's largess of generally dispensing computers already loaded with *Encarta Africana* throughout the nation's public (read black) schools, the shove will be on to indoctrinate the masses, already pre-tenderized by corporate world beat and hip-hop, into this new corporatized diasporic perspective, which fits so well with corporate multiculturalism.

But the portion of his project that is about propelling him into the spotlight may, nevertheless, fail because this is no longer about the individual man Henry Louis Gates Jr. anymore. Just as Aunt Jemima's pancakes has never been about the various women paid to play Aunt Jemima. Rather it is about money, influence, and cultural capital. At the same time, the many and virtually endless wonders of the African world, which are ostensibly being announced to a global audience by this series of products, are getting lost in a poisonous mix of fratricidal venom and the fast fizzling attempt to launch yet another deity in the black cult of personality (Michael Jordan comes to mind).

On TV, if you are continually on camera, you must be likeable. On screen, there is such a thing as "unlikeable," and it becomes very clear very quickly. It's the reason that networks pay such astronomical sums for news anchors and such. Let us suppose that this tour of African wonders had been hosted by Ed Bradley instead of Dr. Skip Gates. I dare say this pill would have gone down a lot easier. Either way, nevertheless, for good or evil *Wonders of the African World* et al. are here to stay, just like *Eyes on the Prize*, at least in part because it is built upon a highly complicated and densely networked structure of encyclopedia, Web site, and CD.

Africana, the encyclopedia, seems an attempt to initiate our own national version of South Africa's Truth and Reconciliation Commission, but not only is this done at a fairly high, and subsequently exclusionary intellectual level, but it is also minus the immediate afterglow of hard-won political struggle or the patina of heroes like Nelson Mandela and Rev. Desmond Tutu. For that matter, the encyclopedia also lacks any compelling argument for or against official apologies to the descendants of African American slaves. On the other hand, the encyclopedia's orientation and speculation, particularly when accompanied by such easier-to-decipher tools as *Encarta Africana 2000* (CD) and *Wonders of the African World*, leave us near incapable of determining who, if anybody, might need to apologize for the behavior of their ancestors because African peoples were as implicated in slavery's dealings as were white Americans, Europeans, and Arabs.

The trouble here is that the more you know, the more the idea of an accurately vast encyclopedia becomes insupportable. Gates's and Appiah's *Africana* is no exception. The project of encyclopedias in general is crosshatched with highways and byways at each step; most of them, if pursued, will turn out to be dead-ends insofar as usable insight. Encyclopedias are also impossible to describe in their endless detail, so I won't even bother to pretend that I've read all 2000 plus pages of it. It is tempting as a black feminist to speculate about why references to the accomplishments of women in general are smaller or less central than those to men, even as there are large and important exceptions to this rule, including a large entry on African women in the visual arts by Betty LaDuke.

Yet consistently, in category after category of music, theater, dance, and the visual arts, women are given less space than their male peers, or their entries lack a picture, or their contribution is made to look subsidiary and diminutive in any one of a range of ways. In the CD version of the encyclopedia, *Encarta Africana*, in which entries are supported by relatively complex visual apparatuses, it becomes even clearer that women haven't been the definitive innovators of culture in *Africana*'s version of things. This assertion is made, nevertheless, without benefit of the substantial new additions on a new and improved *Encarta Africana 2000* CD and accompanying Web site, which includes a total of 800 more Web links and about 7 million more words than the encyclopedia's former 2.5 million.

According to Michel Marriott in the *New York Times* ("World's Worth of Black History: *Encarta Africana 2000*," November 4, 1999), much of the new material draws upon the newly constructed Library of Black America, a 6.3 million-word computerized collection of already existing documents, such as articles, novels, poetry, slave narratives and other nonfiction works of the African Diaspora. I would assume that, nevertheless, as is traditional in the black world when men dominate, the token Goddess Mother/Divas would remain highly visible.

The Goddess Mother Diva of them all (after Lucy) is El Ma'mariya, a wavy, abstract terra cotta goddess figure, dated 4000–3200 B.C.E. (African art collection, Brooklyn Museum), a photograph of which is featured on the *Encarta Africana* CD. Yet her origins and contextual importance remain mysterious once you've consulted the encyclopedia because she isn't included either under her own name or under the copious entry on "Art and Architecture, African." Part of the lack of explication may be simple oversight. The name of the work is "Amratic Nagada." "Amratic" refers to the period of late Neolithic cultures of predynastic Egypt and the Nagada culture was located in South Egypt in the fourth millennium.

Success stories, such as the professional lives of Whoopi Goldberg and Maya Angelou, serve as present-day goddesses, each of who conduct several star turn/talking head segments on the *Encarta Africana* CD in which they define or describe, presumably in the vernacular, weighty concepts or figures central to the thesis of the encyclopedia. Goldberg defines identity and talks in cogent sound bytes about how important Amos and Andy, Stepinfetchit, and Rosa Parks were. Angelou, with equal brevity, defines diaspora; reprises the Million Man March; explains the contributions of Oprah Winfrey, Amiri Baraka, Du Bois's dream of the encyclopedia; her presidential inaugural poem "And Still I Rise"; James Baldwin; and Toni Morrison.

Other prominent black figures who substantially invested in the entire encyclopedia project are Kofi Annan, secretary general of the U.N., as well as the famous triumvirate (or dream team) of Harvard Afro-American Studies' professors: Gates, Cornel West, and Anthony Appiah. Apart from the emphasis on the accomplishments of men over those of women, the second, not unrelated, thing that caught my notice was that music is given prominent and extensive treatment on a level far beyond that of any other of the other arts, in particular visual arts.

Nonetheless, words continue to play a crucial role. In his oral presentation on the CD, Appiah makes the connection that the technology of *Encarta Africana* was a reformulation of Du Bois's idea of placing fragments of music transcription from the "soul songs," or spirituals, at the beginning of each of his essays in his first important book, *Souls of Black Folk* (1903). In *Encarta Africana*, it became possible to insert audios and audiovisuals via multimedia segments—thousands of them, in fact.

Unfortunately, however, the specific approach to music and art of the diaspora seems, more or less by default, that of Quincy Jones. As Jones says on the CD, "the black American experience is written in the music. Everything else is . . . Uncle Tom's Cabin, is written by the victors, the conquerors."

On the other hand, the thing that is immediately evident after only a cursory examination of the final volume is that while exposition on the visual arts is often limited, the actual illustrations used are both extraordinary and rare. Many of them originate with the *Image of the Black in Western Art* collection, begun by the De Menil Foundation, run by Director/Curator Karen Dalton, and now housed at Harvard under Gates's mantle. This collection is closely associated with the four-volume picturebook series that went by the same name, which is now out of print but which only drew upon a small fraction of the entire collection. The encyclopedia includes lots of rarely seen and otherwise hard to obtain illustrations of black life, and yet there is no list of illustrations nor sufficient explanation of their provenance, context, or whereabouts. Whereas actual entries on art are paltry, images of art, including little-known paintings, posters, sculpture, and incredible contemporary and vintage photographs are sprinkled all over the volume.

Despite the copious attention to matters of the Francophone and Latin worlds and diaspora, this is essentially an Anglophone encyclopedia with Appiah, Gates, and Du Bois at the helm. To get some idea of how differently other high-placed camps in academic black studies regard such matters, we must turn to other volumes altogether, such as the autobiographical/poetic series of vivid vignettes in *In Search of Africa* (Harvard University Press, 1998) by Malian Cinema Studies scholar and filmmaker Manthia Diawara, chair of Africana Studies at New York University, who returns to find his roots in what is left of revolutionary Sekou Toure's Guinea after having expatriated to the United States decades before; or *Sojourner Truth: A Life, a Symbol* (Norton, 1996), the psychoanalytically riveting most recent work of black feminist historian Nell Painter, who chaired black studies at Princeton.

In the documentary *Wonders of the African World*, many of Gates's choices plainly had to do with the attempt to favor as vast a reception as possible, without forfeiting the dignified aura of Du Bois's orginal intellectual project and to do for the African Diaspora what the encyclopedists of the Enlightenment did for Europe. Yet although last time I checked we were living in a highly visual society, nothing in the package thus far has been particularly visually appealing — especially at the ordinarily colorful K through 12 level — despite the presence of an abundance of rich and varied visual materials incorporated in the package.

Nonetheless, I offer an alternative to the perspective that dismisses Gates's work precisely because of the dubious ethical proprieties of his corporate successes. Suppose we look at *Africana Encarta, Africana Encyclopedia of the African and African American World*, and the various *Wonders of the African World* not as a tree but as seeds for an entire forest. Suppose whatever this is turns out to be not really about Gates, the individual or even the corporate entity, afterall, but about growth, expansion, new horizons and possibilities for aspirational conceptions of nationalism and internationalism. Suppose we think of this as grounds for finally getting the twenty-volume version that Du Bois originally intended pushed through in Ghana, or even through international cooperation. I am sick to death of can't. Let's try can.

As would also be appropriate in the case of *Encarta Africana*'s CD, I suggest that adult readers save up a block of time in order to make the encyclopedia's acquaintance, and I hope some kind of study guide will soon follow for educators and teachers/parents. Children, I suspect, may not find it particularly user-friendly because its visual presentation is so forboding, dark, and unappetizing. I tried the CD out with my two youngest nieces (eleven and fourteen) and found little there designed to entice them visually into getting interested in the long, densely written passages. On the other hand, my seventeen-year-old niece, a junior at Choate Rosemary Hall, loves it to death and has already used it and its accompanying illustrations in a research paper.

In my view, this work is more suitable for college (maybe not at Harvard and Yale but certainly at CCNY, where I teach) undergraduates and general reference than it is for kids, although it could easily be spruced up to make it attractive to kids, the way the best of their computer games are. Children who aren't black may find some novelty in it at an even younger age, in that it strays significantly from what I assume they are offered in their textbooks in regard to the history of African civilizations and the contributions of the African Diaspora to the New World. But if a prior narrowmindedness about the capacities of the race isn't your guide — and I would assume such a mind-set would be comparatively rare among the purchasers of this volume and CD — the talking heads, no matter how monosyllabic and vernacular their discourse, are just dull. The virtual tours are fun for adults who have achieved the taste to appreciate a stroll through the often monotone ruins of the ancient world. Children will probably find it difficult to make the conceptual leap, certainly if they haven't already been on such trips.

Meanwhile those children who are determined and resolute enough to explore the hidden secrets of *Africana* encyclopedia and *Encarta Africana* have a special treat in store. It should continue to prove uniformly fascinating for more developed and informed readers to ponder the logic of this encyclopedia's growth and development, as well as where it all may be leading.

VI.

QUEER THEORY AND

VISUAL CULTURE

36.

Defacing History

"Facing History: The Black Image in American Art, 1710–1940" was an exhibition with an apparently straightforward agenda. It sought to gather together a representative sample of paintings, sculptures, and drawings that each included a black person as part of their content. This effort could be seen as part of a larger intellectual project — looking at how blacks have been represented in the (mostly white) fine arts — that has been undertaken elsewhere in the past decade, notably in the Menil Foundation's multivolume series, The Image of the Black in Western Art, and in art historian Albert Boime's essential study, *The Art of Exclusion: Representing Blacks in the Nineteenth Century* (1990).[1]

One would expect such an ambitious exhibition to encompass at least three interconnected projects: an archaeology of images of blacks in American art, a consideration of the overwhelming dominance of the white perspective in image-making in American culture, and an engagement with the larger critical issues of racism and multiculturalism in the art field. But in the case of "Facing History," the principal motif was, as the *New York Times* said, "Images of Blacks Refracted in a White Mirror." As with other recent studies of blacks in art, the show lost track of the more complex and challenging issues and became little more than the proverbial search for a needle in a haystack: looking for a white male artist in America who has portrayed race but has transcended racism.

"Were better artists able to transcend stereotypes?" asked Patricia Failing in her review of "Facing History" in *Art News*. The very framing of this question belied the conventional belief that transcendence (in this case a code word for sublimity and esthetic mastery) precludes an artwork's accountability in the realms of politics and everyday life. This sentiment was reiterated by Michael Brenson of the *New York Times*, who inadvertently answered Failing's question in his own review when he claimed, "The tone for the show is set not by all the dehumanizing images, but by the few human ones, which deliver a message simply by towering over the others as art."[2]

For most critics, the main question was not "What do these images tell us about the experience of being black in America?" but more simply, "Is it great art?" This determination of greatness or transcendence seemed to depend, in turn, on a rather simplified realism-versus-stereotype debate in which more "realistic" (less stereotypical or distorted) representations of blacks were those that most succeeded as art and consequently transcended bigotry. Even the show's black curator, the late Guy McElroy, seemed to agree that esthetic mastery is capable of canceling out the pervasive racism of the images. "When you look at this show, you won't feel subjected to a negative experience," McElroy said. "The paintings are too beautiful and the points they make are too strong in presenting the complexities of African-American life."[3]

But I would argue that the very process of using imagery to try to determine whether an artist is racist or not trivializes the way in which racism functions. In the fine art of the nineteenth century, in particular, whatever inclination there was to portray blacks in more realistic or less derogatory terms had more to do with fashions in art and the influence of European styles than with any substantive changes in social attitudes toward blacks.[4] Precisely what is needed in debates about images of blacks is "the recognition that vision *has* a history, that there are different regimes of visuality."[5] The promulgation of stereotypes, for instance, has been only one of the manifestations of racism in fine art. A better way to understand racism in the visual sphere — then and now — is to understand the various historical phenomena that add up to what I call "invisibility."[6]

The chief way invisibility has worked in visual art since the nineteenth century is that blacks often seem not to exist in society because they are for the most part excluded from representation. In any survey of American art, for example, one finds this literal invisibility: blacks are simply absent both as subjects and as producers of art. A second, much more infrequent but no less crucial way invisibility has worked — at least in figurative art — can be seen when blacks are depicted but at the same time trivialized and degraded (made *virtually* invisible) by the terms of their representation. Many of the works in "Facing History" portray blacks in this way: objectified, subsidiary or servile, in the background, or in the shadows. Such strategies of portrayal can be found in the conventional forms of both realism and stereotypical images. Indeed, the overarching concept of "invisibility" makes clear that realism and stereotyping are really two sides of the same coin. Each ignores the larger framework in which representational conventions—what Martin Jay calls the "scopic regimes of modernity"[7]—are constructed and reproduced.

As a black feminist critic, I would hope that the principal purpose for studying images of blacks in visual art is to gain insight into cultural racism. Therefore, the questions we should be asking are: Have racial myths been supported by specific visual constructions that have evolved in Western or American art history? What role, if any, does gender play in visual representations of race? Another key area of discussion should be: Why has there always been such a scarcity of influential black artists in American art history? How can we encourage museums and critics to take seriously the contributions of these artists in the future?

In organizing "Facing History," the Corcoran Gallery of Art in Washington, D.C., actively sought a black audience. Appropriately, they employed a black curator, the late Guy McElroy, a Ph.D. candidate at the University of Maryland, and they asked noted black cultural historian and literary critic Henry Louis Gates Jr. to write the catalogue's introductory essay.[8] Each of these moves by the Corcoran should be commended. But showing images with blacks in them or even inviting a black person to be the guest curator of such an exhibition doesn't necessarily mean that alternative, "other," or black critical perspectives are being explored.

It is my suspicion, in fact, that the exhibition's organizers sought to ensure a pacified audience by deliberately minimizing or suppressing overtly angry or racist images. This was accomplished by focusing on high art (and excluding from the exhibition photography, popular-culture images, and ephemera) and by looking principally at white artists' views of blacks. In this way, the museums that hosted "Facing History" had their cake and ate it, too. On the one hand, the study of racism was limited by excluding the very material (from popular culture) in which racism is most evident and by focusing on the exceptions in fine art—those works in which denigration of blacks is more subtle. On the other hand, because the exhibition was meant to disguise the forcefulness of racism's impact on visual images, expressions of racial difference or political opposition by black artists were all but excluded.

The decision not to use popular-culture images in the show was made rather late in the organizing process, according to McElroy, because the exhibition's corporate and government sponsors did not want to be identified with the really virulent racist messages of the images.[9] In fact, the inclusion of popular-culture images would have necessitated another kind of show altogether (and in my view a far more useful and interesting exhibition), one which would have explored the relationship between representations of blacks in popular culture and representations of blacks in fine art. Sometimes the distinctions weren't all that clear. Some of the most stereotypical portrayals of blacks in genre paintings were reproduced as lithographs for mass circulation. For instance, William Sidney Mount's *The Bone Player* (1856) was one of a series of works commissioned by the Philadelphia publisher William Schaus for lithographic reproduction for the European market.

Even when "Facing History" included paintings such as *The Bone Player*, the fact of the image's circulation as a reproduction and the work's social context were downplayed. By its attachment to the cult value of the autonomous art object, this exhibition missed an opportunity to shed much-needed light on the precise manner in which the collective racism of American white society was constantly being corroborated by the repetition of a relatively invariable set of stock visual images that moved freely back and forth between high culture and popular culture.[10]

By including only high art, the exhibition was misleading, since the sheer volume of popular-culture images of blacks vastly overwhelmed the relatively rare fine-art images of blacks. Throughout the nineteenth century and well into the twentieth century, literally millions of lithographs, posters, political cartoons, postcards, and advertisements depicting blacks were produced. Of these, relatively few were reproductions of paintings like *The Bone Player*. Much more common in popular culture were derisive caricatures of Zip Coon, Jim Crow, or blackfaced performers in minstrel shows. But whether in paintings or popular ephemera, the iconography was roughly the same: blacks singing, dancing, playing music, eating watermelon, and sleeping. In popular-culture images, however, there was a far greater degree of physical distortion. In endlessly inventive ways, these representations supported the widespread belief that blacks were uncivilized and ineducable. A much broader history of images—of high *and* low American visual culture—would have begun to reflect the reality of the violence, both overt and implicit, that black Americans have experienced at the hands of white Americans during the past two hundred years.

The first time I visited "Facing History" was at the Brooklyn Museum on a Sunday afternoon. The mood of the crowd, which included large numbers of black people, mostly in families, was quietly festive, proud, and celebratory. One woman was carrying in her arms, from painting to painting, an unhappy-looking little girl of about five. "We looked at the African art because that's what you like to do," she said to the little girl. "Now we're doing something I like to do."

I suspect that there is a larger black community in Brooklyn than anywhere else in the United States. Harlem seems small and downtrodden in comparison. But the Brooklyn Museum, which presented "Facing History," has little apparent connection to the black community around it. Although I had been living in Brooklyn for about a year, I had never visited the museum. Unfortunately, if you're black, it is one of the least interesting things to do in Brooklyn.

There is so much else to do and see, from Fort Greene, which houses a community of prominent black artists and intellectuals (including Spike Lee); to Prospect Heights, which features the Botanical Gardens; to Eastern Parkway, the route of the carnivalesque and unforgettable West Indian Day Parade (Brooklyn's Mardi Gras). A list of Brooklyn's more fascinating institutions might also include the Brooklyn Academy of Music, where there are often interesting multicultural events; and Boys and Girls High School, which frequently hosts lavish African festivals and black rodeos — it was even the site of Nelson Mandela's first public appearance in New York.

The Brooklyn Museum, which art critic Kellie Jones describes as "aspiring to be the Brooklyn Met," offers little competition to these attractions. As the five-year-old girl accurately perceived, the most interesting thing in the permanent collection for black visitors is the African art, mostly from Zaire. Though contemporary art has increasingly been a priority at the museum, Jones says that "they haven't had either the curators or the interest in black issues to originate their own exhibitions on black subjects." "Facing History" (which was organized by another museum, the Corcoran) was clearly selected to appeal to Brooklyn's black audience but the effect (on me, at least) was just the opposite. With each visit I was struck by the insidious, demoralizing effect of so much sugary racism so ambiguously presented.

In *The Art of Exclusion*, a recently published art-historical study that parallels the concerns of the exhibition, Albert Boime's thesis is that "the visual encoding of hierarchy and exclusion" marked most representations of black people in the nineteenth century and before. By "visual encoding," Boime refers to "a sign system" which "had been put into place to supplement written texts rationalizing slavery and was inseparable from them."[11] In practice this meant that almost invariably — even when representations of blacks in fine art seemed harmless or attractive—the placement of blacks within the activity of the picture, the nature of their action (or inaction), or some other visual formula served to identify the black figure as socially and intellectually inferior.[12]

The questioning of blacks' intellectual ability (and the subsidiary skepticism as to their capacity to create great art) goes right to the heart of nineteenth-century cultural and scientific ideals, which upheld the belief that blacks were biologically incapable of learning and of fitting into American society.[13] During the two decades preceding the Civil War, there was a fascinating correlation between the drawings used to illustrate "objective" scientific studies on racial origins and stereotypical distortions of blacks in popular culture. In both cases, the black person's lack of humanity was signaled by the introduction of the physical characteristics of monkeys, apes, or gorillas. During the same years that this spurious pre-Darwinian American science developed the concept of polygenesis (the theory that the various races evolved as separate species) and claimed a closer relationship between blacks and apes than between whites and apes, visual artists invented the "Sambo" stereotype.[14] In an apparent confirmation of the prevailing scientific hypothesis, Sambo had long arms, bent legs, a sloping forehead, beady eyes, good humor, and an animal-like simplicity. Such flagrantly racist images have all but disappeared from today's visual culture, but the idea that blacks are intellectually or culturally inferior remains entrenched in the institutionalized ethnocentrism, Eurocentrism, and xenophobia that prevails in academia and the arts.[15]

Among the ninety-eight paintings, sculptures, and drawings included in "Facing History," there were numerous pernicious examples of the "visual encoding" noted by Boime. An analysis of these strategies of encoding could begin with the obvious and crude distortions of black physiognomy. Such images are identified with the rise of minstrelsy and Jim Crow in the 1840s, though the earliest versions of these types in painting precede this antebellum boom in reproductions of black images. "Facing History" included such popular paintings as John Lewis Krimmel's *Quilting Frolic* (1813), David Claypoole's *Johnston's Bee Catching* (ca. 1818), William Sidney Mount's *Rustic Dance After a Sleigh Ride* (1830), and Lilly Martin Spencer's *Dixie Land* (1862). In these paintings, the various ludicrously distorted or cliched images of blacks were meant to emphasize the physical differences between blacks and whites as well as to ridicule blacks' intellectual capacity.

Other means of visual encoding, more subtle than physiognomic distortion, included the often formulaic determinism of the placement of blacks in relation to whites in an image. A typical convention is the confinement of black servants to the background or the shadows while white subjects occupy the foreground. This occurs in the early portraits by Justus Englehardt Kuhn and Robert Street and in Richard Caton Woodville's *Old '76 and Young '48* (1849). Another similarly denigrating formula is the white artist's tendency to portray blacks sleeping, as in James Goodwyn Clonney's *Waking Up* (1851), Edwin Forbes's *Mess Boy Asleep* (1867), and Harry Roseland's *Wake Up, Dad* (1896). And then there is the well-worn stereotype of blacks eating watermelon, as in Thomas Hovenden's *Ain't That Ripe?* (ca. 1865). Finally, there is the extremely common circumstance in which blacks occupy a symbolically deferential position in the painting. In Samuel Jennings's *Liberty Displaying the Arts and Sciences* (1792), for example, a white female Liberty offers "knowledge" to a small group of frightened blacks on their knees. In the background, a larger group of blacks, evidently oblivious to the appeal of learning, are playing music and dancing. Such musical stereotypes were frequently employed to depict blacks as clownish performers and to reinforce the belief that they were shiftless and lazy. In all, there were thirteen representations of blacks playing music or dancing in "Facing History."

Against these more familiar and overt forms of racist representation are images that appear to be more sympathetic or "humanistic" in their realistic depictions of blacks. But I would argue that these depictions, though less distorted, are equally racist and even more insidious. According to Boime, the appearance of more realistic images of blacks coincided with the rise of antislavery sentiments in the late eighteenth and early nineteenth centuries. For Boime as well as for the organizers of "Facing History," two paintings are key examples of more realistic, nonstereotypical representations of blacks: John Singleton Copley's *Watson and the Shark* (1778) and William Sidney Mount's *Eel Spearing at Setauket* (1845).

Brooks Watson, a wealthy merchant and Tory leader in England, commissioned Copley to paint *Watson and the Shark* in 1778, during the painter's stay in England. The painting portrays a scene from Watson's youth, when he lost a leg to a shark attack in Havana harbor. Copley's version of the event shows a group of seamen in a boat frantically attempting to rescue the young Watson, who is about to be devoured by the gaping jaws of the shark. Prominently positioned among the seamen is a single black man, who offers a rope to the fallen Watson. Many critics argue that the black man's central position, at the apex of the composition, signifies Copley's intention to confer on him a certain dignity. As McElroy claims in the exhibition catalogue, the black sailor is "a multi-dimensional individual who shares causal equality with a white man."[16]

Although the painting ostensibly portrays an actual event, Boime argues that it should be read as a conservative political allegory about the risk involved in the Empire's loss of the colonies. In this context, the black man "comes off mainly as an exotic servant who awaits his master's next move."[17] Boime insists that the apparently superior position of the black man doesn't signify social advantage but rather the complex intersection of Watson's guilt about supporting the abuses of the slave trade and his apprehensions regarding the future of emancipated blacks. To viewers of the period, it would have been equally evident that it was more frequently black slaves, not rich white gentlemen, who were found floundering in shark-infested waters. White slavers in the triangle trade between Africa, the Caribbean, and the American colonies often threw slaves overboard. If they were sick, they were considered damaged cargo.

While I tend to accept Boime's explanation, the very fact of such polarized debate about whether Copley positioned the black figure to have the upper hand or to play the servant reveals more about the sad limits of such discussions than it does about anything else. Still, *Watson and the Shark* remains virtually the only example of fine art in the American colonies that offers any challenge whatsoever to existing racial hierarchies (and it was painted in England). This fact could and should be the basis for asking an entirely new set of questions regarding the evolution of black images in American art.

The debate over Mount's *Eel Spearing at Setauket* employs similar art-historical cliches about form and biography, though even less convincingly. Mount, who spent most of his life in rural eastern Long Island, is perhaps the most famous nineteenth-century American genre painter. But according to Boime, Mount was a racist Northern Democrat who wrote of his strong opposition to the antislavery movement and who specialized in derogatory portrayals of blacks. Although Mount abandoned the most obvious physical distortion of his black subjects after *Rustic Dance After a Sleigh Ride* in 1830, his representations of blacks usually feature toothy grins, and his black subjects are often shown as clownish entertainers playing musical instruments.

The mysterious subject of *Eel Spearing* is often explained by a letter Mount wrote in 1847 describing how, when he was a young boy, he had been taught to fish for eels by a black slave named Hector. In the painting, which may or may not be a representation of the episode from Mount's youth, the dominant adult figure is not male but a strangely androgynous and forceful female—according to McElroy, without parallel in nineteenth-century American art. Several critics, captivated by Mount's apparent substitution of a black woman for a black man, have speculated that the heroic stature of the female stems from Mount's inability to deal with his homoerotic feelings toward Hector as well as his conventionally racist fear of black male strength.[18]

A more helpful kind of discussion in this instance might focus on why images of black women were so much rarer than those of black men in both popular culture and fine art made in America in the nineteenth century. Whereas European images of blacks in the nineteenth century tend to focus on and exoticize the black female body, American artists were much more likely to avoid the black female body altogether. Black women only really began to surface visually in America with the Aunt Jemima–type images in turn-of-the-century advertising and in Mammy characters in American films of the 1920s and '30s, most typically, *Gone with the Wind*. Within this history of black female imagery, two things about the elaborately clothed black female in *Eel Spearing* seem worthy of further consideration: first, her apparent physical strength, and second, her status as a servant.

The negative view of blacks in the nineteenth century was a collective judgment, widely shared and accepted in a society that aimed at social progress and human perfectibility. In the antebellum period, most white Americans, whether proslavery or antislavery, deeply feared the emancipation of slaves because of the perceived inferiority of black culture. In particular they dreaded a dramatic increase in the size of the then small but fiercely hated free black population, which numbered about 500,000 on the eve of the Civil War.

After the Civil War, some painters, such as Thomas Eakins and Winslow Homer, showed a genuine interest in depicting black culture in ways that went beyond mere convention. In looking at Homer's *Dressing for the Carnival* (1877) or *Gulf Stream* (1899), however, one should remember that he was one of the very few American painters during this post–Civil War period who was painting black subjects at all. This diminishing of representations of blacks in painting during the last quarter of the nineteenth century probably reflects the greater hostility of whites toward blacks during Reconstruction. The 1870s were the beginning of the most harrowing time in American history for African Americans, a time when lynchings, segregation, and political and economic disenfranchisement were rampant.[19]

Homer's paintings reflect but don't necessarily address these problems. Indeed, both Eakins's and Homer's most sympathetic portrayals of blacks are shot through with an acceptance of the subservient and subsidiary role of blacks in American society at the time. Even as some may admire the surface beauty of Eakins's painting of the black man in *Will Schuster and Blackman Going Shooting (Rail Shooting)* (1876), it is impossible to overlook the political and economic reality this picture portrays. The black man is a servant without a name and the white man has the gun.

One of my neighbors in Brooklyn is Art Coppedge, a member of the board of the New York State Council for the Humanities and a black artist who has long been an activist on the art scene. Like many African Americans I spoke to, he was incensed with the scarcity of black artists in "Facing History." He even tried to circulate a petition denouncing the show on this ground — and he had a point. Of the seventy-nine artists in the show, only eight were black: the nineteenth-century painters Edward Bannister, Joshua Johnson, and Robert Duncanson; the nineteenth-century sculptor Mary Edmonia Lewis; the twentieth-century sculptor Sargent Johnson; and the modern painters Archibald Motley Jr., Augusta Savage, and Jacob Lawrence.[20]

One of the implicit assumptions of exhibitions such as "Facing History" is that white images of blacks are more representative, more interesting, and more revealing than black images of blacks. This assumption achieves currency in part because there have always been relatively fewer black artists than white artists in America. Moreover, conventional definitions of fine art often exclude forms — such as quilting, sewing, carving, potting, and other crafts and folk arts — practiced by significant numbers of blacks in the eighteenth, nineteenth, and twentieth centuries. Not surprisingly, however, the works by black artists most often chosen for shows such as "Facing History" are those works that conform most closely to mainstream, white esthetic standards. McElroy suggested as much in an interview when he argued that the techniques and values of black artists "were based on mainstream culture [and] . . . weren't ideologically separate from those of white artists."[21] Instead of replicating the imbalance of black artists to white artists, however, McElroy might have sought to explicate the cultural conditions that created the disparity.

In his introduction to the "Facing History" catalogue, Henry Louis Gates tells a very different story. He says that beginning around the turn of the century, blacks responded to the preponderance of stereotypical images of themselves with alternative visual self-representations. During the period from 1895 to 1925, the appellation "the New Negro" was meant to signify a "self-sufficient, powerfully creative black self." But more often than not, the struggles of black artists to represent this new self were thwarted by art schools, art dealers, and social constraints. As Gates notes, "As long as the decorative mediums of painting and sculpture remained inherently conservative in their positive or negative configurations of black identity, a career in the fine arts remained an extremely tenuous proposition for a black man or woman."[22] Because visual representation was not open to blacks as a form of response to denigration, Gates maintains, blacks during this period generally chose literary modes of refutation.

Afro-American cultural critic and philosopher Cornel West has a different explanation for blacks' frequent shunning of conventional fine-art mediums. West claims that whereas music, religion, and athletics have been indigenous forms of black cultural expression, "the strong, puritanical Protestantism of black religion has not been conducive to the production of pictures." As a consequence, "painting and sculpture are not as widely appreciated as they ought to be in black America [and] pictorial black artists are marginal."[23] West's argument draws attention to the fact that prevailing theories of the historical development of Afro-American culture have their own hierarchies. Orality and musicality come first, then literary works, and after everything else come visual production and visual artists, which are downplayed and ignored—even by blacks themselves.

After the first few weeks that "Facing History" was on view at the Brooklyn Museum, a documentary video narrated by the black actress Ruby Dee was added to the show. Shown in a small room adjoining the main exhibition space, the video seemed to acknowledge the scarcity of black perspectives in the exhibition. After providing a historical summary of racism's causes, the film offered an inventory of black artists, many of them associated with the Harlem Renaissance, who were working in America from the turn of the century into the 1940s: Richmond Barthe, Selma Burke, Aaron Douglas, Meta Warrick Fuller, Palmer Hayden, Malvaux Grey Johnson, Sargent Johnson, William Johnson, Archibald Motley Jr., Jacob Lawrence, Augusta Savage, and James Van Der Zee. Few of these black artists were represented in the exhibition and almost no space was given to the Harlem Renaissance.

In any case, change and greater understanding of racism's effects will never come from a narrow focus on white images of blacks. That's what we already have, and have had all along—in advertising, film, and television as well as in museums and art galleries. Rather, the key to change lies in demystifying the as-yet-unexplored relationships in visual art between white and black images, between "high" and "low" images and between esthetic concepts and historical reality.

Such matters were only further masked, even effaced, by the approach that "Facing History" took toward blacks. An alternative strategy might involve empowering the "other" within the space of the museum. Such an effort would attempt to institutionalize a dialectic between the so-called margin and the center, between the outside and the inside. But "Facing History," which appeared to flow from a new art history informed by political and social approaches (such as feminism and antiracism), was, in the end, extremely ambivalent about drawing upon the very considerable resources of the "other" and bringing what currently lies outside the museum inside.

Originally published in *Art in America* 78, no. 12 (December 1991): 120–29, 184–86.

Notes

1. To a far greater degree than the exhibition itself, the catalogue for "Facing History" provides a complex critical reconsideration of black artists and of the representation of blacks in American art. Guy McElroy, *Facing History: The Black Image in American Art 1710–1940* (San Francisco: Beford Arts Publishers, 1990). This catalogue includes two important essays: McElroy, "Race and Representation," and Henry Louis Gates Jr., "The Face and Voice of Blackness." Both essays are extensively illustrated with just the sort of contemporaneous popular-culture images omitted from the exhibition.

Of the four volumes of The Image of the Black in Western Art that have been published, particularly relevant to this exhibition is volume four, Hugh Honour's *From the American Revolution to World War I* (Part 1: *Slaves and Liberators*; Part 2, *Black Models and White Myth* [Houston: Menil Foundation, 1989–90]. Other books that are relevant to a reconsideration of black representations of blacks in American art are: Karen C. C. Dalton and Peter H. Wood, *Winslow Homer's Images of Blacks: The Civil War and Reconstruction Years* (Houston: Menil Foundation, 1988); Sidney Kaplan, *The Black Presence in the Era of the Revolution, 1770–1800* (Amherst: University of Massachusetts Press, 1990); and Albert Boime, *The Art of Exclusion: Representing Blacks in the Nineteenth Century* (Washington: Smithsonian Press, 1990).

2. Patricia Failing, "Invisible Men: Blacks and Bias in Western Art," *Art News* (summer 1990): 152; Michael Brenson, "Black Images, American History," *New York Times*, 20 April 1990, p. C30.

3. Grace Glueck, "Images of Blacks Refracted in a White Mirror," *New York Times*, 7 January 1990, pp. H1, H37.

4. Instructive here is Linda Nochlin's discussion of Jean-Leon Gerome, a French Orientalist painter who was the teacher of Thomas Eakins—the artist most often cited in "Facing History" as a nineteenth-century American artist who rose above racism. Using the instance of Gerome's so-called realistic (yet patently ahistorical) portrayals of Arabs, Nochlin points out how "realism" can mask the ideological intent of the image by its tendency to be read as "the apparent absence of art." See Linda Nochlin, "The Imaginary Orient," *Art in America* (May 1983): 122.

5. Hal Foster, "Preface," in Hal Foster, ed., *Vision and Visuality* (Seattle: Bay Press, 1989), xiii.

6. In his 1952 novel *Invisible Man*, Ralph Ellison explored the dichotomy of the simultaneous presence and absence of blacks in American culture, which he called "invisibility." As the novel's unnamed hero pursues his search for identity, he is also continually confronting the widespread tendency by American experts (white and black) to misread, misinterpret, and distort the role of blacks in American history and culture.

7. See Martin Jay, "Scopic Regimes of Modernity," in Foster, ed., *Vision and Visuality*, 3–23.

8. McElroy and Gates provide some expansion of the views expressed in "Facing History" in Maurice Berger, "Speaking Out: Some Distance to Go," *Art in America* (September 1990). Guy McElroy died of a heart attack on May 31, 1990, at the age of 44.

9. McElroy, quoted in Glueck, "Images of Blacks," p. H37. Although no popular-culture images of blacks were included in the exhibition, an extensive archive of such representations was compiled and was originally intended for inclusion. Many of these images are illustrated in the "Facing History" catalogue, xiv–xlv.

10. Although the catalogue notes occasionally mention that a painting was reproduced as an engraving or that a sculpture was copied for subscription, this information is not always given. Either way, such information on reproducibility is always de-emphasized in favor of stressing the object's uniqueness.

11. Boime, *The Art of Exclusion*, 15.

12. Such prejudices carry over to this day into how we consider our cultural history. As Henry Louis Gates Jr. recently suggested, racial issues have been almost nonexistent in the humanities because of an ongoing "skepticism about black people's capacity to create 'great art' or 'classics' in any field. American society still perpetuates the most subtle and pernicious form of racism against blacks—doubt about our intellectual capacities." See Berger, "Speaking Out," 81.

13. Even though the scientific basis of the theory of multiple species was long ago discredited, its legacy is the cultural bias of IQ tests. See Stephen Jay Gould, *The Mismeasure of Man* (New York: W.W. Norton, 1981), 30–72.

14. A useful history of the relationship between what Gates calls the "Sambo" stereotype and the development of minstrelsy in the American theater is provided in Joseph Boskin, *Sambo: The Rise and Demise of an American Jester* (New York: Oxford University Press, 1986). Unfortunately, although Boskin focuses on the development of visual images of Sambo, there are very few pictures in his book.

15. After subsequent research, I now see this differently. See forthcoming work on "the problem of the visual."

16. McElroy, *Facing History*, 6.

17. Boime, *The Art of Exclusion*, 32.

18. Ibid., 37. Boime also refers to the studies of Karen Adams and Leslie Fiedler. McElroy's catalogue note on *Eel Spearing at Setauket* summarizes the scholarship on the painting.

19. According to Boskin in *Sambo*, 139: "It was the food industry that made the most extensive use of Sambo in its promotions. Eventually, three human figure trademarks attained national recognition and appeared in cards, on signs, and particularly in newspapers and magazines: Uncle Ben (rice), Aunt Jemima (pancake mix and syrup), and the Cream of Wheat chef." Although these trademarks have been updated and stripped of the most offensive signs of racial stereotyping, their continuing presence and their clear characterization as genial domestic servants encodes a nostalgia for "the good ole days of slavery."

20. It was intended that the most celebrated nineteenth-century black artist, Henry Ossawa Tanner, who studied with Eakins, would be represented in the exhibition by his most famous work, *The Banjo Lesson* (1893). But William R. Harvey, president of Hampton University, which owns the work, protested the exhibition's lack of "real and positive" images of blacks and refused to lend the Tanner work. See Glueck, "Images of Blacks," p. H37.

21. McElroy, quoted in ibid.

22. Henry Louis Gates Jr., "The Face and Voice of Blackness," in *Facing History*, xliv.

23. Anders Stephenson, "Interview with Cornel West," *Flash Art*, no. 133 (April 1987): 55; rev. and repr. in Andrew Ross, ed., *Universal Abandon?: The Politics of Postmodernism* (Minneapolis: University of Minnesota Press, 1988), 283–84.

37.

When Dream Girls Grow Old

I dare say *Waiting to Exhale* was bound to be a hit. That it features not one, not two, but four black actresses in roles other than maids, whores, or their cinematic equivalent is a big part of it. The package includes the top singer (Whitney Houston) and the top actress (Angela Bassett) of the moment. Add a bestselling novel and script adaptation cowritten by the black woman writer (Terry McMillan) of the moment, mix with a black male director who doesn't actually loathe women, and you've got yourself something everybody just has to see. By default.

So McMillan's novel wasn't especially literary. So the script doesn't really have much of a story. So Whitaker's debut as a film director was less than distinguished. Wake up and smell the incense. The black-female movie audience in particular has been languishing on the brink of self-image starvation for years. Aside from *The Color Purple, Daughters of the Dust, Just Another Girl on the IRT, Sankofa*, and a few other fairly recent and mostly obscure films, there hasn't been much to sustain us.

Although rarely taken seriously by anybody but them, the fate of black actresses is nevertheless a key component in this country's unceasing struggle over who will control representations of race, gender, and sexuality. The issue has long since become more complex than whether those images will be "positive" or not, although some of us can't seem to get past that. In a still largely miscegenation-phobic nation, black actresses as women of color embody the contradictory feelings of contempt and desire that issues of race, gender, and sexuality inevitably arouse.

The result can best be seen in what happens to black actresses when they get older. Like black women writers a few decades ago—when Zora Neale Hurston died in poverty and Alice Walker had to rediscover her unmarked grave—black actresses are still likely to die in relative obscurity. The recent prime example is the ignominious death of Butterfly McQueen at eighty-four in a fire while lighting a kerosene heater in a one-bedroom shack outside of Augusta, Georgia.

McQueen, you may recall, starred as Prissy in the retro and racist *Gone with the Wind* (1939). Her now infamous "I don't know nothin' about birthin' no babies!" screeched emphatically in that high-pitched voice, made black women cringe for the next fifty years. Although their work was always first-rate and, at the very least, highly entertaining, black performers such as McQueen, Hattie McDaniel, and Stepin Fetchit (né Lincoln Perry) have had no end of castigation, ostracism, and condemnation for their stereotypical roles in white supremacist films of the '30s and '40s—as though the tight and repressive fit of the roles they were given had actually caused the racist mayhem of the overall political and social context, instead of the other way around.

In the process of misinterpreting the dark side of black cultural traditions, we blacks have been trying our best to flush down the toilet the lion's share of black achievement in twentieth-century popular culture. When I first saw McQueen in *Cabin in the Sky*, she instantly became one of my favorite actresses. The work of McQueen and a host of ordinarily detestable others is better understood in the context of their roles in "race" or black-cast films, where their humorous idiosyncracies weren't poisoned by association. In *Cabin*, the subtle way McQueen plays dimwit to Ethel Waters's hot mama reminds me of one of those old Gracie Allen and George Burns's routines.

But McQueen never got the work or the credit she deserved. Moreover, black actresses of yore have often been considered unworthy of note. Because they were just a bunch of Mammies, Jezebels, and Tragic Mulattoes, the conventional wisdom goes, why honor them? But how about honoring what they were able to do with what they had?

Even the older black actresses we readily claim, the Lena Hornes, the Abbey Lincolns, the Diahann Carrolls, the Cicely Tysons, or the Alfre Woodards, we keep on a pedestal out of sight. The multiple aggravations they have suffered in our name at the hands of the entertainment industry we neither know nor care to know. But what we fail to comprehend is that the

McQueens and the Hornes have indeed fought the good fight the only way they could—through the roles they didn't take as well as the ones they did. McQueen's stand on not accepting denigrating roles is well documented although usually forgotten. It kept her out of work most of her career. Instead she sold toys in Macy's, worked as a waitress in a soul-food restaurant, and did community work in Harlem. I remember McQueen best from the '70s as I walked to classes at City College on Convent Avenue, sweeping the walk of what I thought was her house.

Quite often black actresses never even got a chance to be old. The stunning Dorothy Dandridge, who starred in *Porgy and Bess* (1959) and *Carmen Jones* (1954), which garnered her an Academy Award nomination, died of an overdose of pills at forty-two. Diana Sands, who played the heroic Beneatha in Lorraine Hansberry's *A Raisin in the Sun* (1961), starred on Broadway in *The Owl and the Pussycat* (1964) and performed equally well in Shaw and Shakespeare, died of cancer at thirty-nine. Just in the past year, Madge Sinclair, the wonderful actress who played Kunta Kinte's wife in *Roots* and the voice of the Lion Queen in *The Lion King*, died of leukemia at fifty-seven. Roxie Roker, the mother of Lenny Kravitz, who played Helen Willis on *The Jeffersons*, died at sixty-six. And Rosalind Cash, whom black film historian Donald Bogle once aptly described as our Susan Hayward, died of cancer at fifty-six.

Even when they do manage to get old, they may suffer from complete neglect as was the fate not only of McQueen but also of Fredi Washington who played "light enough to pass" Peola in the 1934 version of *Imitation of Life*. She often advised aspiring black actors to always have some other way of earning a living because racism would impede their opportunities. Frustrated by her own inability to find sufficient work in film (she refused to pass), Washington returned to the stage. In the late '30s she founded, along with Bill "Bojangles" Robinson, Noble Sissle, and Ethel Waters, the Negro Actors Guild, and was executive director of it in the '40s. Consistently active on the Left and in civil rights, Washington also served as drama critic for a local Harlem newspaper published by Congressman Adam Clayton Powell Jr. She died a year and a half ago at ninety.

A triumph in itself, I would say. Respect for longevity may also be why black audiences flocked to see *Having Our Say*, a Broadway show based upon the real lives of two black sisters, who never wed, never had children, and lived to be over one hundred. The play is fashioned, more or less, precisely after their bestselling book *Having Our Say*. In their living room and kitchen, Sadie and Bessie take turns telling the story of their upper-middle-class lives growing up in the South and their womanhood in Harlem. Two of the most superb older black actresses — Mary Alice and Gloria Foster — played the roles for a long time, with Alice nominated for a Tony.

After several months, they were succeeded by Novella Nelson and Frances Foster, both less well known but still quite forceful and impressive in their own right. Yet *Having Our Say* closed at the end of last year after a nine-month run to go on tour, which is a little more quickly than usual with successful black shows. Typically, other actors, preferably ones with more box-office appeal, are brought in to milk as yet untapped audiences. Of course, there aren't any brand-name black actresses with the possible exception of Whoopi.

Conceived partly, I imagine, as an antidote to the Mammy syndrome, *Having Our Say* is hardly a masterpiece of Western literature. It fairly oozes Mother's Day sentimentality, its notion of "positive" images almost as claustrophobic and restrictive as the other side of the coin. But it is safe to venture that it may be a long time yet before we see so many black actresses on Broadway again. Especially if they don't sing.

Meanwhile, I don't know what lies in the future. I guess we should consider ourselves lucky if Whitney and Angela are around to play Bessie and Sadie fifty years from now.

Originally published in the *Village Voice*, 30 January 1996, p. 21.

38.

The French Collection

Upon first viewing *The French Collection*, I was eager to write about it because of the light the eight story-quilts could shed on the relationship of family narrative to myriad practices of cultural critique in response to black community. Also, I reflected upon the various inventive means by which my mother, the artist Faith Ringgold, had forged images taken from photographs of family and friends with the facts of Afro-American and European cultural history into a black feminist fantasy and feminist critique. I gained new insight into how the riddles of my childhood had formed not only my life questions but my mother's and my grandmother's, as well.

Both the stories and the paintings included in *The French Collection* tactfully raise issues that have become central to my own concerns as a cultural critic: (1) the complicated relationship of Afro-American cultural production to European culture; (2) how issues of race and gender were cloaked and embedded in the evolution of European and American Modernism; (3) and how black female subjectivity managed to survive the racial and sexual politics of Afro-American Modernism.

In late June of 1961, Faith took my grandmother, my sister Barbara, and me to Europe for the summer via the SS *Liberte* to Le Havre en route to Paris. Faith was thirty years old and had just finished her master's degree in Fine Art at the City College of New York. She was already an art teacher with a public high school license and she wanted to be an artist. But what kind of artist would she be? What kind of art would she do? If she, a black divorced mother of two, really devoted her life, body and soul, to this vocation, wouldn't she be taking an enormous chance? How could she do this extraordinary thing for which there were no role models?

As a fashion designer, Momma Jones, her mother, had provided a role model of sorts, but there were perhaps hundreds of Afro-American women working in a black fashion industry parallel to the white one in black communities such as Harlem in the '40s and '50s. Moreover, Momma Jones had waited until her children were grown to begin her career and even then, she chose to put family first. She had never had to face the alienation or the isolation of taking on a career, which would be regarded by the black community as neither black enough nor womanly enough. So Faith was understandably reluctant. In order to help her make up her mind, she decided that our little family unit would travel to Paris and Nice, Monaco, Florence and Rome, Zurich and London to see in person the treasures of European art — in fact, to see what she still called the great masters.

In *The French Collection*, which Faith describes in her introduction as "a surreal meditation on why many of us black women have never done the things we'd like to do," the stories and the paintings revolve around the exploits of Willia Marie Simone, a black woman from Atlanta, Georgia, who goes to Paris in 1920 at the age of sixteen to become an artist. In the first story-quilt, "Dancing at the Louvre," Willia accompanies Marcia, a childhood friend from Atlanta who is now living in Paris, to the Louvre with her three children, whereupon the children, who care nothing for da Vinci, proceed to dance in front of the Mona Lisa. In the painting, Faith borrowed the images of Marcia and her three children from contemporary photographs of my sister Barbara and her three children, Faith, Teddy, and Martha.

But the situation portrayed makes me recall my first visits to the Louvre in 1961 during which my sister and I, at eight and nine, cried and begged to be released but eventually learned to love painting, sculpture, and the elaborate edifices that house them. A year or so later, when the Mona Lisa toured the United States, we could tell our classes about how we'd already seen it.

In "Dancing at the Louvre," Mona Lisa is smiling the enigmatic half-smile of a wily and subversive female subjectivity under the repression of patriarchal domination. In the process, she seems to encourage Melissa's children as they romp and dance, their braids flying. In order to survive, the painting says, one must learn to dance and experience pleasure in the inner sanctums of Western culture. Appropriating Western tradition is fine, as long as it isn't taken at face value, as long as it isn't taken seriously.

In the second story-quilt, "Wedding on the Seine," Willia has just been married to a rich Frenchman. Afraid that marriage will mean she'll have to give up her dream of being an artist, she runs away from her wedding party to throw her bridal bouquet in the Seine. But, according to the story that accompanies the quilt, her husband Pierre soon dies, leaving her wealthy and with two children, whom she sends to live with their Aunt Melissa in Atlanta.

In 1961, we were in Rome when we learned that Uncle Andrew, my mother's brother and my grandmother's son, had died and we had to rush back to the United States for his funeral. For a time, after we returned from Europe, Faith corresponded with a Guadeloupean medical student living in Paris who wanted to marry her. Even after Faith decided not to marry Maurice, she continued to entertain the idea of moving to France and sending my sister and me to school in Switzerland. Such plans were shelved indefinitely when Faith decided to marry Burdette Ringgold in 1962.

But when Faith decided to become an artist, the temptation to move to Paris to escape the racism and the disdain for the visual arts in the United States was great. These were the times during which James Baldwin was publishing his essays about his experiences as an ex-patriot in France in *Notes of a Native Son* and *No Place to Be Somebody*, in which he invokes the relationship of European imperialism to American manifest destiny and its less than generous treatment of minorities. Faith avidly read everything Baldwin published and was profoundly moved.

But the proportions and scale in "Wedding on the Seine" adds the issue of gender to this story as well. A miniscule Willia dropping her tiny bridal bouquet into the great waters of the Seine against the backdrop of the massive architecture of the bridge and the city makes the point that Willia's gesture of resistance is small and ineffectual. Happily married myself since December 1989, I appreciate this institutional critique of marriage more than ever. The title "Wedding on the Seine" suggests the ideal fantasy of marriage, but the imposing edifice and structure of the city suggests the official rhetoric of the ceremony and its endless bureaucratization. Within this context, Willia's desperate act presses the question of the fate of the individual black female subject. What will happen to her? Will she, too, be swallowed up by the Seine?

In the third story-quilt, "Picnic at Giverny," Willia is invited to paint in the gardens at Giverny only to find a gathering of American women artists and writers comtemplating the question of the role of women in art. As she paints them, she reflects upon her greatest problem as a black woman artist — what to paint. As the women artists and critics take up the question of the female nude in Western art, it occurs to Willia that she wants to combine a portrait of these fully clothed women with a nude of Picasso sitting on the grass. She will draw her setting from Monet's *Les Decorations des Nymphaeas* and her composition from Manet's *Le Dejeuner sur l'Herbe*.

The images of these women are all taken from photographs of friends and mentors of Faith's who have been supportive of her work as an artist. Seated on the grass just behind Picasso are Moira Roth, feminist art historian and professor of art history at Mills College in Oakland, California; Ellie Flomen-haft, director of the Fine Arts Museum of Long Island; Judith Leiber, owner and designer of Judith Leiber pocketbooks and patron of the arts; Lowery Sims, curator, Metropolitan Museum of Art; Thalia Gouma-Peterson, femi-nist art historian and professor of art history at the College of Wooster; Emma Amos, painter and printmaker; Bernice Steinbaum, dealer and gal-lery owner; and myself. Standing behind them are Ofelia Garcia, president of Rosemont College in Philadelphia; and Johnetta Cole, president of Spelman College in Atlanta.

In the fourth story-quilt, "The Sunflowers Quilting Bee at Arles," the Na-tional Sunflower Quilters Society of America, whose membership includes Fannie Lou Hamer, Sojourner Truth, Mary McLeod Bethune, Ella Baker, Harriet Tubman, Rosa Parks, Madame CJ Walker, and Ida B. Wells, are hav-ing quilting bees in sunflower fields around the world to promote the cause of freedom. Willia goes to meet them in the sunflower fields at Arles. The strange demeanor of Van Gogh, who wants to meet them as well, makes them question the sanity of Willia's desire to be an artist and to live in France.

In the image, Parks, Hamer, Walker, Truth, Tubman, Bethune, and Baker sit in the midst of a field of sunflowers, holding in their hands a quilt of a field of sunflowers. This image is, of course, framed by yet another quilt. Standing among the sunflowers is Van Gogh.

In the story, Faith raises unmistakeably the question of the relationship of black struggle to the individual black female subject and ponders the con-nection between the work of the artist and the work these women have taken on of freeing the world from oppression. My favorite thing in this story is when Sojourner Truth, whose child was sold to a Dutch slaver, wants to know from Van Gogh, who is Dutch, whether or not he knows anything about the child's whereabouts. Although he never answers, Van Gogh, whom Faith describes as a "tormented little man," fades into the field of sunflowers as if he were a sunflower, himself.

In the fifth story-quilt, "Matisse's Model," Willia becomes an artist's model and is shown posing nude for Matisse. Matisse's *La Danse*, in which the girls are all brown, provides the background. "I have always wanted to be beautiful, not like an anonymous beautiful woman but like une belle peinture," Willia muses in the story.

In the light of recent theoretical reflections in feminist art history regarding the stultification of the male gaze in modern art and film, to imagine Willia posing for Matisse raises an interesting problem. Not only is it historically true that black women had no institutionalized opportunities to become artists, it is also a mark of their peculiar oppression that they were rarely even considered worthy of the notorious male gaze. Despite the occasional exceptions in the early twentieth century such as Josephine Baker, performing her banana dance at the Folies Bergere and in several French movies for lustful white male audiences, the more commonplace image of the black woman in Western culture takes its inspiration from the scientific drawings of the Hottentot Venus, which regarded the black female body as pathological.

Not too much later, Manet would help to incorporate a lasting visual binary opposition that would reoccur again and again, especially in subsequent American films, by using the portrayal of a large, buxom, black maid in the shadows to emphasize the delicate nudity and whiteness of Olympia. Even more common still, is no black woman in the picture at all.

So Willia's gesture is a significant one. The implicit connection that Faith is making between being valorized as an object — as "a beauty" — and being taken seriously as a subject, or in this case as a painter, is provocative and thought provoking. Does the objectification of white female bodies in Western art (in contemporary advertising, TV, and film as well as in earlier visual art) handicap white women or give them an advantage (or both?) in their struggle to affirm their subjectivity? In any case, the advantage has not yet been sufficiently explored in feminist theory. It is an exploration that might be very helpful in articulating peculiar forms of black female objectification and subjectivity.

In the sixth story-quilt, Willia has a dream in which her family's dead gather in the Henry Matisse Chapel in Venice. Their talk is of slavery. The image that Faith has created here speaks to the ineffable sadness of being a product of a family in which there has been so much death and so little birth.

The people portrayed in the painting are taken from photographs of dead members of our real family: Susie Shannon, Momma Jones's great grandmother; Betsy Bingham, Momma Jones's grandmother; and Ida B. Posey and B. B. Posey, Momma Jones's mother and father. On the right in the chairs are a young Momma Jones with the baby Ralph (who was born and died before

Faith's birth) sitting on her lap. The images of little Andrew, Faith's brother, and Big Andrew, Faith's father, and Barbara, Faith's sister, are taken from photographs of Aunt Barbara's wedding. Standing on the right in the back, are Faith's father's parents, Baby Doll Hurd and Rev. Jones, as she imagines them to have been. Also standing in the back in a row are Uncle Hilliard, Uncle Cardoza, Aunt Edith, Aunt Bessie, and cousin Mildred and cousin Ida Mae, all sisters, brothers, and cousins of Momma Jones.

The saddest death of all represented here is Momma Jones's and it is fascinating to me how the entire genealogy is constructed around her as the center. Also, that Faith would have chosen of all the photographs she might have used, this image of a youthful Momma Jones with the baby Ralph on her lap, reiterates the recurring themes of *The French Collection* — of what a young, ambitious black woman might have become if not for marriage and children.

Momma Jones was that young, ambitious black woman. In fact, her first ambition had been to be a dancer, but her parents would not allow it. Roughly the same age as Josephine Baker and Zora Neale Hurston, it is not difficult to see the shadows of their lives in hers.

In the seventh story-quilt, "Picasso's Studio," Willia poses nude for Picasso. In the background is *Les Demoiselles D'Avignon*. As she sits, the African sculptures and masks in his studio complain, for Willia's ears alone, of Western imperialism in Africa. The women from Avignon speak to Willia as well, advising her to take a chance on being an artist for if all else fails, she can always fall back on selling the one thing all women have to sell.

I find fascinating here Faith's bracketing of the Picasso painting: first, because *Les Demoiselles D'Avignon* emphasizes in its composition the symbiotic relationship between African art and French Modernism; second, it also acknowledges the instrumental character of Western myths of female sexuality to this process of cultural miscegenation. When Faith makes Willia model for Picasso against the background of *Les Demoiselles*, she connects the issues regarding black female subjectivity raised in "Matisse's Model" to *Les Demoiselles d'Avignon*'s preoccupation with hybridity. In the eighth story-quilt, "On the Beach at Saint Tropez," Willia looks at men's bodies as she explains to her son why she didn't raise him herself but sent him to be raised in Atlanta by his aunt.

"I escaped the cotton fields of Georgia and the side streets of Harlem to live as une artiste in Paris," she tells him. She came to Paris, married Pierre, the boy's father, although she did not love him, and generally did what she had to do to get what she wanted. "If you want to judge me, it is your choice to do so," Willia says, "but it will only make us both sad. I cannot change my past or yours and I abhor criticism. It is so useless to be judged in your later years when you have no time to change."

In this last installment of the first part of *The French Collection*, Faith raises the expectation that she will tell us more about Willia's relationship to her grown up children. I'm looking forward to the revelations of Part II. In the meanwhile, *The French Collection* masters utopian feminist fiction, autobiography, and feminist cultural critique. In her playful juxtaposition of the icons of contemporary European and Afro-American culture, Faith begins to reveal the peculiar secrets of postcoloniality that characterizes the black experience of minority status in a white world.

Originally published in Faith Ringgold, ed., *The French Collection: Part One* (New York: Being My Own Woman Press, 1992).

39.

Modernism, Postmodernism, and the Problem
of the Visual in Afro-American Culture

In 1954 in the case of *Brown v. Board of Education*, the Supreme Court ruled
that segregated schools were inherently unequal, discriminatory, and illegal.
The case made by the NAACP included the findings of Kenneth and Mamie
Clark, black Ph.D.'s. in social psychology who had been using a doll test and
a coloring test to measure how racism and segregation damaged the self-
esteem of black children, ranging in age from three to seven. They found,
among other things, that black children—I don't know how many of them
were girls or if anyone thought about the fact that only girls generally play
with dolls—preferred white dolls to black dolls, and that black children had
a tendency to use a white or yellow crayon to color both a same-sex figure
said to be themselves and an opposite-sex figure said to be a friend.[1]

There has been much debate within the fields of psychology and sociology about the meaning of the Clarks' research, most of it focused upon
the scientific validity of the testing methods.[2] However, it is not at all unusual for the media to refer back to this research as evidence that racism is an
unambiguously deprivational experience, while completely ignoring what
the visual implications of such findings might be. In fact, just this summer,
there was a TV special called *Blacks in White America*, entirely produced by
black journalists at ABC.[3] The documentary opened with a present day re-
enactment of the Clarks' research showing small black children choosing a
white doll over a black one, and interpreting a stereotypical line drawing of

a blond little white girl as prettier or cleaner or nicer. It closed with the narrator's voice—a black female journalist—telling us that she had been one of the little girls who had participated in the Clarks' original research in the early fifties. She confessed that she, too, had preferred the white doll over the black one.

The documentary interpreted this information as corroboration of the fact that blacks are still comparatively poor and disenfranchised in comparison to whites. Profiles of a black regiment of fighter pilots in World War II and of the newly appointed black Chairman of the Joint Chiefs of Staff, Colin L. Powell, were offered as correctives. Amazingly, neither art nor beauty nor aesthetics nor high culture nor pop culture nor media were raised as significant precipitating factors in this process.

Of course, poverty and powerlessness feed a child's perception of what it means to have black skin, but this process is much more complex than a direct correlation could encompass. Rather, it is society's always already operative evaluation of images, further inscribed by skin color (dark or light, white or black, or yellow or red) that would most affect a child's opinion of race. Not only the presence of "negative" black stereotypes in schoolbook illustrations, posters, religious imagery, advertising images, as well as movie and television images but the absence of black images in mass media in general is the crucial dynamic never accounted for.

The power of the image—as well as of the word—seems to be the very thing addressed so well by Toni Morrison's use of the Dick and Jane text in order to characterize white hegemony in *The Bluest Eye*.[4] After all, this was an elementary school reader whose illustrations were at least as unforgettably repetitive and stifling to the imagination as its text. The absence of black images in the reflection of the social mirror, which such programmatic texts (from *Dick and Jane*, to Disney movies, to *The Weekly Reader*) invariably construct, could and did produce the void and the dread of racial questions that the Clarks found in the '50s, particularly in northern black children who were already attending integrated schools. Their studies related how these children sometimes cried when asked to identify the doll that was "Negro" or that was the same race as them. On the other hand, southern children who attended segregated schools displayed less ambivalence, which the Clarks interpreted as a cynicism inappropriate to childhood: "'Oh, yeah, that's me there—that's a nigger,' they'd say. I'm a nigger.'"[5]

We all know in our hearts, as any mere child in our midst today must know, that "nigger," "black," and "schwartze" are often used interchangeably in our language to mean an abject "other," and yet we persist in denying it, just as Kenneth and Mamie Clark, the NAACP, and the Supreme Court denied it in 1954. In 1979, when Donald Neuman designated his exhibition of charcoal drawings at Artist Space as "Nigger Drawings," and in 1989 when Jackie Mason called mayoral candidate David Dinkins a "schwartze," sizable downtown New York controversies followed precisely in order to continue this charade, which has become one of the principal tenets of bourgeois humanism, that color is an innately trivial matter, which signifies nothing.

HOW ONE IS seen (as black) and, therefore, what one sees (in a white world) is always already crucial to one's existence as an Afro-American. The very markers that reveal you to the rest of the world, your dark skin and your kinky/curly hair, are visual. However, not being seen by those who don't want to see you because they are racist, what Ralph Ellison called "invisibility," often leads racists to the interpretation that you are unable to see.

This has meant, among other things, that Afro-Americans have not produced (because they've been prevented from doing so by intraracial pain and outside intervention) a tradition in the visual arts as vital and compelling to other Americans as the Afro-American tradition in music.[6] Moreover, the necessity, which seems to persist on its own volition in Afro-American Studies, for drawing parallels or alignments between Afro-American music and everything else cultural among Afro-Americans, stifles and represses most of the potential for understanding the visual in Afro-American culture. For if the positive scene of instruction between Africans and Europeans in the United States[7] is located in what is now triumphantly called the "tradition" of Afro-American music, the negative scene of instruction is in its visual tradition.[8] This "negative scene of instruction" (so much more common in Afro-American experience) was one in which white teachers refused to teach black students who were in turn just as reluctant to learn from them. As even the smallest child seems to instinctively understand, institutionalized education has always been, first and foremost, a means of transmitting social values, not knowledge or power.

It appears that the only reason black artists aren't as widely accepted as black writers (and this is far from widely enough) is because shifts in art historical judgment result in extraordinary economic contingencies. Consequently, the closed economic nepotism of the art world perpetuates a situation in which, as Howardena Pindell has pointed out, "artists of color face an industry-wide 'restraint of trade,' limiting their ability to show and sell their work."[9]

If black writers had had to rely on the kinds of people and developments that determine the value of art, if writing had to be accepted into rich white people's homes and into their investment portfolios in the manner of the prized art object, I suspect that none of us would have ever heard of Langston Hughes, Richard Wright, Zora Neale Hurston, Ralph Ellison, Amiri Baraka, Sonia Sanchez, John Edgar Wideman, Ishmael Reed, Alice Walker, Adrienne Kennedy, Toni Morrison, Ntozake Shange, August Wilson, George Woolfe, and Trey Ellis. Indeed, we are lucky to have heard of Jacob Lawrence, Betye Saar, Romare Bearden, Richard Hunt, Sam Gilliam, Daniel Johnson, Mel Edwards, and Faith Ringgold.

I WAS TWO years old in 1954. And perhaps because my mother was pursuing a master's in Art Education until I was nine, I grew up being aware of the Clarks' research. I also grew up watching a television on which I rarely saw a black face, reading Archie and Veronica comics, Oz and Nancy Drew stories and *Seventeen* magazine, in which "race" was unmentionable. At the same time, I always had black dolls and I was always given a brown crayon to take to school as an encouragement to color my people brown as I did at home.

In the spring of 1961 my mother, who wanted to be an artist, graduated from City College of New York with her master's in Art Education. That summer my mother planned and carried out an elaborate tour of the art treasures of Italy and France with my grandmother, my sister, and myself in tow. I remember the virtually endless streams of white faces not only in paintings and sculpture but also in the operas, film, theater, and television we saw that summer. I can also remember a French saleswoman being asked by my mother to find a black doll at the Galleries Lafayette in Paris, and being relieved when she succeeded in producing one. I can still recall that doll, which was blacker than most American black dolls.

"Race" was frequently discussed in my family's home, although "racism" was not. As far as I know, no such word had entered common parlance. Moreover, and more personally, any discussion of "race" in the presence of people who were not black embarrassed me. I can remember giving a report on the "races of the world" in my seventh grade class and being so embarrassed by my subject matter that I could hardly speak. I said "colored" to refer to my own people. A black boy in my class corrected me by saying "Negro." I was mortified, for "Negro" was then considered to be the more militant word. My grandmother never used "Negro" at all, although my mother and her friends did. Of course, "black," as a description of race, was still the ultimate and virtually unspeakable insult.

So you can see I come by my fascination with the visual quite automatically. Visual production has always been an obsession in my life because I was a child of the 1954 Supreme Court decision, a child of Kenneth Clark's research — Dr. Kenneth Clark who taught at CCNY where my mother was a graduate student, and, together with his wife, ran the Northside Psycho-logical Testing Service, which shared a building with the private school I attended from the seventh grade on.

I saw Kenneth and Mamie Clark often. If I didn't actually know them, I felt as though I did, was enormously proud of them as was everyone in my family. For they were part of this whole business of being a Negro, I well knew, this whole self-conscious business of something that would later be called "The Black Aesthetic" but which, for right now confined itself to this problem of not liking dolls of the same color as yourself unless carefully educated to do so. This I understood even then for I was also a child of tele-vision, comic books, and magazines, although I was carefully instructed by parents and teachers to know that the pleasure these gave was counterfeit, not to be taken seriously.

Moreover, my mother and my grandmother were artists. My paternal grandmother, Momma T from Jamaica, West Indies, was a Sunday landscape painter. My maternal grandmother, Momma Jones, was a fashion designer. I modeled in all her fashion shows while growing up and was constantly being photographed by the two or three black photographers she always had on hand to document even the most trivial events. Later she would collaborate on quilts and other kinds of fabric art with my mother, the "fine" artist.

In the work of the women in my family, it is actually in the career of my mother, Faith Ringgold, that fashion and fine art were finally conjoined. But for quite a long time before she became interested in the questions of a black aesthetic and a feminist aesthetic, she was a painter who tried to take seri-ously her relationship to the tradition of Western painting, particularly its culmination in Cubism. Our home revolved around the tension this chal-lenge created in her and in her work. I remember in particular, when I was very young, a very bad (Postmodern?), often wet Picasso-esque "study" that contained a mise en abime effect of endless doors within doors, and that occupied the space in our home that should have been occupied by a dining room table and chairs.

ACCORDING TO RAYMOND WILLIAMS in *Marxism and Literature*, hegemony is a process that relies upon the mechanisms of traditions and canons of Old Masters in order to waylay the Utopian desires that are potentially embodied in cultural production.[10] The underlying structure of the very concept of "tradition" lies in wait behind contemporary variations on "tradition"— whether they are named feminist, Afro-American, or Eskimo—in that they are inevitably radically selective in favor of maintaining the dominance of a brutal status quo despite their best intentions to subvert it.

I cannot recall a time during which I didn't perceive Western art and Western culture as a problem in ways that seem to me now akin to the manner in which modernism, postmodernism, and feminism raise such problems. On the other hand, thanks to my mother's unrelenting ambition to be a successful artist and her political interpretation of the continuing frustration of that ambition, I can't remember a time during which I didn't know that artmaking and visual production were also deeply problematic in Afro-American culture. For these reasons and more, James Baldwin's statement in *Notes of a Native Son* that he "despised" black people "possibly because they failed to produce Rembrandt,"[11] had a profound resonance as I was growing up.

More specifically it was Picasso (not Rembrandt) and modernism, in general, that epitomized the art historical moment of greatest fascination. The debate was precisely situated in the paradox that Picasso, Cubism, and subsequent modernists had borrowed heavily from African art. In other words, as it was widely interpreted among a black middle-class intelligentsia in the '50s and '60s, "they," or white Euro-American high modernism, had borrowed from "us," the African peoples of the world, even if "they" were incapable of admitting it.

My interest in modernism only accelerated once I had become knowledgeable enough about the visual and literary production of both Afro-Americans and white Europeans and Americans in this century (no small task) to know that modernism actually took place in the Afro-American as well as in the white American-European milieu. Afro-American modernism is both the same and different, as imitative as it is original, which is consistent with Henry Louis Gates's notion of "critical signification," an attempt to describe the mechanical relationship between Afro-American culture and Euro-American culture. According to Gates—and he has employed "critical signification" almost exclusively in the context of literature and the question of Afro-American literacy—Afro-American culture imitates and reverses the terms of Euro-American culture. This relationship can also usefully be described as dialogical, or as one of intertextuality.[12]

But the problem remains the unilateral unwillingness of Euro-American culture to admit and acknowledge its debt, or even its relationship, to African and Afro-American culture. In fact, this problem—which lies at the heart of the problem of the visual in Afro-American culture—has such a long and convoluted history that its enunciation has become one of the telling features of Afro-American modernism. One of the early practitioners of Afro-American literary modernism, Ralph Ellison, even gave it a name: invisibility.

In *Invisible Man* (1951), Ellison catalogues the dilemma. According to the myth of blackness, it is the opposite of whiteness, or it is so much "the same" that it is "invisible." Both dynamics are, in fact, aspects of this "invisibility's" inevitable and structural binary opposition. On the one hand, there is no black difference. On the other, the difference is so vast as to be unspeakable and indescribable. Invisibility, a visual metaphor, is then employed as a way of presenting a variety of responses to racism and cultural apartheid: there is the problem of translating a musical and oral Afro-American tradition into a written history and literature; there is the problem of Eurocentrism; and there is the problem of not being seen, in all its various connotations.

There is also the problem of being viewed as an object whose subjectivity is considered as superfluous as that of the dancing, grinning Sambo doll that the formerly political Clifton sells on the street corner in downtown New York. And finally, there is the problem of being the patriarch of a black family whose role must be defined in opposition to that of the patriarch of the white family. Therefore, myth constructs the black family on a model contrasting with the freudian/oedipal/modernist drama of individuation, so that, early in the novel, the illiterate storyteller/farmer, Trueblood, impregnates both his wife and his daughter, and thereby gains cachet in the white community which pays him, again and again, to tell them the story of how it happened.[13] However, perhaps the most psychologically damaging residual of this story is that in the process of its unfolding, the subjectivity of the black woman becomes entirely unimaginable.

In *Invisible Man*, women are generally white, and while the text is not especially sympathetic or kind to white women, it seems entirely engaged by the assumption that from a white male progressive point of view, or from the perspective of Euro-American modernism (I am not suggesting that these are necessarily synonymous), the problem of the female (white) other and the problem of the black (male) other are easily interchangeable. In Euro-American modernism, and in Afro-American modernism, as well, for that matter, the position of the other is as unitary and as incapable of being occupied by categories more diverse than "women and blacks" as was the formerly unified, omniscient subject from which it split.

It seems to me not entirely irrelevant to mention here that Ellison's prediction wasn't at all accurate, in that it is a handful of black women writers who follow in the tradition of Trueblood, in being well paid by a white (postfeminist?) audience to tell the stories of the oedipal transgressions of black men. I don't mean to suggest that either black men or black women are doing anything wrong, for the oedipal transgressions of the black male are as inevitable as the black woman's need to break her silence about them (and I am not referring only to incest). But the motives of the whites who are ostensibly being entertained by this storytelling are not necessarily much different from those whites who paid Trueblood to tell his tale, or who stood on the corner watching Clifton's grinning, dancing Sambo dolls. The difference in the motivation is only a function of the extent to which the performance and consumption of these texts are interrogated by a critical discourse emanating from white, black (and brown) feminist and Afro-Americanist discourses. The relative scarcity of such interrogation in the media and in academia is as telling as the relative scarcity of a multicultural "other" presence in the various fields of visual production, from museum administration to films. It is telling us, in fact, that the fabric of invisibility has not altered, that it makes little difference in our hegemonic arrangements if Trueblood is now a woman.

But if we move now from the Afro-American modernist novel par excellence to the Afro-American postmodernist novel par excellence, Ishmael Reed's *Mumbo Jumbo*, there is an interesting black female character who comes into view.[14] It is the dancer, vaudevillian, and Folies Bergere star Josephine Baker, who shares with African art, and with Picasso and the Cubists, a mutual location in the Paris of the '20s. Reed's novel brings all of these variables into dramatic dialogue or juxtaposition with each other during the Harlem Renaissance.[15] Yet the "idea" of Josephine Baker in *Mumbo Jumbo*, and in most of what has been written about her, remains the old-fashioned one wherein she becomes the muse of the white man, whether that is resented as it is by Reed, or celebrated as it is by many others who have written about her.[16]

When one arrives at the postmodern scene, marked as it is by reproduction and simulation, the rampant exploitation of international capitalism, not to mention much speculation regarding the death of the subject, the death of history, and the total blurring of lines between pop culture and high culture, spin-offs of the Josephine Baker model proliferate. Tina Turner, Grace Jones, Jody Watley, Whitney Houston, Diana Ross, and Donna Summer (as well as Michael Jackson) all follow in her tracks. Baker's much photographed performances are not the only starting point, however, of this fascination with black women's bodies—the site upon which blackness was conceptualized as an aspect of the white personality and white Euro-American achievement. There was also the popularity in Europe of an ethnographic photography issuing from the process of the colonial/anthropological exploitation of a third world Asia and Africa that proceeded and overlapped with a burgeoning interest in Europe in African and Oceanic art, which was really about an interest in other ways of seeing and looking that had not before occurred to the West.

Sander L. Gilman points out that in the early decades of the 1800s, even before photography's ascendency, there was a general fascination in Europe with the "Hottentot Venus," as represented by a series of black women who were imported from South Africa and exhibited in the major cities of Europe because of their large and fatty buttocks. In this way, representations of black women with large and fatty buttocks came to signify not only black women but all other categories of women, such as prostitutes, who were thought to be as sexually wanton as black women.

According to Gilman, Manet paints the white courtesan *Nana* with protruding buttocks for this reason, and in *Olympia*, the presence of the clothed buxom black female servant allows for the transgressive sexuality of Olympia. In 1901, Picasso painted a parody of *Olympia* in which she is a fat black woman with the huge thighs of the Hottentot Venus. Gilman describes this painting as a prolegomena to the intersection of issues of race and sexuality in *Les Demoiselles d'Avignon* of five years later.[17] *Les Demoiselles* might be seen as illustrating the occasional advantage of art over institutionalized history or science in that it seems to represent the desire to both reveal and repress the scene of appropriation as a conjunction of black/female bodies and white culture—a scene of negative instruction between black and white art or black and white culture.

Unlike the positive scene of instruction of Afro-American and Euro-American music, in which mutual influence and intertextuality is acknowledged (although not without struggles that further enrich the transmutation), in the negative scene of instruction of Afro-American art and Euro-American art the exchange is disavowed and disallowed—no one admits to having learned anything from anyone else.

Subsequently, Euro-American postmodernism emerges as the lily white pure-blooded offspring of an inbred and dishonest (in the sense of not acknowledging its mixed blood) modernism and poststructuralism. And, more or less simultaneous with this subtle but effective metamorphosis, the Black Aesthetic emerges as the unambivalent, uncompromised link-up between Africa and the "New World" in which Euro-American influences are superfluous and negligible.

GRISELDA POLLOCK, FOLLOWING Julia Kristeva's lead in "Woman's Time," has proposed that there is a third position in feminist discourse beyond the simplistic mechanics of the struggle for equality for (white) women and the celebration of (white) female difference.[18] This third position is the most difficult to describe because it encompasses many positions and strategies potentially. Its goal, however, is to deconstruct the discursive formations that define the hegemonic process and that define, as well, the subversive limitations of previous feminist approaches. Herein lies my opportunity to usher forth "new knowledge," as Pollock names it, in conceptualizations of the visual in Afro-American culture that would consider the interdependency in issues of ethnicity and sex. This "new knowledge" would be constituted in the excavation of the black artistic versus the white artistic experience under the historic headings of modernism and postmodernism—on the theory that this is, in fact, the genuinely counterhegemonic thing to explore at this particular art historical moment. The purpose of this would be to subvert the most persistent arrangement of present day cultural hegemony, with its cultural apartheid and "separate development" as Trinh Minh-ha has described it.[19] Instead of being concerned with commonalities in the developments of Afro- and European American communities in the '20s (or in subsequent periods), each camp of canonizers, whether white or black, male or female, is only interested in claiming autonomous achievement. What gives modernist primitivism any critical import in this cultural revisioning of the visual is the fact that it appears to be an ongoing category in modernist, postmodernist, and feminist discourses, a fundamental way of discounting the "blackness" of the occasional black artist who is accepted within its ranks (as in the case of Jean-Michel Basquiat and Martin Puryear), while rejecting the category of black artist in general.[20]

This said, there also exists in this postmodern moment the problems encountered, for example, by black British filmmaker Isaac Julien, who has experienced the opposition of the Langston Hughes estate for his counterhistorical and counterhegemonic vision of the Harlem Renaissance in his most recent film *Looking for Langston*. Ostensibly the estate objects to the implication that Hughes was gay, but the film is really about the erasure of the gay black subject and in the process the erasure of the body and of sexuality in the dominant discourse. This film made me aware, as I had not been before, of how disembodied cultural figures of the Harlem Renaissance generally are made to appear within black critical discourses, compared with those black artists, such as Louis Armstrong, Bessie Smith, and Josephine Baker, who have been cast in primitivist or neoprimitivist terms and who, as such, have always been of more interest to white criticism.

This disembodiment, with its attendant desexualization of black literature and high culture, occurs in response to the oversexualization of black images in white mass culture. It is an effort, in part, to block the primitivism of the black subject by white critics (this is particularly relevant in Afro-American literary criticism), resulting in the not surprising though still devastating outcome of, once again, marginalizing or erasing as irrelevant or unworthy the female subject. If this process of desexualization and deprimitivism had not been assimilated in the consolidation of black high culture within Afro-American studies, many more black female artists, writers, and blues singers—whose gender seems of paramount importance here—would figure in the discussion of black culture. To focus on the intersections of gender and sexuality would be to bring into relief the terms not only of the sexual victimization of black women (rape, etc.) but of black men (lynchings, etc.) in the South, and evidence how the dread of such scenarios fed into the literary and visual production and the modernist aspirations of the artists, writers, and intellectuals of the Harlem Renaissance.

ON THE OTHER HAND, the absence of black voices in the debate over the "Primitivism in 20th Century Art" show at the Museum of Modern Art in 1984 was no accident. William Rubin, the curator of the show, would have us think that modernism is the culmination of universal aesthetic values and standards. Therefore, it should come as no surprise that, in a few isolated instances, so-called primitive art would be as good as Western art, for the people who made these objects are people, too.[21] Thomas McEvilley, his respondent in *Artforum*, would have us shed Western aesthetics for Western anthropology,[22] although, as James Clifford points out in his contribution to the debate, both discourses assume a primitive world in need of preservation, or, in other words, no longer vital and needless to say, incapable of describing itself.

Clifford is right when he says"The fact that rather abruptly, in the space of a few decades, a large class of non-Western artifacts came to be redefined as art is a taxonomic shift that requires critical historical discussion, not celebration."[23] Yet I am not convinced that "minority" artists of color in the West—who are, in some sense, along with African and third world artists, the rightful heirs to the debate around "Primitivism"—will ever surface in the discussion.

Black criticism has been blocked from discussions of visual modernism by an intricate and insidious cooperation of art galleries, museums, and academic art history. Black art has also been blocked from any discussion of primitivism, which has been colonized beyond recognition in the space of the global museum. At this juncture one is compelled to ask, "Is multiculturalism, as it is being institutionally defined, occupying the same space as primitivism in relationship to postmodernism?" For me, a response to such a question would need to include a careful scrutiny of the history of black popular culture and race relations, and account for the sexualization of both, thus defining the perimeters of a new knowledge that I can only name, at this point, as the problem of the visual in Afro-American culture.

For this reason, more suggestive to me is Hal Foster's reading of the stakes of the debate on primitivism in his book of essays *Recodings* in which he describes *Les Demoiselles* as the landmark of a crisis in phallocentric culture. Primitivism becomes the "magical commodity" whereby white European art will appropriate the ritual function of tribal art and resist the process, which the museum space makes inevitable, of being reduced to a lifeless commodity. "On the one hand, then," Foster writes, "the primitive is a modern problem, a crisis in cultural identity, which the west moves to resolve: hence the modernist construction 'primitivism,' the fetishistic recognition-and-disavowal of the primitive difference. This ideological resolution renders it a 'nonproblem' for us. On the other hand, this resolution is only a repression: delayed into our political unconscious, the primitive returns uncannily at the moment of its potential eclipse. The rupture of the primitive, managed by the moderns, becomes our postmodern event."[24]

And yet finally there is only an implied entryway here for the artist or the critic of color who is not a member of a postcolonial intellectual elite. We who are subject to internal colonization, who are called "minorities" in our homelands further suffer the problems of the modern and of cultural identity. The ununified, unmarked subject of most other analyses of the postmodern continues to render us "invisible" and silent.

Gayatri Spivak ventures the point in "Who Claims Alterity?" that postcolonial intellectuals have the advantage over minorities subject to "internal colonization" because of the tendency for those who control theory to conflate the two spheres.[25] To me the potential difference for white intellectuals is between one's somewhat dark past and one's absolutely dark future. While a white art world may debate the nature of the relationship between "primitive" art and modern art, black artists and intellectuals widely assume that a white world is simply unable to admit that art from Africa and elsewhere in the third world had a direct and profound influence on Western art because of an absolutely uncontrollable racism, xenophobia, and ethnocentrism.

The so-called discovery of tribal objects by modernism is analogous to an equally dubious discovery of the New World by European colonization. What was there was not, in fact, "discovered" but rather appropriated or stolen. But more to the point, the dynamic that emerged was born not only from the probability that European civilization would first repudiate and deny, then revise and reform that which they would eventually label "tribal" or "primitive," but from the even greater probability of a new kind of civilization or art, no longer strictly European, which would be revitalized by its proximity to and contact with an internal alternative. In other words, both European and non-European cultures were transformed by their "new" and closer relationship to one another in the New World. For the most part, the relationship was one of exploitation, appropriation, oppression, and repression. But it is also true that something came into and is coming into being: something neither "primitive/tribal" nor European modern.

While the most concrete sign of that something new is generally referred to as postmodernism, unfortunately this move usually carries along with it the reinscription of modernism's racial apartheid. Although the negation of modernism's former power to explain the cultural world is potentially useful to counterhegemonic strategies, invariably European influenced theorists are so preoccupied with the demise of the Hegelian dialectic that they never really get to anything or anyone else. Moreover, there is another sign just as indicative of novelty that is best represented by the cultural contributions of Afro-Americans to popular culture.

The temptation is great to subsume and reify this contribution under the heading of primitivism, or neoprimitivism, following the pattern of modernist criticism. But it is the kind of development that will only occur because white males continue to absolutely dominate and control all aspects of postmodern criticism. In other words, it is not the kind of choice that black critics or black feminist cultural critics are likely to endorse.

Originally published in Cornel West, Martha Gever, and Trinh T. Minha, eds., *Out There: Marginalization in Contemporary Culture* (New York: New Press, 1990).

Notes

1. Richard Kluger, *Simple Justice*, vol. 1 (New York: Knopf, 1979), 398–403.
2. Ibid., 446–48.
3. Scott Minerbrook, "At ABC: Black Journalists Make News," *Emerge* (October 1989): 33.
4. Toni Morrison, *The Bluest Eye* (New York: Holt, Rinehart and Winston, 1970), 7: "Here is the house. It is green and white. It has a red door. It is very pretty. Here is the family. Mother, Father, Dick, and Jane live in the green-and-white house. They are very happy. See Jane. She wants to play. Who will play with Jane?"
5. Kluger, *Simple Justice*, 448.
6. Cornel West, "Black Culture and Postmodernism," in Barbara Kruger and Phil Mariani, eds. *Remaking History* (Seattle: Bay Press, 1989), 274.

7. Lawrence Levine, *Slave Culture and Black Consciousness: Afro-American Folk Thought from Slavery to Freedom* (New York: Oxford University Press, 1977); and Amiri Baraka (Leroi Jones), *Blues People: Negro Music in White America* (New York: Grove Press, 1963).

8. Howardena Pindell, "Art (World) & Racism," *Third Text* 3, no. 4 (spring/summer 1988): 161: "I have learned over my 20 years in New York not to 'romanticize' white artists, expecting them to be liberal, open, or necessarily supportive because they are creative people. Pests, a group of non-white artists, had hung a poster in Soho on Broome and Broadway last spring which read, 'There are 11,000 artists of color in New York. Why don't you see us?' Someone had written on the poster, 'Because you do poor work.'"

9. Ibid., 160.

10. Raymond Williams, *Marxism and Literature* (Oxford: Oxford University Press, 1977), 115–17.

11. James Baldwin, *Notes of a Native Son* (New York: Beacon Press. 1955), 7.

12. Henry Louis Gates Jr., "Figures in Black: Words, Signs, and the 'Racial' Self," and Robert Stam, "Mikhail Bakhtin and Left Cultural Critique" in E. Ann Kaplan, ed., *Postmodernism and Its Discontents* (London: Verso, 1988). Not only does Gates tend to use interchangeably the terms signifying, intertextuality, and the dialogic, Stam points out in his essay that the term "intertextuality" was first introduced into critical discourse as Julia Kristeva's translation of Bakhtin's concept of the dialogic. Of course, Gates draws heavily upon Bakhtin's notion of the dialogic in order to describe how critical signification works.

13. Ralph Ellison, *Invisible Man* (New York: Random House, 1952).

14. There are many other relevant black female figures in black modernism (Bessie Smith and Zora Neale Hurston, for instance) but my attention here is on how a perspective that focuses on the Afro-American "other" of Euro-American modernism and postmodernism must necessarily exclude (black) female subjectivity in some crucial ways.

15. Josephine Baker is on the cover of *Mumbo Jumbo* by Ishmael Reed (Garden City: Doubleday, 1972).

16. Phyllis Rose, *Jazz Cleopatra: Josephine Baker in Her Time* (New York: Doubleday, 1989); and Brian Hammond and Patrick O'Connor, *Josephine Baker* (London: Jonathan Capo, 1988).

17. Sander L. Gilman, "Black Bodies, White Bodies: Toward an Iconography of Female Sexuality in Late 19th Century Art, Medicine, and Literature" in Henry Louis Gates Jr., ed., *Race, Writing, and Difference* (Chicago: University of Chicago Press, 1986), 251–53.

18. Griselda Pollock, "Differencing the Canon." Paper delivered at CAA "Firing the Canon" panel. Hilton Hotel. New York City, February 16, 1990.

19. Trinh T. Minh-ha, *Woman Native Other* (Bloomington: Indiana University Press, 1989), 89.

20. Peter Schjeldahl, "Paint the Right Thing," *Elle* (November 1989), 214–16; Michael Brenson, "A Sculptor's Struggle to Fuse Culture and Art," *New York Times*, 29 October 1989, Arts and Leisure Section, p. 37.

21. William Rubin, ed., *'Primitivism' in 20th Century Art: Affinity of the Trial and the Modern*, 2 vols. (New York: The Museum of Modern Art, 1984).

22. Thomas McEvilley, "Doctor Lawyer Indian Chief: 'Primitivism' in 20th Century Art at The Museum of Modern Art," *Artforum* (November 1984): 54–60.

23. James Clifford, *The Predicament of Culture: Twentieth Century Ethnography, Literature, and Art* (Cambridge: Harvard University Press, 1988), 196.

24. Hal Foster, *Recodings: Art, Spectacle, and Cultural Politics* (Port Townsend, Wash.: Bay Press, 1985), 204.

25. Gayatri Spivak, "Who Claims Alterity?" in Barbara Kruger and Phil Mariani, eds., *Rethinking History* (Seattle: Bay Press, 1989), 274.

40.

A Fierce Flame: Marlon Riggs

I didn't know Marlon Riggs well but you didn't have to know him well to feel close to him or to find him unforgettable. Now that he is dead at thirty-seven, every occasion on which I saw him is seared upon my brain.

The first time I met Marlon was in 1988 at a black film conference at the Whitney Museum immediately before the public unveiling of his controversial video *Tongues Untied* on channel 13. On that day he performed a talk about gay bashing on *In Living Color* and in Spike Lee's *School Daze*. I say "performed" because whenever Marlon spoke publicly, it was a performance. He was indeed the "conference queen" he sometimes cynically dubbed himself. He drew upon a combination of the insights from his videos delineating black stereotypes in the media (*Ethnic Notions* and *Color Adjustment*) and his videos diagnosing and disarming homophobia in the black community (*Tongues Untied* and *Non, Je Ne Regrette Rien*).

I remember thinking at times that Marlon was rather outré, a bit too dramatic and flamboyant. I was one of the people who quietly preferred Isaac Julien's cool analysis of compulsory heterosexuality in *Looking for Langston* to *Tongues Untied*. The emotional, autobiographical utterings made me uneasy. Why was his flame turned up so high, I wondered. I don't think I knew then that Marlon had AIDS, nor would I have known what to make of it in any case since I hadn't yet tuned into death, much less the peculiarity of the AIDS crisis.

The next time I remember seeing Marlon was when I asked him to speak at the Conference on Black Popular Culture at DIA in December of 1991. Again he performed, this time a piece called "Unleash the Queen." In it he spoke of his specific plight:

"Gaze upon me. Gaze upon this deviant, defiant, diseased Other. T-cell count less than 150. The collapse of kidney function imminent from interior ravaging by multiplying microbes. Disease consumes me."

If you hadn't known he was dying, you might have thought his words too bitter, too drenched in a black sarcastic humor for anybody who was all of thirty-four. I couldn't comprehend that he was actually dying, although I had come to accept that he had full-blown AIDS. I can remember silently comforting myself with the thought that he would live at least another ten years.

"Gaze upon yourself. Dis-ease grips you as well. We are mutually bound, sick, trapped. Except you, many of you, persist in the illusion of safe, sage detachment."

Then Marlon began work on *Black Is . . . Black Ain't*, a documentary on black identity (left unfinished) in which he was profiling me as well as a number of other black intellectuals. He came to videotape me in the blazing heat of August 1992. At my house, he was no longer the conference queen but rather the completely focused yet self-effacing technician. Accompanied by an entirely black crew, he, himself, was small, black, and intense.

I inspected him closely for signs. Still, I would not have guessed he was ill. Squeezed into my cramped steam bath of an apartment in Brooklyn, only just recently having recovered from illness myself, my husband and I fell in love with the resiliency of Marlon's spirit, with his passion and courage. We laughed together that day as we had never laughed and we bonded with him and his crew. I had no idea then that that would be the last time I would ever see him alive.

Marlon's work and his words illustrate for me now a kind of allegory of life in our times. *Tongues Untied* and *Non, Je Ne Regrette Rien* were his way of asking, when are black folks going to get hip to AIDS, to homophobia, and to the beauty of black gay life? When are black folks going to get hip to how little time there is to death? In everything Marlon ever said during the brief years of our acquaintance, and in all the work he produced, I also hear him saying goodbye. That's why his flame was high and his art was not cool. He was burning up.

"Miss Girl must now abandon your/her stage. Indeed, she suspects she has overstayed, by just a bit, her welcome. But what bona fide queen conforms to expected time limits? Before he/she tosses his/her tiara to the next diva in the wings, I ask you—no, beg—no, demand: a little more realness from each of us. Please."

Originally published in the *Village Voice*, 26 April 1994, p. 60.

41.

"Harlem on My Mind"

Harlem on My Mind: Cultural Capital of Black America, 1900–1968, edited and with a new introduction by Allon Schoener and with a new foreword by Henry Louis Gates Jr. New Press, 1995.

Maybe you're wondering why there is a reissue of a catalogue for an exhibition that closed over twenty-five years ago. You might say that the "Harlem on My Mind" exhibition was the "Black Male" show of its day, hugely successful with the public but controversial and slightly suspect among the experts and critics. But the preconditions of the Metropolitan Museum's exhibition were much less propitious. For starters, it was 1969, which meant there was no prehistory of black involvement with the major art institutions.

Whereas the "Black Male" show had Thelma Golden as curator and Hilton Als as editor of the catalogue, "Harlem on My Mind" had to contend with the less-than-ideal knee-jerk liberalism of Allon Schoener, visual-arts program director of New York State Council on the Arts at the time, as both curator and editor of the catalogue. His laborious explanation of all the sordid details of why this show was protested by the Harlem community and why the catalogue was forcibly taken out of print, even though it was selling like hotcakes, is not quite the composed recitation of the facts one might hope for from a man who has had twenty-five years to perfect his alibi.

Apparently, the main reason the catalogue was withdrawn from circulation just two weeks after the exhibition had begun was the original introduction, included in the present version, which was written by a Harlem high school student named Candice Van Ellison. An otherwise laudable term paper was marred, according to John Lindsay and others, by the then surprising assertion of widespread anti-Semitism in the black community. "Anti-Jewish feeling is a natural result of the Black Northern migration," the seventeen-year-old Van Ellison wrote. ". . . [P]sychologically, Blacks may find that anti-Jewish sentiments place them, for once, within a majority. Thus, our contempt for the Jew makes us feel more completely American in sharing a national prejudice."

But more controversial, at least with me, is Henry Louis Gates's characteristically brief foreword to the new edition in which he describes Thomas Hoving's tenure as director of the Metropolitan Museum as "bold and innovative" for having mounted "a different sort of show, a show not devoted primarily to the high art of such great artists as Romare Bearden and Jacob Lawrence, but rather a virtual documentary history of the arts, letters, and social and cultural institutions, through which African-Americans defined themselves between the turn of the century and 1968."

The trouble with that statement is not only that "Harlem on My Mind" doesn't come close to providing an adequate documentary history of black people (much less their arts, letters, and social, and cultural institutions), Harlem, or anything else but also that retrospectives for Bearden and Lawrence weren't even remotely among the range of possibilities at the Met, MoMA, or the Whitney in 1968. "Harlem on My Mind" came first in a time during which black artists were not taken seriously in the museum world.

And "Harlem on My Mind" would have been all there ever would have been without artists of color protesting major museums, a protest in part launched by this exhibition, and a protest which in turn prepared the ground for the black art historians, critics, and curators (as well as their diverse supporters) who have changed the criteria of what will be included in the canon of Western art (I hope) forever.

Also, Hoving was, no doubt, more of a liability than model multiculturalist David Ross, the Whitney's present director. In the blessedly brief preface, which ran in the book at the time and is included in the reissue as well, Hoving spews forth in the typical self-critical liberal mode of the late '60s: "To me and my family, living on 84th Street and Park Avenue, Harlem was a light-year away, uptown. And that was good. For behind the vague misty thoughts concerning other people that came through members of my family down to me, Negroes—colored people—constituted an unspoken menace, the tribe that must not be allowed to come down the Avenue." Classy, huh?

But perhaps the most important difference is that the "Black Male" show was deliberately an art exhibition whereas "Harlem on My Mind" deliberately was not. The museum's press release at the time said, "The Harlem community becomes the artist in this case, the canvas, the total environment in which Harlem's history was formed." As it turned out, this didn't mean that black conceptual artists (for instance, the then unknown David Hammons or even a very young Adrian Piper) were going to be invited to re-create the garbage-strewn vacant lots, the storefront churches, and the rundown neighborhood bars of the Harlem milieu. What it meant was an audiovisual display: photos blown up to poster size — maybe twenty-five to fifty or so for each decade — designed to represent the range of Harlem existence accompanied by wall texts, video, and audio tapes. "Tom Hoving never deviated in his support of my view of the exhibition as a communications environment," Schoener writes in his new introduction, "without artifacts, depicting the history of Harlem. Although we never discussed it, I assumed that we both saw the exhibition as an opportunity to change museums."

"Harlem on My Mind" was mounted at the Metropolitan Museum in 1969, the year I graduated from high school. I saw the show, but it didn't exactly rock my world. But then again, there were a lot of other things going on, like the Vietnam War and Black Power. Nobody was much into an interactive Harlem theme park.

Divided into decades from 1900 to the 1960s, the texts were provided by a series of mostly brief stories taken from New York newspapers. These assorted narratives went back and forth from the celebration of black landmarks and triumphs (such as the Harlem Batallion known as "the Hell Fighters" marching down Fifth Avenue in glory in 1919 after their victory in France, or the news of Joe Louis's victory over Braddock in 1937) to dismal projections about poverty, crime, and political unrest. Apart from the appearance of the occasional female icon — Billie Holiday, Ella Fitzgerald, Bessie Smith, Lena Horne, Sarah Vaughn, Mme C.J. Walker, and so on — as was traditional in days of yore, the women occupied the background.

"Harlem on My Mind" really doesn't stand up as a representative collection of black photos or as a work of illustrated cultural history. It has neither the lushness, the allure, nor the creative genius traditionally associated with Black Harlem. The best way to classify it is not as a major chapter but a footnote in the history of black culture. The black sections in the superstores are crammed with more substantial and clarifying texts on Harlem. You can't miss them. There are lots of other interesting collections of photographs around at the moment (I wish there were more) that could help: among them, *Generations in Black and White: Photographs by Carl Van Vechten,* edited by Rudolph P. Byrd (University of Georgia, 1994); *VanDerZee: Photographer, 1886–1983*, edited by Deborah Willis (Abrams, 1993); and *Reflections in Black: A History of Black Photographers, 1840 to the Present*, also edited by Willis (Morton, 2000). Although it hasn't much to do with Harlem, the work of the less well-known photographer Richard Roberts in Columbia, South Carolina, collected in *A True Likeness: The Black South of Richard Samuel Roberts: 1920–1936*, edited by Thomas L. Johnson and Philip Dunn (Algonquin, 1994), gives a feeling for the period hard to find elsewhere.

As for sources of other documents, photographs, and illustrations of the period, here are some of my favorites: *The Black Book*, edited by Middleton Harris (Random House, 1974), which features a short intro by Bill Cosby, who advises you to, "Browse in it. The pickins' ain't always easy, but they're always good." Given the wealth of photos, illustrations, and arcane documents included here, which range from the full story of the Amistad Rebellion to all sorts of memorabilia from the '20s, '30s, and '40s, I don't think it is even possible to read the whole thing.

Other helpful, sometimes colorful texts are: *A Separate Cinema: Fifty Years of Black-Cast Posters*, edited by John Kisch and Edward Mapp (Farrar Straus and Giroux, 1992); *Black Beauty, White Heat: A Pictorial History of Classic Jazz 1920–1950*, edited by Frank Driggs and Harris Lewine (Morrow, 1982); *Twelve Million Black Voices* by Richard Wright (Thunder Mouth Press, reissued 1981); and *Brown Sugar: Eighty Years of America's Black Female Superstars* by Donald Bogle (Da Capo Press, 1980).

Originally published in the *Village Voice*, 23 August 1995, p. 84.

42.

Questions on Feminism

Question 1: Recent feminist art and critical practices appear to be moving in various different directions: while some artists and writers continue to develop ideas, arguments, and forms related to 1980s feminist theories focusing on psychoanalysis, a critique of Marxist and related political theories, and poststructuralist theories of cultural identity, others have forged a return to 1960s and '70s feminist practices centering on a less mediated iconographic and performative use of the female body. Although significant for feminist practices, the work of the 1960s and '70s did generate theoretical critiques of its overt or underlying thematic of biological or physical essentialism. In light of this, how can we understand recent feminist practices that seem to have bypassed, not to say actively rejected, 1980s theoretical work, for a return to a so-called "real" of the feminine? And what roles do the continuation/elaboration of the 1980s feminist concerns and practices play in the current arena?

Question 2: Recent art, critical, and curatorial practices have renewed the use of the term "accessibility," which is routinely opposed to "elitism" in characterizing some feminist art and critical-theoretical practices. "Elitist" feminist art and critical writing are typically associated with theory, and in particular with psychoanalytic and semiotic/language-based theories and are defined as distanced from popular culture and contemporary politics.

In this sense popular culture is broadened to incorporate "grassroots" feminist politics as well, which is thought to be more capable of crossing distinctions of race, class, and sexual orientation. "Accessible" art and critical writing, and "grassroots" feminist politics often employ autobiographical strategies and conceptions of identity — strategies and conceptions that have been criticized for being insufficiently mediated. What are the implications of the renewal of these oppositions of accessibility and elitism, of low and high art, of the real and the semiotic, for feminist art and critical practices in the 1990s? What questions do these alignments and practices pose about the legacies of 1980s feminist theories?

These questions were sent to a group of artists and writers in the summer of 1994 by the editors of *October*. My response follows.

AS A BLACK FEMINIST cultural critic, in my most recent work I have focused on visual culture: film, TV, the visual arts, design, fashion, and advertising. Two reasons: first, there is still a grave paucity of black and feminist critical discourse on black participation in most areas of visual culture; and second, issues arising from visible intersections of "race," sexuality, and gender in visual culture are particularly compelling in our present moment. These include: in TV and video, the O. J. Simpson chase and trial, the Thomas/Hill hearings, Madonna's or Michael Jackson's or Prince's use of "race" in music videos, or the underground video "The Salt Mines," which examines a homeless community of Latina transvestites; in film, *Crooklyn*, *Daughters of the Dust*, *Just Another Girl on the IRT*, *The Crying Game*, *Sankofa*, or even the recently released *Shawshank Redemption*, just to name a few; in visual art and photography, the "Black Male" exhibition at the Whitney; the photographic work of Robert Mapplethorpe, Lyle Ashton Harris, Carrie Mae Weems, and Lorna Simpson; the installations of Renee Green, Fred Wilson, and David Hammons, as well as the painting of Jean-Michel Basquiat, Emma Amos, and Faith Ringgold, also just to name a few. Analysis of advertising, fashion, race, and design around issues of "race," sexuality, and gender are particularly neglected, although some recent inroads have been made.

In my own work, I attempt to assimilate and critique the theoretical accomplishments of so-called "elitist" feminism, at the same time that I have no wish to alienate "grassroots" feminism. Although I am black, I don't think of my work as more "accessible," not because of anything inherent to my critical practice — not, for instance, because of my use of "autobiographical strategies" or "conceptions of identity" — but because most people are not yet interested in what I have to give: specifically, new knowledges of the black woman's role in American culture, in feminist thought, and in visual culture (and tangentially connected to this, as well, explorations of the larger categories of women of color, queer women, poor women, etc.).

In the formulation of my own critical practice, I find it all but useless to contrast "psychoanalytic and semiotic/language-based theories" with approaches concerned with "popular culture and contemporary theories." Obviously, as the Black Popular Culture Conference (which I organized at DIA in New York in 1990) would suggest, I am very interested in popular culture, but not in contrast, or in opposition, to more theoretical or "elitist" approaches. For one thing, I wouldn't automatically place discourses on "popular culture" in the inclusive column. And for another, I am beginning to feel excluded, myself, by adherents of either camp who fail to delineate what is emotionally at stake in their own work as part of their critical practice. All biographical reflection doesn't necessarily serve to reveal such core issues any more than all theoretical speculation serves to obscure them. Maybe this is just a personal idiosyncrasy of mine, stemming from the realization that death is always hovering, but increasingly I feel as though the preoccupation of high academic theory with masking its own intentions in obscurantist analysis seems a waste of the precious little time we all have left. But I find even more repellent quasi-autobiographical reflection and popular culture "riffs" which pretend to offer self-revelation and risk but which, instead, only serve to further conceal the motives and the underpinnings of critical practice.

So-called "popular culture" and "high culture," in concert, constantly bombard us with a plethora of irrelevant and misleading information and affect. If you're not a "Harold Bloom" who feels capable of spending the rest of your life reading, memorizing, and synthesizing everything into the theory to end all theories, then your job is to distinguish the wheat from the chaff. By this I do not mean something as mundane as distinguishing popular culture from high culture. The job would be much easier if that were the case. Rather it is the barrage of the cross-fertilization of the two binaries, pop culture versus high culture, high theory versus identity politics, mastery versus mediocrity—along with all the other dominant binaries (male/female, black/white, young/old, gay/straight, rich/poor)—which needs to be interrogated. And when I say interrogated, I don't mean some vague academic test. I mean besieged with skeptical scrutiny, not only at the level of high theory but also, conceivably, at the level of the everyday.

Of course, I am aware of the kind of chaos it might cause to everyone if academics were littered along the supermarket lines, let's say, deconstructing product packaging before making their purchases. This is not what I mean. Rather what I mean to suggest is that how and when, and in what combination, one employs "identity politics," "theory," and, let us say, "history," is a delicate and precise matter not easily subject to specific description. You might say that I view critical practice as yet another kind of cultural production and artistic practice; and I view its frequent pretenses of scientific rationalism or positivism (owing to its many roots in the Enlightenment and in various structuralisms), as misguided at best.

There are many critics who are engaged at the level I am advocating: Stuart Hall, Gayatri Spivak, Nancy Miller, Homi Bhabha, to name a few. But the best example of a school of criticism that employs these principles is queer theory and criticism, as exemplified among the ranks of the participants in the recent Masculinity Conference: Eve Kosofsky Sedgwick, Sander Gilman, Wayne Kostenbaum, bell hooks, Maurice Berger, Kendall Thomas, and Sapphire, as well as others who were not present such as Diana Fuss, Alex Doty, Teresa de Lauretis, and Judith Butler.

Originally published in *October* 21 (winter 1995).

43.

Feminism, Race, and the Division of Labor

Women have always worked—in their homes and the homes of others, in fields, facto-ries, shops, stores, and offices. The kind of work done has varied for women of different classes, races, ethnic groups, and geographical locations. And the nature of women's work has changed over time with urbanization and industrialization. What remains the same is that the ways in which women have worked involve a constant tension between two areas of women's lives: the home and the marketplace. —ALICE KESSLER HARRIS, *Women Have Always Worked: A Historical Overview*

Throughout the Jim Crow decades white-authored historiography continued largely to reiterate the most dehumanizing, defeminizing, and demeaning images as simple matters of fact. Black women figured in this body of literature almost uniformly in terms of a set of pejorative slave-women stock characters. While these often overlapped, they may be identified singly as the brood mare, the Jezebel, the bad black mother, and the Mammy— the sole emblem of "good" black womanhood. —PATRICIA MORTON, *Disfiguring Images: The Historical Assault on Afro-American Women*

You are a Wolof woman from Senegal. You have come to Paris in 1895 with your husband as a performer in the Exposition Ethnographique de L'Afrique Occidentale (Senegal and French Sudan) because of the promise of good pay. You have been positioned in front of a camera, and you are thinking about how cold it is; you can't believe that you have to live here in this reconstruction of a West African village, crowded with these other West

African people, some of whom don't even speak Wolof. Every day the white people come to stare at you as you do your pottery. You make fun of some of them out loud in Wolof, which they don't understand.—FATIMAH TOBING RONY, "Those Who Squat and Those Who Sit: The Iconography of Race in the 1895 Films of Felix-Louis Regnault," *Camera Obscura* 28 (January 1992)

"Women's work" may have always been the key divisive issue in the women's liberation movement in the United States. The long-awaited successes and triumphs of feminism and the women's movement in the workplace, in the home, and in the public sphere have helped to free some women, at least hypothetically, to aspire to the heights of their ambitions and talents. Nevertheless, women's work continues to mean very different things depending upon your age, your race, your sexuality, your economic status, and whether it was you or your grandparents or your great-grandparents who came to this country as immigrants, or your ancestors who came here as slaves, or your ancestors who have always been here.

The first wave of the women's movement was brought into being and succeeded in galvanizing large numbers of men and women, in the manner of most paradigmatic shifts, because of inevitable evolutionary developments in our economic arrangements (among these the abolition of slavery and the African slave trade, industrialization, imperialism, urbanization, World War I, and World War II) that necessitated a correlative change in the valuation of the work of women. At the same time, women's desire for meaningful work outside the home and adequate remuneration for work within the home were met, at long last, with some slight encouragements.

Pleas and polemics for equity, forceful and unmistakable, were heard in the public sphere for the first time. The most privileged were invariably the first and most blessed by any change. Such developments took place not only among the white middle class, however; they influenced the lives of all women, especially black women.

The second wave of women's liberation was instigated by such economic and cultural factors as the sexual revolution in the wake of the Kinsey Report, the wide availability of the birth control pill, the legalization of abortion, the civil rights movement and the New Left (both of which were against the Vietnam War), the publication of Betty Friedan's *The Feminine Mystique*, and the birth of the National Organization for Women (NOW) and Redstockings. It was as if the advances of the first wave really began to gel only in the second wave. The accomplishments of black power, Latino power, Native American power, gay power, women's liberation, and the overall vibe of the

Age of Aquarius were mingled in the dubious successes of Lyndon Johnson's "War on Poverty," the Equal Employment Opportunity Commission, and other civil rights' legislation.

To this day, however, the problem for feminist unity has continued to be (aside from the all-too-familiar, unrelenting onslaught of the New Right) a brutal economic stratification, both in this country and worldwide, in which some lives are considered more precious than others, and the work of some women is not considered important enough to warrant a living wage or the basic protections of the law. Leading the list of those least valued would be teenage mothers, women in prisons, welfare mothers, mentally or physically ill women, domestic workers, illegal aliens, alcoholic or addicted women, and sex workers. I need hardly add that more often than not, these categories overlap and extend into all social arenas. Even women who are cultural workers and producers in the art world—usually considered among the ranks of the privileged—have had the value of their work consistently called into question, never more so than in the context of the recent culture wars. The National Endowment for the Arts's repressive tendencies are often inclined to adversely effect those who are most likely to rely on public monies: women and minority artists.

So when Lydia Yee told me of her plan to mount an exhibition titled "Division of Labor: 'Women's Work' in Contemporary Art" at the Bronx Museum and asked me to write an essay for the catalogue, I was most eager to have the opportunity to consider, briefly, "women's work" and its impact on the accomplishments of contemporary women artists. Her inclusion of softer, sewn, stitched, mixed-media, and so-called "craft" oriented works from the 1970s brings back memories of a more courageous art world; it also allows us to imagine clearly, for the first time, the ongoing influence of this work on a wide array of subsequent explorations of gender and ethnicity in contemporary art, from May Stevens and Nancy Spero to Barbara Kruger, Jenny Holzer, and Cindy Sherman to Lorna Simpson, Carrie Mae Weems, Pat Ward Williams, and Fred Wilson.

Having come of age in the art world as the daughter of the artist and art world feminist activist Faith Ringgold, I have been in a very good position since the 1960s (I was eighteen in 1970) to appreciate the way in which the works of so many contemporary women artists have come out of their own observations and insights, either as feminists or as womanists, into the inequities, injustices, and ambivalent pleasures of the world of women's work. As a teenager, I had the great pleasure of watching the women artists' movement unfold from the early days of the Artworkers' Coalition, Women for

Art Revolution (WAR), and Art Strike, when Women Students and Artists for Black Art Liberation (WSABAL), which Faith and I started, insisted that the alternative Venice Biennale of 1970 protesting the U.S. invasion of Vietnam and Cambodia include not only white male "superstars" but 50 percent women and 50 percent people of color. Today, I am not as proud of the quotas as I once was, but at least we were shaking things up. When I observe such women artists as Jenny Holtzer, Louise Bourgeois, and Lorna Simpson being featured at international biennials, and the participation of curators of color in other major exhibitions, I like to think that we helped lead the way.

I was also there by Faith's side when Ad Hoc Women started in 1971, under Lucy Lippard's leadership, a group whose actions would subsequently change the elitist and exclusionary composition of Whitney Biennials forevermore. Eventually such activity would lead to the formation of such groups as the Guerrilla Girls and Women's Action Coalition (WAC). I became a black feminist, in this harried way, as the daughter of a black feminist. Again, I was there beside my mother when she, Jean Toche, and John Hendricks planned and executed the historic Flag Show at the Judson Memorial Church, in which Kate Millet, Yvonne Rainer, Iris Crump, and so many other women artists participated. I was the first arrested, along with Jean and John, for "desecration of the flag" on the night the U.S. Attorney General's office closed down the show. I thought it was all very exciting until I was actually arrested. Then, as I watched, Faith persuaded the officers to trade her arrest for mine, took her diamond ring and her wedding band off her fingers and gave them to me, and was taken away to jail, to "The Tombs." That was one of the most frightening nights of my life. I called everybody I could think of until she was released and the rings were safely back on her fingers. Faith, then known as one of the Judson Three, had always been more radical than I was.

For Faith, mothering and her responsibility to the family unit had always come before her work as an artist. Although she had tried to do both while I was growing up, the family invariably came first until I was old enough to be interested in the art world. Then, as she made her way into the current art world scene of activism and protest, she took me along, but she was still my mother. She would not have traded her own arrest for anyone else's. I will never forget that moment, standing there as Faith traded me for herself—the hush of the sanctuary, the shadows, the quiet voices of the officers, and the look in my mother's eyes as she pushed me behind her, as if to shield me with her body. "A constant tension," as the historian Alice Kessler Harris wrote about the dilemma of women's work, "between two areas of women's lives: the home and the marketplace."[1] In those rotten, beautiful days of Vietnam, Cambodia, and Richard Nixon, I was only nineteen.

In this society, it is still common to dichotomize and polarize motherhood and art, reproduction and politics, but the mother who is a politically active artist cannot. Is it, then, glass ceiling time or time to rewrite the rules?

Since having taught a course on black feminist theory at the Graduate Center of the City University of New York, I have become fascinated by the idea of labor issues as a means of defining, in very specific terms, the kinds of differences that have sometimes plagued the possibility of unity in the women's movement. In the first half of the course, we read such historical texts on black women's labor as Deborah Gray White's *Ar'n't I a Woman?: Female Slaves in the Plantation South* (1985); Elizabeth Fox-Genovese's *Within the Plantation Household: Black and White Women of the Old South* (1988); Jacqueline Jones's *Labor of Love, Labor of Sorrow: Black Women, Work, and the Family, From Slavery to the Present* (1985); Paula Giddings's *When and Where I Enter: The Impact of Black Women on Race and Sex in America* (1984); Patricia Morton's *Disfigured Images: The Historical Assault on Afro-American Women* (1991); Angela Davis's *Women, Race, and Class* (1981); and Sara Evans's *Personal Politics: The Roots of Women's Liberation in the Civil Rights Movement and the New Left* (1979).

Needless to say, a large part of everything written about the history of black women in the United States concerns their work inside and outside of the home, but mostly outside of the home. From White's history of black female slaves, we learn the gloomy story of how little can be gleaned from the historical record — black female slaves didn't often have the time, the means, or the education to keep diaries or write letters. Most of what we know about them comes from diaries and letters written by whites, court records from when they got into trouble, the few female slave narratives helped to publication by white female abolitionists at the time, and the oral slave narratives collected from elderly slave survivors in the 1930s by the Works Progress Administration (WPA).

From Fox-Genovese, we begin to fathom the true dimensions of the alienation of the black female slave. "Slave women could not experience gender as a seamless wrapping of their selves," she writes. "Slavery forced upon them a double view of gender relations that exposed the artificial or problematic aspects of gender identification, for by stripping slave men of the social attributes of manhood in general and fatherhood in particular, it afforded women no satisfactory social definition of themselves as women." As such, there was rarely any identification on the basis of gender between black and white women in the antebellum South: "Women were bound to each other in the household not in sisterhood, but by their specific and different relations to the master."[2]

From Jacqueline Jones, we learn that during the late nineteenth century and for much of the twentieth century, the working lives of black women were virtually immune to industrialization: "As paid labor became increasingly associated with the time-oriented production of goods, the black nurse, maid, and cook remained something of a labor-force anachronism in a national . . . context. The Afro-American woman found herself confined to this type of toil by virtue of her sex and race."[3] If black women weren't working in white people's homes, then they were usually employed doing backbreaking work in the fields, picking cotton or some other crop, or they were forced to do gloomy, foul-smelling, poorly paid jobs, considered beneath the dignity of whites, in factories: stemming tobacco or shucking oysters.

Giddings's book brings sharply into focus the early feminism of black club women in the nineteenth and twentieth centuries and their concern for the plight of poor and working class black women by virtue of race, mission, and sisterhood. Davis covers similar ground from a slightly more leftist perspective and Morton explains both the myth and reality of the stereotype of "Mammy," and how necessary her survival is, in one guise or another.

The book by Sara Evans helps to clarify, for me, along with the oral history *My Soul Is Rested: Movement Days in the Deep South Remembered* (1977) by Howell Raines and the recently published biography of Fanny Lou Hamer, the pivotal, although thankless, role black women played in the civil rights movement.[4] They were the "Mommas" who fed and housed the civil rights workers. And they were also the brilliant, seasoned fighters who orchestrated many of the successes of the civil rights movement from behind the scenes because the men desired visibility much more than they did. The Hamer biography, which tells the story of how this civil rights leader died sick, poor, and alone, is enough to make you weep. Her elaborate funeral at which all the black male leaders presided was scant recompense indeed: too little, too late.

These historical readings serve to help us understand the profound differences in black feminist approaches. By and large, black women have had a very different work history. We have been domestic workers and agricultural laborers, not decorative "ladies." And even when we managed to rise to the station of "ladies" in all outward appearances, seldom did it keep us from hard work. For the most part, we haven't had to struggle with the infantilizing paternalism of an overbearing patriarchal figure clutching a fist full of dollars but rather with lynchings, burnings, and race riots. For the most part, the men we've known have been beside us or beneath us, or sometimes even above us, but rarely in genuine control. Although this isn't to say that black men have not been as tempted by misogyny and sexism as other kinds of men.

Jones was my grandmother's married name, the name she had not used since her divorce from my grandfather Big Andrew years before I was born. Only my sister and I called her Momma Jones. As a Harlem fashion designer and a local seamstress, her professional name was Madame Willi Posey, her maiden name preceded by a Gallic, fashion-conscious twist. Momma Jones hadn't had much of a problem with men since her divorce, but she was always counseling women who did, either the young women who modeled in her fashion shows or the more mature women who made up her clientele.

One evening when I was a child, a young woman—large, brown, and quite handsome—came to tell my grandmother Momma Jones her problems. This young woman cried in my grandmother's parlor that she didn't know what to do about her husband beating her. But because her husband was thin and small, Momma Jones asked her, "Why don't you hit him back?" She knew all right that she was stronger than him, she told Momma Jones, but she didn't want him to know that.

All around me in Harlem as I was growing up, husbands were coming home drunk at night and beating their wives; men were beating women as though it was as necessary as mealtime. My husband Gene has told me that the same thing was going on down in South Carolina where he was born, and in Florida where he was raised. I offer no justification for battering. But there was something about that woman explaining why she wouldn't hit her husband that has haunted me all these years.

Sometimes black women just think that they are stronger than their men because of myth and stereotype. Sometimes they are actually stronger. There are all kinds of strength. The most important kinds are not necessarily always physical, political, or economic, but moral, ethical, experiential, and intellectual.

The sacrifices black women have made for others are unfathomable. Because of this I never really comprehended the patriarchal assumption that men were stronger than women until I was much older and better schooled in the mores of the dominant culture. Were they really? This is the question that one must answer anew each day as a black feminist, as a feminist of color.

In the same black feminist theory class, we also read Ntozake Shange's For *Colored Girls Who Have Considered Suicide/ When The Rainbow Is Enuf*

(1975), the extraordinary "choreo-poem," which continued on Broadway as a play and announced black feminist discontent to the world. We also read the most prominent black feminist theory situated within the humanities, such as Toni Cade Bambara's prescient anthology *The Black Woman* (1970); my own *Black Macho and the Myth of the Superwoman* (1979) and *Invisibility Blues: From Pop to Theory* (1990); bell hooks's *Ain't I a Woman: Black Women and Feminism* (1981) and *Black Looks: Race and Representation* (1992); Hazel Carby's *Reconstructing Womanhood: The Emergence of the Afro-American Woman Novelist* (1987); Audre Lorde's *Sister Outsider: Essays and Speeches* (1984); Toni Morrison's anthology *Race-ing Justice, Engendering Power: Essays on Anita Hill, Clarence Thomas, and the Construction of Social Reality* (1992); and Adrienne Rich's influential essay "Disloyal to Civilization" in *On Lies, Secrets, and Silences: Selected Prose, 1966–78* (1979).

In the milieu of these supportive, insightful texts, we were able to begin to contemplate the painful and dangerous divide for the study of women of color that exists in the conventional organization of academic disciplines. On the one hand, social science approaches focus on historical, ethnographic, and sociological data, whereas the humanities approaches often confine themselves to semiotic analyses of discourse, creativity, and representation. We really need both approaches in tandem, along with the study of the history of science, law, and medicine, to do justice to the legacy of women of color. Indeed, I would argue as a feminist that we should read minority women writers, not only as works of art (and therefore capable of spiritual and philosophical guidance) but also as sociological works and political works, for surely, as black womanist critics such as Joyce Joyce correctly point out, this was part of the spirit in which they were written.

My view is that, in the case of black women as a class (and this may be true of other groups of women of color and minority women in this country: Native American, Asian American, Latin American, Arab American, African, queer women of color, for example), the work of literature occupies much greater intellectual and philosophical space than it would in the dominant culture because of the lack in communities of color of all but the most rudimentary vestiges of such academic discourses as philosophy, linguistics, psychology, political science, critical theory, economics, and so on. Indeed, I think the same is probably true of works of art in general — music, film and video, visual art, and the performing arts.

When Harriet Jacobs wrote the slave narrative *Incidents in the Life of a Slave Girl* (1861) under the pseudonym Linda Brent, in order to earn money to feed her children and to plead the case of women in slavery, her concerns were no more or less practical than those of Frances Harper when she wrote *Iola Leroy; or, Shadows Uplifted* (1892) or Pauline Hopkins when she wrote *Contending Forces: A Romance Illustrative of Negro Life North and South* (1900). Each was written to stem the tide of the stereotype promulgated in white circles of black female sexual licentiousness.

As the innovations of European modernism were slowly assimilated by black aesthetic practice, the concerns of Nella Larsen when she wrote *Passing* (1929), Gwendolyn Brooks when she wrote *Maud Martha* (1953), Paule Marshall when she wrote *Brown Girl, Brownstones* (1959), Toni Morrison when she wrote *The Bluest Eye* (1972) remained pragmatic but were increasingly psychological and deconstructive, as well. Each of these writers wrote about the black female yearning for meaningful work in the context of a worthwhile existence and the problems that arise when that desire is twisted and blocked. How women of color, their bodies, their minds, and their work, should be valued is still a volatile and disturbing issue in much of the world.

Yes, as Alice Kessler-Harris points out, women have always worked: as slaves, as servants, as tillers of the land, and as what Virginia Woolf called "ladies in the house." But when would their true greatness, their true genius be recognized, as Linda Nochlin asked, rhetorically, in her 1971 essay, "Why Are There No Great Women Artists?"[5] The answers are complicated and more than a little frustrating. I do not expect to see the much-needed changes in my lifetime. In the meanwhile, women's work in contemporary art helps the veterans of the culture wars, the sex wars, and the gender wars to contemplate a future utopia. In communities of color, the visual artist, in particular, is the visionary, the prophet, the cultural and intellectual architect of the new, the old, and the misunderstood — the one who tries to make sense of the trouble-ridden world. Together with the most progressive women artists of other nations and ethnicities, and artists who reflect on gender and sexuality in their work, artists who are women of color give us something to look forward to, a little more than we might ordinarily expect from the art world and from the public sphere. For instance, I become almost nostalgic when I think of Judy Chicago's *Womanhouse* in 1972 on the West Coast (which I never saw but read so much about).

Faith, too, began to combine feminist art world activism with the search for a black feminist aesthetic. After returning from two trips to Africa, coupled with her sewing and crafts collaborations with her mother, my grandmother, Momma Jones — for her classes at Bank Street College in which her students made masks, costumes, beaded, and sewn art — Faith began to incorporate these strategies into her work as an act of black feminist will. At this time, she began the *Weeping Women* series of masks, which led to *Mrs. Brown, Elsie, Delores*, and *Catherine*, all finished in 1973, and the various sewn versions of Wilt Chamberlain and his make-believe white female bride, Wiltina.

In 1972, Faith and I went to Europe together and saw the Tibetan tankas hanging in the Rijksmuseum in Amsterdam. Faith was immediately struck by the desire to appropriate the various formal strategies of this Asian work. First, she borrowed the vertical writing and the ploy of the pastoral landscapes for her *Political Landscapes* series, which featured black feminist inscriptions. Then she began doing soft paintings that could be rolled and that were framed in cloth by Momma Jones in her *Slave Rape* series. The first of these were three large oil paintings of herself, myself, and my sister Barbara in the nude, looking as though we were slave women in the African forest about to be apprehended by slave catchers.

Faith was acting upon inclinations toward uniquely feminist aesthetics, subject matter, and materials that had been taken up, as well, by Martha Rosier, Joyce Scott, Mimi Smith, Mary Kelly, Miriam Schapiro, and Harmony Hammond (all in this show). Faith was inspired in her *Who's Afraid of Aunt Jemima?* by both Edward Albee's *Who's Afraid of Virginia Woolf?* (1962) and Betye Saar's *The Liberation of Aunt Jemima* (1972). Saar's Aunt Jemima is a revolutionary with a rifle in one of her beautiful Joseph Cornell-esque boxes, whereas Faith's Aunt Jemima is a businesswoman and an entrepreneur, kind of like the flipside of Delilah in the 1934 version of the movie *Imitation of Life*, who decides that she'll take her share of the pancake money after all.

The early 1970s were interesting days indeed for women in the art world, a time during which a feminist aesthetic began to be discussed seriously, without smirks or laughter, in alternative art circles. Later on, in the 1980s, this work would be condemned as essentialist, as if identity would ever be anything but the eternal mystery. But in the 1990s, in these mournful times of AIDS, homelessness, workfare, death penalties, Uzi machine guns, and "three strikes and you're out," a lot of this work is oddly reassuring. Many of the insights of the 1970s—the use of "crafts," perhaps largely the contribution of women's culture around the world, as well as the freedom to use mundane, commonplace materials from the world of housework—have been incorporated into the strategies of the postmodern. The struggle to demystify the pedestal status of "fine art" has come from the initiatives of feminist art as well.

Much of the work in Lydia Yee's show draws upon the complex dialectic of women's work and women's culture. Some of the pieces, such as Oliver Herring's *Covered Coat* (1994), Gay Outlaw's *Skillet Pillar/Spinal Column* (1993), Mimi Smith's *Kitchen* (1973), Joyce Kozloff's decorative works, and

Amalia Mesa-Bains's *The "Castas" Closet* (1995) focus on the material culture of women's work. Emma Amos's *Horizon* (1985–87), Judy Chicago's *Menstruation Bathroom* (1972), Mary Kelly's *Post-Partum Document* (1974–79), and Faith Wilding's *Womb Room* (1972) take on issues regarding women's bodies. Xenobia Bailey's *Sistah Paradise's Bag of Funk* (1994), Joyce Scott's *Nanny Gone Wrong* (1992), Mimi Smith's *Knit Baby Kit* (1968) all speak to the emotional dimensions of gender.

In the blinding glare of polarities of feminist anti-essentialism versus identity politics, I choose the tactile, the specific, and the densely clear: soft art, women's art, hard truths, women's work.

Originally published in *Division of Labor: "Women's Work" in Contemporary Art* (New York: The Bronx Museum of the Arts, 1995).

Notes

1. Alice Kessler-Harris, *Women Have Always Worked: A Historical Overview* (Old Westbury, N.Y.: Feminist Press, 1981), 41.
2. Elizabeth Fox-Genovese, *Within the Plantation Household: Black and White Women of the Old South* (Chapel Hill: University of North Carolina Press, 1988), 373.
3. Jacqueline Jones, *Labor of Love, Labor of Sorrow: Black Women, Work, and the Family, From Slavery to the Present* (New York: Basic Books, 1985), 127.
4. See Kay Mills, *This Little Light of Mine: The Life of Fannie Lou Hamer* (New York: Dutton, 1993).
5. Linda Nochlin, "Why Are There No Great Women Artists?" *ARTnews* 69 (January 1971). Reprinted in Linda Nochlin, *Women, Art, and Power and Other Essays* (New York: Harper and Row, 1988), 145–178.

44.

Doin' the Right Thing: Ten Years After

She's Gotta Have It

There's been tons of speculation over the years about who Spike Lee is and what his films mean, a lot of it pretty wrongheaded in my view. Some whites fear him. Some blacks are jealous of him. Everyone from Amiri Baraka to Joe Klein has suggested that we stop him, or at the very least watch him closely. Despite, or perhaps because of this burdensome surveillance, Lee became the most prominent African American filmmaker ever with his first film. Ten years later, he still is.

In April of 1986, I was invited on *Donahue* with Tony Brown and a representative of the NAACP to talk about *The Color Purple*'s gender troubles. Tony Brown hated the movie without ever having condescended to see it, and the rep from the NAACP already smelled of liquor at ten in the morning. The audience was packed with the far better informed members of the Black Filmmakers Foundation, one of whom was the still unknown Spike Lee. On my personal copy of the videotape, there is a perfect close-up of him in the audience. He was quiet that day.

Later that year, *She's Gotta Have It* was released and Spike Lee's career took off for the stratosphere. Around the same time, Lee's sound bite–spitting alter ego exploded upon the scene, writing tell-all film memoirs (beginning with the revealing *Spike Lee's Gotta Have It: Inside Guerrilla Filmmaking*) and making vituperative assaults on Whoopi's blue contact lenses,

Steven Spielberg, and *The Color Purple* as the epitome of what was wrong and racist about Hollywood.

Remember 1986? That was also the year black folk suffered through Prince in *Under the Cherry Moon*, Eddie Murphy in *Golden Child*, Whoopi in *Jumpin' Jack Flash*, and Rae Dawn Chong in *Soul Man*. Then *She's Gotta Have It* opened in New York City. And as Nelson George notes in *Blackface*, "The world of black film changes forever."

For most of us in New York film audiences, it was like when *Nanook of the North* was first shown in 1922 to packed houses, or when American audiences first saw Italian neorealism: a breath of fresh air. Something entirely new, yet certifiably authentic. Despite the considerable flap over the apparent homophobia and the intolerable sexism of having the plot turn on Nola Darling's being raped into submission, *She's Gotta Have It* became an instant black classic by default. There was no competition.

The Spike Lee phenomenon began with the mistaken assumption, on his part and everybody else's, that blacks making their "own" films would improve the quality of black representations in the public sphere. In 1986, some of us still thought black filmmakers might go that route, but in mid 1996, it's clear we are neither there nor headed there. Ten years and umpteen black films later (eight more for Lee alone), we've witnessed the rise of the Hudlin brothers, Matty Rich, John Singleton, Van Peebles Jr., and the Hughes twins, as well as the emergence of such dignified figures as Carl Franklin, Julie Dash, Haile Gerima, and a host of others, with not a single substantive challenge to the centrality of Lee's inimitable paradigm of obstreperous autonomy combined with commercial or critical success. We can now see that the notion of blacks making their "own" films presupposed the existence of a monolithic black community, unified enough to possess a common ideology, ethics, morality, and culture, sufficient to override such competing and divisive interests as class, gender, sexuality, age, and education.

Also implicit in this formulation of blacks having their "own" films was the nagging question as to whether such representations would somehow make black people's lives better overall. Regardless of whether a film has any value as art, it can, if it chooses, closely mirror or reflect the problems and inequities of its society. People make the mistake of thinking that a film can therefore also correct inequities. This is because we, as a culture, are still trying to figure out what representation fully means in still new and exponentially expanding forms: what such forms can and can't do, what we should and should not ask of them.

Debates over the appropriateness of politically inflected art, attempts to censor racist, sexist, or violent representations, as well as tensions over issues of quality, identity, and diversity in popular culture are all expressions of that quandary. But the escalating public dissonance around issues of gender, sexuality, and especially class is an inspiration rather than a problem to the artist, unless you consider the "black community" to be your stock-in-trade, and Spike Lee has long since jumped off that train.

AFTER THE RIPE success of *She's Gotta Have It*, Lee managed to piss off a lot of people with his next two films. Although it did well at the box office, *School Daze* was dismissed by pundits as a silly, house-party-animal-house kind of film about college kids getting into wacky fun. Other experts were alienated by his adoption of the musical genre or annoyed by his critique of black college life, and some just didn't like him airing the well-known fact that some blacks have their own hang-ups about skin color.

But the more I watched it, the more I fell in love with it. I ignored the scene in which the Jigaboos homophobically dis the home boys and the sad culmination of the plot in which the sorority queen allows a frat pledgee to screw her as part of a sinister bargain with Big Brother Almighty, the head frat man. Logic has never been all that important in musicals, anyway.

I treasure it for the first forty-five minutes in which the best songs occur, including the stunning dance-battle scene between the Wannabees and the Jigaboos and, especially, the girl-group number in which Tisha Campbell, Jasmine Guy, and two other foxy young ladies do flawless dream-girl gyrations. "Boy, you know I love you," Campbell purrs to the music, her body tightly swaddled in silk lame, flicking back her long blond extensions. One day I plan to buy the video for no other purpose than to replay that sequence as many times as I like.

As for *Do the Right Thing* (1989), it needs no defense and, just as Lee insisted at Cannes and every other place he went, it should have won a bushel of awards. Despite the attacks of such ax-grinding critics as Joe Klein in *New York* magazine and Stanley Crouch *in The New Republic* and the *Voice*, who predicted that the riot in the film would lead to a real one, *Do the Right Thing* is clearly a stroke of cinematic genius from beginning to end, as well as a time capsule of late-'80s racial strife. The more you watch it, the better it looks, beginning with the opening sequence of Senor Love Daddy (Sam Jackson) as community DJ, stringing the narrative together, much like the radio banter in Michael Schultz's *Car Wash*.

Responses to Lee's work calmed down considerably with *Mo' Better Blues* (1990), despite a skirmish in the *New York Times* over whether the two parasitic jazz club owners (the Turturro brothers) were anti-Semitic in conceptualization. In fact, Lee is more an aesthete than a demagogue, no matter what he yells at Knicks games. The plot shows signs that his one-man war against bourgeois propriety was wearing down. Protagonist Bleek is a successful jazz musician who values his craft over either of his two girlfriends, only to find that when he loses his lip, what matters most is the love of a good woman and a family. Denzel Washington makes his debut as a sex symbol/leading man, but he wasn't half the revelation that newcomer Wesley Snipes was as the fascinating other guy who gets the other girl.

In *Jungle Fever* (1991), the film about interracial relationships that made almost everybody crazy, the two central themes of Lee's mature work are first articulated. The first of these, the always morbid and sometimes deadly conflict between parent (usually the father) and child is sounded like a death knell throughout the complicated plot. There are the following insidious relationships: between architect Flipper Purify (Wesley Snipes) and his daughter, whom he fears losing to the streets of Harlem; between brother Gator (Sam Jackson) and his codependent mother (Ruby Dee) and dogmatically religious father (Ossie Davis), who ultimately kills him; between Paulie Carbone (John Turturro) and his father (Anthony Quinn), who continues to mourn obsessively the loss of his wife; between Angie and her father, also a widower.

The other major theme is the possibility of soul death and the subsequent loss of all one's dreams, through drugs, too much sex, or some other narcotic seduction. So here we have Flipper and Angie, whose racial identities and social equilibrium are threatened by their infatuation with each other, their "jungle fever"; the crack addiction of Gator and his girlfriend, Vivian (Halle Berry); the racist banter of Paulie's friends in the candy store, seduced by the collegiality of fascism; and Paulie's father's inability to break free from his obsessive grieving for his dead wife. Clearly, Lee continues to have a difficult, albeit creatively profitable, relationship with his own father's legacy and with the memory of his mother.

In *Malcolm X*, the parent-child conflict is writ larger than ever before in Malcolm's infatuation and subsequent break with Elijah Mohammed. Malcolm's possible soul death goes through progressive stages — his life as a child when his father is killed and his mother loses her mind, as a young man when he is a misguided hustler and petty hoodlum, and as a follower of the Black Muslims. In the final stage, in Lee's version, Malcolm (Denzel Washington) loses his life but not his soul in a spectacular ten-minute-plus melee.

After going up against the Nation, Farrakhan, the studio system, Amiri Baraka, and half of America to make *Malcolm X*, Lee mellowed out. In *Crooklyn*, his most autobiographical film, cowritten with his sister Joie and his brother Cinque, the charming little girl protagonist (one of the best child actors I have ever seen) locks horns with her mother (Alfre Woodard), who will soon die of cancer. It's also a portrait of a disturbingly contentious, overwhelmingly male (four brothers), and strife-ridden family. Critics complained of *Crooklyn* that it seemed aimless and undigested but it documented the everyday life of a certain kind of marginally middle-class black family (the kind I came from) in ways pretty hard to equal. Constantly bickering, teasing, and yelling, these folks are the opposite of the family on *The Cosby Show*.

In *Clockers*, based upon Richard Price's grim novel about drugs and street life in Newark, Lee returns to the almost exclusively male scenario of *Malcolm X*, *Mo' Better*, and *Do the Right Thing*. Strike will negotiate his way through a bevy of complicated father figures, including his brother Victor and two cops, one white and one black, in order to break free from the demonic father, drug dealer Rodney. The cinematography by Malik Sayeed and the performances were particularly stellar. Yet *Clockers* went nowhere.

"A lot of people perceived *Clockers* as a hood film," Lee commented recently at his offices at 40 Acres and A Mule. "Hood films are kind of over. This was one of the reasons I was hesitant about doing it. Audiences, black and white, are getting pretty fatigued of that genre. Rightly so, they want to see some different stories coming out of black culture besides a shoot-em-up, hip-hop film."

Lee's demeanor is cool, calm, and self-effacing. You could almost mistake him for sleepy if it weren't for the obvious focus and intensity in the timbre of his voice. "I thought we could transcend the hood genre and make something greater. We don't take the stance that young black men just have to resign themselves, that they are either going to die prematurely or they are going to spend the rest of their lives in prison."

People may think that the mellower Lee has lowered his sights, become less ambitious about transforming the film industry. But, in fact, the two projects he is currently pursuing—an on-the-bus movie about the Million Man March and a biopic of the great black baseball player Jackie Robinson—don't suggest he's making any concessions to the commercial bottom line.

Get on the Bus written by Reggie Blythewood looks at a group of black men during a seventy-two-hour bus ride from L.A. to D.C., on their way to the march. Lee succeeded in getting all the financing for the film from black male investors, including Johnnie Cochran, Wesley Snipes, Danny Glover, and Will Smith, in order to reinvoke the emphasis of the march on self-reliance and empowerment. It will open on October 16th, the anniversary of the original march, a day for which yet another march, this time focusing on the family, is being planned. "But everybody can't go to the march," Lee states with a sly smile. "So they can go to the movie theaters."

Lee says he plans to take on homophobia and sexism in the movie and concedes that the march organizers may not be entirely happy with its representation. While he continues to think more of Farrakhan than I do, he's still astonishingly laid-back, mild, and charming, even when he disagrees with what you're saying.

SINCE I AM SUPPOSED to be the original black feminist boogeygirl, it must be a measure of Spike Lee's sagging returns at the box office coupled with his evolutionary growth that I am beginning to really appreciate his films. But *Girl 6* is really my favorite thus far. Why? It's a girl film with lots of cute, funny women. It's a homoerotic film for straight women who enjoy looking at other women. If you're not so straight, male or female, you should enjoy it as well. Not only is there little of the moralistic baggage that has marred Lee's work in the now distant past, *Girl 6* is cool jazz rather than juvenile hip-hop, sophisticated rather than sassy. The soundtrack by Prince is mean. Lee halfheartedly tacks on the soul-murder theme here in *Girl 6*'s confusion over rhetoric versus reality and her obsession with a little girl who falls down an elevator shaft in the projects. But this dark, self-reflexive comedy, complete with *Natural Born Killers*-type spoofs of blaxploitation scenarios starring Girl 6, makes his specific intentions inscrutable, vague, and almost beside the point. *Girl 6* remains predominantly color-purple womanish. Even Alice Walker might approve.

Aside from the remarkable talents of Theresa Randle as protagonist, Isaiah Washington as ex-husband, and a noteworthy supporting cast, the secret ingredient in *Girl 6* is the writing of Suzan-Lori Parks, the recent heir to Adrienne Kennedy's throne as the reigning princess of the black avant-garde theater. Parks is the epitome of postmodern femme, lightning quick on sex as well as gender, as her *Venus*, currently playing to packed houses at the Public, amply demonstrates. If Francis Ford Coppola or some other white director had done a *Girl 6*, it would have been heralded by the media as a quantum leap in the women's film genre. I expect the definitive white-girl, phone-sex movie to emerge, as though *Girl 6* had never happened, within the next two years to massive publicity. A wicked cross between Ariyan Johnson in *Just Another Girl on the IRT* and Marlene Dietrich in *Blonde Venus*, Theresa Randle's character changes wigs as much as Naomi Campbell and is just as gorgeous. But because the film was directed by a black man and it's about black women, you know the rest. In fact, so much so that *Girl 6* has come and gone from the movie theaters in record time. Flopsville is all she wrote.

When I saw *Girl 6*, I was accompanied by Faith, my fourteen-going-on-forty-year-old niece from Harlem. The two of us sat in the half-empty Plaza Twin in Brooklyn in the middle of a Sunday afternoon laughing louder than anybody else at the same jokes, not something we often do. More often we laugh at each other — she at me for being lame and I at her for being so cynical. I was wondering why none of the reviews had given me any idea how darkly humorous and engaging this film actually was.

The rest of the scant audience, composed of strays and teenage mothers with their children, seemed listless and bored. Not at all the audience of smart females of color and hip white girls this film deserved, they weren't getting it because it wasn't linear and action packed. It wasn't violent or even sexually explicit. No woman was humiliated or destroyed. Rather the women were at the center, the men marginal to the plot. Even Girl 6's ex-husband appears only sporadically. There are no fathers, no mothers, no conventional families. Moreover, it didn't even have recognizable stars except Madonna who makes a cameo as a telephone-sex madam, and it didn't fit any of the conventional genres. You could call it a black comedy but the laughs were pure bittersweet chocolate. It really didn't have much of a story.

An aspiring actress, who gets sick of being asked to take off her clothes to get a part, joins on with a phone-sex agency as Girl 6 in order to make a living and to give her talent some creative outlet. After all, phone sex does involve acting. Because the money is good, she begins to invest more and more of her time in phone sex, even getting emotionally involved with some of her clients, mostly white men. When she switches to doing phone sex out of her own apartment, she is drawn into a black hole that almost gets her killed. Almost but not quite. At the end, she is in the cab on the way to JFK and LA to tackle the bona fide career as an actress. Although there are huge wrinkles and chasms in the plot, I can relate to its allegorical dimensions. Along with my niece and every other black woman I know, I am looking to figure out the role we'll play in the future; being sexy and young fades as predictably as good weather. What then? If the answer is pleasure, whose pleasure?

These are Parks's themes in *Venus*, as well, in which Saartje Baartmen, a South African refugee, is brought to London in the nineteenth century in order to be displayed as a freak because of the huge configuration of her butt. In Parks's rendition of this true story, Saartje is just as needy as the white men who lose themselves in the fold of her posterior flesh. Both *Girl 6* and

Venus monkey around skillfully with the way in which the black woman's face and figure are so readily obfuscated by the myth of an endless black sexuality. *Girl 6* is also about the fantasy and pleasure of virtual reality versus the mundane, tar-baby realities of lived experience from a black-female point of view. These are represented by the humdrum frustrations of everyday life, the most telling aspects of which are Girl 6's skimpy apartment in a walk-up (telephone in the hall), her homey black male neighbor who collects baseball cards and has become her best friend, and her failed marriage with a furtive kleptomaniac who leads a marginal existence.

While making nine films at breakneck speed, Lee has grown before our eyes from a man-child to an adult, gotten married, and become a successful and critically acclaimed film director with a solvent production company and record studio, a store, and several ancillary businesses all located within his native Fort Greene. The fact that he stayed, built his kingdom in the black community, and didn't run, has lent his affect a quiet strength in recent years.

The reality is that feature films have never anywhere served the function of making people's everyday lives better, except to the degree that diversion and entertainment improve the quality of life. Given the prohibitive costs, film has become, more now than ever, not only a three-headed monster of art, politics, and business, but also a hybrid of all the arts, as well as most of the new communication technologies.

Given this picture, what should be the goal and the mission of the black filmmaker? It is almost too obvious to say. An artist has no choice but to try to be as fully expressive of his or her own vision as possible. Therefore, the goal of the black filmmaker should be to fulfill his own, individual vision. Lee is doing this and shows every sign of continuing.

In the process, he has managed to usher in a new kind of black — not brat — pack, abundantly talented and pleasantly heterogeneous: Larry Fishburne, Jasmine Guy, Tisha Campbell all got major boosts from *School Daze*, as did Sam Jackson, Rosie Perez, Roger Smith, and Martin Lawrence from *Do the Right Thing*. Denzel Washington and Wesley Snipes were helped by *Mo' Better Blues*; Halle Berry and Lonette McKee by *Jungle Fever*; Delroy Lindo, Angela Bassett, and Theresa Randle by *Malcolm X*.

"I always thought that if I got into the position of being able to hire who I wanted," Lee says, "that it was my duty to make sure that I gave talented people opportunities not only in front of the camera but behind the camera. Malik Sayeed — *Clockers* was his first film." Sayeed, who is only twenty-seven and started as an electrician on *Malcolm X*, also did splendid work as cinematographer on *Girl 6*.

Yet everybody wants to know the secret to his magical powers of endurance and imagination. How about his real-life family drama, his daddy and the drug bust, his tightfistedness, his Booker T. Washington ambitiousness, his arduous struggles with feminist interpretations of his works? But Lee's secret is no secret. He has proclaimed it in everything he has done from the very beginning. It's pure ambition, fortitude, and talent, the very best combination you can have these days (provided your location is in the metropolitan first world), regardless of your race, class, gender, and/or sexuality.

Originally published in the *Village Voice*, Film Supplement, 21 May 1996, pp. 10–15.

45.

The Gap Alternative

In the images of style we see a world where the marketplace becomes its own, closely watched, opposition. That world is utopian: cost is no object; work holds no restrictions; desire has no conscience; each moment is self-governed. — STUART EWEN, *All Consuming Images*

There is real power in remaining unmarked; and there are serious limitations to visual representation as a political goal. — PEGGY PHELAN, *Unmarked: The Politics of Performance*

Let's face it. Advertising is usually a shady enterprise. Although I don't personally believe that evil is irreversibly written on its soul, for the most part it tends to operate like a passive-aggressive friend who is actually your worst enemy, the one who likes to bring you to your knees in pain but always with a smile.

Various kinds of unsavory manipulation are part and parcel of advertising's bag of tricks. In particular, among those print ads aimed at consumers of women's clothing, which take up more pages than anything else in most women's magazines, the repertoire is usually confined to two possible mind-sets.[1] These are: the "don't you wish you were rich" ads for expensive clothing; and the "don't you wish you were young and beautiful" ads for downmarket clothes.

Because of my longstanding fascination with women's magazines, and my insistence on speaking about it publicly in the past five years or so, I have become well aware that many people, especially most-feminists and black intellectuals, think that the solution to the advertising problem is simply to get rid of it. But this is no longer a viable solution, if indeed it ever was. The main reason is that no contemporary industry has its finger more on the pulse of the multinational postcapitalist computerized zeitgeist of the twentieth century than advertising. As technological advances in computers, communications, film, video, CDs, and CD-ROMs come zooming down the pike, the ad agencies are always the first to swoop them up in their chilly embrace.

But the truth is that despite the mendacity of almost all the information advertising provides, it nevertheless continues to define us. What worries me more, however, is advertising's moral depravity. So much so that everybody hates advertising except the people who depend upon it to make a living. If advertising were more subtle and ethically rigorous, it would be much more persuasive and interesting. We have seen this in the enunciative power of many public service messages for charities and philanthropic endeavors of one kind or another. The most moving recent use of advertising strategies has developed around the AIDS crisis.

But for anybody who cruises magazines as habitually as I do, the advertisements that seem able to employ this kind of power stick out like a sore thumb. The self-congratulatory multiculturalism of the Benetton ads has been attracting a lot of attention for a long time, but they never quite cut the mustard for me, although I was glad to see so many models of color getting work. But their voyeurism and fetishism, what Peggy Phelan calls "the colonialist/imperialist appetite for possession,"[2] became much too transparent. Black or brown skin photographs so beautifully that when advertisers finally use black images, it is difficult to resist sensationalizing or fetishizing the color and texture.

Moreover, as Phelan explains, visibility can be a trap:

> As critical theories of cultural reproduction become increasingly dedicated to a consideration of the "material conditions" that influence, if not completely determine, social, racial, sexual, and psychic identities, questions about the immaterial construction of identities—those processes of belief which summon memory, sight, and love—fade from the eye/I.[3]

The clothing companies that have shown the most freedom in deviating from the manipulative norm are those that have a product that is reasonably priced and nearly essential. The series of Gap ads that use old photos of various ultra-hip celebrities, many of whom are dead, provide the exemplary instance.

The Gap has been chief among recent business success stories in apparel sales. As its name signals, it found a veritable gap in the marketplace for selling the kind of clothing that everybody wants to wear most of the time — durable, comfortable, informal, rugged, virtually timeless classics such as khakis, sweats, jeans, T-shirts, flannels, and so forth — at reasonable prices in an endless chain of conveniently located stores. No razzmadazzle, no bullshit, no smoke and mirrors. Just product with very little malarkey or markup. Granted (as my husband the bargain shopper reminds me), you can find cheaper versions of everything at the Gap somewhere else if you have several hours to kill, but you can't beat the Gap for the utter absence of tedious frustration surrounding the act of the purchase. So, on general principles, I have always thought well of the Gap.

But when I started to notice this series of ads in the spring of 1994, it immediately got my attention. As far as I could tell, the ads appeared only in *The New Yorker* and the *New York Times Magazine*. They were all exactly alike in this respect: each was a black-and-white photographic portrait of a cultural icon in a revisionist canon of American modernism, a modernism that included generous numbers of artists who were black, Asian, female, or queer, as well as artists who weren't necessarily high cultural but whose achievements in popular culture we now recognize as having been of the highest quality.

These ads, in which each of these icons — male or female — was wearing khakis, never even appeared in any of the women's magazines. Moreover, virtually none of the subjects could have been actually wearing Gap khakis since all the photographs, except perhaps the one of Allen Ginsberg, were taken before the company's existence. The product — to the extent that there was a "product" — was clearly being marketed as evocative, historically remote and unseen rather than immediate, material, and substantial.

I haven't yet figured out whether I find black-and-white photos emotionally resonant because most of my old family photos are in black-and-white or because there is something intrinsically evocative about black-and-white photos. Whichever the case, these pictures, leaked (so that you could have easily missed them) one at a time and a week at a time, of Miles Davis, Sarah Vaughan, George Balanchine, Marlene Dietrich, Sal Mineo, Montgomery Clift, Truman Capote, Leonard Bernstein (the dead ones), as well as Gordon Parks, Isamu Noguchi, Paul Bowles, Bobby Short, Frank Sinatra (in their youth) caused a lump to rise in my throat and a dampness to appear in the corner of my eyes.

And the fact that the campaign lingered on throughout the summer but faded in the autumn (along with everything else sweet) as the more frenzied campaigns aimed at the back-to-school/Thanksgiving and Christmas crowd gobbled up all the attention, only made them that much more miraculous. They never felt big or splashy or common. Moreover, they seemed to advertise, finally, something people of my generation and cultural education already had — Davis's, Vaughan's, and Bernstein's music; Parks's photographs and films; Capote's and Ginsberg's writing; etc.

Each one featured the following messages: in the right-hand lower corner, there was a box marked "Gap Khakis" and somewhere near the head of the subject, were the words "Montgomery Clift [or Sarah Vaughan or Miles Davis] wore khakis." In the various pictures, the artist is clearly wearing a version of khaki pants, rolled up around the ankles in the case of Bowles, Parks, Capote, and Short, paint-spattered in the case of Noguchi, accessorized with sneakers in Sinatra's case, with pearls in Vaughan's case, with socks and ballet slippers in the picture of Balanchine.

These ads are sexual in that they feature the bodies as well as the faces of these celebrated individuals. In order to see the pants they are wearing, we must see the entire body. The emphasis is, in fact, on the body, or on how these special people inhabit their bodies. These pictures are perhaps not the most distinguished on photographic terms; but in terms of the aesthetics of the body, they are beautiful and fascinating indeed in a society and a context in which visibly represented bodies are only supposed to be young, perfect, and thin. An exuberant Capote leaping through the air in perhaps the most famous of these photos is emblematic of their energy.

Montgomery Clift is shown standing on a ladder in a kind of twisted three-quarter profile, dipping a paintbrush in a can of paint with his right hand, his sleeves rolled up as if he were about to get to work. And yet we know that Clift (who appears to be in his mid-twenties) was not a house painter at this stage of his life but a very famous and talented movie actor. Moreover, most of the wall looks wallpapered and there is dark wood trim along the ceiling. There is no tape and no drop-cloth; no attempt has been made to cover the areas that could easily be splattered by paint. As a result, I surmised that this picture must have been a production still of some sort taken during rehearsal. Clift is not looking at the camera and his left hand is in his hair, which I was able to determine mostly by the shadow the hand made on the wall behind, a sign that he is standing in an intense and artificial light, perhaps movie lights.

Clift is maddeningly handsome, his face sensitive and poetic, his physique trim and just short of bony. His image recalls to me all the roles he has played that I've enjoyed: the unfaithful suitor who is ultimately rejected by the older and wiser Olivia de Haviland in *The Heiress*, the psychiatrist who must decide whether to lobotomize the beautiful Elizabeth Taylor in *Suddenly Last Summer*, the young man in *A Place in the Sun* who kills a chubby (although magnificent) and supposedly pregnant Shelley Winters in the middle of a lake in a rowboat.

Although these films, and so many others of that period, featured exclusively white casts, the resonant, evocative play of light and dark in black-and-white film may have facilitated our imagining otherwise. As we watched these films on TV as children, they taught us the essentials of human character and conventional melodrama, crucial information for understanding the inner dynamics of American popular culture and modernity; lessons I will never forget and of which I enjoy being reminded.

The Vaughan portrait, dated 1950, is definitely an impromptu shot. Vaughan is sitting with her shoes off, one of her feet up on a piano stool, the other swinging slightly above the floor, intently focused on a piece of sheet music. Her mouth is open as if she were singing. The rest of the scene is in fuzzy focus, but it appears to be a music studio situation. There are pearls around Vaughan's wrist. She is young, which tells me this picture was taken when her voice was unbelievably clear as a bell, and I am reminded of the times I saw her sing and what an incredible musician she was, one of the greatest jazz singers who ever lived.

One thing I loved about Vaughan on stage was the way she inhabited her body. Although not a classic beauty, nevertheless she always seemed so strong and attractive, so comfortably situated in her body as the sweat poured down her brow and as she wiped it gingerly from around the wisps of hair that framed her face.

Although the Bernstein photo is credited with the words "Mary Engel, estate of Ruth Orkin," the copyright line also says that "Leonard Bernstein is a registered trademark of the Amberson Group, Inc. courtesy of the Beta Fund," whatever this means. The picture shows a youngish Bernstein conducting, obviously in rehearsal, his shirt open at the collar and wrinkled, his feet shod in penny loafers. Several of the cellists in front of him are wearing sunglasses. Perhaps this means they were outside.

The picture was apparently taken around the time Bernstein did the children's concerts on public television. As a child, I watched them all. Several years later, he wrote *West Side Story*, which emerged just in time to accompany me into adolescence. Even though I was still a child, I was extremely aware of the discussions in the black community, in which it was suggested that Bernstein, or more probably the movie studio, had chosen to portray whitened Puerto Rican teenagers instead of gang-banging blacks in order to soften the multicultural blow. Nevertheless, my sister and I practically wore the album out, and I still know all the songs by heart. I will always love Bernstein for his music, his politics, and his joie de vivre.

In fact, I just love all these pictures. I can't help myself. And I think it was a marvelous idea on the Gap's part to revive these vintage photos for the sake of middle-aged people like myself who remember these artists in their prime, or perhaps even for the young people who have grown fond of Tony Bennett and other relics of a bygone age, in the name of a product we have apparently never been without all along.

As for my favorite, I can't say whether it is the one of Dietrich, who has become a personal hero of mine (her daughter makes her sound so fascinating), or Miles Davis, who was so gorgeous in his youth and whose autobiography is still so riveting. In the one of Dietrich, she is standing on a stage with her hands on her tiny hips, looking fifty-ish but infinitely glamorous still. Her khakis are sleek, very elegant, and cut off above the ankles. Around her tiny feet are the bits of tape that mark where the actors should stand and move when they deliver their lines. She seems resolute and, for some reason, she reminds me of my grandmother, who was also a very elegant person, a fashion designer who modeled herself after Coco Chanel. By contrast, the portrait of Davis is casual. It shows him with the magnificent Miles forehead cupped in his right hand, his left leg thrown over the back of a folding chair, a scarf tied, devil-may-care, around his neck.

These lovely silky old photos, revived and reanimated gingerly and with taste, represent the increasing democratization of the portrait. As such, they exemplify a gradual cultural change: on the one hand, we are growing more and more deeply invested in the superficialities of the image; on the other, through the facility of new technologies, most of us stand to experience a much larger expressive tradition of images than would otherwise have been possible. For the Gap's contribution to all this, I say thanks. Thanks for the memories.

Originally published in Donna de Salvo et al., *Face Value: American Portraits* (Southampton, N.Y.: Parrish Art Museum/Flammarion, 1995), 112–18.

Notes

1. A few years ago, in the inaugural issue of the new *Ms. Magazine*, Gloria Steinem wrote an article explaining why *Ms.* would no longer include any advertising. In the process, she recounted a fascinating history of the problems *Ms.* had had in coping with advertisers and, thus, the subtle ways in which they can impact on editorial decisions, particularly and especially in women's magazines. No other kind of magazine is so influenced by its advertisers. Personally, I believe it is because women will put up with it.

2. Peggy Phelan, *Unmarked: The Politics of Performance* (New York: Routledge, 1993), 5.

3. Ibid., 6.

46.

Art on My Mind

"Art has no race or gender," bell hooks proclaims in the introduction to her new book *Art on My Mind*. "Art, and more especially painting, was for me a realm where every imposed boundary could be transgressed. It was the free world of color where all was possible." This seems a strange statement coming from an avowed leftist cultural critic, somebody who has always prided herself on never forgetting, and never allowing anybody else to forget, her race or gender.

hooks's own art work (yes, she is an artist) adorns the cover of *Art on My Mind*. I'm not quite sure what it is—photograph, a collage, a painting, an etching, or a drawing—but it reminds me of photographs I've seen of the shack in which Madame C.J. Walker, the first black female millionaire, was born. Or the work of the black female artist Beverly Buchanan, who draws and sculpts southern country shacks from her native Georgia. Although hooks never offers any explanation regarding the origins of the image (I assume selecting it for the cover was an afterthought), one thing is pretty certain: it is designed to imprint upon our consciousness her humble working-class origins in Hopkinsville, Kentucky.

hooks tells us that she was stifled as an artist by the failure of her working-class community to see value in fine art and subsequently compelled by the harsh indifference of "white supremacy" and "capitalist domination" to destroy all but one of her own early paintings. This one painting she has kept hidden in the basement of her house all these years. The book's opening drama is staged around her rediscovery of this work. The description goes:

> The outline of two houses, shacks, is visible. It is autumn. The yellow light of early fall emerges in the midst of earthy brown and red shades. There is chaos and turbulence in the image. It is a time of change and transition. Yet nothing can disturb the inner sanctuary—the place where the soul lives. These are the dwelling places of the spirit. Returning to them, I come again to the memory of a free world of color where ultimately only our engagement with the work suffices—makes art matter. (xvi)

As artist and as critic, hooks chooses the ahistorical fantasy of the neophyte. But art has always meant, and will continue to mean, many things to many different kinds of people—as determined by tribe, nation, location, class, race, gender, social organization, religious beliefs, and individual idiosyncrasies—over the years and throughout the world. In the process of including peoples of color and their myriad art practices within the notion of the artist (and we need not necessarily have only one Eurocentric notion of the artist), it would be more helpful if aesthetics were viewed as flexible, freewheeling, indeterminate, and polyvocal. But that isn't exactly hooks's style.

As are most feminists, I am quite familiar with hooks's other books— from *Ain't I a Woman* (1981) to *Black Looks* (1992) to the assortment of hastily assembled collections of recent years. Like many of her readers, I have grown accustomed to making excuses for the doctrinaire, self-righteous attacks on various members of her ever-expanding hit list, as well as her repetitive sloppiness in the use of such catch-all condemnatory phrases as "white supremacist patriarchal domination"—but I have not been happy.

I have been waiting for somebody else in the feminist world to take on this one-woman black feminist cottage industry, to challenge and expose her relentless guilt-mongering as well as her contempt for other black feminists. Yet as fearless as we may seem to others, black feminists are terrified of her. Or are we afraid that we may kill the goose that laid the golden egg? Translation: could the exposure of the excesses of one prominent black feminist scholar call into question the intentions of all other black feminists, and with it the precious hard-won academic appointments, anthologies, conferences, grants, and travel budgets, as well?

Of course, at City College of New York (where hooks has recently been appointed Distinguished Professor of English at a salary of $95,000, although she teaches sparingly) most of us needn't worry about such things any more, since the recent Giuliani/Pataki budget cuts have axed prerequisites to the bone. Which leaves me much more willing than most to sacrifice the questionable solidarity of black feminist discourse to the ever-diminishing pursuit of the real—as in, let's get real. Given the array of opportunistic Sapphires (and Kingfishes) on the lecture-circuit gravy train, this difficult job must start somewhere, especially now that hooks seems to be steering toward the same mainstream to which Cornel West and Skip Gates and a lot of other names too painful too mention have already retreated.

Art on My Mind consists of hooks's usual formula of recycled pieces—catalogue essays and reviews of Lorna Simpson, Carrie Mae Weems, Emma Amos, Jean-Michel Basquiat, Felix Gonzalez-Torres, Alison Saar, and Andrés Serrano—as well as either new or re-published interviews with Weems, Amos, Saar, printmaker Margo Humphreys, and architect LaVerne Wells-Bowie. The best of the interviews by far is with the painter Emma Amos, who provides fascinating details about her memories of being an expatriate artist in London in the 1960s, as well as her participation as the token woman in the all-black-male Spiral Group, which included Romare Bearden and Norman Lewis, in the 1970s. The few color and black-and-white reproductions included in the book provide valuable illustrations of the achievements of the artists hooks has selected.

But a substantial portion of the book is devoted to the autobiographical reveries/critical musings for which hooks is well known. Her consistently self-indulgent writing has at least two distinct registers, the disarmingly playful and the correctly polemical. For instance, in a chapter called "Black Vernacular: Architecture as Cultural Practice," she begins: "Designing the house of my dreams in a high school art class, I did not think that any decisions I made were political." Yet she will follow this with: "I have chosen to write about this concern with space in order both to acknowledge the oppositional modes of psychic decolonization that marginalized, exploited, and oppressed black folks envisioned and to document a cultural genealogy of resistance." (147)

In these sections, she adopts the histrionic tone of the hypervigilant advocate prepared to defend and protect the rights and creativity of women artists of color against the inevitable incursions of insensitive white critics and voyeurs who would appropriate their vision, or, as she calls it, "eat the other." As for other critics of color: basically, we don't rate. The effectiveness of most of us is dismissed on the grounds that our bourgeois backgrounds disqualify us from engaging in the antiwhite, supremacist critique that is most needed. Or, as hooks puts it,

Much of the critical writing on the work of African American artists is limited in vision and scope. Black academics writing about art within a conservative educational hierarchy that is deeply mired in white supremacist thinking about aesthetics and art practices often choose traditional ways of approaching the work of African American artists. As a result, little critical work from a more progressive standpoint emerges. (111)

I expected the title *Art on My Mind* to be a reference to the controversial "Harlem on My Mind" exhibition at the Metropolitan Museum of Art in New York in 1968, which many have cited as the starting point for artists of color organizing to protest their exclusion from the major mainstream art institutions. Allon Schoener, a freelance curator, and Tom Hoving, then the director of the museum, decided it would be a good idea to do a black show about Harlem that was not about art but which took a sociological view of the black community, primarily using photographs, audio recordings, and videotapes. Black artists picketed because they had neither been considered for nor consulted about the show.

But hooks doesn't mention the "Harlem on My Mind" exhibition or any other significant landmark in the history of black artists or artists of color. In fact, she seems totally unaware of that history: how the protests at the Metropolitan led to protests at the Whitney Museum of Art and the Museum of Modern Art, which led to feminist protest in the art world led by artist Faith Ringgold (my mother) and art critic Lucy Lippard.

It seems no accident that the white critics hooks targets for attack—Maurice Berger, Lucy Lippard, and Robert Farris Thompson—are precisely the ones who have emerged as crucial defenders of artists of color. Berger, a highly respected multicultural art historian and critic, is the author of *How Art Becomes History* (1992), which includes several chapters on issues of race in the museums and in-depth discussions of the work of artists, administrators, and critics of color, as well as other political approaches to art history. Yet hooks is dismissive of Berger's recent anthology, *Modern Art and Society: An Anthology of Social and Multicultural Readings* (1994), which features on the cover a drawing by the black feminist artist and philosopher Adrian Piper, whose work hooks never mentions. "Positioned as a critical intervention," hooks writes, "Berger's anthology functions similarly to more conservative texts in the way in which it both appropriates and excludes the voices of black females writing about art." And of Lippard, author of the undeservedly ignored *Mixed Blessings: New Art in a Multicultural America* (1990), hooks says "When we critique and challenge the critical writings of our progressive white peers, we are often admonished for not recognizing the 'good' they do. It is the missionary ethic of colonialism all over again."

But her worst ire is saved for Robert Farris Thompson, the author of *Flash of the Spirit: African and Afro-American Art and Philosophy* (1983) and her former colleague at Yale University, whom she deems "less threatening to the art establishment" because he is "a privileged white male scholar." The unfairness of her critique of Thompson is striking: for instance, she complains that the paperback edition of *Flash of the Spirit* carries a one-sentence endorsement from the *New York Times Book Review*: "Convinces the reader there is real and important significance in the term African American." "This quote is not counterhegemonic. It does not decenter the West. It reaffirms Eurocentric thinking and, as a consequence, perpetuates white supremacist biases." (115)

One minute, hooks is beyond politics in the realm of art for art's sake. The next minute, she is slinging p.c. hash with the best of them. Needless to say, there is a creepy essentialism implicit in all of this. While it may be true that no black woman actually wrote an essay that was included in Berger's collection, is that the only question we are ever supposed to ask of an art-historical text? And in an equation in which the whites who should be scrutinized most harshly are the ones who value the work of people of color, are the best white people the ones who make no bones about their lack of knowledge and interest in "the other"?

As for the several handfuls of people of color — museum curators, critics, and artists — who have been forerunners in the art world, who fought the battles, who made the inroads and took all the heat over the years — the critics David Driskell, Rick Powell, Judith Wilson, Leslie King-Hammond; the curators Guy McElroy, Thelma Golden, Lowery Sims, Deborah Willis, Kelly Jones, Kinshasa Conwill, Mary Schmidt Campbell, Pat Cruz; and the legions of artists of color — you won't learn much about them in this book.

The absence of footnotes and appropriate documentation is more annoying than usual. I don't buy hooks's "empowering the uneducated" line. The only person being empowered by her failure to use footnotes and a bibliography is her. Footnotes and bibliographies take extra time to prepare and cost more money. Not only that, the reader might get a better idea of when hooks, herself, is "eating the other."

Originally published in *The Women's Review of Books* (October 1995).

47.

Pictures Can Lie

The recent visual prominence of the black male body — quite suddenly seemingly everywhere from glossy advertisements to art galleries and museums to fashion shows to the crime pages of the daily tabloids — is regarded ominously by this black woman old enough to remember Emmett Till. Despite the myriad social, economic, and cultural advances of black men also evident all around us, in the realm of postmodern representations, where sampling and pastiche have become the norm, the black male image seems now more than ever in danger of becoming the checkpoint for much of society's free-floating hostility.

The various social disasters associated with Clarence Thomas, Louis Farrakhan, Mike Tyson, Michael Jackson, Colin Ferguson, Rodney King, and O.J. Simpson haven't helped the situation much. Even the media hoopla over the Million Man March and the Black Male Show was as much about the pictures as the text and the welcome prospect of yet another opportunity to fetishize the black male body. As the most uncomfortable "Other" for the largest constituency (most whites, people of color, and quite a few blacks at the upper end of the age and class strata), the black male body has become the site for an erotic fantasy holiday that takes place mostly in the head.

Take, for instance, a beautiful 8x10 color photo, such as the one taped to my refrigerator door of MC Hammer in shades, bare chested in a gorgeous paisley jacket. When I look at it, as a middle-aged, happily married bohemian-type black woman who hung the picture in the first place because it turned me on, I have every reason to enjoy, and no reason to fear, Hammer's obvious pleasure in his ability to adopt the posture of the gorgeous hunk. But for those of us (sometimes including me) who fear that an encounter on a lonely street late at night with a young black male can be dangerous, desire intermingles with loathing in illicit ways. For a white supremacist, how can he possibly deal, since he's not supposed to feel anything but hatred for Hammer?

In Western culture, images of women's bodies of whatever color have traditionally functioned as "other." Precisely because sexual feelings for the female body were considered gender-appropriate in the primary audience (male), any accompanying ambivalence and anxiety were tolerable and easily assimilated. I began to realize that something major had changed in the cultural priority of fetishizing the female body when Mapplethorpe's notorious photographs of nude black men exploded on the scene.

It is possible to argue that this rearrangement in visual tastes has roots much farther back, during that period of disenfranchisement following Reconstruction in which black men were ritualistically lynched and castrated. Blackface minstrelsy, the most popular entertainment genre then, belongs in the picture as well. In blackface minstrelsy—from the very beginning a male-dominated form—white men mimicked and mocked the bodies and speech of the black male. It provided not only comic relief for would-be lynchers but representations of the black male body for a long time to come.

But these days, the situation is considerably more complex and nuanced. The fetishizing of the black male body is generally accompanied by one or more of five narratives: (1) the rap and hip-hop/rebel without a cause/youth culture narrative, seen as representative of the essential truth of black male existence, regardless of age; (2) the entrepreneurial gangster narrative, almost invariably evoked by any story of black male economic success; (3) the familiar athletic prowess narrative, in which brawn, with its tragically limited shelf life, is sometimes placed before intellect; (4) the endangered species narrative; (5) and the hero.

The endangered species narrative has been in circulation, under one name or another, since the riots in the '60s, partly to rationalize the perpetual existence of a black underclass and partly to trivialize a range of nihilistic trends (which are impacting white culture as well) in black life. Richard Wright's Bigger Thomas provided the fictional prototype back in the '40s.

The black hero has been inextricably linked to timeworn convictions regarding the nobility of self-sacrifice and premature death (the good die young), reanimated by Harriet Beecher Stowe's creation of Uncle Tom back in 1852. Of course the prototype here is none other than JC himself, still the ultimate figure in black life. Other significant models include Martin Luther King and Malcolm X. The gist is that no black hero is allowed to live for very long.

Defeatist and depressing on the one hand, altruistic and ethical on the other, this myth of the black hero is partly why so many blacks (including myself) were convinced that if Colin Powell ran for president, thus elevating himself to national hero status, he would surely be murdered. We've had black heroic figures who haven't died prematurely or tragically—Du Bois, Frederick Douglass, Booker T. Washington, Mary McLeod Bethune, Angela Davis, and so on. Thus far, however, their bios haven't yet achieved the crossover appeal (accomplished through communications and advertising, national holidays, X hats, etcetera) that would make them significant emotional touchstones for Americans of all colors. This rigid schemata in the current politics of dominant black-male representations is partly why I, as a black feminist, have come to see invisibility as not just a handicap but also a strategic necessity for blacks who would be intellectuals, artists, or just any ole body who wants to get something accomplished within the confines of racism. The ideal would be to mix visibility with invisibility—success in the dominant discourse with the metamorphosing folk wisdom of black oral traditions—in just the right balance. Too much visibility of the wrong kind, and at the wrong time, can not only be dangerous to your health but also to the general well-being of blacks as a class.

Multiple examples of this phenomenon come from the reporting of crimes, especially black-on-white crimes. Sports, entertainment, and feature coverage also readily provide cases in which black men are making a spectacle of the fact that they are not treating themselves and others close to them well. Leaving O.J. aside, past instances that stand out in my memory have been the bankruptcy stories of Sammy Davis Jr., James Brown, and Redd Foxx, the murder of Marvin Gaye by his father, the endless installments of the Jackson family neuroses, the megalomaniacal eccentricities of Prince, and the drug arrest of Spike Lee's father.

Sometimes it seems as though some journalistic venues live only for the opportunity to dissect the black male scandal—the Ben Chavis or the Al Sharpton. Understand, I am not saying that all this news isn't news, or even that it shouldn't be reported. Indeed, I hang on every word of such news just as much as everybody else. But there is so little within dominant representations—for all the superficial variety—to counterbalance the way such stories validate already deeply rooted mythical narratives and beliefs about black men as "Other."

Originally published in the *Village Voice*, 2 April 1996.

48.

The Hottentot Venus

While I don't suggest you make *Venus* your only black play this year, by all means see it in anticipation of the future concerns of a black feminist theater. To ease your way into life on the black side of the footlights, you might want to see as well Savion Glover and friends in the raucous, bluesy, tap-dancing *Bring in 'da Noise, Bring in 'da Funk*, or August Wilson's *Seven Guitars*, a backyard drama full of dark laughs, set in the '40s. Although these are guy plays, they will provide a point of comparison, thus preparing you to better appreciate the shock of the advanced, extraterrestrial blackness of the work of Suzan-Lori Parks. Otherwise you're liable to make the mistake of being a little freaked out by a play in which the central preoccupation is somebody's butt.

Ostensibly, *Venus* is based on the real case study of Saartje Baartman, also known as the "Hottentot Venus." A woman of the so-called Hottentot tribe of South Africa, Baartman was brought to London and Paris in the early nineteenth century for the purpose of placing her butt on public exhibition in circuses and sideshows. Needless to say, these were no ordinary buttocks but huge, spongy appendages that seemed to possess a life of their own, so aggressively did they stand out from the body. This was not at all the kind of butt of which Josephine Baker said, "It's true that there are rear ends so stupid, so pretentious, so insignificant that they're only good for sitting on."

Their large, complex configuration (probably a fair portion of which was cellulite) was considered at once a freak of nature and therefore an entertaining performance by the standard of the day, a scientific oddity, and emblematic of the combined racial and sexual inferiority of Africans. Sander Gilman, professor of the history of psychiatry at Cornell University, tells us that the Hottentot was designated "the antithesis of European sexual mores and beauty . . . the essential black, the lowest exemplum of mankind on the great chain of being."

When Baartman died of tuberculosis in Paris at the age of twenty-six, her autopsy was written up in a French scientific journal by Henri Ducrotay de Blainville in 1816 and then by Georges Cuvier in 1817, with a particular focus on the exact disposition of her clitoris and labia to emphasize their presumed similarity to those of an orangutan. Her parts were then pickled and placed in the collection of the Musee de l'Homme in Paris, where they remain to this day.

In his controversial study *Difference and Pathology: Stereotypes of Sexuality, Race, and Madness* (1985), Professor Gilman writes about how the protrusion of Baartman's buttocks was viewed as correlated with the malformation of her clitoris: both were considered indications of a pronounced sexual appetite, even a lesbian lust. Thus Gilman draws a potential link between the dark continent of female sexuality in Freud and the dark continent of Africa in the mind of nineteenth-century Europe that has fascinated an ever-expanding circle of black feminist cultural critics, art historians, and artists. Several years before *Venus* there was an installation by the artist Renee Green on Baartman, whose buttocks have provided the touchstone for a variety of discussions and essays on the peculiar status of the black female nude in fine art and popular culture.

But the implications of Baartman's fate go much further. In 1829 there is record of yet another woman from Baartman's tribe exhibited as the "Hottentot Venus"; she was the prize attraction at a ball given by Duchess du Barry in Paris. Other Hottentots and Bushmen, male and female, were dissected and catalogued, even as they were being exterminated in South Africa by the colonial occupation. Whereas the autopsies of the men took little interest in penises, the genitalia and the buttocks of Hottentot women attracted much attention because of the late-Victorian desire to pathologize female sexuality and stigmatize the clitoris. Therefore black female sexuality became the standard for deviant sexuality in women in general. Voila: such sacred modernist images as Manet's rendering of Olympia's maid and Picasso's *Les Demoiselles d'Avignon*, in which the excessive sexuality of the white woman is signaled by blackness.

Meanwhile, the so-called Hottentots are said to have been the ancestors of the present-day clans of the Khoikhoi and San people in South Africa. Baartman was only the first in a long line of Africans whose remains were analyzed and stored in British and European research institutions and museums. The Griqua National Congress, whose 20,000 members claim to be the last vestiges of the Khoikhoi people, distinguish themselves both from the black South African majority and those of mixed races and are fighting for their identity as an endangered ethnic minority within the new South Africa. Indigenous to the Cape region, they mixed over time with the Xhosa, who are one of the largest groups, and the San, or Bushmen, who are also bordering on extinction.

But don't waste your precious brain cells trying to correlate the tale I've told with the one Parks tells of Baartman as a lusty, lovely lady who falls in love with the mad scientist who will ultimately dissect her. Just sit back and enjoy Parks's outrageous script and Richard Foreman's deft staging and directing. Don't be afraid to laugh at the plentiful humorous sight gags. Parks's point is at once archaeological and devilishly playful, a Brechtian process of refamiliarizing what is ordinarily considered a mundane body part in order to plunge us backward into a period of history we've chosen to forget.

While the actress Adina Porter does a moving job of endowing Baartman with humanity, the play isn't necessarily about the empirical experience of the actual woman, what it was really like for Saartje Baartman to be exhibited nude, to be stared at by white men fascinated with her buttocks. More important to Parks, I imagine, is to come to terms with the variables that created the situation.

Baartman's was not an isolated case. Lots of Africans, Indians, and Southeast Asians were placed on exhibition both here and abroad, in circuses and sideshows, in the context of large World's Fair–like international expositions or, less decorously, in the context of "freak shows." These were people who were born with some kind of deformity or another: Siamese twins, Mongoloids, etcetera. Our own P. T. Barnum was one of the innovators in this industry. The key thing was that you had to be able to see the difference. Visual differentiation was the foundation of most thought about race and sexuality during this period. Perhaps this was partly why "Jewishness," a less visible difference, and mulattoes in a U.S. context were regarded with such horror.

One of the preconditions in this picture was the emergence and consolidation of what some have called the spectatorial imagination of the West, the gaze, the need to study and examine "the other," fueled by the popularity of such inventions and developments as photography, the electric light bulb, popular journalism, and film. Also, performance practices then enthusiastically embraced much more than what we define as legitimate theater today, a lot of it having quite a bit in common with the display of Baartman's buttocks.

Despite its apparent lightness and humor, *Venus*, like Parks's previous work, *The America Play*, actually draws upon a wide range of divergent, comparatively new and unexplored discourses: stereotypes of race and gender in Western culture, the plight of the black female body in representation, and the ethnographic subject of the social sciences as a by-product of colonial power, wherever there were inconveniently located indigenous populations who couldn't or wouldn't get with the program.

Originally published in the *Village Voice*, 21 May 1996, p. 31.

49.

Angels in America, Paris Is Burning,

and Queer Theory

And of course one of the many echoes resounding around the terrible accident of HIV and the terrible nonaccident of the overdetermined ravage of AIDS is the way it seems "naturally" to ratify and associate — as *un*natural, as unsuited for survival, as the appropriate objects of neglect, specularized suffering and premature death — the notionally self-evident "risk group" categories of the gay man and the addict. — EVE KOSOFSKY SEDGWICK, *Tendencies*

Sexuality must not be described as a stubborn drive, by nature alien and of necessity disobedient to a power which exhausts itself trying to subdue it and often fails to control it entirely. It appears rather as an especially dense transfer point for relations of power: between men and women, young people and old people, parent and offspring, teachers and students, priests and laity, an administration and a population. — MICHEL FOUCAULT, *The History of Sexuality*

Foucault's notion of sexuality as "an especially dense transfer point for relations of power" is useful to understanding the impact of AIDS on contemporary sexual discourse. As a sexual (or more accurately sexualized) disease, AIDS has given vent to yet another highly charged subspecies of sexual discourse. It also seems as though precisely to the degree that AIDS has become over-determined is also the degree to which we seem inclined to completely lose touch with the facts of the emerging impact of AIDS on society.

It is to be expected that representations would diverge significantly from the core reality they are attempting to recreate — representations partly serve the function of elaboration and mystification — but in the case of representations of AIDS, the problem is further exacerbated by "dense transfer points of power" not only "between men and women, young people and old people, parent and offspring" but also between black and white, and between the rich and the poor. Ideally, in AIDS discourse, boundaries of race and class are, and must be, repeatedly traversed (or denied) in order to accommodate the developing demographic realities of a global AIDS crisis.

My concern herein is to consider the relation of the theoretical discourse around AIDS to popular and prominent representations of AIDS, in this case specifically *Angels in America*, Part I and Part II, by Tony Kushner, a successful Broadway show a few years ago. I've chosen to look at *Angels in America* more closely because I found it unashamedly avant-garde in its methodology and radical, especially for Broadway, in its politics. I both liked and enjoyed the show, particularly the first half.

A variety of other works have attempted to straddle the breadth and seriousness of AIDS: among these have been the movie *Philadelphia* by Jonathan Demme, the TV movie *Boys in the Band* on HBO, as well as numerous works of theater and art, including the famous AIDS quilt project. For me, knowing AIDS (or any pressing social reality or disease) is a large part of the problem of the translation from theory to art. How can we know it? Through art or statistics or interpretation? What do we know? And can such knowledge be imparted to the general public? Moreover, what can modes of representation or cultural reproduction, in this case a Broadway play, either give to, or take from, current theoretical discourse around AIDS?

In this context, I would also like to introduce, as a counterbalance to *Angels*, which considers the lives of white, middle-class gay men primarily, the relative success in this field of an entirely different kind of cultural production: the documentary film *Paris Is Burning* by Jennie Livingston, which was not ostensibly about AIDS but about a black and Puerto Rican transvestite subculture in Manhattan. *Paris Is Burning* was also hugely successful and controversial. Its audiences are strictly comparable to a Broadway audience in the sense that they were preselected by relatively obscure tastes for gay or queer theory or commentary.

In any case, such an audience is decidedly more general and representative than the present elite (educationally and politically) audience for queer theoretical texts on AIDS by such critics as Eve Kosofsky Sedgwick, Simon Watney, Paula Treichler, Douglas Crimp, and Susan Sontag, and as such, perhaps a step in the right direction.

For the first time really, I got personally interested in AIDS four summers ago when I discovered that I had lupus, a chronic, incurable autoimmune (albeit not necessarily fatal) disease commonly classified as a variety of rheumatoid arthritis. During the six weeks before diagnosis I had swollen glands and a constant temperature of about 101. My doctor at HIP (Health Insurance Plan, a New York area HMO) tested me for HIV, having incorrectly ruled out lupus. For two weeks I read the literature on AIDS trying to figure out whether I might have it or not. Mostly I relied upon *Women and AIDS*, the book by ACT UP, but in my pain and panic I was unable to figure out I didn't have it. Indeed, AIDS and lupus do have opposing actions. Whereas AIDS means you have an entirely inactive immune system, with lupus your immune system is hyperactive, but this formula is not nearly so reassuring as it sounds.

Somehow I couldn't distinguish the two and I doubt if most other people would be able to either, since both can feature fever, swollen glands, lesions, joint pain, hair loss, and a host of immunological difficulties. In fact, there's a part of my brain that continues not to rule out AIDS even though women make up a relatively small percentage of AIDS victims in the United States, and I haven't engaged in anything that could be considered high-risk behavior for over twelve years. Even when you figure on women of color being ten times more likely to contract HIV than white women, the odds are still quite small for monogamous women in my age group.[1]

The uncertain boundaries of incurable, and not well understood, diseases such as lupus and AIDS is part of the problem. The mythological constructs of diseases rely heavily upon our lack of information about them. Just as AIDS is considered the big bugaboo now, cancer was the most feared and mythologized disease before that, and before that polio and before that tuberculosis and before that syphilis or indeed whatever was the rage in the hospital wards and the streets at the time. This does not mean, however, that less compelling (for the moment) diseases escape being mythologized. They don't. Cancer and all terminal and incurable diseases are still infinitely more demonized than auto accidents, which kill more people.

That same summer, I saw the *Millennium Approaches*, the first half of *Angels in America* by Tony Kushner. Kushner is best friends with a former graduate student at the City University Graduate Center named Kimberly Flynn, who had been my student the first semester I began teaching there. I was sick that semester, as I have been off and on for ten years (with lupus), and she was still recovering from a head injury. We commiserated over the difficulties of illness in an unsympathetic institutional space (i.e., CUNY).

Apparently, Tony Kushner commiserated with Flynn as well. According to an article in the *New York Times Magazine*, Flynn was a fellow student at Columbia University with whom he "spent thousands of hours discussing Marxism and feminism and sexual politics and who remains his closest friend." Flynn suffered a brain injury as a result of a taxicab accident in 1984 (from which she has finally recovered), about which Kushner has said, "The business of helping her handle the sequellae to the accident was my most direct experience with serious health problems" and "elements of her story . . . have become incorporated in 'Angels.'" As such, Kushner concludes that the play could not have been written without Flynn.

I suggest that Flynn played the role of his muse, on the one hand, and of full collaborator on the other. Although *Angels* bills itself as a "Gay Fantasia," it is also very much about being sick, in particular, sick with AIDS. Indeed, one of the problems that *Angels* can be said to have from the outset is what some might consider a failure to distinguish *being* gay from *having* AIDS. I would also suggest that this is also the site upon which *Angels in America* has a problem with race, because race and class are crucial variables along with sexuality in the AIDS crisis.

Angels in America is written in a postmodern, elliptical style, although interactions between characters are still naturalistic and easy to follow. Unrelated scenes occur simultaneously and sometimes the dialogue of one scene will alternate with that of another superficially unrelated scene. Dream, reality, fantasy, nightmare, and delusion alternate and overlap until the distinction between them recedes into irrelevancy. Women in male drag playing male roles adds to the effect of a Brechtian hyperreality. Although especially *Perestroika*, the second part of the play, is filled with pithy one-liners, and all the scenes are short and humorous, as it now stands, *Angels in America* would not be suitable in a commercial film or television format, unless the adaptation were for PBS or channel 4 in Britain, or some equally pristine medium.[2]

Angels toured off-Broadway and began in a series of workshop productions at the Mark Taper Forum in Los Angeles. It opened on Broadway in April 1993 and shot directly to success, which suggests its ameliorative powers as a form of sexual discourse. Although *Angels in America* had eleven mainstream producers from the Shakespeare Festival Theatre to Rocco Landesman of the Jujamcyn Theatre (one of the Broadway chains), and it won several Tony Awards and the Pulitzer Prize in 1993 and several more Tony Awards for the second part, *Perestroika*, in 1994, no one really expected this high-minded play to do much more than break even.

This category of Broadway play, which threatens to break new ideological ground on gender, class, race, and sexuality (other recent examples include *The Sisters Rosensweig, The Song of Jacob Zulu, Jelly's Last Jam, Grapes of Wrath, M Butterfly, Twilight,* and *Rent*), continues to be of interest, however, because of the way in which Broadway, off-Broadway, and regional theater seem to serve as a kind of a workshop for ideas that will subsequently recirculate in diminished form via TV and film. Sometimes on the further reaches of this category, a play may also play host to ideas with which TV and film may never be comfortable. *Angels* falls into this latter category. Despite the fact that it is not too good for Broadway, at least for a season, in its present form it is still wholly unsuitable for the bottom line marketplace aesthetics of most U.S. film and TV, which consists of the following: the need to fit comfortably and supportively around commercial breaks, the ubiquitous happy ending, conformity to the action/adventure vs. melodrama vs. situation-comedy narrative ghettoes, the idealization of the hero/es(star/s).

The *Millennium Approaches* focuses upon three central characters simultaneously, sometimes all in the same scene. First, there is the relationship between Prior and Louis. Prior is an ex–drag queen and Louis is his lover who works as a word processor. Prior is in the third stage of AIDS, having developed Kaposi Sarcoma. The gist of their story is that Louis allows himself to intellectualize his distaste for the physical characteristics of Prior's illness and leaves him. On the other hand, Prior must face a delusion-filled encounter with death, which includes the appearance of a rather splendid looking angel. While Louis is Jewish, and the play begins with a funeral in his family presided over by a rabbi, Prior is high-church WASP and from a family that he can trace back to the thirteenth century. Prior's distant ancestors visit him during his delusions and share with him aspects of the plagues (all of which sound remarkably like AIDS) they've witnessed and suffered in their times.

The second relationship, on which the play focuses, is between Joseph and Harper, both of whom are Mormons. Joe is a chief clerk in the Federal Court of Appeals. Harper is his agoraphobic valium-addicted wife. Joe, of course, is gay but in the closet. Harper's ability to pick that up unconsciously is exacerbating her own illness. She wants to know why he takes such long walks. And she, herself, has fantasies/delusions that she will go on a long vacation to Antarctica to see the break in the ozone layer.

The third relationship is with this same Joe and Roy Cohn, a lawyer and a power broker in the Reagan administration. In the scene with his doctor in which Cohn, who is an unethical conservative Republican in the Reagan camp, discovers that he has AIDS, it is established that Cohn views AIDS as a disease of "hemophiliacs, IV drug users and homosexuals." As such, he greets his diagnosis with the accusation that his doctor is calling him a homosexual and threatens to destroy the man's career if he ever puts such an accusation into words even in the privacy of his office.

Cohn says about himself,

> This is not sophistry. And this is not hypocrisy. This is reality. I have sex with men. But unlike nearly every other man of whom this is true, I bring the guy I'm screwing to the White House and President Reagan smiles at us and shakes his hand. Because *what* I am is defined entirely by *who* I am. Roy Cohn is not a homosexual. Roy Cohn is a heterosexual man, Henry, who fucks around with guys. (Kushner, 46)

He suggests, as well, that the doctor is too hung up on labels. Not only does Cohn insist that he is a heterosexual man who fucks guys instead of a homosexual, he also insists that he has liver cancer instead of AIDS, since, in his view, only homosexuals have AIDS. Whereas Cohn refuses to admit to himself or anybody else that he's gay or that he has AIDS, Joe, the Mormon, finally admits to his wife and his mother in Utah that he is gay. And while Louis leaves Prior in the lurch, he finds Joe with whom he begins to have an affair.

The second half of the play, *Perestroika*, begins with an impassioned speech by an Asian male, described in the text as unimaginably old, with a long white beard in a simple black uniform, who is announced as "Aleksii Antedilluvianovich Prelapsarianov, the World's Oldest Living Bolshevik." He waxes eloquent over the bygone age of the "beautiful Theory" of Marxism and mourns for the young of the present generation, postperestroika, who are left with nothing but "Market Incentives" and "American Cheeseburgers" to comfort them. "If the snake sheds his skin before a new skin is ready, naked he will be in the world, prey to the forces of chaos. Without his skin he will be dismantled, lose coherence and die" (Kushner, 13–15). His advice to all is to not make any attempts to move forward without a new theory.

This precaution seems to be somewhat seriously meant by author Kushner as *Perestroika* does not, in fact, move forward or outward but rather circles around the same scenarios so persuasively invented in *Millennium Approaches*. Immediately after the old Bolshevik's speech, the curtain goes up to reveal Prior as he was at the end of the first half, very sick in bed, and receiving a visitation from an angel who crashes through the ceiling of his apartment. Directly Joe and Louis are shown to be having a passionate love affair and Harper falls into a grave depression. Joe's mother from Utah, who sold her house and came to New York in *Millennium Approaches*, ends up taking the crazed Harper back to Utah to work in a Mormon wax museum. Ultimately, Joe leaves Louis and tries to return to Harper and Louis tries to return to Prior. Harper rejects Joe and Prior rejects Louis. *Perestroika* doesn't really have a climax or an ending in the traditional sense.

Perestroika also feels a lot more self-indulgent and flabby than *Millennium Approaches* and much more heavy handed politically as though the author were tying up loose ends. The point of the interwoven narratives in the second half, I believe, is not only that Prior chooses to live instead of dying with AIDS but also the deconstruction of most previous master narratives, from the "beautiful Theory" of Marxism to the Joe McCarthy Republicanism of Roy Cohn, from Jewish religion to the Mormon religion. You may dip and sample to make your way through life, but old-fashioned mythologizing is banished.

If race were a significant feature in this scenario one might expect the scenes between Roy Cohn, who is hospitalized, and Belize, the mestizo character who serves as his nurse until he dies, to be more central or cathartic. But the fact is that Belize, as a person of mixed race and non-European American origin, never becomes a real satellite for anything that is really going on in this play.

Instead, as the one character who is presented as entirely healthy both physically and mentally, he serves as the antidote that the "primitivism" of the Other has always been imagined to be by modernism and postmodernism. It follows in the unconscious logic of the play that if he is a person of color, he is therefore quite naturally more pragmatic, more realistic, more solid, more earthy, less given to intellectual rationalization and moral uncertainty. In this manner, his race is at the same time both deeply significant and not significant at all because it isn't really connected to anything structural in the play.

AMONG CURRENT THEORETICAL discourses around AIDS, there are a number that are helpful to an evaluation of *Angels in America*. In *Illness as Metaphor* (5–9) and the more recent *AIDS and Its Metaphors* (93–99), Susan Sontag makes the point that we use metaphors about illness both as a way of distancing ill people *and* as a way of making illness, itself, seem more familiar. In *Disease and Representation: Images of Illness from Madness to* AIDS, Sander Gilman suggests that we rely upon solid fixed notions (stereotypes) of illness in order to externalize, objectify, and distance illness and the ill.

Gilman also says that we need stereotypes; we demand them to be more fixed, immutable, and rigid than historical specificity would ordinarily permit. Nothing is more tension producing in this regard than illness because, as

Gilman says, we're all subject to it, and the most pernicious types of stereo-types of women, blacks, gays, Jews, and people of color equate the condition of the "other" with the condition of illness. In this scenario, Jewishness or gayness or blackness or female gender becomes a kind of disease that impairs the intellectual abilities and endangers physical well-being. (Or, as in the case of Belize, the stereotype reversed, he is mentally and physically invulnerable.) Further, Gilman argues that the stereotypical visual images of incurable illness (specifically syphilis, mental illness, tuberculosis, cancer, and AIDS) provide models for other kinds of stereotypical images (3–10).

If such a cultural conjunction—the synchronization of visible illness and visible cultural difference—is somehow incorporated into the self-image of the minority community itself, it would be awfully hard to root them out without also deconstructing prevailing concepts of illness and the ways in which images and illness correlate. What worries me about *Angels in America* is that it may be popular for all the wrong reasons: there is the danger that it might encourage a certain upper-middle-class audience not only to indulge in a further mystification of the demographics of AIDS but also to blur together gayness and AIDS, making them synonymous.

The racial composition of the current AIDS population and its global effects is closely attended to in the works of Simon Watney and Paula Treichler (Watney, 85–86). Our present awareness of the global impact of AIDS comes precisely out of the fact that we live in a postmodern technological age. Previous generations were not in a position to be so readily aware of the extent of an epidemic (McNeill). Of course, most of us still choose to be unaware of the suffering of others around the world as much as possible. In the Age of Information, death is not necessarily considered significant. It depends on *who* is dying and where.

In *Aids and Its Metaphors*, Sontag makes the argument that metaphors about illness lend themselves to the most pernicious energies in human society. Nevertheless, she suggests that given the lack of medical and scientific knowledge to dispel the uncertainties, the best one can do to ward off the evil effects of mythology is to resist and demystify the metaphors in favor of whatever facts are actually known. "The purpose of my book was to calm the imagination," Sontag writes, "not to incite it. Not to confer meaning, which is the traditional purpose of literary endeavor, but to deprive something of meaning: to apply that quixotic, highly polemical strategy, 'against interpretation,' to the real world this time. To the body" (102).

The process by which AIDS becomes the mega-disease that serves as the mega-metaphor of our peculiar times is fascinating. As Sontag goes on to elucidate:

AIDS is such an apt goad to familiar, consensus building fears that have been cultivated for several generations, like fear of "subversion" — and to fears that have surfaced more recently, of uncontrollable pollution and unstoppable migration from the Third World — that it would seem inevitable that AIDS be envisaged in this society as something total, civilization threatening. And raising the disease's metaphorical stature by keeping alive fears of its easy transmissibility, its imminent spread, does not diminish its status as, mainly, a consequence of illicit acts (or of economic and cultural backwardness). That it is a punishment for deviant behavior and that it threatens the innocent — these two notions about AIDS are hardly in contradiction. Such is the extraordinary potency and efficacy of the plague metaphor: it allows a disease to be regarded both as something incurred by vulnerable "others" and as potentially everyone's disease. (151–52)

Which brings us to the key metaphor in the AIDS lexicon, which is plague. Sontag explains well how the notion that AIDS is an uncontrollable, easily transmissible plague is part of the political formula of the conservative right. Even the manner in which HIV infection, ARC, and AIDS can and sometimes are all conflated into what is understood to be the automatic death sentence of AIDS, as though to imply that it is necessary that we submit to being policed and regulated from the moment we're infected, is part of turning a once cold war focused on exogamous enemies in Eastern Europe, China, or Cuba into a hot and intense, high-tension war focused inward to combat the poor, the homeless, people of color, gays and lesbians, and people with HIV. As Sontag writes, "Plagues are invariably regarded as judgements on society, and the metaphoric inflation of AIDS into such a judgement also accustoms people to the inevitability of global spread. This is a traditional use of sexually transmitted diseases: to be described as punishments not just of individuals but of a group ('general licentiousness')" (142).

Angels in America responds well to Sontag's observation regarding metaphor and disease by both playing with the clichés and resisting them. As Sontag says, "Apocalypse is now a long running serial: not 'Apocalypse Now' but 'Apocalypse From Now On.' Apocalypse has become an event that is happening and not happening" (176). The milieu of *Angels in America* was apocalyptic, but the play's elliptical narrative construction resists normal apocalyptic trajectories and conclusions.

Even Cohn's speeches about having AIDS and being homosexual have to do with a display of naked power and influence. In the rawness of his manipulations of power, he never falls back on the idea that he is being punished for anything. Although certainly Ethel Rosenberg's presence haunting him upon his deathbed suggests a kind of punishment, all of the characters, on the Right or on the Left, resist the metaphorical understanding of AIDS or gayness, except to the extent that the very fact of the characters' mental and physical illnesses could be understood to play metaphorically with gayness.

For example, the closest to a metaphorical condition is that of Harper, who it is implied is mentally ill. But even she has a nice concrete reason for being delusional—too much valium, too much staying at home. Her husband is a closeted gay and therefore cold toward her. Therefore, she wants to go to the coldest place of all to see the break in the ozone layer in Antarctica.

Yet Weber describes *Angels in America* as an epic that "considers the AIDS plague as the defining metaphor for a national spiritual decline during the 1980s and as the starting point of a social order for the next century" (29). Obviously, this suggests a very different reading from my own. The ominous figuration of this metaphor is confirmed in the form of the painting by Milton Glaser of the advertisement for *Angels* of a dark, human, winged figure who crouches over in what Gilman insists is one of the classic postures of illness (18–20).

Even more relevant to Kushner's problematic in the first half of *Angels in America* are the following observations of Sander Gilman.

The fixed structures of art provide us with a sort of carnival during which we fantasize about our potential loss of control, perhaps even revel in the fear it generates within us, but we always believe that this fear exists separate from us. This sense of the carnivalesque provides us with exactly the missing fixity for our understanding of the world that the reality of disease denies. For illness is a real loss of control that results in our becoming the Other whom we have feared, whom we have projected onto the world. The images of disease, whether in art or in literature, are not in flux, even though they represent collapse.

In regard to Gilman's statement, "The images of disease, whether in art or in literature, are not in flux, even though they represent collapse," in *Angels* Kushner tries to capture the flux and the collapse and to resist the fixity, although Weber's description and the publicity billboard for the show might suggest otherwise. All the characters and their situations in the *Millennium Approaches* are always in flux, always naked. Prior, who is sick with AIDS, is always in flux, first dressed in drag and then hallucinating and delusional, although his delusions in the form of his ancestors in other plague-ridden times are quite meaningful to us—not just crazy.

In the second half, Harper, Joe, Louis, Prior, and Cohn all remain somewhat in flux, not entirely fixed, although Kushner is less successful here at keeping the treadmill going. But where the *Millennium Approaches* and *Perestroika* are really less successful are in their failure to incorporate Gilman's or Treichler's awareness of the global and racial realities of AIDS. Also the work of video artist and activist Ellen Spiro in *Diana's Hair Ego* and *Invisible Women* and much other video work can be viewed in this spirit. Even Jonathan Demme's *Philadelphia* used lots of people of color in the clinics and in the street scenes.

When Belize attempts to be intermediary in Prior's and Louis's breakup, Louis and Belize have a discussion about race that is both confusing and esoteric.

Louis says to Belize,

But ultimately race here is a political question, right? Racists just try to use race here as a tool in a political struggle. It's not really about race. Like the spiritualists try to use that stuff, are you enlightened, are you centered, channeled, whatever, this reaching out for a spiritual past in a country where no indigenous spirits exist — only the Indians, I mean Native American spirits and we kill them off so now, there are no gods here no ghosts and spirits in America, there are no angels in America, no spiritual past, no racial past, there's only the political, and the decoys and the ploys to maneuver around the inescapable battle of politics, the shifting downwards and outwards of political power to the people . . . (?)

I get the feeling here that what Louis is trying to figure out about race is what Kushner is trying to figure out about race. The second half of the play, *Perestroika*, also supports the conclusion that Kushner can't take it any further than seeing "race" as a distraction, a metaphor, an obfuscation of the racist. As the play calls heavily upon Jewish, Christian, and European master narratives, myths and identities, there is an extreme gap in its awareness of racial or black racial identity.

Indeed, it seems to me as though Kushner is trying to figure out whether to allow race more reality than an American political past and a Jewish ethnic and European WASP past would ordinarily allow. In other words, the hegemonic view of race is that it really doesn't exist as a legitimate conceptual category because it has only negative content (racism) and no positive content (cultural genius). Also, how can blacks have a race when no other group thinks of themselves as having one?

Even more disturbing is the way in which Kushner seems to, almost inadvertently, confine AIDS to being a gay middle-class American disease. The reality of AIDS is unfortunately all too global, not only because the realities of our time are global but also because millions of people of color who do not ostensibly consider themselves gay are afflicted with the disease. Now the question, it seems to me, for Tony Kushner, is how to avoid the metaphorical, apocalyptic, gloom-and-doom apprehension of this medical reality and instead to speak of it in terms of Belize and his relationship to the other white characters.

I think the way to have done this would have been to bring in the family of Belize, or failing this, the ghosts who haunt Belize. Instead of his playing the one super strong character who has it all together and is never afraid, show how he has struggled with his gay identity like everybody else: how his family feels about him, etc., as Kushner has done with all the other characters except Roy Cohn, who is rightly stereotyped as the reactionary villain. Everybody is haunted except Belize. Even Cohn has Ethel Rosenberg, whom he's been responsible for putting to death, who trails him around. Instead, as Belize comments at one point, "I am trapped in a world of white people! That's *my* problem" (Kushner, 93), and it gets a laugh because, of course, it is true of the play as well as the world.

Louis says there are no angels in America, no spiritual past, and yet *Millennium Approaches* ends with a lovely makeshift mechanical angel coming through Prior's roof. Obviously this is meant to invoke the spiritual, as are many of the other religious touches in the play. Even the focus in both halves upon the devastating impact of Louis's abandonment of Prior during his illness, which is compared to God's abandonment of the world, suggests that the ideals of morality, spirituality, and ethics are given greater weight than the pragmatic realities of race, class, or even sexuality. What I had hoped Kushner was hinting at here were alternative structures of knowledge, even "subjugated knowledges" as Foucault might describe them, not just a kind of deconstructive or postmodern spirituality, remixing the old traditional elements. But, in fact, in the second part it does seem as though the spirituality he intended does boil down to something like old-fashioned ethics and morality.

The success of *Angels in America* suggests, once again, the power of the deconstructive approach to amuse, titillate, and entertain without significantly altering relations of power. Kushner constantly emphasizes and plays with the various inconsistencies of binary systems such as heterosexual/homosexual, male/female, masculine/feminine. As Sedgwick points out,

> to understand these conceptual relations as irresolvably unstable is not, however, to understand them as inefficacious or innocuous. . . . To the contrary, a deconstructive understanding of these binarisms makes it

possible to identify them as sites that are *peculiarly* densely charged with lasting potentials for powerful manipulation—through precisely the mechanisms of self-contradictory definition or, more succinctly, the double bind. Nor is a deconstructive analysis of such definitional knots, however necessary, at all sufficient to disable them. Quite the opposite. (*Epistemology*, 103)

Nevertheless, I am ambivalent about coming to the conclusion that *Angels in America* represents nothing but a more enlightened form of cooptation. I prefer to consider *Angels in America* in the context of AIDS discourse, queer theory, and cultural production in literature, theater, film, performance, and video over the long haul. For example, when compared to *Philadelphia* or *Boys in the Band, Angels in America* was much more profound and ambitious. Whereas *Angels* may suffer in a comparison with the works of Watney, Sedgwick, and Sontag, there is also the long-term consideration of Kushner's career as an individual dramatist. By this I mean to say he is a wonderful playwright, fully capable of miracles.

The linguistic categories that are understood to "denote" the materiality of the body are themselves troubled by a referent that is never fully or permanently resolved or contained by any given signified. Indeed, that referent persists only as a kind of absence or loss, that which language does not capture, but, instead, that which impels language repeatedly to attempt that capture, that circumscription—and to fail.—JUDITH BUTLER, *Bodies That Matter*

If representational visibility equals power, then almost-naked young white women should be running Western culture.—PEGGY PHELAN, *Unmarked*

. . . a deconstructive understanding of these binarisms makes it possible to identify them as sites that are *peculiarly* densely charged with lasting potentials for powerful manipulations—through precisely the mechanisms of self-contradictory definition or, more succinctly, the double bind.—EVE KOSOFSKY SEDGWICK, *Tendencies*

I no longer believe in the notion of inherently counterhegemonic or oppositional cultural work, or the idea of cultural production that can produce revolution. Instead, I believe in the transformative powers of something a little more difficult to substantiate or track: counterhegemonic readings and subtly oppositional uses of cultural texts or material culture. It is the accumulation of a large number of such interpretations that might finally have some impact politically. After all, it makes sense, doesn't it, that if a lot of people change their minds all at the same time, then something different is likely to happen? For me, the slowness of this process helps to explain precisely why nothing ever seems to change as well as what can be done about it. Moreover, it is my view that most sentient academics actually agree with me, although it is not always so popular to say so publicly.

Many prominent feminist cultural critics continue to babble on about the potential of the oppositional and the revolutionary in cultural production, meanwhile explaining the lack of concrete political progress and, indeed even the more and more strident swing to the Right, as a product of the misguidedness of one kind of cultural production or another, and the lack of the popularity of the counterhegemonic. If only the counterhegemonic were more popular. But then, as we all suspect, it wouldn't be counterhegemonic any more.

The evaluation of such a work as Jennie Livingston's *Paris Is Burning* is precisely the question because issues of "race," long ignored by the Left, continue to be a major stumbling block for transgressive theories and practices. Invariably, most of the avant-gardes of the twentieth century of poetry, painting, performance, film or dance, have been scarcely better than the Jesse Helmses on issues of "race," or in terms of including people of color in any way, although people of color have been slightly more likely historically to find themselves the faintly ridiculous object of the gaze, as in the occasional Aunt Jemima or Uncle Ben.

A documentary presenting an ethnographic study of the subterranean world of black and Puerto Rican queers in New York who organize themselves into "houses" ruled over by "mothers," and who live to "walk" in balls, *Paris Is Burning*, directed by a white lesbian, has been subject to some of the same kind of criticism as Robert Mapplethorpe's photographs of gay black men in the nude. They are considered invalid appropriations of black queer visibility, or in other words, because their authors are white, it can't be alright. Livingston's or Mapplethorpe's intentions are somehow inherently racist, or the eager and enthusiastic reception of the audiences who have witnessed Livingston's or Mapplethorpe's work is racist.

But the perspective of the author is not necessarily the only point-of-view represented here. No one can deny how urgently compelling these visual images are for most of us. Moreover the willingness to dismiss the challenge of this work following the lead of a few influential black cultural critics is distressing (hooks, 60–64; Mercer, 184–97).

I can see a problem with Livingston's attempt to bracket the experience of her cross-dressing subjects on the basis of what she interprets as their desire to be white. For some reason (perhaps because she, herself, is white), their desire to be white takes precedence over equally articulated but ephemeral desires, such as to be b-boyz, military men, bangee girls, or a real-looking naked woman, none of which have much to do with whiteness.

Let's just suppose, for a moment, that our attraction to these images is neither evil nor detestable, and that we won't burn in hell. There is this residual puritanism in some black feminist and black gay thought that seems to suggest that anything at all pleasurable in the context of race, especially having to do with the visibility of race, must be relentlessly probed and interrogated for reactionary implications. There is an unwillingness to allow any internal differentiation in categories of racism. It seems odd to suggest that visual or narrative stereotype in representations ought to be considered a sin precisely to the same degree, and in the same manner, as a lynching of a black person or the burning of a black church. To do so is to trivialize the lynching or the church burning, and to make a mockery of serious critique.

I am one of those people Judith Butler refers to in the beginning of *Bodies That Matter* who has a profound problem with the "linguistic idealism" of poststructuralism (27), especially when it is put forth as the determining factor in political questions that might more properly choose to reference history, reality, and experience. While I can accept the gravity of the poststructuralist critique of such essentialist categories, and even find it occasionally useful as a scholar of black studies, women's studies, and gay studies to remind others that any convincing and seamless narration of facts and events probably includes some fictional elements, nevertheless, this does not mean that history, reality, and experience don't exist or should be entirely discounted. Just because language can only approximate reality, just because reality constantly eludes representation, that doesn't mean that we should stop trying to find out what is really real.

I gather that this argument over the feasibility and usefulness of poststructuralist debate is a central one in queer theory. Judith Butler, Peggy Phelan, and Eve Kosofsky Sedgwick are three of my favorite queer theorists, each of whom represents a different approach to the problem of poststructuralism within queer theory.

Judith Butler, who is the most pro-poststructuralist of the three, wants to hold to the idea that the discursive logic of binary oppositions and other metaphorical operations of language provide the key underlying reality of our existence and are impossible to circumvent. Only by a convoluted philosophical argument is she able to hypothesize that there may, indeed, be something "outside" the discursive, something which is "abject," and something which may or may not account for the illusive "bodies that matter" referred to in the title of her book (28–30).

Meanwhile, Peggy Phelan begins to raise questions in *Unmarked* that offer a genuine challenge to the pervasiveness of poststructuralist discourse, but in terms of articulating her argument through her illustrations, she somehow loses her way. I now suspect this may be because she is caught some-where in the middle between Butler's and Sedgwick's approaches perhaps without fully realizing what is at issue because what is at issue is so rarely ar-ticulated in an academic context. In particular, her invocation of the unseen, the invisible, the silent, and the dead as a potential space for new interpre-tations is a much more compelling notion than she is able to encompass in her arguments.

Of the three, Sedgwick, my chosen ideal, is perhaps the most reticent on issues of race, although she has offered some truly suggestive insights that have far-reaching implications for issues of race in *Tendencies* and *Episte-mology of the Closet*, such as her "Axiom 1: *People are different from each other*."

> It is astonishing how few respectable conceptual tools we have for dealing with this self-evident fact. A tiny number of inconceivably coarse axes of categorization have been painstakingly inscribed in current critical and political thought: gender, race, class, nationality, sexual orientation are pretty much the available distinctions. . . . But the sister or brother, the best friend, the classmate, the parent, the child, the lover, the ex, our fami-lies, loves, and enmities alike, not to mention the strange relations of our work, play, an activism, prove that even people who share all or most of our own positionings along these crude axes may still be different enough from us, and from each other, to seem like all but different species. (22)

To me this is a really important observation, the starting point for realiz-ing that psychoanalysis, semiotics, and deconstruction are still crude ana-lytical tools for discerning difference in the fuller sense in which Sedgwick is speaking of it. As early as 1990, Sedgwick was already calling into question the transgressive implications of poststructuralist and postmodernist ges-tures at the same time that she was also able to deploy them more brilliantly than most (23–24).

On the other hand, both Phelan and Butler have tackled race directly with varying degrees of effectiveness, Phelan to discuss *Paris Is Burning*, Robert Mapplethorpe's photographs, and conceptual artist Adrian Piper's work, and Butler to discuss Nella Larsen's novella *Passing* and *Paris is Burning*.

Phelan's book begins with a highly tantalizing first chapter called "Broken Symmetries: Memory, Sight, Love" in which she sets up her project:

> UNMARKED attempts to find a theory of value for that which is not "really" there, that which cannot be surveyed within the boundaries of the putative real. By locating a subject in what cannot be reproduced

within the ideology of the visible, I am attempting to revalue a belief in subjectivity and identity which is not visibly representable. This is not the same thing as calling for the greater visibility of the hitherto unseen. UNMARKED examines the implicit assumptions about the connections between representational visibility and political power which have been a dominant force in cultural theory in the last ten years. (2)

This proposal was a fascinating one to me, in particular, not only because I am a black woman, and as such, unduly mired in the terms of identity politics but also because I increasingly define myself as a critic of visual issues in cultural production. In my *Invisibility Blues*, my thesis was that black women are generally invisible within the dominant discourse. But the difference between Phelan and me is that my notion of the dialectical relationship of invisibility and visibility is taken not from the common sense visual meanings of those terms but rather from the brilliant insights of an African American writer/philosopher named Ralph Ellison who wrote a novel in 1952 (the year of my birth) called *Invisible Man*.

A landmark in African American modernism, in the novel the unnamed protagonist struggles with the myriad ways in which he seems to be, as an individual, invisible to both the white and the black bourgeois status quo that control the part of the South in which he is educated, as well as in New York where he later seeks to find work. In the end, he realizes the real question may be how he has been invisible to himself, and he learns to use invisibility as a tool, as a mode of access rather than allowing himself to be manipulated by invisibility. This book and its thesis about black identity and history has been incredibly influential in African American cultural criticism (Gates, 235–60; Baker, 172–99). Besides being a masterpiece of literature, it is also a theoretical masterpiece. Although he substantiated his powers as a critic in two books of essays—*Shadow and Act* and *Going to the Territory*—he never wrote another novel. It was as if there was no way of continuing the precarious insights of invisibility.

One of the drawbacks of Ellison's thesis, however, was his almost deliberate resistance to issues having to do with concrete visibility. Invisibility is used by him rather as a metaphor for almost everything but actually being seen or not seen—voicelessness, lack of agency, a lack of historical comprehension, and a lack of institutional power. The concrete visibility, or the image, of blackness is never the issue for Ellison and always a problem.

This problem of addressing issues of visuality or visibility is a longstanding one in African American culture. It is almost as if the concerted collective response over time to the demeaning visualization of blackness in advertising, blackface minstrelsy, and other forms of popular culture has been to effect a blanket denial of the importance of visibility. Almost always in African American cultural criticism one finds that it is the unvisualizable abilities that are most celebrated—rhythm, musicality, soul, authenticity, intelligence—and that visual meanings—such as beauty, color, lightness and darkness—are regarded with suspicion.

In the first chapter of Phelan's book, she goes on to point out, accurately I think, that the increasing tendency on the Left to embrace visibility (and identity) politics and the notion that visual representation is equivalent to more power and progressive change is dangerous. One might translate this to mean if the art world is racist, the way to redress that is to include greater numbers of black artists in exhibitions, as has been the case lately at the Whitney, for instance, where both Jean-Michel Basquiat and William Johnson have had massive retrospectives in recent years, and the last Whitney Biennial included more artists of color than ever before. Or one can simply include more images or "representations" of blacks, or people of color, as was the case in the "Black Male" show two years ago at the Whitney.

And yet, as Phelan would point out, in fact all sorts of invisible issues of power and domination are left entirely untouched by these seemingly "new" arrangements. For one thing, the invisible power behind the scenes at the museum hasn't necessarily changed. For another, the invisible power the museum represents in the society to ameliorate and draw attention away from its other inequities hasn't changed either.

Phelan reaches perhaps the same conclusion that African American cultural criticism has been inclined to favor all along when she invokes Lacan's notion of the "Real" to critique the reality of visible representation. Where Phelan offers a continuation of the project that Ellison began is when she proposes that we consider the blind spot within the visible/real as an opportunity to redesign the representational real. This is an enormously suggestive proposal.

The problem with representation as she puts it is:

The pleasure of resemblance and repetition produces both psychic assurance and political fetishization. Representation reproduces the Other as the Same. Performance, insofar as it can be defined as representation without reproduction, can be seen as a model for another representational economy, one in which the reproduction of the Other as the Same is not assured. (3)

Phelan's use of the title UNMARKED is built upon a paradox within Lacanian psychoanalysis and Derridean deconstruction, both of which have highlighted the fact that within the discourse of binary oppositions (white-black, straight-gay, male-female, young-old, sane-insane, healthy-sick, normal-aberrant, beautiful-ugly), the most powerful term, the one that bears a disproportionate weight in the equation, is the unmarked one. Although the more powerful term is generally unmarked, or unremarked in discursive paradigms and visual fields, it is nevertheless marked with intrinsic value. In the economy of invisible powers and qualities, it is the dominant term that is really and truly marked in invisible ink. So when Phelan suggests invisibility and unmarkedness as a domain of the subversive and the oppositional, it is through a notion of appropriating the invisible powers of the dominant, as well as understanding the implicit trap in mistaking visibility for power.

Because of the ocular and discursive limits of visual representation and visibility, most of us are continually passing for something or another anyway, whether you choose to or not. Quite possibly, it is only within the safety and anonymity of the closet that one can hope to sort out all the intricacies (the unconscious?) of who we might be in relationship to "the other." The point to be made about binaries is not that they are always reasserting their own logic and reality regardless of human agency but rather that they have only the "reality" we invest in them. Nevertheless, they are superimposed again and again by discursive practices, no matter how inadequately but with our complicity, upon a veritable world of differences.

In Phelan's argument about the castration of all symbolic exchanges, whether they are discursive or imagistic, I believe she misses the point because of the degree to which she, herself, has made clay feet of identity politics. "In other words, the gaze guarantees the failure of self-seeing. Lacan says, 'I am unable to see myself from the place where the Other is looking at me'" (15). I had hoped that her argument was leading to proposing the impossibility of cohesive and coherent singular identities. I thought it was leading to pluralizing identities in a manner in which I consider Jennie Livingston's *Paris Is Burning* to be exemplary.

But instead, Phelan has constructed a swan song for identity: "Lacan and Freud called this immateriality the unconscious; it speaks through the symptom. I am calling this immateriality the unmarked; it shows itself through the negative and through disappearance." More comprehensibly perhaps, she explains that because her sister died when she was a kid, "I've spent a lot of time trying to understand what a captivating presence my sister's ghost was and is" (12).

I would argue that the usefulness of Phelan's unmarked—the invisible, the dead, the negative—is that visibility is defined by invisibility, that life is defined by death, that the corporeal is defined by the incorporeal. I would propose just such a loose notion of the "outside" of the discursive, or the "bodies that matter" as Butler might call it, as the antidote to the poststructural certainties of binary oppositions, which work, predictably, like machines, not like people.

I think the problem with Phelan's reading of *Paris Is Burning* is that she too readily identifies with Jenny Livingston's attempt to control the extremely volatile and unstable sub-cultural world she has discovered.

Counterintuitively, the balls reveal the performers' longing to be made unremarkable—to pass as "normative" (and thus be unnoticed) rather than to be seen as "other" (and constantly surveyed by the upholders of the normative). Excessively marked as "other" outside the arena of the balls, the walkers employ the hypervisibility of the runway to secure the power and freedom of invisibility outside the hall (Phelan, 93).

But these drag balls aren't just the visual manifestation of failure, loss and shame, although they may be deeply inscribed often by the deprivations of economic poverty, which is the very thing that makes them so suggestive for counterhegemonic interpretation. What these black and Puerto Rican drag queens have managed to build is also about strength, resourcefulness, performativity, and creativity under fire. Just imagine the consequences if such energy and desire could be harnessed for progressive politics. Livingston doesn't begin to "read" this subculture adequately. For one thing, this subculture has a long, fascinating and resilient history within the context of a once segregated world of all-black fashion designers, shows, models, and photographers.

Livingston attaches certain meanings to this subculture that don't fit, but the film exceeds those meanings by miles. For instance, where does one stand at a ball? Where is the audience? Everyone in the audience is a participant in the ball. Everybody will ultimately be a walker. Under these circumstances, what subject position does one occupy at the ball through Livingston's marginal gaze?

Also in regard to imitation, who is imitating whom? Who and what do these "children" want to be? As Corey makes clear, they used to be drag queens but now all of "the Real" is a possible playground for fantasy, imitation, and performance. What is it they are trying to hide, as Phelan sees it? First, they are all men. All they need do is put on the typical unisex outfit and walk down the street. People are not all that great at picking up gayness or even effeminacy. But Phelan conflates the black gay world with this world of poor black male cross-dressing and that is as grievous an error as it would be to assume that all white gay men, or Native American gay men were cross-dressers. Cross-dressing and transexualism are at least as marginal in the black world as they are in the white world.

So these "children" are men who choose to dress up like women and pretend to be women who then, sometimes, pretend to be women pretending to be men. It seems to me that the formulation of performativity and address is much more complicated and carnivalesque than either Livingston or Phelan are able to take in. Or as Phelan says herself, "But despite these limitations, *Paris Is Burning* is still an important film — if only because it comes so close to being an astonishing documentary about something that may be unfilmable" (103).

Butler also has problems fully acknowledging the uniqueness of *Paris Is Burning* on the grounds that drag is not necessarily heretical:

> As *Paris Is Burning* made clear, drag is not unproblematically subversive. It serves a subversive function to the extent that it reflects the mundane impersonations by which heterosexually ideal genders are performed and naturalized and undermines their power by virtue of effecting that exposure. But there is no guarantee that exposing the naturalized status of heterosexuality will lead to its subversion. Heterosexuality can augment its hegemony through its denaturalization, as when we see denaturalizing parodies that reidealize heterosexual norms without calling them into question. (231)

She wants to claim subversive powers for the "performativity" of queer theory while denying it to the actual queer performances in *Paris Is Burning*. Although the film exhibits "defiance and affirmation," Butler writes, "there is also the kind of reiteration of norms which cannot be called subversive, but which lead to the death of Venus Xtravaganza, a Latina/preoperative transsexual, cross-dresser, prostitute, and member of the House of Xtravaganza" (Butler, 125).

Even more of the players in *Paris Is Burning* will die in the years immediately following the release of the film, mostly of AIDS, but with the significant difference after the film that each time one of them dies, her obituary is featured in the *New York Times* because of her participation as an actor in *Paris Is Burning*. When a dead dehydrated male body is found tucked away in the closet of Corey (my personal favorite in the film), after her death, she is even featured on the cover of *New York Magazine*, surely a first of some kind.

While I feel as though Butler's treatment of *Paris Is Burning* skirts the main issue, her reading of the Harlem Renaissance writer Nella Larsen's *Pass-*

ing directly confronts the issue of race that has been so problematic for feminist psychoanalytic criticism. Many psychoanalytic feminists

> have claimed in various ways that sexual difference is as primary as language, that there is no speaking, no writing, without the presupposition of sexual difference. And this has led to a second claim which I want to contest, namely, that sexual difference is more primary or more fundamental than other kinds of differences, including racial difference. It is this assertion of the priority of sexual difference over racial difference that has marked so much psychoanalytic feminism as white, for the assumption here is not only that sexual difference is more fundamental, but that there is a relationship called "sexual difference" that is itself unmarked by race. (Butler, 181)

Operating from this perspective, she asks us to consider the question in relation to the text of Nella Larsen's short novel *Passing*: "how might we understand homosexuality and miscegenation to converge at and as the constitutive outside of a normative heterosexuality that is at once the regulation of a racially pure reproduction?" (Butler, 167)

But the problem for me here is that it is a mistake to read miscegenation as the psychic equivalent on the "outside" of anything so vast as homosexuality. Rather miscegenation, or more specifically "passing," is equivalent to the queers who can pass, or the epistemology of the closet. Rendering miscegenation and homosexuality as equivalent terms has its rightness, in the sense that both involve the realization of illegitimate desires, but both cover too vast a terrain for generalizations. Miscegenation, on the one hand, can be both invisible and highly visible, in the case of the child who bears evident signs of being of mixed race. Homosexuality can also be all too visible, as in the case of the cross-dressers and transexuals in *Paris Is Burning*.

But when Butler comes to the conclusion that she agrees "with both McDowell and Carby not only that it is unnecessary to choose whether this novella is 'about' race or 'about' sexuality and sexual conflict, but that the two domains are inextricably linked, such that the text offers a way to read the racialization of sexual conflict" (174), I am surprised by her conclusion. Although I agree with it, it is my feeling that the same can be said about many things in American life and culture, including the phenomenon of the drag ball so aptly documented by *Paris Is Burning*. I completely agree with her when she suggests that "the social regulation of the psyche (or the super-ego) can be read as the juncture of racial and gendered prohibitions and regulations and their forced psychic appropriations" (181). But the reading of Nella Larsen's text is the only place in which she seems to be able to advocate this.

Notes

1. This situation has changed, especially for middle-class black women.
2. The recent HBO version of *Angels in America* was very well done, and took into account the need to enlarge the character of the black nurse. Love it! I wish they would play it more.

Works Cited

Baker, Houston. 1984. *Blues, Ideology, and Afro-American Literature*. Chicago, Ill.: University of Chicago Press.

Butler, Judith. 1994. *Bodies That Matter: On the Discursive Limits of "Sex."* New York: Routledge.

Carby, Hazel. 1987. *Reconstructing Womanhood: The Emergence of the Afro-American Woman Novelist*. New York: Oxford University Press.

Davis, Angela. 1981. *Women, Race, and Class*. New York: Random House.

Ellison, Ralph. 1952. *Invisible Man*. New York: Random House.

——. *Shadow and Act*. 1961. New York: Random House.

——. *Going to the Territory*. 1988. New York: Random House.

Foucault, Michel. 1980. *The History of Sexuality*, vol. 1: *An Introduction*. New York: Vintage Books.

Gates, Henry Louis. 1987. *Figures in Black: Words, Signs, and the "Racial" Self*. New York: Oxford University Press.

Gilman, Sander. 1988. *Disease and Representation: Images of Illness, from Madness to AIDS*. Ithaca, N.Y.: Cornell University Press.

hooks, bell. 1991. Is Paris burning? *Z Magazine* (June), 60–64.

Juhasz, Alexandra. 1992. "WAVE in the Media Environment: Camcorder Activism and the Making of *HIV TV*." *Camera Obscura* 28: 135–52.

Kushner, Tony. 1993. *Angels in America: A Gay Fantasia on National Themes*, Part One: *Millennium Approaches*. New York: Theatre Communications Group; 1994, Part Two: *Perestroika*. New York: Theatre Communications Group.

McNeill, William. 1977. *Plagues and People*. New York: Anchor Books.

Mercer, Kobena. 1991. "Looking for Trouble." *Transition* 51: 184–97.

Phelan, Peggy. 1993. *Unmarked: The Politics of Performance*. New York: Routledge.

Sedgwick, Eve Kosofsky. 1990. *Epistemology of the Closet*. Berkeley: University of California Press.

——. *Tendencies*. 1992. Durham, N.C.: Duke University Press.

Sontag, Susan. 1989. *Illness as Metaphor and AIDS and Its Metaphors*. New York: Anchor.

Treichler, Paula. 1992. "Beyond *Cosmos*: AIDS, Identity, and Inscriptions of Gender." *Camera Obscura* 28: 21–78.

Wallace, Michele. 1990. *Invisibility Blues: From Pop to Theory*. New York: Verso.

Watney, Simon. 1989. "Missionary Positions: AIDS, 'Africa,' and Race." *Differences* 1, no. 1 (winter): 82–100.

Weber, Bruce. 1993. "Angels' Angels." *New York Times Magazine*, 23 April, pp. 29–30, 48–58.

50.

Toshi Reagon's Birthday

Toshi Reagon is a precious miracle worthy of this rocky fin de siècle, the second generation of a black feminist tradition that began with Sweet Honey in the Rock, an a cappella singing group founded by Toshi's mother Bernice Johnson Reagon. At Toshi's recent birthday concert at Cooper Union, magnificent Momma Reagon entered to a standing ovation and proceeded to warm up the crowd with a singalong to the accompaniment of an African Shakeree held in her lap.

Sweet Honey in the Rock has always had a special talent for combining old-time singable spirituals and protest songs with new-fangled lyrics and rhythms. When you listen to their music, it will take you awhile to realize that their only instrumentation is provided by a few miscellaneous African type noisemakers because these women are so good at making all manner of earthy, rhythmic sounds with their mouths and throats.

Over the years at a range of women's music festivals and feminist movement events, they have become expert at forging inspired political music, songs mining the roots of the black political left in form (spirituals, gospels, blues, jazz, work songs, and shouts) as well as content. Sweet Honey amply demonstrates their prowess in this field on their recent twentieth-anniversary album, *Still on the Journey*, which consistently smokes, from the rap inflected "A Tribute," telling the story of their genesis as "twenty-one African American queens whose individual journeys merged at an intersection of struggle through song," to the stunning "Another Man Broke His Word," with lyrics and words by daughter Toshi, who also has served as producer of Sweet Honey's most recent albums.

But the song I liked the best on that album, which speaks directly to Bernice's many irons in the fire, is "I'm Going to Get My Baby Out of Jail," lyrics and music by Len Chandler, a song from the civil rights movement about a pregnant civil rights leader named Gloria Rackley in Orangeburg, South Carolina, who was arrested in 1965 for being in the white waiting room at the local hospital, who then refused to allow her husband to pay the five dollar fine, and pursued her innocence through the Fifth Circuit Court of Appeals. In the process, both Rackleys lost their college teaching jobs to the struggle.

Toshi and Bernice continually hailed such men and women throughout their performance, and they let you know they expect something of you as an audience, too. Before Bernice had sung two lines of an old spiritual, she stopped to say, "don't let me be just up here singing, without you joining in," and she started over. This time we sang with her, as she called, "now the harmony," which was flowering even as she spoke. Momma Bernice talked almost as much as she sang. It was not a performance but a conversation with girlfriends, males included.

Then she introduced the birthday girl, Toshi, who came out and sang with acoustic guitar and her mother for awhile. Toshi is a big beautiful woman who flings her dreadlocks in the air when the beat becomes intense. As she sings, her warm, generous spirit flies out to embrace you, and you start to get the feeling that all she really cares about is the music, a kind of poetic justice.

A real chip off the old block, Toshi said she preferred giving to receiving on her birthday. In exchange for correct answers from audience members to trivia questions on the civil rights movement and African American culture, she passed out hip little prizes such as bracelets made by her favorite jeweler and books by favorite authors Jewelle Gomez and Toni Morrison.

This audience was positively spellbound by this mother/daughter duo on a rainy Friday night in the East Village as they broke for an intermission. It was a real family affair, just what Dole and Gingrich proposed, but with lots of New Age families mostly consisting of women of all ages, shapes, and colors.

After the break, Toshi returned with her backup group, on congas, drums, electric and acoustic guitars to sing all her best songs from her two albums *The Rejected Stone* and *Justice*, with the passion and forthrightness that are her particular burden in this world. Since I won't pretend to being a cognoscente of recent rock, I would describe her unique style, which never fails to get me in the gut and make me want to both cry and dance, as heavy late everything-I-ever-loved-about-rock-n'-roll, folk singing and folk/rock, a synthesis of the best bits of Nona Hendryx, Odetta and the Temptations, with inflections of Pete Seeger, Bruce Springsteen, and Bob Marley thrown in for good measure.

Toshi's songs always seem to be about such politically subversive items as pleasure, peace, and black folks sticking together in the face of AIDS, but the real political specificity is in the rhythms, the harmonies, and the almost palpable nostalgia for demos of old, which she must have attended with Bernice as a child. Finally, it is talent, an unfailing musicality, urbanity, wit, and the sweetest voice this side of the Mason-Dixon Line that makes this combination work for Toshi every time.

Despite an audience of about five hundred in the Great Hall at Cooper Union, the event still had the ambience of a birthday party for your best cousin, the one who can sing. And you missed it. But you will have a chance to catch her again in April at the Fez, and you had better.

51.

Cheryl Dunye: Sexin' the Watermelon

It's no accident that Cheryl Dunye's first feature, *The Watermelon Woman*—the only black film I've ever seen capable of counteracting the waiting-to-exhale blues in a single session—was denounced on the floor of Congress and in the *Washington Times* (June 14, 1996) for misusing NEA funds to promote a gay agenda. As Dr. Alvin Poussaint remarked at the time, "People feel homosexuality is not black. It's not natural in the black community . . . , and there is no history of black lesbians in Africa." In anticipation perhaps of the continued befuddlement in the black community over issues of sexuality, and the controversy likely to follow in its wake, *The Watermelon Woman*'s deliberate humor and frivolity depart significantly from the influence of its most obvious role models, the films of avant-garde feminist pioneer Yvonne Rainer. Dunye features herself as the androgynous star in what is, on the one hand, a girl-gets-girl romantic comedy, and on the other, a tongue-in-cheek mockumentary about one Fae Richards, also known as "the Watermelon Woman," a fictional actress in "race" films of the '30s.

Cheryl, also the name of the protagonist, is first drawn to Richards after having seen her performance as a young, pretty mammy in a '30s melodrama called *Plantation Memories*. She is then attracted to Richards's story through a need to discover an all-but-lost black female past in film and thereby to clarify her own goals as a black lesbian would-be filmmaker. In order to counteract the absence of a sufficient black female or feminist or lesbian archive, Dunye invents a scenario for a black lesbian in the Hollywood of the '30s. She pairs her with Martha Page, a fictional white director modeled vaguely after Dorothy Arzner. Dunye reports that she cribbed this particular idea from the scandal-mongering *Hollywood Babylon*, a film classic in which the author repeats the rumor that Hattie McDaniel and Marlene Dietrich may have once had a thing. As Cheryl remarks in one of the film's many direct-address video moments, black women's "stories have never been told."

The love story in the present, echoing Page and Richards's affair in the '30s, involves Cheryl coupling with white girl Diana (Guinevere Turner), but the more profound dynamic is between Cheryl and Tamara (Valarie Walker), her black lesbian buddy and coworker at the local video shop. Tamara, the essentialist, doesn't understand Cheryl's attraction to white girls, whereas Cheryl is the universalist dreamer. They disagree about everything from Afrofemcentricity to how best to be black lesbians, while they smoke joints and share a forty. Tamara hews to the more traditional approach of staying with your own kind. Cheryl, who dreams of being a successful filmmaker, is willing to risk writing her own script.

The film's relaxed and freewheeling structure—strung together with luxurious slo-mo sequences of Cheryl dancing on an urban rooftop—nods playfully to other significant precedents in films about black women, such as Isaac Julien's *Passion of Remembrance* in its frank preoccupation with issues of sexuality and representation, Spike Lee's *She's Gotta Have It* in the use of direct address, Julie Dash's *Daughters of the Dust* in its focus on black female material culture (clothes, hair), and Leslie Harris's *Just Another Girl on the IRT* in its forthright portrait of urban black female attitude.

Yet *Watermelon* goes significantly beyond any of these. For instance, Cheryl's taste for "race" movie mammies and Tamara's fascination with black porn, would find no place in the films of Dash or Lee. In my view, Dunye is to be considered a leading figure, along with other highly influential and talented second-generation black feminists like writer Rebecca Walker and rock-folk musician Toshi Reagon, in the latest generation of black feminist artists and intellectuals. These extraordinary women have thrived upon the accomplishments of a highly developed realm of black feminist cultural production, most of which is still a secret to mainstream arts audiences.

It is an aesthetic revolution spawned by the texts of June Jordan, Alice Walker, Toni Morrison, Toni Cade Bambara, and the poetry of Lucille Clifton, Sonia Sanchez, and Sapphire, as well as the stirring, politically committed music of the black feminist a cappella group Sweet Honey in the Rock, now in its third decade. In *The Watermelon Woman* itself, Dunye showcases a host of feminist talent, black and white. Poet Cheryl Clark plays

Richards's black lover; historian Sarah Schulman plays the director of the CLIT Archive; Ira Jeffries, a Brooklyn playwright, plays Ms. Shirley, a retired postal worker; Brian Freeman of the performance group Pomo Afro Homos plays Lee Edwards, the head of a race films archive; Jocelyn Taylor, a video artist, plays Tamara's girlfriend Stacy; and Toshi Reagon is a street singer reminiscent of the early Bob Dylan.

Behind the scenes, Michelle Crenshaw served as cinematographer. Zoe Leonard took the fake pictures of Fae Richards. Alexandra Juhasz coproduced with Barry Swimar; Dunye also wrote the script. *The Watermelon Woman* has already swept a number of gay and lesbian film festival prizes, as well as winning the Teddy Bear Award at the Berlin Festival in 1996, and I expect it will do just fine among the sophisticated audiences at the Film Forum in New York and at the Whitney Biennial, where it will be among the featured films this year.

The only unfortunate thing about *The Watermelon Woman*, in terms of the likelihood of its capturing a commercial crossover audience, is its name. The humiliations of racist illustrations and films beginning at the turn of the century have meant that African Americans can go a little crazy over mainstream attempts to retrieve the reputation of the watermelon in any context whatsoever. It is no doubt a mark of Dunye's one-woman assault upon most aspects of prevailing gender styles in black film that she chooses to leave the ironic defense of her title in the highly capable hands of none other than Camille Paglia, one of the most besieged lesbian feminist voices in the country.

In a short talking-head interview in the second half of the film, Paglia, from her office at Swarthmore, says the sort of thing we've come to expect of her: contrary to black cultural commentary, watermelon should not be seen as a symbol of shame but of abundance; a mammy should not be regarded as an image of denigration but as a bountiful goddess figure.

Indeed, Paglia even goes so far as to say that "the great actress" Hattie McDaniel in her mammy role in *Gone with the Wind* reminds her of her own Italian grandmothers in the kitchens of her youth. Such women were, and are, to be admired and emulated, not scorned.

That Dunye and I and a few others may happen to agree is not likely to carry much weight with anybody but our immediate families. Yet it's reassuring that *The Watermelon Woman* originates from the work of a black screenwriter and illustrates the thesis that mammies have been underestimated, overlooked, and insufficiently showered with love.

Originally published in the *Village Voice*, March 1997.

52.

The Prison House of Culture: Why African Art?
Why the Guggenheim? Why Now?

What, after all, does it matter that this pair of concepts — Africa, art — was not used by those who made these objects? They are still African; they are still works of art. Maybe what unites them as African is our decision to see them together, as the products of a single continent. Maybe it is we, and not their makers, who have chosen to treat these diverse objects as art. But it is also our show; it has been constructed for us now, in the Western world. — KWAME ANTHONY APPIAH, *Africa: The Art of a Continent*

That tribal art influenced Picasso and many of his colleagues in significant ways is beyond question. But that it caused no fundamental change in the direction of modern art is equally true. Picasso himself put it succinctly when he said: "The African sculptures that hang around . . . my studios are more witnesses than models." That is, they more bore witness to his enterprise than served as starting points for his imagery. — WILLIAM RUBIN, *Primitivism in 20th Century Art*

The primitive does what we ask it to do. Voiceless, it lets us speak for it. It is our ventriloquist's dummy — or so we like to think. — MARIANNA TORGOVNICK, *Gone Primitive*

Due, in part, to the gloomy judgments of African culture by such eighteenth-century philosophers as Kant, Hegel, Hume, and Rousseau, African art has only been considered art — a sign of individual genius, sophistication, and creativity — for less than a hundred years in the West. For the record, the legend goes that Henri Matisse, Georges Braque, and Pablo Picasso were the first to champion its greatness, albeit in a narrowly qualified way. Of course, they were inspired by the densely packed collections of "artifacts, tribal objects and curiosities" at the Expositions Universelles of 1889, 1897, and 1900, as well as the craze for colonial exhibitions of "native" populations of all sorts, across Europe and the United States.[1]

It is crucial to consider the creation by Matisse, Braque, Picasso, and others of a new Modernist vision in art from the aesthetic lessons of African sculpture (as well as Native American and Oceanic objects) within the context of an increasing flow of popular cultures from the New World. Around the turn of the century, there was already a steady — although much less well documented — flow of highly stylized popular cultural imagery of blacks in such arenas as advertising, sheet-music covers, ephemera, and illustrations.[2] Europeans were also increasingly given the opportunity to see real-life black Americans in performance in touring blackface minstrelsy troupes, in bands of Jubilee Singers sometimes raising money for worthy causes, as in the case of the Fisk University Jubilee Singers, and sometimes just supporting themselves, as was the case with the hundreds of spin-offs.

No one has really thoroughly investigated the extent to which various and sundry black performers from the United States toured Europe, the Pacific Islands, and even South Africa, but such books as Henry Sampson's *The Ghost Walks: A Chronological History of Blacks in Show Business*, as well as other recent research on black performance history, hint at the considerable dimensions of this phenomenon.[3] I wouldn't be surprised to learn as well that there were also parallel performance practices streaming into Europe from its various colonial possessions, and would love to find out more about this. We know at least from recent scholarship that extravaganzas of human display — from Buffalo Bill's Wild West Show (which toured the world) to the ethnographic spectacles organized by such entrepreneurs as Imre Kiralfy for the White City, a permanent exhibition site from 1908 to 1914 in London — were commonplace during the years immediately preceding and following the turn of the century.[4]

The point here is related to the one that James Clifford makes in *The Predicament of Culture* when he invokes the body of Josephine Baker in the context of the development of modernism in Paris in the '20s: these African art objects were not being examined in splendid isolation.[5] Indeed, they were forced to operate upon Europeans in a context literally swarming with activity, insight, and myriad visual imagery generated by parallel and related cultural practices stemming from the impact of the presence of colonized subjects within the purview of their various empires. These phenomena included not only the various performance practices of the colonized and the

formerly enslaved that managed to travel to Europe but also cultural perspectives generated by aestheticisms of Orientalism and primitivism that
were already in place as part of the philosophical and ideological logic of
imperialism, colonialism, and domination.[6]

Nonetheless, art-historical expertise has conventionally depoliticized the
moment of modernist catharsis and transformation by placing it very precisely in or around 1906, the year that Picasso began work on the celebrated
inaugural canvas of the conjunction of primitivism and modernism, *Les Demoiselles d'Avignon*.[7] You can take your pick of originary scenarios from the
copious art-historical literature. The Matisse story goes as follows:

On his way to pay a visit to Gertrude Stein in the Rue de Fleurus, (he)
noticed a "Negro" object in the window of Emile Heymann's shop of exotic
curiosities at 87 Rue de Rennes, and bought it for a few francs. Upon arriv-
ing at the Stein apartment he showed it to Picasso, who while looking at it
displayed a certain enthusiasm.[8]

We date this event by the fact that Picasso had just finished his extraordinary portrait of Gertrude Stein. Whereas, according to Colin Rhodes in
his brief but dense little book, *Primitivism and Modern Art*, it is "now generally accepted that it was probably the Fauve painters Maurice de Vlamick
and André Derain who first acquired African pieces in Paris early in 1906
. . . and that they were quickly followed by Matisse, who had become
interested in West African sculpture after a trip to North Africa in March
1906."[9]

As for a more subjective account, Picasso's lavish epiphanies, as reported
by André Malraux and Françoise Gilot, begin to hint at modernism's anxiety
of influence around tribal objects and their association with their presumably primitive and uncivilized African creators. Picasso has said:

> When I became interested forty years ago in Negro art and I made what
> they refer to as the Negro Period in my painting, it was because at the
> time I was against what was called beauty in the museum. At that time,
> for most people a Negro mask was an ethnographic object. When I went
> for the first time, at Derain's urging, to the Trocadéro museum, the smell
> of dampness and rot there stuck in my throat. It depressed me so much
> I wanted to get out fast, but I stayed and studied. Men had made those
> masks and other objects for a sacred purpose, a magic purpose, as a kind
> of mediation between themselves and the unknown hostile forces that
> surround them, in order to overcome their fear and horror by giving it
> a form and image . . . I knew I had found my way. Then people began
> looking at those objects in terms of aesthetics.[10]

A far cry still from the respect this art deserved, such views were nevertheless better than the way the rest of the official white world of scholarship and expertise felt about it. Traditionally, the study of "fetishes" and "tribal objects" was left to anthropologists, geologists, archaeologists, and naturalists.[11] Its distribution and circulation were left to looters, from military men to missionaries, under cover of imperialist occupation, and the collectors and dealers who relentlessly pursued them.

Indeed, the fate of these objects was not unrelated to the fate of the human bodies also removed from Africa under less than ideal circumstances — some of them sold or just handed over and some of them kidnapped. Whereas the slaves might expire on the trek to the coast, or in the arduous middle passage,[12] lots of African objects, many of them made of wood or equally perishable materials, were destroyed by the fires of zealous missionaries, or even by their African patrons (not necessarily their skillful creators) when they had outlived their ritual usefulness.

As a sideshow to the general chaos that accompanied Europe's annexation and colonization of the African continent in the late nineteenth century, the best and the most interesting (we can only but vainly hope) African objects were salvaged for exhibition or sale, even as entire villages of Africans (as well as Native Americans, Pacific Islanders, and Eskimos or Inuits) were sometimes shipped over to Europe, England, and the United States and placed on display in zoos and circuses.[13] No doubt, many of the objects that made it either to the New World, Britain, and Europe were probably destroyed one way or the other. It is not too surprising then that until very recently, the practice of African art discourse, to the degree that such a thing could be said to exist, had been plagued by the Eurocentrism, phallocentrism, and solipsism that had always marked other Western discourses about Africa.

For instance, following the sacking of Benin by the British in 1897, when close to one thousand intricate bronzes that had originally hung on the wooden pillars of the palace were discovered, it was a while before the speculation died down that these works must have been made by visiting Europeans. Also, the monuments and pyramids found in what is now the South of Egypt, formerly the black kingdom of Nubia, were repeatedly credited to the fairer-skinned (and thus presumably more talented) Egyptians.[14]

In 1910, when the German ethnographer Leo Frobenius found a nearly life-size bronze head in a naturalistic style in the grove of Olokun (the Yoruba sea goddess), he decided that Olokun was Poseidon, and that the head was in fact from the long-lost colony of Atlantis. We could easily fill a book or two with documented examples of the kind of racism that passed for scholarly expertise.[15]

As a consequence, there is and continues to be, especially in this country, an appalling chasm in regard to the study and appreciation of African art. Consider for a moment the arrogance of a CD-ROM set called *The History of Art*, starting out with a volume on *Ancient Greece* that doesn't even bother to acknowledge the existence of Africa, except through its references to Egypt as the decadent negation of the glorious humanism of Greek art.[16] Moreover, this disdain for African art isn't just a white thing.

Consequently brought low by all this mess, some colored Americans don't have much use for African art either. Some of the various comments I've heard from blacks in relation to the Guggenheim exhibition have been, "I was infuriated by the wall labels," or "The Guggenheim is just trying to get credit for being multicultural when they have never done anything for artists of color."

"They should hang a big sign over the whole show saying, 'This work is all stolen!'" said one of the organizers of a conference on the arts in Africa hosted by 651 at the Brooklyn Academy of Music, in conjunction with the Guggenheim exhibition. Was she suggesting that great art can't be claimed or assimilated unless we know precisely who did it because it lacks the essentializing aura of the individual artist? I don't think so. After all, if rap artists can sample copyrighted materials, why can't we sample this unsigned but neither unloved nor unlamented work for whatever—contemplation, mediation, images, role models, philosophical insight?

Rather, the devastating and traumatic emotional consequences of their transport—just how these objects came to be in our midst—can outweigh their beauty and spiritual power for some descendents of the survivors of our holocaust. Also, I think the woman from 651 was actually trying to make the kind of distinction Manthia Diawara, director of the Africana Studies Program at New York University, was getting at in his talk at the same conference about working on a documentary profile of the life of Sekou Touré, former president of Guinea.

A group involved in a coup d'état to overthrow Touré was arrested by him, Diawara explained to me, and ultimately executed, for their alleged, although never proven, participation in an art smuggling scheme. The irony is that at the same time that some newly liberated Muslim African nations declared it illegal to export traditional African art objects in order to increase the wealth of the state, they also forbade the use of them for worship in a traditional context.

According to Diawara, the works collected at the Guggenheim and in other museums serve to displace black modernity. From this perspective, these nameless objects, having no authors, and no continuity with known traditions, alienated from their own intended functions in antiseptic plexiglas exhibition cases, are at once lifeless and immortal, like the albatross around the neck of the mariner in the Coleridge poem. The greatest difference, then, between the bodies of our ancestors and these tribal objects is that the bodies were allowed to die (therefore enabling us to replace them), whereas the tribal objects can never die, given their curious half-life on the back shelves of Western art. Presumably as a consequence, black art as a discourse with self-defining agency is prevented from existing both in the present and the past.

My take is both different and the same for one reason only: I am the daughter of a black feminist artist, Faith Ringgold, who considered African art pivotal to her creative development. Just as Black Power and black cultural nationalism were in their ascendancy in the late '60s and early '70s, and everybody was talking about going back to Africa for its music, its dance, its food, its people, its clothing, its air — indeed, everything but its visual art — a small circle of black intellectuals and artists got interested in these objects as "art" — that is, as signs of an African genius, sophistication, and talent to be drawn upon as models for our own African American creativity. In other words, I see the down side but I see the up side too.

What exists in American, European, African, and Asian collections should probably be considered no more than the tip of the iceberg as far as production is concerned. If we can say that only 10 percent of silent films have survived, then maybe 1 percent or less of the objects we now describe as African art are still in existence. It might even be useful to think of them as ruins, the product of archaeological excavation, the better part of which no longer exists. The museum and gallery collections should be regarded as our best clues to the actual dimensions of visual art activity prior to the '50s or '60s in Africa. Its study should be formulated, at least for the citizens if the Diaspora and all of our friends, in the context of mourning the soul death of our ancestors and, admittedly, as a sign of our cultural decimation.[17] Such was, perhaps, the thinking of the former director of the Museum for African Art, Susan Vogel, when she selected Maya Lin, the creator of the Vietnam Memorial in Washington, D.C., to design their new space in SoHo. The walls are dark and the rooms womblike, a perfect place to have a good cry.

In recent decades, particularly in the United States, a generation of scholars who combine the tools of anthropology, political geography, archaeology, art history, and deconstruction in a kind of cultural studies of the ethnographic have been making significant headway toward integrating divergent discourses with unvarnished truth about the various colonial histories of the acquisition of African art. A particular publication that may have speeded the entire process along was Martin Bernal's *Black Athena*, with its reinterpretation of the links between the Greco-Roman world and the African and Semitic worlds. Subsequent investigational exhibitions at such institutions as the Brooklyn Museum, the Metropolitan, the Smithsonian, and particularly the Museum for African Art, have gradually altered the landscape, although usually not in a way that can help us with the problem of what to say about African art's impact on modernism. To spell out this impact is important not only because Western culture of the modernist variety continues to dominate the world's vision but also because this missing link to the characteristic structures and relations between visual discourses will help us to better comprehend the entire program's ongoing and dynamic effectiveness (hegemony) in the present.

This project has been left in the not always capable hands of those who come to it from the modernist side: Hal Foster in *Re-Coding*, James Clifford in *The Predicament of Culture*, Sally Price in *Primitive Art in Civilized Places*, Marianna Torgovnick in *Gone Primitive: Savage Intellects, Modern Lives*, as well as, most infamously, William Rubin in *Primitivism in the 20th Century Art*, the two-volume catalogue that accompanied the exhibition of the same name at the Museum of Modern Art in 1984. All the same, not nearly enough scholars, intellectuals, and artists have taken up the question of "primitivist modernism," given its potential importance to multiculturalism.

Within this context, *Africa: The Art of a Continent* presents quite a conundrum in that it works as a microcosm of the problem with the field of African Art as a constituent element in modernism. On the other hand, there is the archaeological, anthropological, social science-y approach to African art, which sees it as an artifact of culture with a small "c," and therefore a gateway to the more mysterious side of history, sometimes called prehistory, before the world's great written traditions began to keep the records to which we still refer.

The modernist people think the social science folks are too dismissive of aesthetic value, and the social science folks think the modernists don't care a fig for history, much less for the subjectivities and agency of the original makers of this work. The usefulness of the social science model is included in the late discovery of structural anthropology that its field of operation is that which is ultimately unknowable or untotalizable about cultural difference. The fact I love, but which many seem to hate, is that cultures come in an endless combinatory variety of arbitrary meaningfulness. For this reason

as well, I love all the myriad signs that "difference" is finally irreducible —
such as those on display at the Guggenheim.

There are those who will be enraged by this exhibition's overt display
of ignorance, and the vast, unapologetically white walls of Frank Lloyd
Wright's structure, almost blinding in the daylight. It is correct to say that
this is not your ideal didactic exhibition, but what fascinated me is the extraordinary opportunity given us to fill in our own narratives, to contemplate precisely that which is not known about African art, in the way in which
a Toni Morrison or a Charles Johnson have done for slavery and the Middle
Passage.

According to Harvard philosopher Kwame Anthony Appiah, the concepts of both Africa and art are first, inventions of the West, second, relatively recent in origin, and third, not relevant to the actual creation of the
works of the exhibition. "So we might as well face up to the obvious problem," Appiah writes, "neither Africa nor art — the two animating principles
of this exhibition — played a role as ideas in the creation of the objects in
this spectacular show."[18] Good point, I suppose, but still, I am not quite so
willing or ready to yield all rights to a continental philosophy or aesthetics
solely to the West.

The fate of African art objects was not unrelated to the fate of the human
bodies also removed from Africa under less than ideal circumstances — some
of them sold or just handed over and some of them kidnapped. The Harvard
Black Studies threesome of Henry Louis Gates Jr., Kwame Anthony Appiah,
and Cornel West served as special consultants for the exhibition, and each
wrote a short essay for the catalogue, of which Appiah's is the most interesting. This may be as good a time as any to alert you to the fact that there
are almost as many kinds of Afrocentrism as there are types of toothpaste,
and some of them have about as much in common with Leonard Jeffries's or
even Molefi Asante's way of thinking as you would expect to find between
caviar and filet mignon. Appiah, the least well known of the threesome at
Harvard, is a leading figure in this context. A professor of philosophy and
African American studies, he was born in Ghana, is Asante by birth, and is
best known for his reflections on genetic indeterminacy of racial identity.

To even call whatever these folks stand for "Afrocentrism" is stretching
it a lot, given that they don't necessarily buy into the essentialist rhetoric of
margin vs. centers, or even the very notion of a fixed identity. In any given
number, *Transition* is just as likely as not to have more articles authored by
phenotypically white folk than black. But they do seem to have the will to reclaim Africa from the more provincial, xenophobic, and occasionally hate-

mongering Afrocentrists we spawn so easily on this continent—the point being, I believe, not only the preservation of the creative legacy of the African continent, but also, finally, casting some light upon its present grievous political and economic condition, which continues to go largely unremarked in the United States.

Yet Appiah may be more willing to yield the right of way to the West in regard to aesthetics precisely because he is African, not African American, and no poor dispossessed African either. Moreover, his notion of Africa not as a continent but as a bursting bundle of ethnicities, tribes, and nations is accurate. As an Asante, he grew up surrounded by the treasures of Asante art, and knowing that they were his birthright. If one gets rid of both the notion of Africa and of aesthetics, quite naturally the claim of any African American to precisely ethnic art from the African continent seems perversely illegitimate in comparison to Appiah's, and, after all, the art is both material property as well as symbolic legacy.

But I believe that such concepts as art and Africa are a little more complicated, more "cooked" than raw, and as such many different hands have contributed to the present recipe. Africa and Europe are not on opposite sides of the world but nearly attached by land; they were never unknown to one another. The continent of Africa is part of the "Old World," not the New.

Given this scenario, in which blacks haven't necessarily had more of a notion of what to really make of the presence of African art in European and American museums than most whites, how are we to interpret the obvious shortcomings of the Guggenheim exhibition? Having originated at the Royal Academy of Arts in London in 1995 and traveled first to the Walter-Gropius-Bau in Berlin, *Africa: The Art of a Continent* was curated by a white artist, Tom Phillips, one of the eighty members of the not-at-all progressive Royal Academy, with the aid of a curatorial advisory committee with such heavyweights as Michael Kan, director of the Detroit Institute of the Arts, Frank Herreman of the Museum for African Art in SoHo, and the highly respected Ekpo Eyo, professor of Archaeology at the University of Maryland and the former director of the Nigerian National Museum and the Federal Department of Antiquities.

Yet one African art insider tells me disdainfully, "They didn't talk to any of the people they needed to talk to, and the exhibition shows it." Other sources inform me that Susan Vogel, former director of The Museum for African Art, and one of the chief proponents of new approaches to African art, wasn't able to remain on the advisory committee for the exhibition because of her insistence that it include contemporary African art. She was the curator of the stellar exhibition *Africa Explores: 20th Century African Art* back in 1993, jointly held at the New Museum and the Museum for African Art.[19] On the other hand, the Guggenheim's chief curator for the exhibition, Jay Levinson, while both smart and charming, is no African art expert (he did the Columbus Centennial exhibition at the Smithsonian and will do the big Chinese exhibition planned next summer for the Guggenheim). Did the Gugg make a boo-boo, or was this just their awkward way of proclaiming their new interest in increasing their audience of color from a level of nil?

Including a display of over five hundred mostly eye-popping traditional objects from Egypt to Zimbabwe, the aggregate of which is guaranteed to defy all ready generalizations about the unity of African culture, the hyperbolic ultra-modernist space of Frank Lloyd Wright's Guggenheim confronts and commingles with African art on a gargantuan scale for the first time since the *Primitivism* show at the Museum of Modern Art in 1984, in which masterpieces of modernism were coupled with similar works of African, Native American, and Oceanic art.

I never saw the modernism show. I was in Oklahoma at the time, and wouldn't have dreamed of flying back to see it then, although I could kick myself now for having missed what must have been the spectacle of a lifetime. By way of compensation, I have spent a considerable amount of time with the two accompanying volumes of essays published by MOMA. Most of the essays endlessly equivocate about whether African art influenced modernist art. The arguments vacillate between the assumption that if a particular artist hadn't seen a particular "tribal" object before he did the painting or sculpture in question, then clearly we are talking about affinities rather than influences in combination with the repeated, seemingly contradictory concessions that yes, there were definitely some clear influences.[20]

Needless to say, this was not the high road even in 1984, and no major museum in 1997, at least in the United States, would ever again make the mistake of doing such an exhibition, in which the "tribal" arts were historically compared to the superlative accomplishments of the West. The chart Alfred Barr used to illustrate the various contributing factors that made up European modernism, and which accompanied a 1937 Cubist exhibition, definitely won't do any more either.[21] At the same time, there hasn't been any new breakthrough synthesis of modernism and African, Oceanic, and Native American art perspectives to take their place. Even at the time of the *Primitivism* show, the widespread critique still centered around substituting for a modernist bent the much more politically correct focus on the works' original intentions in African society.

Clearly, the West was profoundly affected by visions of new people and places embodied in these objects, but just exactly how did this work? How should or can it be described, given our conventional descriptions of aesthetic schools, influences, and progressive development? Yes, modernism was a heady, no-fault combination of New World African, Far, Near, and Middle Eastern imperialism, exploration, and exploitation further accelerated by such spectacular adventure-promoting inventions as the steam engine, the railroad, electricity, telegraph, telephone, the light bulb, film, photography, and sound recordings, but there is also the fact that, to put it indelicately, cultures steal from one another. When they do so, they don't leave an IOU so you can collect later, either. It is what culture is, what culture was perhaps invented to do by its willing subjects.

At the beginning of *The Prison House of Language*, cultural theorist Fredric Jameson talks about how one discourse model supersedes another. It doesn't occur all at once. First, there has to be a good deal of mucking about trying to make the previous model fit the new circumstances. In the nineteenth century, the dominant Western paradigm in visual culture was mimetic. Although the world is populated by multitudes of people who are still pretty stuck on the realism model, in fact, around the turn of the century, European modernism had already begun to embrace new models of ideal form that drew upon anything handy. The response was not the immediate replacement of one model by the other but rather the endless recombination of the various elements of the two, to which we owe many of the treasures of European modernism found in the museums of the world today.

I would argue that the mix that made European modernism was not just a matter of inanimate African art objects, violently kidnapped and forced into the unempathic cultural context of the ethnographic museum. The importation of African cultural values was part of the picture as well, facilitated by the presence of African bodies and the will of the African spirit, in both New World and Old. While these immigrants almost never succeeded in continuing their visual forms, they did manage to bring their music and their dance with them, or at least to adapt them to the new circumstances. It was called gospel, blues, jazz, samba, calypso, and so on.

On the African side, who can be sure? Perhaps in the eighteenth and nineteenth centuries, their artists (and I will persist in thinking there were such people in all civilizations worthy of the name), under cover of religious ritual, were having a Renaissance somehow prompted by their sorrow over the loss of our ancestors?

The story is: the show was well worth seeing. Aside from the astonishing beauty, poetry, and blues-laden sadness of the objects, there were the dozen or so loans from African museums and collections, a rarity in exhibitions of this kind. Included in this category were the Lydenburg Heads (c.a. 500–700 C.E.) from the Eastern Transvaal, the cave painting of the Linton Panel, and the "Rock Engraving of a Giraffe" of the San, dated back as far as 3000 B.C.E. I was most fascinated by the magnificent Kongo crucifixes from Zaire.

The usual suspects were in evidence in all their brilliance: the Benin and Ife bronzes; the Nok terra cottas; the Akan gold weights; the Yoruba, Igbo, Baule, Dogon, and Luba wood sculpture; the Dan, Bamana, and Senufo masks; as well as the perfunctory nods to the masterpieces of Egypt, old Nubia, and Ethiopia, which gave this exhibition the right to claim that it spanned the continent. There are those who may complain that the exhibition was too much of a grab bag (such as Holland Cotter in the *New York Times*), and I definitely see the point, but it isn't as if the Guggenheim were showing us African art for the first or the last time. Indeed, the Metropolitan, the Museum of Natural History, and the Brooklyn Museum (and that's just New York), despite their paternalistic rhetoric, are excellent sources of permanent displays of African art. Try them. After all, no matter what anybody else tells you, the art in question is really the art of living.

Originally published in *Renaissance Noire* (fall 1997).

Notes

1. William Rubin, ed., *Primitivism in 20th Century Art: Affinities of the Tribal and the Modern* (New York: Museum of Modern Art, 1984), 125–64. In this essay by Jean Louis Paudrat, which details the progress of the earliest importations of African art objects into Europe, he remarks as well of the Exposition Universelle of 1889, "The duplication of a few dwellings claimed to be typical of Senegal, Gabon, or the Congo also caught the public's fancy. On the square of the Pahouin village, a few Okande, Aduma, or Vili tribesmen could be seen, performing dances or engaging in craftsmanship. Some of them would carve on demand exotic ivory souvenirs."

For insight into the U.S. context at the time, see Phillip Verner Bradford and Harvey Blume's *Ota Benga: The Pygmy in the Zoo* (New York: Delta, 1992) for an informative and well-written account of the adventures of a Pygmy from what was then called the "Belgian Congo," who was exhibited at the Bronx Zoo, the Museum of Natural History, and the 1904 St. Louis Fair, and who ended his life by suicide despite having found a fair home among the black community in Lynchburg, Virginia. The fascinating thing about this account is the endeavor to imagine the experience from the point of view of Ota Benga himself, as someone who imagined himself to be in charge of his own life.

Also, for a sampling of information about the various fairs around the world, see Burton Benedict, *The Anthropology of World's Fairs: San Francisco's Panama Pacific International Exposition of 1915* (Berkeley, Calif.: The Lowie Museum of Anthropology and University of California Press, Berkeley, 1983); Paul Greenhalgh, *Ephemeral Vistas: The*

Expositions Universelles, Great Exhibitions, and the World's Fairs, 1851–1939 (Manchester, England: Manchester University Press, 1988); Fatimah Rony, *The Third Eye: Race, Cinema, and Ethnographic Spectacle* (Durham, N.C.: Duke University Press, 1996); and Robert Rydell, "The Culture of Imperial Abundance: World's Fairs in the Making of American Culture" in *Consuming Visions: Accumulation and Displays of Goods in America, 1880–1920*, ed. Simon Bronner (New York: Norton, 1989).

2. Jan Nederveen Pieterse, *White on Black: Images of Africa and Blacks in Western Popular Culture* (New Haven: Yale University Press, 1992); Raymond Bachollet, Jean-Barthelemi Debost, Anne-Claude Lelieur, and Marie-Christine Peyriere, *Negripub: L'image des Noirs dans la publicité* (Paris: Editions Somogy, 1992).

3. Henry Sampson, *The Ghost Walks: A Chronological History of Blacks in Show Business, 1865–1910* (Metuchen, N.J.: Scarecrow, 1988); Ike Simond, *Old Slack's Reminiscence, and Pocket History, of the Colored Profession from 1865 to 1891* (Bowling Green, Ohio: Bowling Green University Press, 1974); Robert Toll, *Blacking Up: The Minstrel Show in Nineteenth Century America* (New York: Oxford University Press, 1974); Mel Watkins, *On the Real Side: Laughing, Lying and Signifying—The Underground Tradition of African-American Humor That Transformed American Culture from Slavery to Richard Pryor* (New York: Simon and Schuster, 1994); and Allen Woll, *Black Musical Theatre: From Coontown to Dreamgirls* (Baton Rouge: Louisiana State University Press, 1989).

4. Amy Kaplan and Donald E. Pease, eds. *Cultures of United States Imperialism* (Durham, N.C.: Duke University Press, 1993); Paul Greenhalgh, *Ephemeral Vistas*, 90; Patricia Leighten, "The White Peril and L'Art Negre: Picasso, Primitivism, and Anticolonialism," *Art Bulletin* 72, no. 4 (1990): 610–30.

5. James Clifford, *The Predicament of Culture: Twentieth Century Ethnography, Literature, and Art* (Cambridge, Mass.: Harvard University Press, 1988), 192–202.

6. Edward Said's *Orientalism* (New York: Pantheon, 1978) is the crucial work on the history of orientalism, although his approach is decidedly Middle Eastern and literary, not visual. Such works as Ella Shohat and Robert Stam's *Unthinking Eurocentrism: Multiculturalism and the Media* (New York: Routledge, 1994); John MacKenzie's *Orientalism: History, Theory and the Arts* (Manchester, England: Manchester University Press, 1995); and Linda Nochlin's "The Imaginary Orient," *Art in America*, May 1983, serve to fill the gap. As for primitivism, aside from the works already mentioned, I would recommend as well the recent double issue of *Wide Angle* 18, no. 2–3, "Movies Before Cinema: Part I and Part II."

7. Two really useful feminist interpretations of *Les Demoiselles d'Avignon* are Anna Chaves's "New Encounters with *Les Demoiselles d'Avignon*: Gender, Race, and the Origins of Cubism," *Art Bulletin* 72, no. 4 (1994): 597–611; and Ann Gibson's "The Avant-Garde," *Critical Terms in Art History* (Chicago: University of Chicago Press, 1996).

8. Rubin, *Primitivism in 20th Century Art*, 216.

9. Colin Rhodes, *Primitivism and Modern Art* (London: Thames and Hudson, 1994), 111.

10. Rubin, *Primitivism in 20th Century Art*, 216.

11. Annie E. Coombes, *Reinventing Africa: Museums, Material Culture, and Popular Imagination* (New Haven: Yale University Press, 1994); Alison Griffith, "'Journeys for Those Who Cannot Travel': Promenade Cinema and Museum Life Group," *Wide Angle* 18, no. 3 (1996), 53–84.

12. Tom Feeling's stunning collection of drawings, *The Middle Passage* (New York: Dial,

1995), as well as Sam Anderson's vivid and imaginative little book *The Black Holocaust for Beginners* (New York: Writers and Readers, 1995).

13. Fatimah Tobing Rony, "Those Who Squat and Those Who Sit: The Iconography of Race in the 1895 Films of Felix-Louis Regnault," *Camera Obscura* 28 (1992): 189–263; Deborah Willis and Carla Williams, *Reimaged Memories and Desire: The Black Female Body* (forthcoming), "The History of Human Display" and "Orientalism" chapters; Deborah Willis and Carla Williams, *The Black Female Body: A Photographic History* (Philadelphia: Temple University Press, 2002).

14. Sylvia Hochfield and Elizabeth Riefstahl, *Africa in Antiquity: The Arts of Ancient Nubia and the Sudan* (New York: Brooklyn Museum, 1978).

15. Tom Phillips, ed., *Africa: Art of a Continent* (Munich: Prestel and the Guggenheim Museum), 122.

16. *History through Art*, Power-CD, CD-Rom, 1994.

17. I should note that cultural decimation of this and related kinds (loss of land, country, language, cultural heritage, family) is much more common than is usually considered in the context of African American discourse, and is by no means unbearable, or even the worst thing that can happen.

18. Phillips, *Africa*, 6.

19. Susan Vogel, ed., *Africa Explores: 20th Century African Art* (New York: Museum for African Art, 1993).

20. In particular, I would point out Rubin's celebrated argument about "affinities" in the introductory essay in *Primitivism in 20th Century Art*.

21. Charles Harrison et al., *Primitivism, Cubism, Abstraction: The Early Twentieth Century* (London: Open University, 1993), plate 86 (101).

53.

Black Female Spectatorship

In a special issue of *Camera Obscura* in 1989 on the "female spectator," the editors posed a series of questions to contributors, one of which was:

> The very term "female spectator" has been subject to some dispute insofar as it seems to suggest a monolithic position ascribed to the woman. In your opinion, is the term most productive as a reference to empirical spectators (individual women who enter the movie theatre), as the hypothetical point of address of the film as a discourse or as a form of mediation between these two concepts? Or as something else entirely?

The array of responses was fascinating and informative, but what attracted my attention even more was that, although quite a number of the fifty-nine contributors mentioned "race" as an unsettling factor to previous conceptions of "spectatorship," there was only one black writer, Jacqueline Bobo, the prominent black feminist communications theorist, among them.[1]

"Unfortunately," Bobo writes, "when the female spectator is usually spoken of and spoken for, the female in question is white and middle class. As a black woman working within the discipline of cultural studies, my goal is to expand the scholarship on the female spectator beyond this."[2] In the process, Bobo, whose work on film and spectatorship I admire immensely, was inadvertently responding to the question posed by the editors of *Cam-*

era Obscura by saying that she saw "female spectatorship" as a "reference to empirical spectators," not as a "hypothetical point of address of the film as a discourse."[3]

I concur with Bobo's interest in the historical realities of black female spectatorship, but I am not as willing as she to cede the psychoanalytic framing of spectatorship. I feel that a psychological approach, even a specifically psychoanalytic approach to black forms of spectatorship is much needed, but I would add that we need not use psychoanalysis as we have found it. In fact, the range of acceptable interpretations of what psychoanalysis is and what it can do is already quite vast. Yet all the approaches I've found, from the use of feminist psychoanalysis in cultural criticism to the theorization of feminist psychologies, continue the pretense of color blindness. In theories of psychoanalysis in general, as well as in the practice of psychoanalysis, race has no reality. This is an unacceptable state of affairs. Even if it turns out to be impossible to theorize "race" as a fundamentally psychological phenomenon, it seems to me that "race" should always be viewed as a present and relevant (social, historical, material, ideological) context for psychological phenomena and psychoanalytic interpretation.

Feminist film criticism generally employs psychoanalysis in a rigorous and precise manner. Either to a lesser or greater extent, it uses Jacques Lacan's rereading of Sigmund Freud in order to analyze "textual" or filmic issues, or issues of discourse, with little reference to possibly relevant social and historical contexts. When one reads it, it appears as though such interpreters are coming up with timeless and universal psychological criteria. At the same time, the disclaimer that feminist film critics have lately begun adding that their observations about spectatorship have no application or interest for people of color and only apply to a narrow bourgeois realm of a white Euro-American middle class goes too far, I think. The white Euro-American middle class of the past century is not yet some obsolete aboriginal tribe on the verge of extinction. Its values have been for some time, and continue to be, ideologically dominant.

On the other hand, I am willing to agree with Griselda Pollack and other critical perspectives in art history that the historical and material specificity of the multiple visual realms of the past and the present have not been adequately articulated or described by feminist film criticism's use of "the gaze" or "spectatorship." Because my concerns are related to a discussion of society and culture in the present, it seems important to keep in mind the historical context of film (especially films that include references to race), as well as the impact of other cultural forms and intellectual discourses on film. I would like to examine how issues of race might be relevant to multiple concepts of spectatorship (the historical/social and the textual/psychological) first, by telling a story.

In the fall of 1990, I participated in a feminist art history conference at Barnard at which I was to lead a workshop on race, gender, and modernism along with the white art historian Ann Gibson. Immediately prior to my own session, I attended the session of a white female friend that was on popular culture with a focus on music. My friend, whose training is in art history and critical theory, did her presentation on Sinead O'Connor, and her co-presenter talked about Madonna. My own recollection is that the session was packed and that I was the only person of color present. After brief presentations by my friend and the other white woman presenter (much more of an expert in music than my friend), a general discussion took place that handled popular culture and rock and roll with a kind of reverence and awe that I can now see, in retrospect, had much to do with the rarity of popular culture discourse at an art history conference.

At the time, however, what annoyed me as somebody who was inadvertently representing race through my body in the room, as well as choosing to represent race at my session that would follow, was that everybody in that room was talking about rock and roll in particular, and popular culture in general, as though black people had never existed and never made any contribution to it. What stands out in my mind is their wondering aloud where the rhythm that was apparent in Elvis Presley and in Madonna had come from? One particularly astute art critic (who just happened to be male) suggested that we refer to Rosalind Krauss's work on rhythm in Picasso.

By this time, I was absolutely steaming but I was also afraid to speak, afraid to say that the rhythm that Elvis exhibited (not to mention the rhythm in Picasso) had come from the same place, from Africa, that rock and roll was largely the invention of African Americans, that it was impossible to talk sanely about popular music in the United States without dealing with race.

Now, I am not altogether sure why I was so afraid to speak then. I know that I am now beginning to lose that fear, but at that time I was very much in the grip of it. I also know that I was often successful in hiding my fear, and as a consequence no one ever knew or believed (especially white people) that I was afraid.[4] I can remember, however, telling myself that I should save my energy and my anger for my own session, although I didn't recognize at the time that the critical space of my session (high modernism/primitivism) was qualitatively different from the critical space of this session (the only session at the art history conference on popular culture).

Both women followed me into my session, whereupon I immediately began the calculated time release of my barely suppressed rage. I was still afraid to speak, by the way, which made my fury, no doubt, all the more difficult to bear for my listeners. The thing that I can best remember saying, which seems to me still instructive for my remarks here, was: "You [white women] are interested in Madonna because she is white. You are not interested in Tina Turner, not because she's less interesting but because she is black." Of course, my friend felt completely betrayed, attacked, and confused by the way in which her session had resurfaced in my session. Matters were not helped by the fact that my session, as was hers, was well attended by feminist art historian high-muckety-mucks (as Zora Neale Hurston might have called them). So the whole antagonism took on the aura of a professional challenge.

Meanwhile, the other white woman, the copresenter, engaged me in lengthy and not unfriendly conversation afterward. Obviously baffled, she insisted, again and again: "Of course, I am well aware of the contribution blacks have made to rock and roll. I don't know why I didn't mention it."

At a more recent meeting of the Society of Cinema Studies in New Orleans, on a panel on "multicultural feminist theories" chaired by Ella Shohat, I tried to spell out what I saw as the analogous relationship of this narrative to the situation then at hand in regard to explaining the problem of black female spectatorship. The idea that every story, every narrative cloaks a deep structure, a simpler and more logical narrative that will then reveal the hidden meaning and order of the less astute and self-conscious narrative, is not only a foundational idea in high modernisms but also an idea I am highly drawn to. On the other hand, I am well aware that from a postmodern perspective, or a multicultural perspective (these two dissimilar discourses have this in common), master narratives may not necessarily unlock the meaning of lesser narratives, and, instead, knowledge is seen as an endless series of narratives, great and small, linear and fragmented, stretching on into an alternately meaningful and meaningless, heterogeneous infinity. After all, when you think about the appeal of textuality as the very thing you can never get rid of, or live without, you can't help but wonder whether the meaning of the story (or the novel, the film, or the song) was ever the point at all.

Nevertheless, I would like to persist in arguing in favor of modernist readings and the continuing usefulness of master narratives such as history and psychoanalysis. During the Society of Cinema Studies panel, I tried to suggest one partial modernist reading. First, as we all know, I said, in established practices of feminist film criticism (as in the field of feminist art history) race is generally ignored or trivialized in the form of the "race/gender/class mantra." But even more disturbing, I said, is that—both before the past few years when race wasn't being mentioned in feminist film discourse and now that it is being mentioned in the work of Mary Ann Doane, E. Ann Kaplan, Sandy Flitterman-Lewis, Judith Butler, Jane Gaines, and Lucy Fischer—I still continue to have the feeling that "I" (the "I" of my subjectivity as an individual black woman who is too dark to "pass for white") am still being ignored or erased or silenced.

Moreover, I continued, I suspect that as in the construction of the famous Freudian reference to "a child is being beaten," it might be a good idea to acknowledge that this effect may have many points of origin, some of them internal to individual/collective black female psychology. It is also important to remember that the process of being silenced or erased or ignored is not some analytical abstraction. After all, I said, it makes "me" angry, so angry that "I" usually can't speak rationally or honestly about it, especially at those moments when it is occurring. And if you remember that in this case the "I" is probably not just I alone, then you begin to realize that this blockage may represent a massive obstacle to black women and white women's becoming reconciled to one another's positions.

In this construction, I pointed out that I was well aware that I was leaving out everybody else except white and black women. Questions arising from interactions among white women and other kinds of women of color, other kinds of women of color with black women, and women of color from different places among themselves were all the more complicated. Differences of sexuality and class also wouldn't make it any easier.

But what I neglected to do was to provide the problem of being silenced, erased, or ignored with a historical context because, of course, I no longer view myself as silenced, erased, or ignored. I was speaking then, at the Society of Cinema Studies, about being silenced in the past, about coming to understand how my own rage had silenced me to such a degree that even when I was speaking the loudest, I was not really saying what I needed to say.

Moreover, to dichotomize visibility and invisibility, or voice and silence, in such a way as to suggest that the former inevitably leads to power and the latter inevitably leads to disempowerment is perhaps misleading. While I think that visibility and voice are important strategies for emergent discourses, invisibility and silence (as in, for instance, working behind the scenes or foregrounding the talents of others) can be useful strategies, too. I hardly need to add that structures of domination can be both invisible and silent and yet quite as powerful.[5] The key thing is not to forget that voice and visibility are being employed as metaphors for empowerment, and that invisibility and silence are metaphors for lack, repression, and powerlessness.

So here "I" was, then, at the feminist art history conference in 1990, or on the feminist film criticism panel in New Orleans in 1993, and "I" was in possession of one legitimately rational argument, concerning the importance of race as a historical and material reality, and one illegitimately irrational argument, concerning the importance of my own individual subjectivity as a black woman, without which neither I nor any other black woman could function as an intellectual in either the fields of art history or film criticism. The rational voice spoke while the irrational voice twisted the knife in the wound. By virtue of entering either profession, I was immediately faced with the adult job of defining both race and my own black female subjectivity. Did it matter then that I was not especially well equipped to do either? Moreover, was there some way that I hadn't yet recognized how to avoid personalizing these issues?

Nevertheless, at the art history conference (in 1990), I began confidently with the statement, "You're interested in Madonna," or as I might have said at the cinema studies conference in New Orleans, "Rita Hayworth and Lana Turner" (in 1993) "because they are white, not because they are interesting. You're not interested in Tina Turner" (in 1990) or "Hattie McDaniel and Butterfly McQueen" (in 1993), "not because they aren't interesting but because they are black." In either context, the feminist art history conference in 1990 or the cinema studies conference in 1993, what manner of statement is this? Is it true? How is it true? Moreover, what did I hope to gain by saying it, besides isolation and ridicule?

I think that both statements were true, and that they start to take us to the root of the problem — specifically, that white women are often interested not in black women but, quite naturally, in themselves. Moreover, that preoccupation, as opposed to the possibility of being interested in black women, has been as much a structural aspect of a so-called female spectatorship as either the "gaze" or the objectified "image."

Granted, it is easy enough to observe that black female intellectuals aren't usually interested in Madonna, Rita Hayworth, or Lana Turner, but they usually aren't any more interested in Tina Turner, Hattie McDaniel, or Butterfly McQueen than white female intellectuals. I suspect that for black women, at least as adults, the possibility of identification, at any level, is much more problematic than it is for white women. On the other hand, "I" (the "I" who is interested in the problem of black female subjectivity) am interested in Tina Turner, Hattie McDaniel, and Butterfly McQueen because I want to understand how the hate/love feelings for them are constructed in film discourse and, by so doing, how black female self-hatred (or perhaps self-hatred is too strong a word here and I really mean something like ambivalent self-esteem) is constructed by the videos and films in which they appear.

Most important of all, I don't see the recent preoccupation in critical circles with "passing," or the construction of the nearly white or actually white actress playing the black female—as in the two versions of *Imitation of Life*—as a problematization of race that necessarily brings us anywhere near the questions I am trying to pose about black female subjectivity. Most black women are not passing and never have been able to pass or look nearly white. Hasn't the precise nature of the problem of race all these years been the impossibility of "passing" for most of us? After all, the question of black women who look white, or nearly white, or as "good" as white (for example, Lena Horne, Dorothy Dandridge, Fredi Washington) seems to pose virtually the same question in terms of spectatorship as the white woman herself. In such a context, race becomes an abstract concept that makes as little visual or linguistic difference as possible.

I am well aware, however, that passing, miscegenation, and lightness have been privileged in African American discourse as well. In novels by African Americans such as *Lola Leroy* (1890) by Frances Harper, *Contending Forces* (1900) by Pauline Hopkins, *The Autobiography of an Ex-Colored Man* (1921) by James Weldon Johnson, and *Passing* (1919) by Nella Larsen, as well as in the film *The Veiled Aristocrats* (1932) by the black filmmaker Oscar Micheaux, passing becomes a key issue in African American culture. Nor do I mean to suggest that the problems associated with passing and being light enough to pass don't constitute a valid black experience. In an essay called "Passing for White, Passing for Black," conceptual artist and philosopher Adrian Piper recounts such problems in fascinating detail.[6] A recent documentary called *A Question of Color* by black filmmaker Kathe Sandler and a book called *The Color Complex: The Politics of Skin Color among African Americans* by Kathy Russell explore these issues as well.[7]

Also, as I have become more familiar with the lives and careers of the actresses who were forced to play the mulatto roles, such as Fredi Washington, Lena Horne, Nina Mae McKinney, and Dorothy Dandridge, I come to realize the courage, fortitude, and political acumen of these women. Light versus dark was never a seamless and carefree operation in the black world, however it was read in the white world. What I do mean to suggest is that it is harder still to focus on the black woman who is in the majority but who, nevertheless, remains in the margins of discourse and representation, who is invariably viewed by many as desexualized and trapped in a maternal role.[8] In *Imitation of Life*, the woman in the margins, the so-called mammy figure played by Louise Beavers in the earlier version (directed by John Stahl) and

Juanita Moore in the Douglas Sirk version, seems to resist explication and examination. On the one hand, you may say there really is nobody there, as Sandy Flitterman-Lewis said in a recent talk about Mahalia Jackson at the end of *Imitation of Life* (1959). On the other hand, Jackson's position as a coda figure precisely mirrors the plight of black women in the dominant discourse.

On closer examination, the so-called mammy stereotype inevitably gives way to the frequent textual complexities of particular black female performers and their collaborators. In *Imitation* (1934), in a moment of homoeroticism Louise Beavers rubs Claudette Colbert's feet and speaks warmly of the pleasures of sexual satisfaction. Cloaked in such scenes, in the guise of servitude and ignorance, is the experience and worldliness of the black woman as well as the privilege and innocence of the white woman.

In regard to the work of Ethel Waters in *Cabin in the Sky* (1943) and in *Pinky* (1949), I would challenge the description by both Donald Bogle and Thomas Cripps of her as a stereotypical mammy. In *Cabin*, Waters is clearly still a hot momma, although not as thin or as young as Lena Horne, her competition. In *Pinky*, she plays an old woman, but her spiritual wisdom and beauty and her quick-witted intelligence give her as much dignity as the white character played by Ethel Barrymore, who is ostensibly her employer but has become more of a friend. While *Imitation of Life*, *Cabin*, and *Pinky* are not black films in the sense of having been produced under total black control, neither are they really films about black people. These films, nevertheless, incorporate significant traces of a potentially subversive black talent, dance, and musical performance. These landmark performances by black women also indicate a slowly shifting terrain for visual representations of black women. The proof of the pudding, it seems to me, is that such films were the exceptions rather than the rule, and that despite their financial success, production of "problem" films and black musicals never progressed to the next logical step but were somehow squelched during the McCarthy era.

Such films as *Imitation* are still films about conventional and tradition-bound stereotypes of black life, about how white people feel about black people. *Imitation of Life* only engages with black female subjectivity, in any real sense, at the level at which Louise Beavers or Juanita Moore (much less successfully in the 1959 version) manage to assert themselves as actors, or at the level of Mahalia Jackson's brilliant solo at the end. Needless to say, *Cabin*, cast in the classic Hollywood musical mold, does not get much closer to the realities of black life.

One may argue that classic Hollywood is not about real white people either. I would argue that there is an additional dimension to the unreality and reification of Hollywood representations of race. As Stuart Hall explained at the Black Popular Culture conference in 1991, "what replaces invisibility is a kind of carefully regulated, segregated visibility." That statement applies especially well to black women in popular culture, even as it also applies to the configuration of images of white women, black men, and everybody else in the dominant discourse.

In this regard, I would like to pose a further question: what if the black female subject is constructed much like the white female subject? Or what if the similarities between the psychoanalytic construction of the black female subject and that of the white female subject are greater than the dissimilarities? Moreover, if you accept the thesis that psychoanalytic film criticism proposes of a closed Eurocentric circuit in Hollywood cinema in which a white male-dominated "gaze" is on one end and the white female "image" is on the other end, what happens to the so-called black female subject? Does she even exist? And if she does, how does she come into existence?

Helpful to me in thinking about the problems suggested here has been the writing of black female conceptual artist and theorist Lorraine O'Grady in "Olympia's Maid: Reclaiming Black Female Subjectivity" and in her unpublished "Postscript," and the writing of black feminist art historian Judith Wilson in "Getting Down to Get Over: Romare Bearden's Use of Pornography and the Problem of the Black Female Body in Afro-U.S. Art."[9] In looking at the status of the black female nude in art history, which is handled very differently from the white female nude, O'Grady insists that the only constant in Euro-American theoretical analysis has been "the black body's location at the extreme," whereas Wilson remarks on how black fine artists have also avoided the black female nude because of its negative associations, perhaps with the sexual exploitation of slavery.

O'Grady, who says her goal is to "deal with what Gayatri Spivak has called the 'winning back of the position of the questioning subject'" is thus prompted to suggest that "the black female's body needed less to be rescued from the masculine gaze than it had to be sprung from an historic script surrounding her with signification while at the same time, and not paradoxically, erasing her completely."[10] While I think that O'Grady is onto something here when she suggests that the issue for black women is one of establishing subjectivity, I haven't always been able to see the notion of a black female subject as separate from the notion of a white female subject. Would this mean, after all, that there were Asian, Indian, and African female subjects as well? Is subjectivity really divided by race, nationality, ethnicity? I don't think so. I'm not saying that subjectivity isn't divided. I think it probably is divided in some manner, but I'm not sure that it can therefore be viewed as historically and materially specific, and that it divides easily by ethnicity, nationality, or any other constructed or natural rubric. Certainly, "spectatorship" as it is constructed by the dominant discourse does not.

On the other hand, things like class allegiances and identity, sexuality, and experience seem to make a profound difference in how the female subject is constituted visually and how those images circulate. Even more significant here is O'Grady's suggestion that the status of the white female "image," or the objectification of the white female body, is part of the circuit of subjectivity for women. In other words, although the white male "gaze" (or the gaze of the dominant culture) objectifies and, therefore, dehumanizes the white woman, in fact, that objectification also implicitly verifies the crucial role white women play in the process or circuit of spectatorship. In other words, the process of objectification also inadvertently humanizes as well a built-in advantage that is then denied to women of color in general, but to the despised (or desired) black woman in particular.

So the problem of white female subjectivity is one of reversing the terms somehow, or reversing the connection or the hierarchy between male and female, whereas in the case of the black female body, or the body of the other, the connection is to a third, much less explored level in the hierarchy, the sphere of the abject, which includes, as Sander Gilman and Michel Foucault have pointed out, the pathological.[11]

As such, reversal is no cure and cannot take place. Black female subjectivity remains unimaginable in the realm of the symbolic. O'Grady's approach as an artist seems to be to attempt to upgrade the status of the black female nude, or at least to get us to think about how and why the black female nude is devalued. Can you imagine Louise Beavers in a sexy dress in *Imitation of Life*? And yet Bessie Smith played just such a role in *Saint Louis Blues*, not to mention in life.

Lately, I have been working on my mother Faith Ringgold's series of story quilts, *The French Collection*, in which she illustrates the adventures of a protagonist named Willa Marie, born in 1903, who goes to Paris to become an artist and who alternates working as an artist's model with her own painting (true of many female artists). In the process, the subsequent images toy with this circuit of subjectivity that O'Grady proposes as so crucial, for Willa Marie is configured as both subject and object by the text and the images.

In a multicultural context, the response of many is to historicize the question of subjectivity (which I believe is crucial as well) and, in the process, dispense with the synchronic explanations of psychoanalytic complexity and abstraction. But, then, how do we account for the play of the unconscious in black cultural production and in the everyday lives of black people? The play of the unconscious roughly refers to the highly ambivalent relation of plans to practice, and stated intentions to unconscious motivations, in African American cultural and social life.

I ask the question about the unconscious precisely because of the problem of interpreting the sexual and gender politics of recent mainstream black cinema. Clearly, the construction of spectatorship in *Malcolm X* cannot be wholly explained by relying on empirical data. We can guess that the construction of gender and sexuality in Spike Lee's *Malcolm X* has more to do with Lee's own issues around gender as well as cinematic traditions in the specularization of women's bodies, and black women's bodies, in Hollywood cinema than it has to do with Malcolm X's life. Moreover, there is apparently the mediation of how Malcolm X also fictionalized his own life in his *Autobiography*, which provides the documentary basis for the film.[12] Gender and sexuality were also very problematic in Malcolm X's self-conceptualization.

On the one hand, regardless of the specific problem of interpreting *Malcolm X*, it is no longer surprising that Spike Lee, as well as other black male filmmakers, succumbed to reinscribing precisely the same hegemonic fantasies about the nature of sexual difference as other filmmakers in the dominant discourse of Hollywood cinema. From the perspective of the question of what is happening to the real, historically determined black female spectator, there is little here to interfere with her conventional construction. But from the perspective of the question of what is happening in terms of the construction of the subject both internal to the discourse of the film and internal to her unconscious psychological processes as a viewer, I suspect that a complicated series of changes is occurring. On the theory that the Eurocentric circuit of white male "gaze" and white female "object" has a psychic cost, variations in that system surely make a difference, but what difference?

Meanwhile, *Daughters of the Dust*, a film by independent black filmmaker Julie Dash, attempts to provide a corrective to the *Boyz*. The film deliberately sets out to tackle the problem of upgrading the black female image and gets bogged down in excessive visuality. Yet again, something crucial has to be occurring on the level of "the hypothetical point of address of the film as a discourse." After all, if it makes no difference how a film deploys its black bodies, why have they been so relentlessly excluded in the past?

Of course, the important thing about all of this is that some of the rules regarding the conventional Hollywood characterization of the black female are finding their way into recently released black films. Black film theorist Ed Guerrero, at a recent Society of Cinema Studies panel on blaxploitation film, referred to the most recent crop as following a credo of ghettocentricity.

And yet the opportunity still exists in the examination of the work of these or any other black filmmaker for thinking about the black women's bodies in the margins, for reformulating notions of spectatorship to encompass the impact of "race" on subjectivity.

Originally published in Devoney Looser and E. Ann Kaplan, eds., *Generations: Academic Feminists in Dialogue* (Minneapolis: University of Minnesota Press, 1997).

Notes

1. I am not accusing *Camera Obscura* of racism. Cinema and communications studies are still largely white fields, and the reasons for this (racism is only one of many) originate at a much deeper level in the structure of our cultural arrangements than the particular racial views of any set of academic editors. Forced to make a selection of black feminist intellectuals engaged in debates around female spectatorship in 1989, there weren't a lot of possible candidates, although I might have asked Valerie Smith, Judith Wilson, Coco Fusco, Hortense Spillers, Mae Henderson, Lorraine O'Grady, and myself, as well as other black feminists already engaged in visual studies of one kind or another, or in psychoanalysis.

2. Bobo, *Camera Obscura* 11 (1989).

3. Ibid.

4. Years of therapy have been crucial in helping to finally dispel, or at least hold at bay in critical academic situations, the paralyzing stage fright I used to experience. I think that stage fright had to do with many things. Race was only one of them.

5. See Peggy Phelan, *Unmarked: The Politics of Performance* (New York: Routledge, 1993).

6. Adrian Piper, "Passing for White, Passing for Black," *Transition* 58 (1993): 4–32.

7. Kathe Sandler, director, *A Question of Color* (California Newsreel, 1993); Kathy Russell, *The Color Complex: The Politics of Skin Color among African Americans* (New York: Harcourt Brace Jovanovich, 1992).

8. In a talk at the CUNY Graduate School in 1993, E. Ann Kaplan greatly contributed to my understanding of how the maternal melodrama serves to construct the black female in film.

9. Lorraine O'Grady, "'Olympia's Maid': Reclaiming Black Female Subjectivity," *Afterimage* 2 (1991); Lorraine O'Grady, "Postscript to 'Olympia's Maid': Reclaiming Black Female Subjectivity," unpublished manuscript; and Judith Wilson, "Getting Down to Get Over: Romare Bearden's Use of Pornography and the Problem of the Black Female Body in Afro-U.S. Art," in Dent, *Black Popular Culture*.

10. O'Grady, "Postscript."

11. Sander Gilman, *Difference and Pathology: Stereotypes of Sexuality, Race, and Madness* (Ithaca, N.Y.: Cornell University Press, 1985); Michel Foucault, *Discipline and Punish: The Birth of the Prison*, trans. Alan Sheridan (New York: Vintage, 1979); and Michel Foucault, *The Order of Things: An Archaeology of the Human Sciences* (New York: Vintage, 1970).

12. Malcolm X, *The Autobiography of Malcolm X* (New York: Ballantine, 1991).

54.

Bamboozled: The Archive

A crucial development early in the twentieth century in the history of black performance was when stereotypical images went from derisive drawings to photographs or, after the mid-1890s, into film footage of actual blacks engaged in the perennially American performance of blackness in part for a white audience but increasingly, as well, for a black audience.[1] Whereas the dominant (European derivative) culture increasingly chose the option of using set designs and orchestral accompaniment throughout the nineteenth and the twentieth century for their cultural presentations, since slavery times black performers of the masses had always used our faces, hands, feet and bodies for accompaniment as well as illustration.[2]

The black body is, itself, and continues to be, Afro-America's (and the African Diaspora's) greatest work of visual art — conventionally understood through movement and dress, but not solely confined therein. For movement and dress are just the tip of the proverbial iceberg (forced underground by the prohibitions of slavery), which also includes a diasporic visual tradition vaster, deeper, and more modern than any ever dreamed of, to be found only sparingly in the museums to date, but rather within what collectors William and Paul Arnett have called the "African American vernacular art of the South," in the graveyards, junkyards, and quilting bees below the Mason-Dixon Line, but that's a story for another day.[3]

Today, we'll stick to black performance, a tar baby if ever there was one.

This pointing to the depths and vastness of an African American visual tradition, in order to contend with a lack of access to visual resources and materials, is, I believe, what black performers have always done — although they have been frequently misunderstood (and have just as often misunderstood their own motives) as racially derogatory and lacking in self-esteem. Think of the often neglected work of Bert Williams, the celebrated black comedian of the teens and the twenties who is cited visually multiple times in Spike Lee's *Bamboozled*, including in the form of one of the few surviving examples (*A Natural Born Gambler*, 1916) of a series of silent motion pictures he starred in. But is Williams's rare contribution to diasporic culture fully given credit where credit is due? I don't think so.

Bamboozled takes on the hundred-year-plus history of blackface minstrelsy but doesn't seem as clear as I would like about who did what to whom. But filmmaker Spike Lee is not alone in his lack of clarity. He shares the field with acres of other learned negroes as well. The white schools don't teach because they don't know our cultural history. Because most of us don't know it ourselves, who would they learn it from and where would they learn it? When the *Bamboozled* panel was staged at New York University, Spike Lee's own alma mater with an audience full of his heirs apparent — presumably apprentice and would-be filmmakers, actors, writers, and performers of various stripes — the scene was for me, as a recent graduate of the Ph.D. program there in Cinema Studies, tinged with a bitter irony.

Apart from the occasional class in Africana Studies, or the Gallatin School, or Donald Bogle's classes in the Film Program, or Robert Stam's and Ed Guerrero's classes in Cinema Studies, or Andrew Ross's classes in American Studies, New York University doesn't teach much African diasporic culture of the North American variety. Performance Studies doesn't usually celebrate or interrogate either Bert Williams or Richard Pryor. As such, *Bamboozled* might serve as an apt contemporary illustration of the failure of all parties to comprehend the stellar significance of black performance. It is quite simply the reason why we made it and the survivors of the Amistad didn't.[4]

Bamboozled is in some ways a visual feast for anyone who has paid any attention consistently to black visual culture and black performance history, although Lee's shot at the banality and corruption of commercial TV is a cheap and easy one. With one hundred TV channels, DVD, the Internet, rap, spoken-word, theater of various stripes, satellite dishes, CD-ROMs, and god knows what else to choose from for information and entertainment, I no longer have time to watch commercial TV and know very few people who do. While this may be a somewhat elitist view, nevertheless, as a culture I think we are moving in the direction of individually calibrated entertainment (i.e., TiVo), not more homogeneous opiate of the masses.

To tell this story one more time for those who haven't seen it or haven't heard it, *Bamboozled* is Spike Lee's most recent and not particularly successful movie. It's star and alter-ego is Damon Wayans who plays the uptight Pierre Delacroix, black TV producer and Harvard graduate who must work under the obnoxiously and arrogantly white Mr. Dunwitty (Michael Rapaport), senior vice-president of the network, who insists upon his superior knowledge of the black vernacular based upon his familiarity with gangsta rap and the like. Inspired by two street performers who work the corner outside studio headquarters (tap dancer Savion Glover and comedian Tommy Davidson), Wayans comes up with a plan to out-Dunwitty Dunwitty: a blackface minstrel variety show set in a watermelon patch and starring the street performers renamed Mantan and Sleep and Eat.

In typical Spike Lee fashion, Delacroix's motivations for doing this are never made clear and vary incoherently. Delacroix is essentially a comic wooden stereotype of an Ivy League educated, upper-class Negro designed by someone who has very little comprehension of this character type. Those who believe that self-esteem is a matter of racial identity (I am not one of them) would say that Delacroix has a self-esteem problem. In my view, his greatest trouble is that he was poorly written.

The thin looking blown-up DVD shots wander around aimlessly throwing out provocative images at a dazzling rate with little explanation. One of these series is provided by the extensive black memorabilia of derogatory dolls, toys, sheet music images, etc., which inexplicably proliferates in Delacroix's office as the plot thickens and the minstrel show becomes a massive commercial TV success. Another oft repeated image is Mantan or Sleep and Eat burning the cork, smearing it on their faces and adding the red lipstick, as though each time it was metaphorically setting the race further and further back. The show's routines draw upon some famous predecessors, in particular the original of which can be seen in the black cast film *Stormy Weather* (1943). The title itself refers simultaneously to a racially derogatory painting by artist John Henry Michaels and a sound bite from a speech performed by Denzel Washington in Spike Lee's *Malcolm X*. All in all, *Bamboozled* is an archive of black performance history and visual culture, so tightly scrambled and compacted it is virtually inscrutable.

Jada Pinkett is, nevertheless, a breath of fresh air as Delacroix's assistant until the muddled plot really kicks in. Another really fun scenario concerns the Mau Maus, the pseudo black power rap group featuring Mos Def, who plays Pinkett's brother and calls himself Big Black Africa, as well as other reasonably well known rappers (Canibus, DJ Scratch, MUMS, McSerch, who is white, Charli Baltimore, who is the only female). The performers who audition for the show and don't make it are another source of great pleasure, which, however, comes to naught.

Of course, the punishment for black self-hatred has to be the ultimate. Sleep and Eat jumps ship before things become too intense but Mantan is murdered by the Mau Maus on commercial TV via some kind of Internet feed. The Mau Maus, excepting the white one who pleads to be killed along with the rest, are then murdered, presumably by the police. Then Jada goes after Delacroix and shoots him, presumably for getting Mantan killed. Because I think the connections between black performance history and black visual culture are rich and important, the film was tremendously frustrating to watch.

The history of black performance is the history of American culture. Notice I did not say black culture but rather *American* culture, and this is right where the problem pops up and never dies because there just ain't enough American culture to divvy up into black and white (not to even bother about Asian-American and Italian-American and Native-American-American and all that) because as some of the wiser heads among us have hinted, whatever meaningful cultural separations there were between "black" and "white" culture in the long lost, long-forgotten first two centuries of North American slavery, they ceased to significantly differentiate racially as far as cultural production. There was, and still is, Jim Crow housing and schools and politics yes, but Jim Crow culture? Not. Those centuries—for which there is no photography and little material culture whatsoever—are remembered only in the rhythms of our bodies, our voices, and our faces. Everything there is for us to know about all this was deeply encoded long ago through culture. The computer folk might say encrypted.

The trouble with blackface minstrelsy remains for many black cultural historians that it is assumed to be the paradigmatic instance of an inauthentic, racist, and hostile representation of blackness. Scholars can argue endlessly about the degree to which such performers were or were not, in fact, influenced by direct observations of blacks in their cultural milieu in the North or the South, and/or the degree to which their intentions were good or bad. But if, indeed, blackface minstrelsy epitomizes inauthenticity, what did become of the authentic narratives and cultural artifacts, material and existential, of the slaves in the postbellum period by the time of the early decades of the twentieth century when film and commercial culture had really begun? How were these "knowledges" of the former slaves collected, and disseminated, and what, if any relevance, did this process have to the formulation of black images and race-based narratives in film and other media?

Following directly in the wake of the popularity of blackface minstrelsy from as early as the 1820s onward, there was, as well, an emerging fascination with other kinds of black cultural production. Skepticism remains appropriate, given the widespread proliferation of black performance styles during this period and all subsequent periods. Invariably, whatever relative authenticity there may have been in the first appearance, or public performance, of a mode of cultural expression, its "authenticity" quickly became a vanishing point, just before its incorporation into the sphere of popular performance practices, both on the stage and in the streets. By as early as the late 1860s, when it came to black culture, surely no one knew for sure what came from where.

Another verifiable instance of this kind of borrowing back and forth from authentic "folk" culture to popular "stage" culture was the case of the Jubilee Singers. In 1871, the Jubilee Singers began to tour the country and the world doing concerts to raise money to build Fisk University. I won't rehearse the narrative of how these songs were translated into standard Western musical compositions and operatic form, whereupon the vernacular tradition in black music went underground and resurfaced via gospel music and the sanctified churches.

Moreover, by virtue of a process now lost to historical memory, all sorts of imitation Jubilee Singer groups sprang up almost immediately. The endlessly proliferating Tom companies of the period invariably had one or more "Jubilee Singers" scenes, to the point where the term must have been virtually meaningless by the turn of the century. In a review of a performance by the Hyer Sisters Company in the *New York Tribune*, in late October of the same year, the reviewer said of the two black sisters who headed the troupe that they were "by no means mere 'Jubilee' singers . . ."

Both Mark Twain and Joel Chandler Harris were significant innovators in the use of black dialect in mainstream American literature. Charles Chesnutt, Paul Lawrence Dunbar, Frances Harper, and Pauline Hopkins, all somewhat less known now and then, should be remembered for their usually more sensitive and accurate use of dialect as a tool for exploring character rather than shutting it down. Whereas Dunbar was really famous at the turn of the century for his poetry in dialect, Chesnutt, whose writing was somewhat more politically astute, had greater difficulty surviving professionally as a writer. I have no doubt, nonetheless, that Chesnutt, Dunbar, Hopkins, and Harper were deliberately revising and critiquing Harris's and his imitators in their own work, just as the silent race films of the '20s, including those of Oscar Micheaux, and the painters of the Harlem Renaissance were commenting on the oeuvres of Chesnutt and Dunbar.[5] In terms of reinforcing the link between orality, performance, and visual culture, it should be noted that many literary and musical texts with racial subject matter were often heavily illustrated. Dunbar, in particular among the black authors, was famous for his so-called "Christmas" volumes, which featured his dialect poems illustrated with photographs produced by members of the Hampton Institute Camera Club. A combination of student and faculty photographers took many rural scenes of surrounding Hampton, Virginia. During the early and middle years of segregated black schools in the South, photography was a particular preoccupation, as was visual media in general.[6]

Yet the really crucial thing to remember when thinking about Joel Chandler Harris's use of the framing device of Uncle Remus, which appears to be the earliest in this link-chain of minstrelsy type images post-Reconstruction (of course, Harriet Beecher Stowe's stoical and passionately serious Uncle Tom is his obvious precursor) is that it is the first formal and literary inscription of a process that must have been widespread: that of listening to what the former slaves had to say. I would imagine that the former slaves were everywhere in the South, growing older, and increasingly visible as the century wore on. Whether you sought them out or not, whether you solicited their narratives or not, whether they would even talk or not (my great-great grandmother Susie Shannon would not talk about slavery at all though she lived to be 110), they were living embodiments of a bloody history nevertheless, and everything and everybody around them must have been haunted by a palpable sense of the memories imprinted in their eyes, their faces, and their bodies.

Just as resulting scenarios of who the slaves had been, and who the freed blacks would be, were unfolding on the popular stage (frequently in segregated theaters), at world's fairs, in music, literature, in illustration, and so on, at the very same time a young anthropologist named Franz Boas was developing a theory of cultural relativism that would eventually sound a death knell for the evolutionisms of racial hierarchies. At the turn of the century, Boas "effectively directed the anthropology of race away from theories of evolution and guided it to a consensus that African Americans, Native Americans, and other people of color were not racially inferior and possessed unique and historically specific cultures . . . Furthermore, one could not project a value of higher or lower on these cultures—cultures were relative."[7] Of course, it took another fifty years for these ideas to accumulate any social resonance among white citizens.

But the crucial thing for this discussion, as Lee Baker writes in *From Sav-*

age to Negro: Anthropology and the Construction of Race, 1896–1954, is the emergence of an interdisciplinary African American Studies, a cornerstone of which was composed of ethnographies of ordinary blacks, including ex-slaves, both North and South. The relevant group of intellectuals included most prominently Carter G. Woodson, Arthur Schomburg, Rayford Logan, Ralph Bunche, E. Franklin Frazier, Charles Johnson, Kelly Miller, Zora Neale Hurston, Arthur B. Fauset, Katherine Dunham, and St. Clair Drake, but there were many, many others white and black, male and female.[8]

I like to call it the archive. Ishmael Reed called it "the text" in *Mumbo Jumbo*. *Bamboozled* was steadily bumping up against the archive that most of us don't even know we have that is buried in the libraries and museums and store rooms of black churches and schools throughout the South. Some of it is in state and local historical societies. You never know where or when you might luck up on some it. For instance, one of Micheaux's early films was found in Belgium. Some of the pages of the archive are grim. James Allen, the picker, brought some of it out when he published *Without Sanctuary: Lynching Photography in America*.[9] Edward Ball let loose some of it when he went South to trace his family's history as slaveholders in South Carolina and ended up tracking the ancestors of hundreds of former Ball slaves back to Africa.[10] On the other hand, some of it is just moldering away right under our noses in the basements and attics of our nearest and dearest.

As Baker emphasizes of the movement of black studies to decipher the archive, which began in the '20s, "The anthropological analysis of folklore provided evidence for their claim that the rich and complex traditions and music of African-Americans was the US's most distinctive cultural gift to the rest of the world."[11] Ultimately this project led to the collecting of the narratives of the former slaves in the '20s by students at Howard and Fisk, pioneered in part by a black woman anthropologist named J. Ophelia Settle, who taught at Howard University, although little is known of her today. It wasn't until the '30s, in the wake of the Depression, that the WPA made the collection of narratives from the former slaves themselves (now all but dead) a national priority.

Nevertheless, traditions and discourses of evolutionism, eugenics, and the crude "white supremacy" efforts of local and regional southern politics and the mob, versus the emerging intellectual discourses of the New Negro and cultural relativism, and everything in between, composed competing perspectives on the world that all the early filmmakers and artists concerned with the portrayal of race could draw upon. While some white male film-makers and artists were much more successful and prolific in the dissemination of their work in the teens and the '20s than were black male filmmakers and artists, both camps were purveyors of a newly technologized popular culture, and both in different ways were rooted in the iconoclasms of the Western frontier, where real men made their own laws.[12] The strategic use of the menu of available black stereotypes—for the minority of producers who were even interested—were the terms upon which the two would launch their opposing campaigns in the contemporary culture wars over the stories of the slaves and the former slaves, and thus in turn, the founding narrative of this nation.

Bamboozled tries to tell the story in the present, through the narrative of shallow Pierre Delacroix but the story, like the archive, is about the past.

Originally published in part in *Renaissance Noire* 1, no. 2 (1997): 162–176.

Notes

1. Some of the films, partially referenced by Lee's *Bamboozled* and some of which no longer survive in viewable prints are *Watermelon Eating Contest*, Edison, 1896; *Watermelon Feast*, American Mutograph and Biograph, 1896; *New Watermelon Contest*, Edison, 1900; *The Watermelon Patch*, Edison, 1905; other actualities of this genre were *A Morning Bath*, Edison, 1896; *Dancing Darkies*, Edison, 1896; *Buffalo Exposition* (plantation scenes), 1901; *Jamaican Travelogues*, 1901. Lee uses a clip from *Laughing Ben*, American Mutograph and Biograph, 1902. Other early films particularly relevant to uses of blackface minstrelsy would be *Interrupted Crap Game*, Selig, 1903; *A Scrap in Black and White*, Edison, 1903; *The Negro's Revenge*, Pathes-Freres, 1906; *The Pickaninny Dance* (from "The Passing Show," Edison, 1894; *Elsie Jones, No. 1* "America's greatest "Buck" dancer," 1894; *Elsie Jones, No. 2*, Edison, 1894; *James Grundy (No. 1)/Buck and Wing Dance* from "South Before the War"; *James Grundy (No. 2), Cake Walk; Grundy and Frint* (Breakdown from "South Before the War"), Edison, 1895; *Ballyhoo Cakewalk*, Edison, 1903; *Darky Cakewalk*, ND, 1903. See Charles Musser's *Edison Motion Pictures, 1890–1900: An Annotated Filmography* (Washington: Smithsonian Institution Press, 1997); *Before the Nickelodeon: Porter and the Edison Manufacturing Company* (Berkeley: University of California, 1991); *The Emergence of Cinema: The American Screen to 1907* (Berkeley: University of California, 1990).
2. See BET's *Comic View*, Spike Lee's *Kings of Comedy*, or any of the old *Def Jam Comedy* shows for contemporary examples of such pro-active performance.
3. This really is a story of its own, which includes the work of such artists as my mom, Faith Ringgold, who inhabits the world of the museums but who still thinks of herself as a messenger from the fields (as Amiri Baraka once dubbed her) through and through, as well as the so-called "naives" and "primitives" or unschooled artists featured in Paul and William Arnett's multivolume collection *Souls Grown Deep: African American Vernacular Art of the South*, vol. 1 (Atlanta: Tinwood Books, 2000).
4. See Manthia Diawara's brilliant *In Search of Africa* (Cambridge, Mass.: Harvard University Press, 1998) for further explication of the profound singularity of African American

modernism. When the head of the Amistad rebellion got back to his village in Africa, it had been decimated by slave catchers.

5. Of course, the link that is always emphasized is with Thomas Dixon's novels *The Leopard's Spots* and *The Klansman* and D. W. Griffith's *Birth of a Nation*, but ultimately Twain and Harris were much more profoundly influential than either Dixon, clearly a madman, or Griffith, best remembered by film scholars for his hundreds of other, wiser film works.

6. Richard J. Powell and Jock Reynolds, eds., *To Conserve a Legacy: American Art from Historically Black Colleges and Universities* (Cambridge, Mass.: MIT Press, 1999). See the section on "Conservation and Photographic Archives," including articles on "The Hampton Camera Club," "Preserving the Cyanotype," and "Chronicling Tuskegee in Photographs." My hypothesis about Dunbar's Christmas books is that they served not only as suitable reading for children but also for the many still nearly illiterate adults in the rural South who were still struggling to learn to read.

7. Lee Baker, *From Savage to Negro: Anthropology and the Construction of Race, 1896–1954* (Berkeley, Calif.: University of California Press, 1998),100.

8. Ibid.

9. Ibid., 138–42. Also browse through the chapters in Alain Locke, ed., *The New Negro* (New York: Atheneum 1977), and Nancy Cunard, ed., *Negro: An Anthology* (New York: Continuum, 1934; 1996), in order to get some idea of the dimensions and preoccupations of this discourse.

10. James Allen et al., *Without Sanctuary: Lynching Photography in America* (Santa Fe, N.M.: Twin Palms Publisher, 2000). See also Anne P. Rice, ed., *Witnessing Lynching: American Writers Respond* (New Brunswick, N.J.: Rutgers University Press, 2003).

11. Edward Ball, *Slaves in the Family* (New York: Ballantine Books, 1999).

12. Baker, *From Savage to Negro*, 144.

INDEX

Abolitionist movement, 155

Abortion, 283; right to, 203, 298

Actors Equity Association, 250–51

Ad Hoc Women, 207. *See also* Lippard, Lucy

Aesthetics, 11; Christian right and, 213; criteria for, 190; identity and, 260; racism and, 190; separatist, 251

Affirmative action: need for, 181; opposition to, 299

African American artists, 77, 200, 239; Basquiat, Jean-Michel, 187, 199, 206; Bearden, Romare, 115, 349; Billops, Camille, 191; Birch, Willie, 193 n.1; Chase-Riboud, Barbara, 207; Colescott, Robert, 204–5; Conwill, Houston, 200; "The Decade Show" and, 260; Edwards, Mel, 191; exclusion of, 260; female, genius and, 188–89; and greatness, 188–89; Green, Renee, 191, 195, 200, 206; Hammons, David, 187, 200, 214; Harris, Lyle Ashton, 200, 204; Jones, Seitu, 191; Ligon, Glen, 200; market forces and, 213; McCauley, Robbie, 205; O'Grady, Lorraine, 191; Pindell, Howardena, 194 n.5, 207; Piper, Adrian, 187, 200, 214; public funding and, 203; public opinion of, 184–94; Puryear, Martin, 187; Ringgold, Faith, 191, 199; Saar, Alison, 207; Saar, Betye, 207; Samba, Cheri, 187; Simpson, Corinne, 200; Simpson, Lorna, 200; Weems, Carrie Mae, 200, 206; Williams, Pat Ward, 200, 206; Willis, Deborah, 206; Wilson, Fred, 200

African American body: in rap videos, 135–36; nudes, 190, 202, 204–6, 210, 262 n.2

African American characters in film, 130, 216, 281

African American comedians: Foxx, Redd, 136; Mabley, Moms, 136; Markham, Pigmeat, 136; Murphy, Eddie, 136; Pryor, Richard, 136

African American comedy: influence on rap, 136; oral tradition and, 136; sexual references in, 136

African American culture, 196, 275–85, 369; "critical signification" and, 245; development of, 244; discourses of, 371; matriphobia and, 280; modernism and, 269–70; mother worship and, 280; nationalism and, 291; nomadic principles and, 245; popular, 185; poststructuralist theory and, 169; problem of the visual in, 224–25; professionals and, 294; white supremacist versions of, 224

African American entertainers: in black entertainment history, 271; blackface minstrelsy, subversion of, 271–72; Lucas, Sam, 272; marginalization of, 281; *Tom* companies, 269, 271–72

African American female(s): actresses, 353–54; black female slave, 179; blues poetry and, 147; cultural participation of, 280; critical discourse and, 180; exclusion from academic life, 180; family structure and, 279–80; feminism, resistance to, 147; heroines and, 266; in Hollywood film, 130, 131, 223–37; images of in popular culture, 264–74; literature by, 179–80; myth of, 279–80; Orientalist imagery of, 269; photographers, 206; poets, 147; on prime-time television, 186; rape of, 258; rap music and, 134–37; as rappers, 136; service to white community, 280; single mothers, stereotyping of, 215–16; silencing of, 136, 170; stereotypes as "Aunt Jemima," 207; stereotypes as "coons," 227–28; stereotypes as maids, 131–32, 228, 231–32; stereotypes as "mammies," 275–85; tragic mulattas, 270–71; textual representations of, 281; whores/good girls, 216. *See also* Feminism, African American; women of color

African American film: African American directors and, 186; African American literature and, 169; filmmakers, 200,

208; homosexuality in, 208; independent black-cast, 231–32; problem of black visuality in, 186; "race" films, 231; unconscious, and the, 282. *See also* Films

African American history, 179–80; oral tradition of, 5–6

African American intellectuals: conservatism of, 244; discourse and, 192; exclusion of women, 180; political correctness and, 198; as public intellectuals, 156; women, intellectual contributions of, 180

African American literary criticism, 181, 198; black feminism and, 180–81; homosexuality and, 192–93

African American literature, 290–96; innovations in, 295; ghettoization, threat of, 180; nineteenth-century, 290; political motivation for, 295; trauma in, 279; by women, 179–83

African American male(s): fatherhood in film, 216–17; homicide rates, 215; homosexuality and, 302–3; incarceration rates of, 134, 215; rap music and, 134–37; misogyny of in rap videos, 135; stereotypes of, 226–27; underclass, 128, 299

African American masculinity, and rap music, 135; Shaharazad Ali's view of, 135

African American music, 13–16, 22–23, 98–99, 192

African American politics, 181; Barry, Marion, and, 252; conservative, 185; and the Left, 185; nationalist, 185; Sharpton, Al, and, 169, 298, 300

African Americans: anti-Semitism and, 211; in *Black Nativity*, 162; Christian fantasies of, 131; conservative, 185, 300; as culture producers, 245; dominant culture, relation to, 245; drop-out rates of, 144; education of, 144, 246; family structure of, 279, 283; in film, 130, 131; illiteracy and, 134; middle class, 185;

poverty and, 134; on prime time television, 127; and psychoanalysis, 191–92; self-hatred, 200; standardized tests and, 144, 293; trauma and, 279; white images and, 200. *See also* Black images

African American studies, 83, 181–82, 292–93; black popular culture studies, 197; importance of women's movement to, 293

African Art, 369, 371

African diaspora, 14, 23; cultures of, 199; diasporic subject, 261; Hughes, Langston, and, 162; imperialism and, 210; rape and, 258

Afrocentrism, 16, 144, 180, 196; educational reforms, and, 144; multiculturalism and, 251

AIDS, 77, 192–93, 205, 298–99, 301–2, 379, 380, 399; capitalism and, 249; *New York Times* and, 90; visual constructions of, 193

Akomfrah, John, 23, 24, 168

Ali, Shaharazad, 140, 297–308; *A Blackman's Guide to Understanding the Blackwoman*, 136, 216, 297–308; on domestic abuse, 300; silencing of black women, 136; stereotyping of black women, 216

Angelou, Maya, 21, 147, 283; *I Know Why the Caged Bird Sings*, 152, 293

Anti-Semitism, overreported, 156; relation to racism, 145

Apartheid, 137

Apollo Theater, 98–99, 162

Assimilation, 144–46

Autobiography, 4, 110; in *The French Collection*, 363

Baartman, Saartje, 77, 206

Baker, Ella, 151, 360

Baker, Houston, 83, 198; on homosexuality, 192

Baker, Josephine, 76, 195, 361, 371

Baldwin, James, 103, 107, 233, 237 n.32, 359

Bambara, Toni Cade, 15, 110, 151, 159; *Black Woman*, 293; *Gorilla, My Love*, 152; *Salt Eaters*, 152, 279

Baraka, Amiri, 100, 107, 110, 123, 291, 367. *See also* Jones, Leroi

Barthes, Roland, 149, 266

Basquiat, Jean-Michel, 187, 199, 206

Bassett, Angela, 283, 353

Baudrillard, Jean, 196

Beloved, 23, 169; Crouch, Stanley on, 297; history and, 179; myth and, 179; politics of location and, 179–83; slavery and, 179. *See also* African American female(s); Black images; Morrison, Toni

Bernstein, Richard, 252, 262, 299

Birth of a Nation, 224, 226–27, 237 n.20, 273–74; *Birth of a Race*, as response to, 227–28

Black British: filmmakers, 167; theory, 168, 198

Black community theater, 162

Black feminism. *See* Feminism, African American

Black films. *See* Films

Black image: in film, 130–33, 232, 273, 275–85; Kruger, Barbara and, 185; media distortion of, 169; nudes, 190, 262 n.2; objectification in mass culture, 186; political unconscious and, 130; in popular culture, 200, 265, 275–85; in rap videos, 135; on television, 186. *See also* Black nude; Stereotypes of African Americans

Black Macho and the Myth of the Superwoman. See Books

Black nationalism, 185, 297, 300

Black nude: question of, 190; female, 206; female vs. white female nude, 190; male, 204

black physiognomy, 344; black skin, 365; negro, 367, 368; "race," 367

Black popular culture: black nationalism and, 185; conference on, 184, 198, 205, 276; hybridity of, 185

Culture: African American, 16; black, 5, 122; black visual, 115–23; high, 196; mass, 169, 196; oral representations of, 223; pop, 169

Culture wars, 202–14, 299; over race, 209

D'Amato, Alfonse, 202, 206

Dandridge, Dorothy, 120, 354

Dash, Julia, 402; *Daughters of the Dust*, 201, 353

Davis, Angela, 110, 128, 137, 159, 212, 394; *Women, Race, and Class*, 151–52; historiography of slavery, critique of, 153

Davis, Miles, 14, 128, 412

Deconstruction, 5, 198

Dee, Ruby, 217, 349

Dent, Gina, 116, 193, 198

Dia Center for the Arts, 180, 193, 197, 201, 252, 276, 380

Diawara, Manthia, 17, 25, 76, 236 n.9, 237 n.20; *Black American Cinema*, 235

Dietrich, Marlene, 412, 415

Difference: and equality, 181; institutional definitions of, 182; as process, 182

Dinkins, David, 211, 366

Douglas, Ann, 93, 94

Douglass, Frederick, 292

Drobenick, Jim, 25, 238–48

Du Bois, W. E. B., 25, 106, 196, 244, 290, 349

Dunye, Cheryl, 77; *Watermelon Woman*, 208

Durbin, Karen, 21, 106

Education: African American children and, 144, 246; curricular reform of, 144; domination and, 246; politics of, 246; representation issues and, 247; and socialization, 145

Edwards, Mel, 191, 367

EEOC (Equal Employment Opportunity Commission), 392; and Thomas-Hill hearings, 139

Ellington, Duke, 14, 21

Ellison, Ralph, 191, 366; *Invisible Man*, 236 n.7

Equal Employment Opportunity Commission (EEOC), 392; and Thomas-Hill hearings, 139

Equality: claims, 182; knowledge and, 181; need for discourse of, 181; struggle for, 181

Essentialism, 76, 77, 291

Ethnicity, 167, 238–48, 379

Euro-American modernism, 370, 372

Eurocentricism, 146, 298, 369

Evans, Sara, 394, 395

Evers, Medgar, 13, 103

Exhibits/artwork: "The Decade Show," 25, 205, 259–60; *Les Demoiselles d'Avignon*, 362, 372, 375; "Division of Labor," 392; "Exposition ethnographique de L' Afrique Occidentale," 390; "Facing History," 339–45, 348–49; "The French Collection," 76, 357, 358; *Generations in Black and White*, 384; "Harlem on My Mind," 77, 383, 384; *Menstruation Bathroom* (1972), 400; *Non, Je Ne Regrette Rien*, 379, 380; *Old '76 and Young '48* (1849), 345; *Olympia*, 195, 229; *Piss Christ* (Serrano), 202; *Political Landscape Series*, 399; *Post-Partum Document*, (1974–79), 400; *Quilting Frolic* (1813), 344; "The Sunflowers Quilting Bee at Arles," 360, 445; *Watson and the Shark* (1778), 345, 346; *Weeping Women*, 398

Family romance, African American, 186, 192

Fanon, Frantz, 191, 257; *Black Skin, White Masks*, 255, 262; psychoanalysis and, 278

Jackson, Samuel, 217, 404, 408

Jacobs, Harriet, 92, 397; *Incidents in the Life of a Slave Girl*, 139; sexual abuse and, 139

Jamaica, 1, 2, 5, 14, 23

Jameson, Fredric, 196; political unconscious, and, 146

Jefferson, Margo, 106, 115

Jeffries, Leonard, 16, 82–84, 146

Jewish-Americans, assimilation, and, 145; whiteness of, 145

Jim Crow, 2, 6, 281, 342, 344, 345, 390

Jones, Jaccqueline, 92, 152, 394, 395

Jones, Leroi, 235 n.2. *See also* Baraka, Amiri

Jones, Lisa, 20, 140

Jones, Momma, 161–62

Jordan, June, 15, 23, 104, 147, 152, 159, 283; and the Sisterhood, 152

Jordon, Michael, 118, 204

Julien, Isaac, 23, 24, 193, 255, 373; *Looking for Langston*, 192, 201; *Passion of Remembrance*, 208

Jumpin' Jack Flash, 402

Jungle Fever, 196, 215–19, 408

Just Another Girl on the IRT, 282–83, 353, 387; and "Mammy" stereotype, 282

Kennedy, John F., 13, 98, 101, 103

Kennedy, Lisa, 192–93

Kennedy, Robert, 13, 103

King, Martin Luther, Jr., 5, 13, 103, 149

King, Rodney: postverdict rebellion, 284; videotaped beating of, 212, 215, 284

Koppel, Ted, 89, 127

Kovel, Joel, 259, 263

Kristeva, Julia, 248, 372

Kruger, Barbara, 392; black images and, 185; omnipresent whiteness and, 195

Ku Klux Klan, 226, 251, 273

Larsen, Nella, 154, 196, 398

Lawrence, Jacob, 348, 349, 367, 383

Lee, Spike, 18, 77, 211, 235 n.1, 298, 402–6; *Jungle Fever*, 196, 215–19; portrayal of Italian Americans, 217

Levin, Michael, 83, 182

Lippard, Lucy, 186, 393; Ad Hoc Women, 207

Literary criticism, 180. *See also* African American literary criticism

Literature, 167–68; colonialism, relation to, 247; and pedagogy, 246

Literature. *See* African American literature

Location, politics of, 167–83; *Beloved* and, 179–83; black feminism and, 168; cultural criticism and, 168; and theory, 167

Locke, Alain, 196, 349

Lorde, Audre, 15, 24, 104, 147, 152–53, 201, 283, 397; *Sister Outsider*, 153

Los Angeles Police Department, and Rodney King beating, 215, 284

Lynching: in *Birth of a Nation*, 273; high-tech, 184; spectacle, 210

Mackintosh, Cameron, 250, 262 n.1, 299

Madonna, 158, 387

Magazines/journals/newspapers: *Afterimage*, 253; *Amsterdam News*, 143, 297; *Aperture*, 16; *Art-in-America*, 76; *Black Scholar*, 151; *Cahier du Cinema*, 24; *Chronicle of Higher Education*, 151; *City Sun*, 297; *Daily News*, 89, 113, 300; *Ebony Magazine*, 170, 231; *Emerge*, 17, 26, 129; *Entertainment Weekly*, 21, 148; *Esquire*, 157; *Essence*, 109; *Harvard Advocate*, 17; *Herald Tribune*, 89; *Ms. Magazine*, 17, 106, 108; *The Nation*, 109, 113, 180, 298; *New Republic*, 144, 151, 211, 297, 303, 403; *Newsday*, 298; *Newsweek*, 105, 107, 300; *The New York Element*, 104; *The New Yorker*, 113, 151, 403; *New York Magazine*, 403; *New York Post*, 16, 169–70; *New York Times*, 16, 22, 26, 88, 89, 105, 106, 109, 113, 137, 142, 144, 151, 162,

181, 218, 252, 339, 340, 403, 412; *October*, 23, 77; *Rat*, 104; *Renaissance Noir*, 78; *Social Text*, 23; *Third World Newsreel*, 25; *Time*, 212; *Vanity Fair*, 113; *Vibe*, 113; *Village Voice*, 18, 20, 77, 106, 107, 113, 403; *Washington Post*, 109; *Women and Art*, 104; *The Women's Review of Books*, 17, 77; *Women's World*, 104

Malcolm X, 5, 13, 98, 103, 149, 300, 404; *Malcolm X* (film), 405, 408

"Mammy" stereotype, 93, 275–85, 354; *Birth of a Nation*, and, 280; black male inferiority, relation to, 280; emergence of in nineteenth century, 268–69; *Gone With the Wind*, and, 230, 280; hostility generated by, 280; Kincaid, Jamaica and, 230; "male mammy," 302; Morton, Patricia, on, 279–80; *The Moynihan Report*, and, 280; myth and reality of, 280; *Raisin in the Sun*, and, 280

Manet, Edouard, 360, 372; *Olympia*, 195, 229

Mapplethorpe, Robert, 153, 202–4, 207, 210, 214, 262 n.2, 298, 387

March on Washington (1963), 13, 151

Mariani, Philomena, 23, 193, 198; *Critical Fictions: Discussions in Contemporary Culture*, 183

Marley, Bob, 14, 15

Mass culture: African American objectification in, 186; black images in, 186

Matisse, Henri, 190; "Matisse's Model," 360, 362

McCarthy era, 234, 244; "Black Lists," 25, 98

McDaniel, Hattie, 230–31, 354

McElroy, Guy, 340, 341, 345

McHenry, Susan, 17, 20, 106, 108

McKee, Lonette, 216, 219, 408

McQueen, Butterfly, 76, 130, 228, 230–31, 354, 355

Mercer, Kobena, 23, 25, 255

Metropolitan Museum of Art, 360, 383

Millet, Kate, 104, 393; *Sexual Politics*, 153

Million Man March, 76, 212–13, 405

Minh-ha, Trinh T., 236 n.12, 261, 461; "theory as non-theory," 240

Minstrelsy, 121, 224, 342

Mirsky, Mark, 18, 104, 106

Misogyny, 22, 75; feminist criticism of in rap, 135; in rap videos, 135; in rap lyrics, 135; relation to racism, 145

Modernism: high, ideology of, 265; high, incorporation of popular culture, 267; high/low schemata, 196; modern art, 203; popular culture and, 265; post-modernism and, 198; race/gender and, 195

MOMA (Museum of Modern Art), 187, 204, 207, 229, 374, 383

Morgan, Robin, 104, 108, 110

Morrison, Toni, 23, 104, 105, 147, 159, 211, 292, 297–98, 365, 367, 397, 398; *Beloved*, 179; *The Bluest Eye*, 152, 279, 293; Sisterhood and, 152; *Sula*, 152; trauma and, 279

Morton, Patricia: 92, 93, 390, 394; and black female slave, myth of, 279–80; *Disfigured Images*, 274, 279, 283

Motherhood, 275–85; cultural shame and, 285; teenaged, 282–83

Mount, William Sidney, 342, 344, 346

Moynihan Report, 280; African American women, images of, 280; "Mammy" stereotype and, 280

Moynihan, Patrick, 92, 153

Mulatta stereotype, 268–69; in *Uncle Tom's Cabin*, 270–71, 274

Multiculturalism, 25, 238–48; aesthetics of, 238; alternatives to, 251; antimulticulturalism, 211; art world and, 249, 251; bourgeois, 239; class and, 239; cultural left and, 251; culture wars and, 202–14; dominant discourse and, 251; educational reforms and, 144; global

culture and, 198–99; modernist, 265; multiculturalism and, 275–85; non-Western influences on, 267; political correctness and, 197, 198; production of, 265; roots of, 266–67; psychoanalysis and, 275–85; travels of, 264–65; visuality, and, 188, 200; Western control of, 267

Postcolonialism, 24, 25, 363

Postmodernism, 196; Black British, 24, 37; multiculturalism and, 239; postcolonial critique of, 239; race/gender and, 195; scene, 371

Poststructuralism, 5, 25, 26, 372; African American culture and, 169; multiculturalism and, 239

Powell, Colin L., 2, 143, 365

Primitivism, 6, 238, 374; Neoprimitivism, 373

Prince, 16, 387, 402, 406

Prissy, 354. See also *Gone with the Wind*

Pryce, Jonathan, 250–51, 262 n.1, 299

Psychoanalysis: black female subject and, 255; cultural resistance and, 254; and film, 235; historicization of, 254; influence on film criticism, 224, 279; object relations, 26; and race, 234, 275–85; and race and gender in film, 223–37

Psychology, African Americans and, 186, 191–92

Puryear, Martin, 187, 373

Queer theory, 76, 94

Quinn, Anthony, 217, 404

Race, as category, 146; conjunction with gender, 195; erasure of in 40s film, 234; gendering of, 235; male psychology and, 234; political unconscious, relation to, 146; psychoanalysis and, 277–78; sexual difference and, 225; and sexuality, 128; visual representation of, 184–94, 225–

37; Western intellectual discourse and, 278

Racism, 2, 21, 90, 367; aesthetics and, 190; antiracism, 350; black-on-Asian, 251; the death penalty and, 132; in fine art, 340; imagery and, 342; scientific, 190, 210

Rainier, Yvonne, 24, 25, 252, 393; *Privilege*, 253, 257, 258–59, 262

Rape, 169–70. *See also* Sexual assault

Rap music, 132–37; attire in, 135; bell hooks on, 135; black comedy and, 136; as creative outlet, 134; cross-over popularity of, 134; as education, 134; and feminism, 134–37; misogynist lyrics in, 136; oral tradition and, 136; positive messages in, 134; sexism of, 134–35; sexuality and, 135

Rappers, female: M. C. Lyte, 136; Monie Love, 136, 137; L.A. Star, 136; Oaktown's 3.5.7, 136; and protofeminist messages, 137; Queen Latifah, 136, 137; Salt-N-Pepa, 136, 137; subjects discussed by, 137

Rappers, male: Ice Cube, 136, 157, 160; Ice-T., 134; Kool Moe Dee, 128, 135; Kwanee, 135; L. L. Kool J, 128; M. C. Hammer, 136–37; Positive K, 137; Public Enemy, 135; w.i.s.e. Guyz, 134

Rauschenberg, Robert, 97, 101

Reagan, Ronald: Reagan-Bush era, 129; Reaganomics, 203; Reagan revolution, 211

Reconstruction, 155, 209

Reed, Ishmael, 105, 367, 371; *Mumbo Jumbo*, 195

Reggae, influence on rap, 134

Rembrandt van Rijn, 190, 369

Reynaud, Berenice, 24, 25, 252–53, 255

Rich, Adrienne, 24, 153, 171; black analysis, appropriation of, 169; *Blood, Bread and Poetry*, 167–68; *North American Tunnel Vision*, 168; on mother-child dyad, 278; "politics of location" and, 167

Steinem, Gloria, 108, 153–54

Stereotypes of African Americans, 120–21; in American Art, 347, 339; "Aunt Jemima," 347, 365; *Birth of a Nation* and, 224, 226; "Black Women in Popular Culture," 264–74; bucks, 226–27, 273; coons, 226–27; in film, 130–31, 223, 226, 282; Jim Crow, 342, 344; maids, 131–32, 228, 231–32; mammies, 226–27, 230, 275–85; on prime-time television, 127, 186; protests against, 227; in rap videos, 135–36; Sambo, 223, 344; Stepin Fetchit, 130; Toms, 226; tragic mulattoes, 226–27; Uncle Ben, 120; visual, 190, 229; whores, 231; Zip Coon, 342. *See also* Blackface

Stowe, Harriet Beecher: *Uncle Tom's Cabin*, 269

Student Nonviolent Coordinating Committee (SNCC), 151

Subjectivity, black, 256; black female, 255, 258

Television: Amos 'n' Andy, 127; The Arsenio Hall Show, 127–29; CNN 89; The Cosby Show, 89, 127, 186, 405; The Ed Sullivan Show, 90; The Jackie Gleason Show, 89; The Jeffersons, 127, 355; In Living Color, 17, 379; McNeil/Lehrer, 88; Nightline, 89; The Odd Couple, 89; Phil Donahue, 109, 401; Roc, 89; Sally Jessy Raphael Show, 300; Star Trek, 89; Star Trek: Voyager, 89; The Steve Allen Show, 90; Taxi, 89; The Today Show, 88, 108

Theory, 167–68; in cinema, 169; of cinema in literature, 169; Minh-ha, Trinh, 240; multicultural, 240–41; people of color and, 240; postmodern, 240; poststructuralist, 169; sexual difference and, 254

Third World Women's Alliance, 151

Third World, 2; Jamaica, 3

Thomas, Clarence, 19, 138–40, 184–85, 205, 212; *See also* Thomas-Hill Hearings

Thomas-Hill Hearings, 138–40, 205, 387; African American interpretation of, 185; black feminism and, 212; culture wars and, 211; as "high-tech lynching," 184, 211; gender and, 185; progressive agenda and, 211; psychological tensions and, 186; visual representation of, 185; as watershed event, 184

Toche, Jean, 104, 393

Tongues Untied, 201, 207–8, 378, 380

2 Live Crew, censorship of, 135, 299

Topsy: as abused child, 270; blackface and, 272; as comic relief, 272; as female trickster, 270; in 1914 film version of *Uncle Tom's Cabin*, 271

Trauma, 278; in African American literature, 279

Trippi, Laura, 260–61, 263

Trueblood, 370, 371

Truth, Sojourner, 137, 155, 160 n.1; "Ain't I a Woman" speech, 155; iconography of, 155, 269; Painter, Nell, on, 155

Tubman, Harriet, 137, 269, 360

Turner, Tina, 283–84, 371

Turtuto, John, 217, 404

U.S. Government, 102, 185, 393

U.S. Imperialism. *See* Imperialism, U.S.

Uncle Tom's Cabin: Christ imagery in, 270; novel by Stowe, Harriet Beecher, 269; film version (1903): blackface in, 271; cakewalk in, 271; mulatta/mulatto figures in, 269–71; popular culture and, 269–70; *Tom* companies, 269; Topsy as female trickster, 270

Unconscious, 277–79

Universities: Brooklyn College, 104; CCNY (City College of New York), 9, 24, 83, 101, 103, 104; Cornell University, Conference on "Visualizing Blackness" 123;

Michele Wallace is Visiting Professor
of Africana Studies at Cornell University.
Her previous books are *Black Macho and
the Myth of the Superwoman* and *Invisibility
Blues: From Pop to Theory.*

Library of Congress Cataloging-in-Publication Data
Wallace, Michele.
Dark designs and visual culture / Michele Wallace.
p. cm.   Includes bibliographical references and index.
ISBN 0-8223-3427-5 (cloth : alk. paper)
ISBN 0-8223-3413-5 (pbk. : alk. paper)
1. African American women. 2. African American arts.
3. Popular culture—United States—History—20th century.
4. Feminism—United States. 5. Wallace, Michele.
I. Title.
E185.86.W344 2004   305.896′073′09045—dc22
2004011108